The Penguin Book of Kites

For Sophie

The Penguin Book of Kites

David Pelham

Penguin Books

PENGUIN BOOKS

Published by the Penguin Group
Penguin Books Ltd, 27 Wrights Lane, London W8 5TZ, England
Penguin Books USA Inc., 375 Hudson Street, New York, New York 10014, USA
Penguin Books Australia Ltd, Ringwood, Victoria, Australia
Penguin Books Canada Ltd, 10 Alcorn Avenue, Toronto, Ontario, Canada M4V 3B2
Penguin Books (NZ) Ltd, 182–190 Wairau Road, Auckland 10, New Zealand

Penguin Books Ltd, Registered Offices: Harmondsworth, Middlesex, England

First published 1976
20 19 18 17 16 15

Made and printed in Singapore by
Kyodo Printing Co. (s) Pte Ltd.

Member of BPCC Ltd
Set in Monotype Times

Designed by David Pelham

Contents

Acknowledgements

I would like to extend my gratitude to the following for providing information and illustrations for this book. The Royal Aeronautical Society; the Science Museum, South Kensington; The Royal Aircraft Establishment; the R.A.F. Museum; The Science Reference Library; Le Musée de l'Air; La Bibliothèque Sainte Geneviève; The Smithsonian Institution; the National Geographic Society; Mr Robert M. Ingraham, American Kiteflyers Association; Ms Andrea D. Bahadur, Go Fly a Kite Store, Inc.; Mr Domina Jalbert, Aerology Lab. Inc.; and Mr S. N. Harrison of Brookite Ltd.
I would especially like to thank my wife Marion, for her enthusiasm, advice and great patience, together with Tal Streeter for his generous contribution.
My grateful thanks are also due to James Cochrane, Frances Balfour, Anne Lowe, David Bann and David Wood for all their help in the preparation of this book.

Of the many friends and enthusiasts who have contributed material and information, I would particularly like to express my warmest thanks to Maria Yalopoulos for her research, translation and friendship, Andrew Holmes for his fine draughtsmanship, and John and Elsie Rose, makers of magnificent kites, for their enthusiasm and generous advice.

Foreword

The kite has been in existence for twenty-five centuries or so, and most of us at some time in our lives have attempted to fly one, yet its history and principles remain relatively obscure even today. In spite of its long and fascinating history of practical application, its instruction and entertainment value, the challenge and rewards of designing, building and flying kites are known to few westerners over the age of twelve.

The uses of the kite have been many and varied, contributing greatly to man's need to extend his physical and mental reach. Apart from its religious and ceremonial significance, and as an object for divining and celebrating fertility, birth and destiny, the kite has been, and may again become, a hard-working tool of mankind. It has been used for signalling over vast distances, providing military observation, fishing, measuring, and divining the secrets of the atmosphere – providing traction and lift in thousands of applications.

Undoubtedly though, the kite's greatest contribution has been its role as precursor of the aeroplane. Sir George Cayley, described by the French historian, Charles Dollfus, as 'The true inventor of the aeroplane and one of the most powerful geniuses in the history of aviation', incorporated a traditional English arch top kite into his kite-glider of 1804, establishing 'the first modern configuration aeroplane of history . . .'*

While Cayley's kite has gone on to reach its zenith, this does not preclude the kite form from offering modern man a worthwhile, relaxing and mentally satisfying endeavour. Indeed, the strange attraction of the kite can be attributed, in part at least, to its paradoxical quality of providing exercise *and* relaxation to both mind and body.

The kite is an aircraft, and as such it is governed by the principles of heavier-than-air flight, and it is only through an understanding of these basic principles that it becomes possible to devise new and beautiful configurations that embody the grace and efficiency of absolute simplicity.

* Gibbs-Smith, C.H., *Sir George Cayley (1773–1857)*, London, 1968, p. 7.

Even though its origins are obscure, it is generally accepted that the kite was first invented in China long before the beginnings of written history. It seems probable however that some cultures discovered the principles of kite flying quite independently, whilst others developed existing patterns to suit their own requirements. Silk was being produced in China as early as 2600 B.C. and as bamboo cane was in abundance it does not seem an unreasonable conjecture that kites were being flown by the Chinese around 1000 B.C.

Many theories have been put forward as to the original inspiration of the kite, ranging from runaway sails from a fishing boat to a Chinese farmer's hat being carried off by the wind. While all theories must remain speculative, in an early text the famous Chinese engineer Kungshu Phan of the fourth century B.C. is credited with the invention of a wooden bird that flew for three days without descending. This is generally accepted as having been a kite; while another well documented account from the second century A.D. refers to the wooden bird of Chang Hêng, which appears to have been a rudimentary ornithopter with mechanized wings. It is interesting to relate this story with the first western account of kite flying, recorded by Aulus Gellius in the second century A.D., which refers to the 'flying dove' of Archytas of Tarentum, and in which the same basic type of aircraft is described.

Chinese folklore abounds in stories of kites flown for both pleasure and purpose, the more expedient applications answering mainly military needs. One of the more ingenious uses of the kite was demonstrated by the Han general Han

Traditional Chinese bird kite.

Chinese bird kites being flown at Haikwan, nineteenth century.

Hsin in the year 169 B.C. He is said to have used a kite to gauge the distance between his forces and the walls of a palace, in order to measure the distance that his sappers might have to dig, so that his troops might enter. Chinese legend also tells us that Liu Pang, founder of the Han Dynasty in 202 B.C., was opposed by a general Huan Theng, a fierce defender of the previous order. Huan Theng and his army were eventually surrounded by the usurper's forces, and were threatened with annihilation. It is said that a fortuitous gust of wind carried Huan Theng's hat from his head, giving him the idea of building a large quantity of kites fitted with sounding devices. These would probably have taken the form of finely shaved bamboo strips held taut between the ends of a bow, and were flown in the dead of night above the army of Liu Pang, who, on hearing the mysterious wailing in the sky, supposedly panicked and fled.

Though man-carrying and man-lifting kites have apparently been used in China in countless military and civil applications since the earliest times, accounts also exist of enforced manned flights. As a method of punishing prisoners, Emperor Wen Hsuan Ti of the Kao Yang Dynasty is recorded as having derived great pleasure from ordering his prisoners to 'fly' from a tower while harnessed to large bamboo mats, offering them freedom should they survive.

Marco Polo in 1282 not only gives a graphic account of the cruelty and hazards involved in manned kite flights, but also gives an extremely accurate description of kite flying technique.

'And so we will tell you how when any ship must go on a voyage, they prove whether her business will go well or ill. The men of the ship will have a hurdle, that is a grating, of

A Chinese figure kite,
early twentieth century.
Smithsonian Institution.

withies, and at each corner and side of this framework will be tied a cord, so that there be eight cords, and they will all be tied at the other end to a long rope. Next they will find some fool or drunkard and they will bind him on the hurdle, since no one in his right mind or with his wits about him would expose himself to that peril. And this is done when a strong wind prevails. Then the framework being set up opposite the wind, the wind lifts it and carries it up into the sky, while the men hold on by the long rope. And if, while it is in the air, the hurdle leans towards the way of the wind, they pull the rope to them a little so that it is set again upright, after which they let out some more rope and it rises higher. And if again it tips, once more they pull in the rope until the frame is upright and climbing, and then they yield rope again, so that in this manner it would rise so high that it could not be seen, if only the rope were long enough. The augury they interpret thus: if the hurdle going straight up makes for the sky, they say that the ship for which the test has been made will have a quick and prosperous voyage, whereupon all the merchants run together for the sake of sailing and going with her. But if the hurdle has not been able to go up, no merchant will be willing to enter the ship for which the test has been made, because they say that she could not finish her voyage and would be oppressed by many ills. And so that ship stays in port that year.'[1]

From China, via Indo-China, the kite soon appeared throughout Japan, probably brought into the country by Buddhist missionaries in the early years of the T'ang Dynasty (A.D. 618–907), and subsequently spread to the Pacific

1. Polo, M., *The Description of the World*, introduced by A. C. Moule, London, 1938, Vol. 1, pp. 356–7.

Minamoto-no-Tametomo's son, lashed to a kite, escapes from exile on the island of Hachijo (after a print by Hokusai).

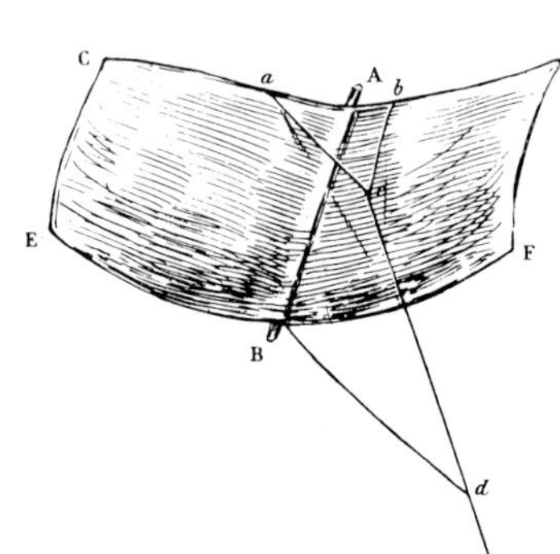

Two traditional Chinese configurations, often flown with a hummer, like the example opposite.

generally, appearing in various forms in Korea, Burma, through Indonesia, Melanesia and Polynesia, acquiring ever greater religious and ceremonial significance as it went.

Fear of invasion from the air may well have been a reality to the ancient Orientals. It is said that there was once a Japanese law forbidding the construction of kites capable of carrying a man. As in China, there are many stories in the folklore of Japan, recounting the daring exploits of brave individuals being borne aloft on kites for both national glory and personal gain.

A degree of ambiguity still exists today when manned kites are referred to, though the difference between a man-*carrier* and a man-*lifter* seems obvious. The early eastern giants invariably bore the passenger within or upon the kite itself, and consequently are classifiable as man-*carriers*. Subsequent western pioneers discovered that a load within the structure of a basic kite interfered drastically with the aerodynamic properties of the craft, and therefore employed kites to provide initial lift and stability only, the passenger being hoisted some way up the kite line when this had been attained. This technique is referred to as man-*lifting*. Nevertheless, in kite flying there always appears to be an exception to the rule, the exception in this case being Alexander Graham Bell, whose Cygnet, because of its remarkable stability, proved itself to be easily capable of supporting its passenger within the structure of the kite itself.

A well-known story from Japan relates how the famous robber Kakinoki Kinsuke used a man-carrying kite in an attempt to steal the scales from the golden dolphins atop the

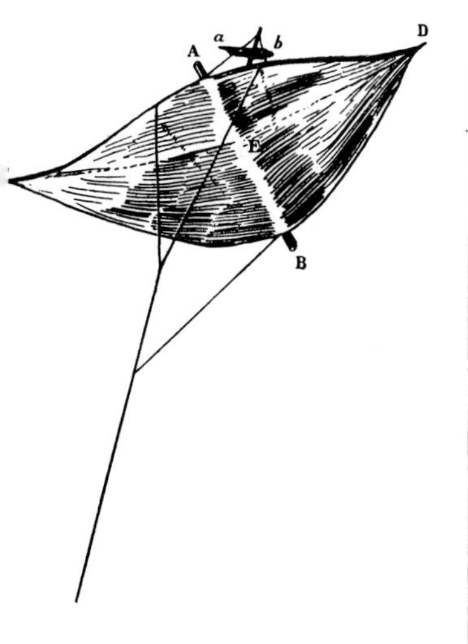

Early aerial invasion.
Japanese kite-borne archer
(after a nineteenth-century print).

towers of Nagoya Castle. Fate seems to have been against him however, for although he appears to have landed safely after successfully dislodging a number of scales, he was later arrested and punished by being boiled in oil together with his entire family. Approximately two hundred years later, in 1927, another thief had more luck. He succeeded in making off with fifty-eight scales from the same dolphins, though his method in no way reflected the panache of Kinsuke.

Another early example of man carrying is described in the story of Minamoto-no-Tametomo, a famous samurai warrior of the Genji clan who, together with his son, was exiled to the island of Hachijo. Not wishing that his son should spend the rest of his days in such a desolate spot, Tametomo constructed a large kite which successfully, so the legend goes, bore the boy aloft across the sea to the mainland. As a consequence the Hachijo kite traditionally bears a likeness of Tametomo upon its surface.

A more prudent Japanese application of the kite's lifting properties was demonstrated by the practice of lifting tiles and bricks to workmen involved in constructing towers, by means of large baskets supported by enormous kites flying overhead.

Certainly the high-water mark amongst the Japanese giants was the famous Wan-wan kite, developed by Nagajima Gempei around the turn of the last century. With an overall width of 24 m (60 ft), and a tail of 146 m (480 ft), it weighed approximately 2·80 metric tonnes (6160 lb), and required a team of about 150 men to launch and fly it.

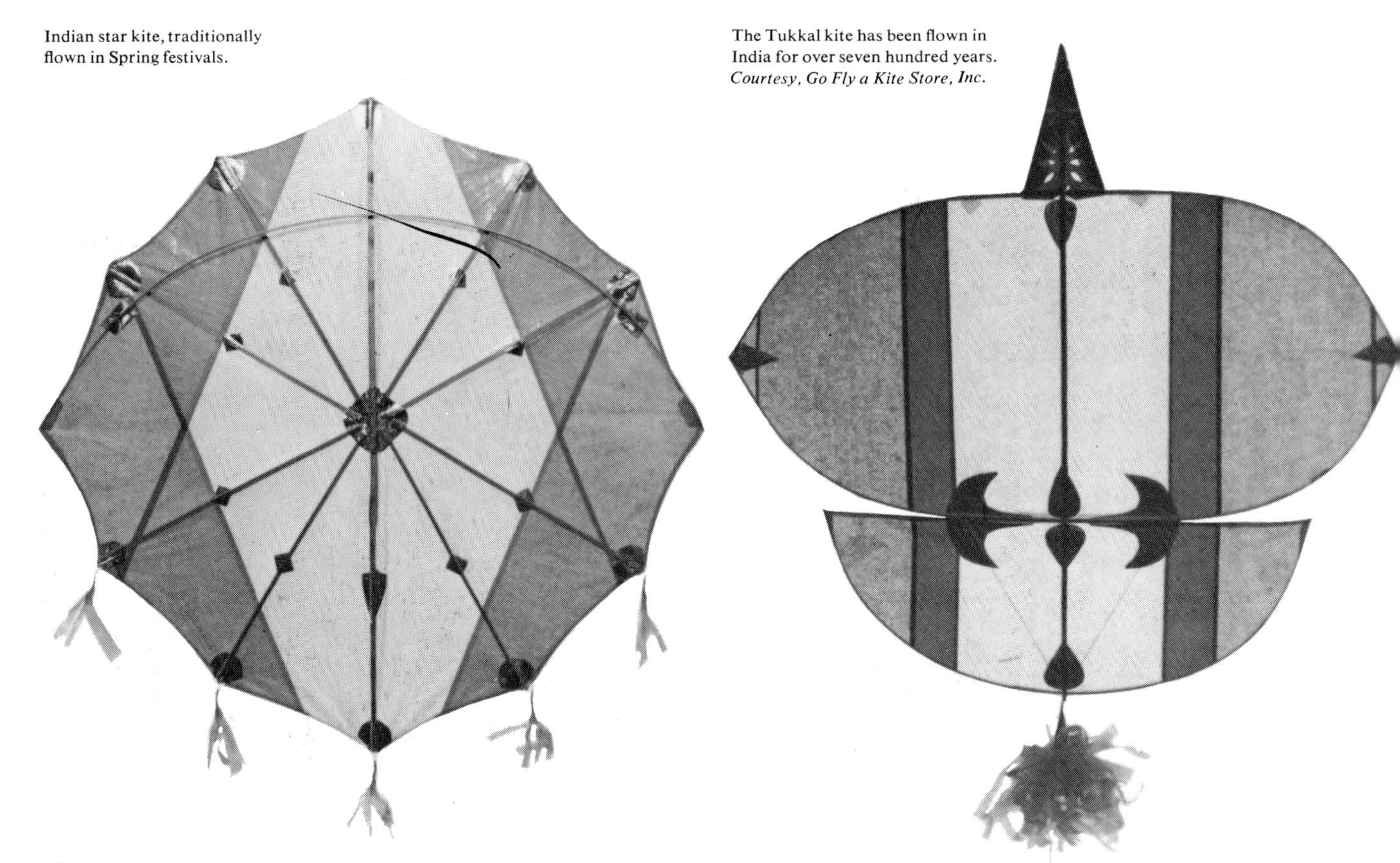

Indian star kite, traditionally flown in Spring festivals.

The Tukkal kite has been flown in India for over seven hundred years. *Courtesy, Go Fly a Kite Store, Inc.*

On the fifth day of the fifth month, the Boys' Festival is celebrated in many areas of Japan. Households which have been favoured with the birth of a male child in the preceding twelve months become the centre of attraction, and huge kites are flown to celebrate the births. All households with male children fly highly coloured windsocks from poles in honour of their sons. Usually these take the form of fish, representative of the carp, a particularly hardy fish that annually battles upstream to its spawning grounds against almost overwhelming odds, symbolic of the sons' progress through the 'river of life'.

Japanese Yakko, or footman kite, representing the servant of the Samurai warrior.

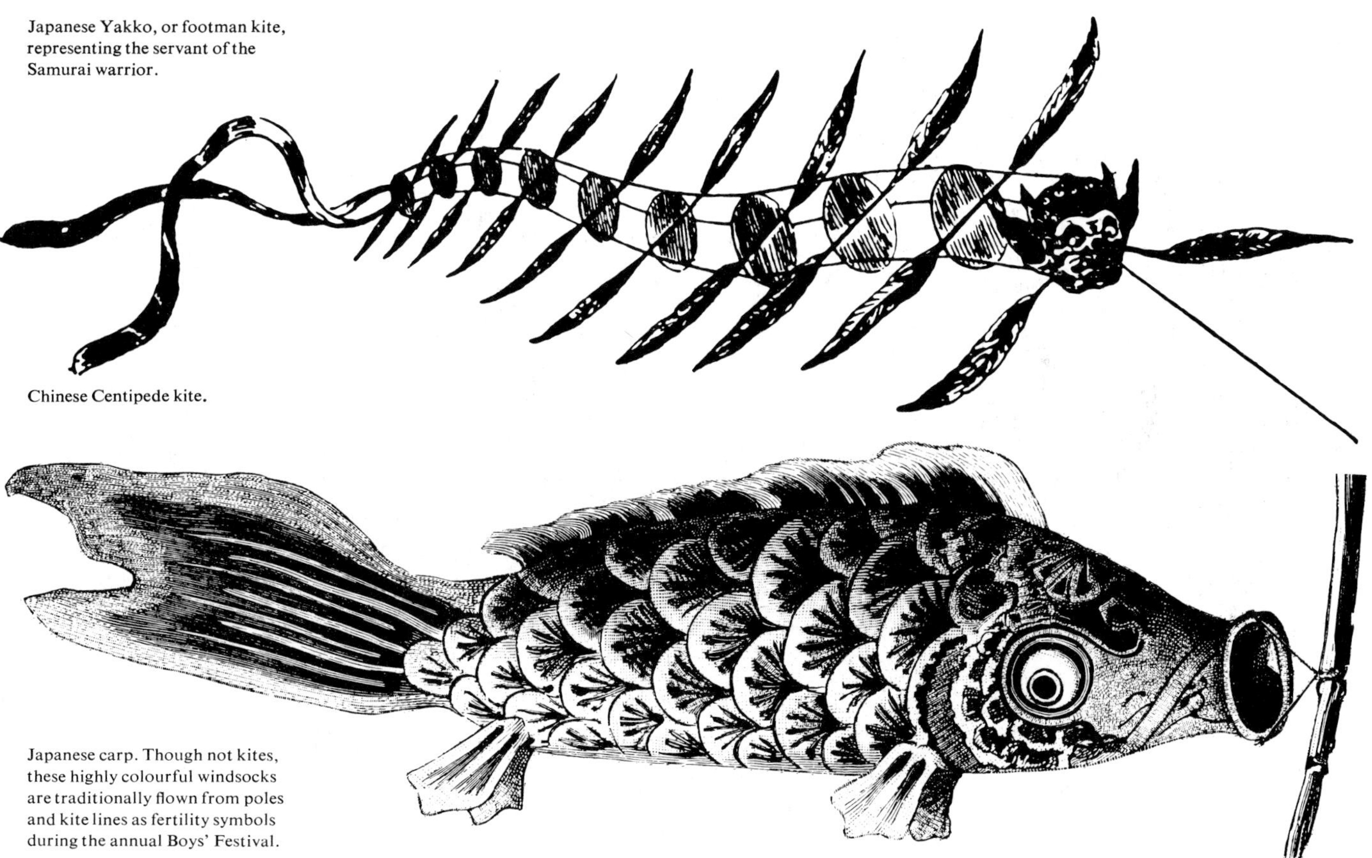

Chinese Centipede kite.

Japanese carp. Though not kites, these highly colourful windsocks are traditionally flown from poles and kite lines as fertility symbols during the annual Boys' Festival.

Probably the most famous fighting kite is the Nagasaki Hata. This is an exceptionally manoeuvrable kite capable of flying at amazing speeds with considerable directional control. Equipped with cutting devices such as ground glass or porcelain glued to the line below the bridle by means of egg white, rice or other natural adhesives, it is a fearsome opponent in competition. The object of a kite fight is to sever the line of an opponent, resulting in the loss of his kite. The Nagasaki fighting kite, however, bears little resemblance to other traditional Japanese kite forms. It is highly balanced, extremely light, virtually square and flown diagonally, as opposed to the traditional Japanese configuration which is basically rectangular and flown longitudinally. It bears a close resemblance to the classic Indian Fighter, differing only in the absence of the Indian support fin at the tail, and in having its two leading edges supported by a guideline of string, while the Indian version has its leading edges unsupported.

It is fairly certain that the Nagasaki fighting kite is a derivation of the Indian Fighter. Considering that the first Westerners who set foot in Japan in 1543 were restricted to Nagasaki alone, it seems likely that these early Portuguese, Dutch and English traders introduced the kite from India. This conjecture is strongly supported by the fact that the Nagasaki Hata (Hata is the Japanese word for flag) is traditionally coloured red, white and blue, in the manner of the Dutch ensign. Whatever the origin, kite flying remains an obsession in Nagasaki even today, with the whole month of March being appropriated for kite flying festivals.

1

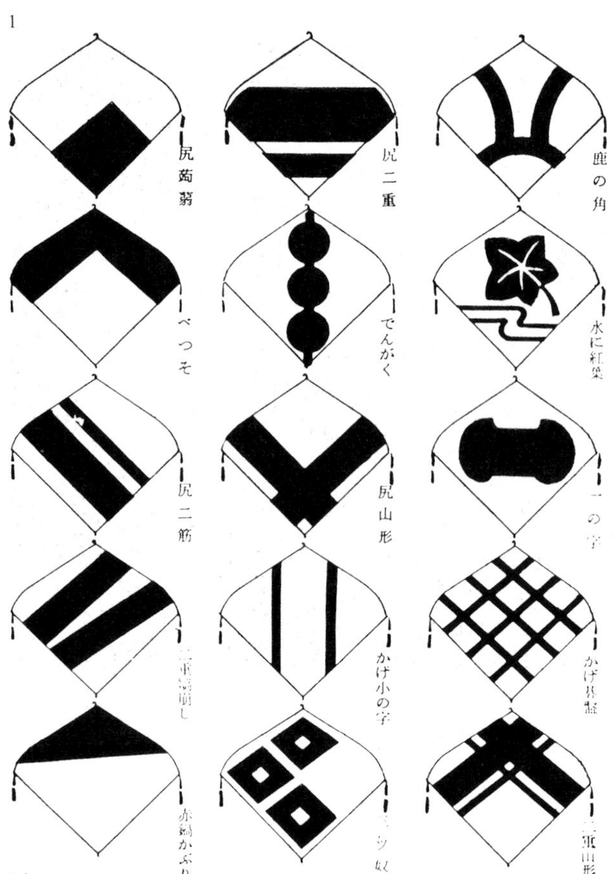

2

1) A page from a Nagasaki kite maker's pattern book.
2) The Nagasaki Hata, a highly responsive fighting kite, traditionally decorated with simple, bold designs which are, in the main, red, white and blue.

In Korea, at the beginning of each new year, it has long been the custom to write the name and date of birth of each male child on the surface of a paper kite. These are then flown in the air. When they are at their highest the line is released and the kite is borne away with the wind. The object is that they should drift as far as possible before coming to earth, the kite drawing away with it any bad luck or evil spirits which might adversely affect the child's future. To pick up such a kite, if found, is to attract the owner's ills to oneself.

Kites were most probably introduced to Korea, again by Buddhists, about the middle of the first millennium A.D. The Korean kite is similar to the Japanese rectangle, though it traditionally has a circular hole in its centre. It is large and fast, flown tailless for fighting from a coloured silk line.

Another weight-lifting application of the kite comes from Korea. In the *Samguk Sagi*, written in A.D. 1145, appears an account of how in the first year of Queen Zindong, the twenty-eighth ruler of the Silla Dynasty, a general Gim Yu-Sin (A.D. 596–637) was given the task of quelling an uprising. While he was engaged in this task a shooting star fell. This was considered to be an extremely bad omen, and consequently the rebels, together with Gim Yu-Sin's own forces, became dangerously agitated. The *status-quo* was only restored after the general was inspired to hoist a fireball into the air by means of a large kite one dark night. This was accepted by all as the shooting star returning to the heavens, and a violent situation was avoided.

3

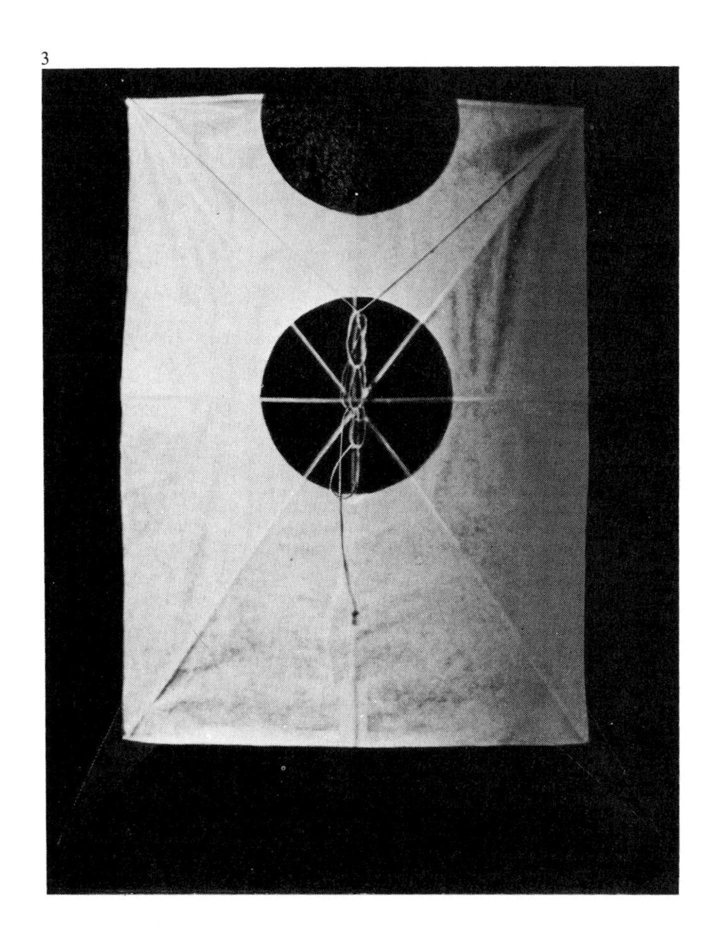

4

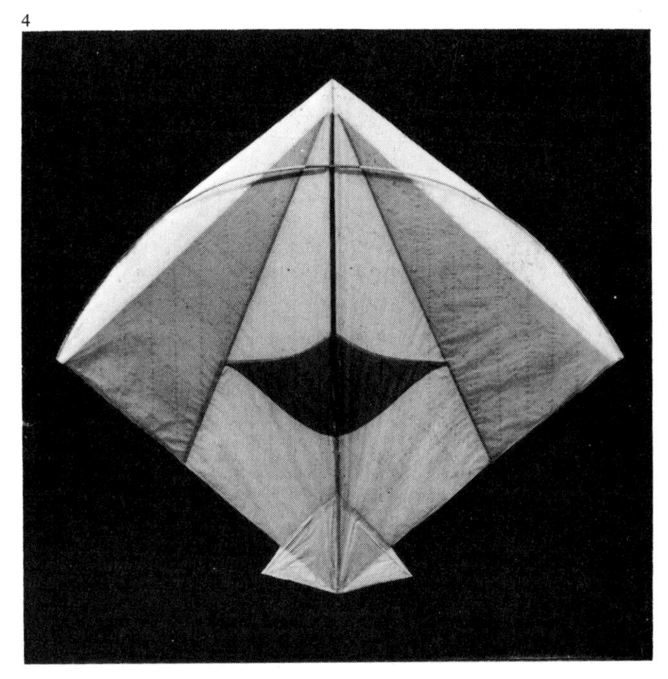

3) A traditional Korean fighting kite. The small 'ears' at the trailing edge give additional stability.
4) A typical Indian Fighter, made up of patch panels of brightly coloured tissue paper.
Courtesy, Go Fly a Kite Store, Inc.

Thailand also has an ancient association with kite flying, not only as a source of entertainment but also as part of magical folklore. Kites are flown at the time of the monsoon in an attempt to invoke the winds to blow hard and long, blowing away the rain clouds of the monsoon in order to save their crops from flood.

As has been said, it is quite probable that kites were independently invented in other Asian countries. In Malaya particularly there is a widely held belief that the Malayan kite was invented and developed quite independently from any outside influences. The facts on these matters will probably never be ascertained; however, what is certain is that each general area developed its own particular form for the kite, individual characteristics arising from the various roles that the kite played in the different cultures.

Fighting and fishing kites appear to have been prevalent throughout the Malay Archipelago long before its recorded history. The cruder form of fishing kite was little more than a large leaf, threaded with strips of fine bamboo for rigidity, with a hook suspended on a good length of line at the tail end. This technique, still used throughout Asia today, not only gives the fisherman an extraordinarily long cast but also ensures that no giveaway shadows fall on the water.

One of the more spectacular ethnic kites, this Maori bird has a wing span of 2·83 m (6 ft 10 ins.). *British Museum.*

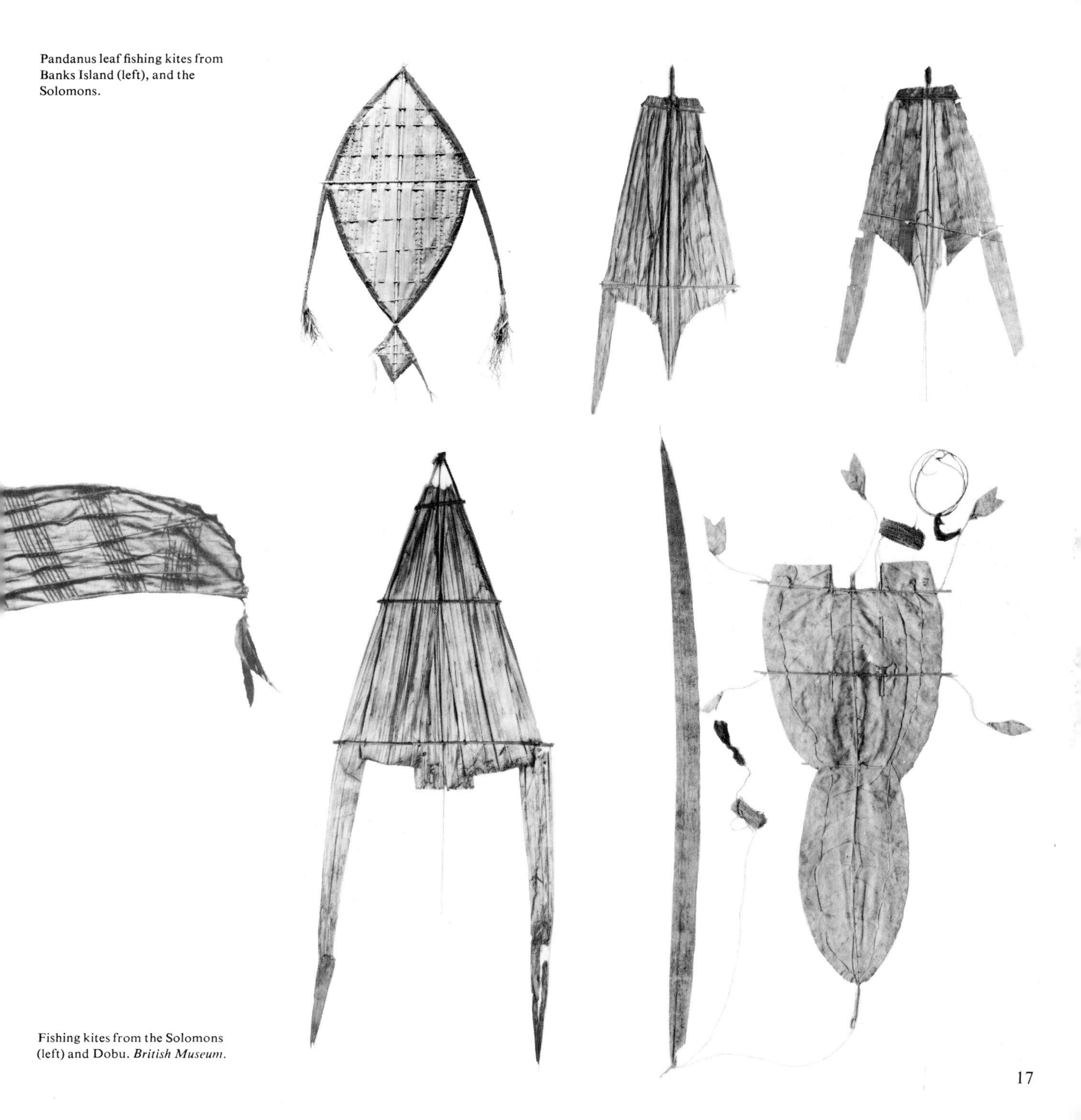

Pandanus leaf fishing kites from Banks Island (left), and the Solomons.

Fishing kites from the Solomons (left) and Dobu. *British Museum.*

The kite so well known in the West as the Malay was being flown throughout Malaysia, Indonesia and Java many centuries ago. This is the classic trapezoidal shape which was flown flat or bowed. The bowed version, an extremely efficient and buoyant design, is flown without a tail in a light wind. This is virtually the same kite as the one William A. Eddy introduced into the West in the 1890s.

Also throughout Malaysia, and particularly in Java, another kite has been flown for centuries. This is the plane-surface arch top, flown with a tail, similar to the shape which became so fashionable in England in the eighteenth century, known as the English arch top. This is a very close relative of the most popular French form, the pear top, which is virtually identical, but for a small protrusion at the head of the kite. As these appeared in Europe around the turn of the fifteenth and sixteenth centuries it seems plausible that they were introduced by the same traders who were responsible for introducing the Indian Fighter to Nagasaki.

PHOTO: HANS NAMUTH

Large and colourful paper kites are traditionally flown by the Guatemalan Indians of Santiago de Sacatepequez. The kites are annually flown from the cemetery of this small village on All Saints' Day in an attempt to invoke ancestral spirits, and also to celebrate the coming of clear skies after the rainy season.

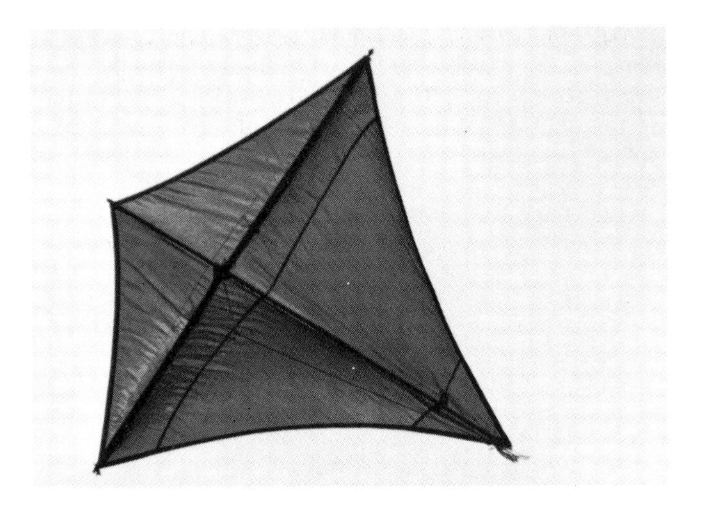

A modern Malay kite.

PHOTO: HANS NAMUTH

According to European tradition the invention of the kite is attributed, as we have seen, to the Greek mathematician Archytas of Tarentum, who, around 400 B.C., is said to have constructed a wooden bird, based on his studies of birds in flight. It has been suggested that his invention may well have been inspired by seeing Chinese bird kites; however there is little reliable information on Archytas' contribution to either the invention or the development of the kite.

In his definitive study *Kites: An Historical Survey*, Clive Hart describes how, throughout Europe, as far back as A.D. 105 the Romans were flying decorated windsocks as military banners. These were usually in the form of animals, wide mouthed and mounted on poles in order to catch the wind. Flowing cylindrical tails of finely spun cloth gave them the appearance of being alive, writhing like dragons above the horsemen. They were intended not only to inspire awe in an enemy, but also to provide archers with a vane, in order that they might determine the strength and direction of the wind. These windsocks were adopted quite extensively throughout Asia and Europe, being occasionally depicted in medieval illumination and tapestry. As early as 1326 *dracones* are to be seen bearing wings, no longer supported on poles but flying free from lines. These may well be the earliest known ancestors of the modern box kite. It is also possible that some of these early depictions represent not windsock kites but a form of hot-air balloon. A source of flame may possibly have been placed in the mouth of the dragon, giving it the appearance of breathing fire, while the hot air passing through the body lent it support.

The first recorded account of the hot-air balloon principle

1

comes to us from as early as the second century B.C. In the Taoist compendium *The Ten Thousand Infallible Arts of the Prince of Huai-Nan* we learn that

'Eggs can be made to fly in the air by the aid of burning tinder . . . Take an egg and remove the contents from the shell, then ignite a little mugwort tinder (inside the hole) so as to cause a strong air current. The egg will of itself rise in the air and fly away.'[2]

Towards the end of the fourteenth century the Europeans appear to have discovered for themselves the high drag ratio and general inefficiency of the windsock kite, whether supported by hot air or wings, and Hart, in his highly detailed study of early aeronautics, *The Dream of Flight*, suggests that the earlier inefficient kite had either evolved into or had been ousted by the considerably more buoyant pennon kite by the early years of the fifteenth century. This pennon kite was in effect a basic flat or plane-surface kite that supported a long colourful tail. As with present-day kites of the serpent variety the kite itself may well have been painted to resemble the head of a dragon or some other ferocious mythical beast.

The first accurate and reliable European description of the pennon kite appears as a captioned illustration in Conrad Kyeser's account of military technology, *Bellifortis*, of 1405. Though the illustration at first sight appears to represent a wingless windsock kite, the method of attaching a three-legged bridle characteristic of that used with a plane-surface kite is

2. Thai-Phing Yü Lan; (Thai-Phing Imperial Encyclopedia), see Needham, J., *Science and Civilisation in China*, Vol. 4, Pt 2, Cambridge, 1965, p. 596.

2

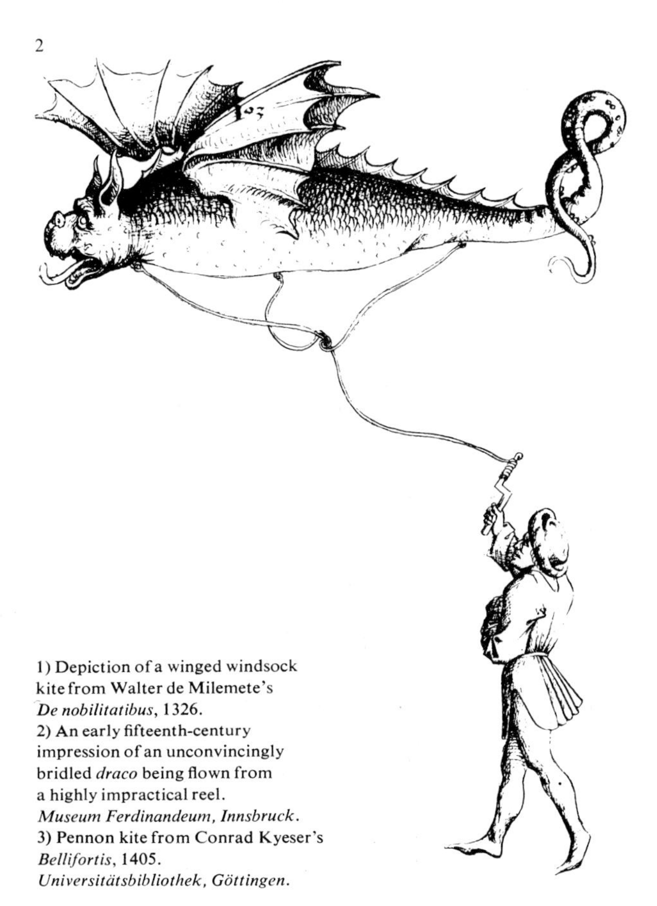

3

1) Depiction of a winged windsock kite from Walter de Milemete's *De nobilitatibus*, 1326.
2) An early fifteenth-century impression of an unconvincingly bridled *draco* being flown from a highly impractical reel.
Museum Ferdinandeum, Innsbruck.
3) Pennon kite from Conrad Kyeser's *Bellifortis*, 1405.
Universitätsbibliothek, Göttingen.

both described in the text and illustrated in a sketch to the right of the main figure.[3] When one compares Kyeser's account of the pennon kite with the first written description of a plane-surface kite to be published in Europe, contained in a Viennese manuscript of 1430, there seems little doubt that the same basic configuration is being described.

The Viennese manuscript details the method of constructing a parchment plane-surface kite supporting a tail of cloth and silk, together with a description of three alternate harnessing points for use in different wind conditions. Whether this configuration was arrived at as a direct evolution of the winged windsock kite, or whether it was influenced by imported plane-surface kites is unlikely to be ascertained.

3. Hart, C., *Kites: An Historical Survey*, London, 1967, p. 66.

Giambattista della Porta described a 'flying sayle' in his *Magiae Naturalis* of 1589, a simple though very beautiful rectangular kite, apparently based on the traditional Chinese form. He advocated that the kite be used for lifting fireworks, lanterns at night, and even kittens and puppies. The latter he suggested might be a spur to the idea of human flight. An illustration in John Bate's *The Mysteryes of Nature and Art* of 1634 is by way of a diagram, showing a lozenge kite lifting a tail liberally spiked with 'fire crackers . . . which will give divers blowes in the ayre'. This diagram is held to be the first illustration of the conventional kite ever to be published in England, and only the second to appear in Europe. The first appeared in 1618 in an engraving of Middelburg, Holland, giving further support to the idea that Dutch merchants played a large role in introducing the kite into Europe.
By the seventeenth century the kite had become quite

1

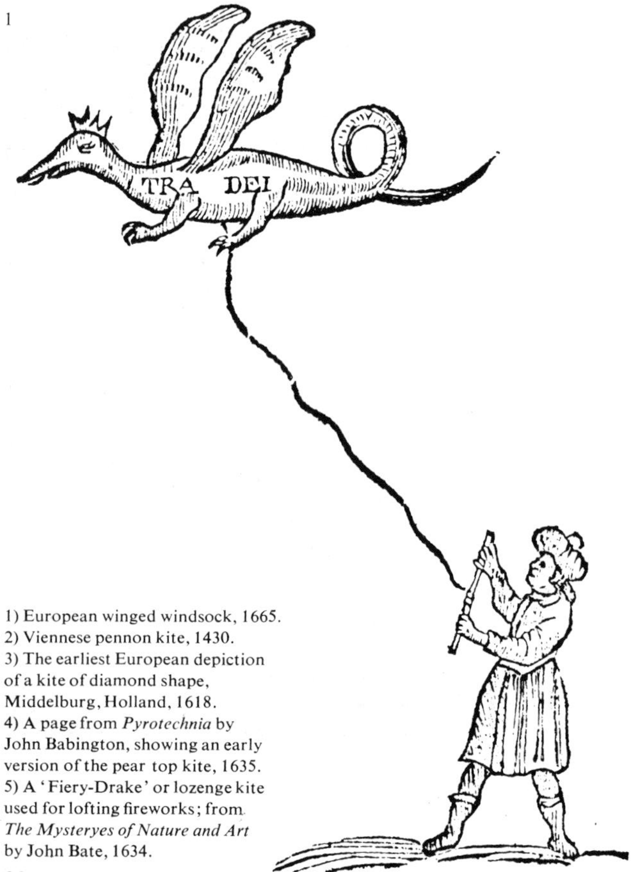

1) European winged windsock, 1665.
2) Viennese pennon kite, 1430.
3) The earliest European depiction of a kite of diamond shape, Middelburg, Holland, 1618.
4) A page from *Pyrotechnia* by John Babington, showing an early version of the pear top kite, 1635.
5) A 'Fiery-Drake' or lozenge kite used for lofting fireworks; from *The Mysteryes of Nature and Art* by John Bate, 1634.

2

3

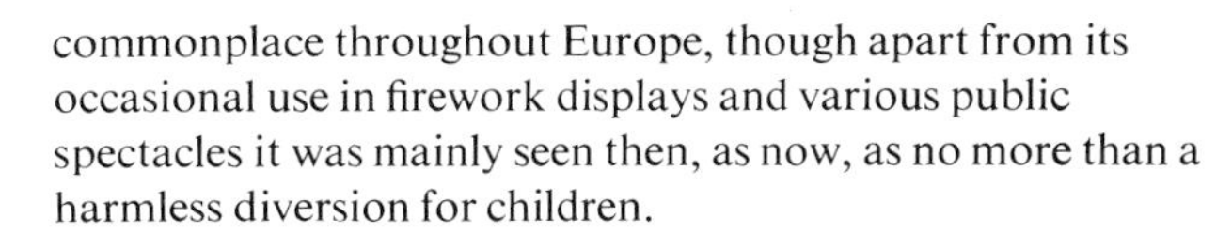
commonplace throughout Europe, though apart from its occasional use in firework displays and various public spectacles it was mainly seen then, as now, as no more than a harmless diversion for children.

With the exception of Isaac Newton, who appears to have made some virtually unrecorded experiments concerning the most economical form for a kite while still a schoolboy, the seventeenth century failed to recognize the scientific potential of the kite.

By the beginning of the eighteenth century kite flying was an enormously popular pastime throughout Europe. But even though it was developed extensively for scientific research throughout the latter half of the eighteenth century, as a pastime it was still almost entirely limited to children.

4

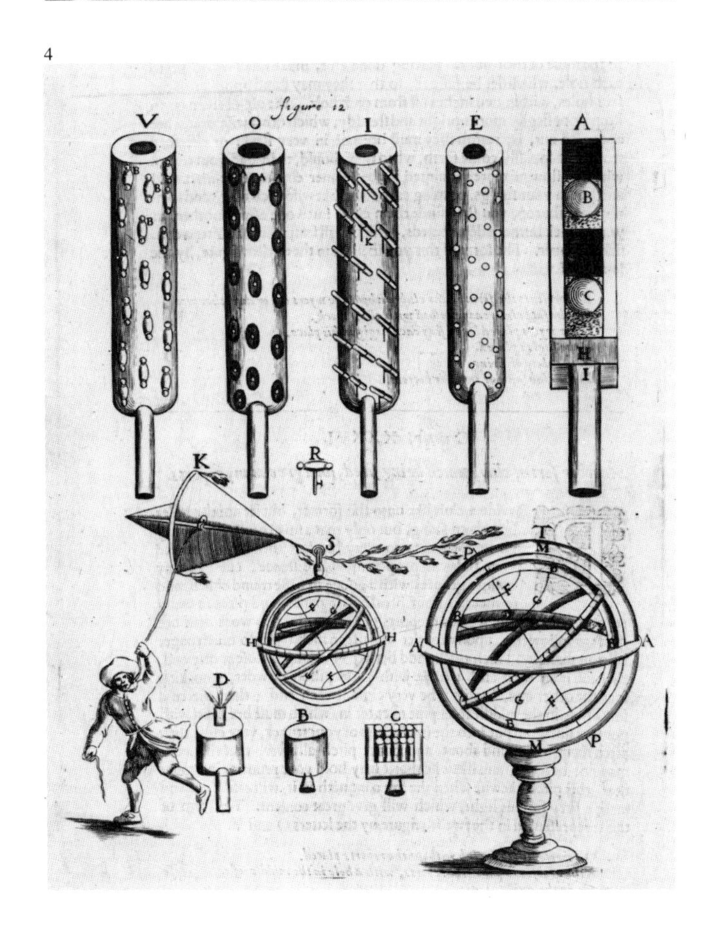

5

It was not until 1749 that the first scientific application of the kite was recorded. This was in the form of a meteorological experiment conducted by Alexander Wilson at Camlachie, in Scotland. Wilson measured the variations of temperature at different altitudes by raising thermometers on half a dozen kites flying in train to a height of 915 m (say 3,000 ft). Flying in train is the technique of flying two or more kites from a common line. Wilson's experiment was also the first recorded account of the train technique being used.

Wilson's efforts preceded by three years what must undoubtedly be the most famous scientific application of the kite of all time. In June of 1752 Benjamin Franklin lofted his electric kite in order to prove that lightning was the same 'electric matter' as that obtained from generation. Soon after his success he described how his experiment might be repeated.

'Make a small Cross of two light Strips of Cedar, the Arms so long as to reach to the four Corners of a large thin Silk Handkerchief when extended; tie the Corners of the Handkerchief to the Extremities of the Cross, so you have the Body of a Kite; which being properly accommodated with a Tail, Loop and String, will rise in the Air, like those made of Paper; but this being of Silk is fitter to bear the Wet and Wind of a Thunder Gust without tearing. To the Top of the upright Stick of the Cross is to be fixed a very sharp pointed Wire, rising a Foot or more above the Wood. To the End of the Twine, next the Hand, is to be tied a silk Ribbon, and where the Twine and the silk join, a Key may be fastened. This Kite is to be raised when a Thunder Gust appears to be coming on, and the Person who holds the String must stand within a Door, or Window, or under some Cover, so that the Silk Ribbon may not be wet; and Care must be taken that the Twine does

1

2

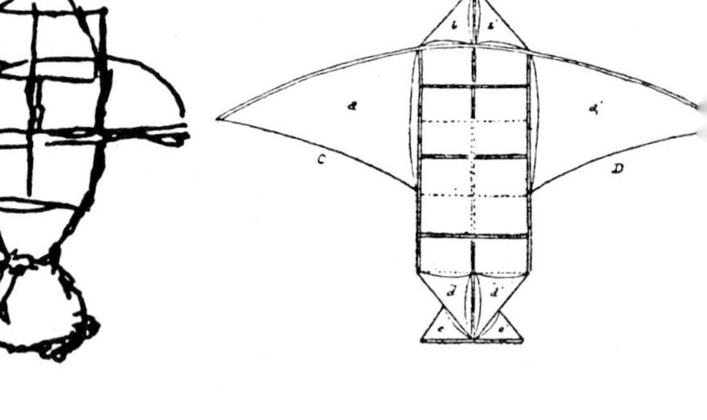

1) Benjamin Franklin, aided by his son, carries out his famous electrical experiment of 1752.
2) An aircraft configuration by Cayley in 1839 (left), anticipated remarkably a French kite design of the early twentieth century.
3) Cayley's first model glider of 1804, comprised of a simple arch top kite mounted on a rod. Steerage and stability were provided by the adjustable tail-unit. This remarkable configuration marked the beginning of a true understanding of aeronautical theory.
4) Cayley's design for his 'governable parachute' or man-carrying glider as it appeared in *Mechanics Magazine* in 1852. The craft has since been constructed and flown successfully.
Science Museum, London.

not touch the Frame of the Door or Window. As soon as any of the Thunder Clouds come over the Kite, the pointed Wire will draw the Electric Fire from them, and the Kite, with all the Twine, will be electrified, and the loose Filaments of the Twine will stand out every Way, and be attracted by an approaching Finger. And when the Rain has wet the Kite and Twine, so that it can conduct the Electric Fire freely, you will find it stream out plentifully from the Key on the Approach of your Knuckle. At this Key the Phial may be charged, and from Electric Fire thus obtain'd, Spirits may be kindled, and all the other Electric Experiments may be perform'd, which are usually done by the Help of a rubbed Glass Globe or Tube; and thereby the *Sameness* of the Electric Matter with that of Lightning completely demonstrated.'[4]

4. Franklin, B., *The Papers of Benjamin Franklin*, edited by L. W. Labaree, Vol. 4, New Haven, 1961, pp. 360–69.

Other electrical experimenters followed, but their kites were basically crude and inefficient, mainly made of paper, and the combined disadvantages of compensatory tails and heavy wire lines restricted their experiments to altitudes of no more than 300 m (say 1,000 ft).

The earliest significant experiments made with the form of the kite were undoubtedly those of Sir George Cayley made between 1799 and 1809. Even though his development of the shape of the kite was virtually a by-product of his devotion to the concept of heavier-than-air-flight, in his classic pronouncement 'The whole problem is confined within these limits, to make a surface support a given weight by the application of power to the resistance of air,' he expressed the essence of aeronautic theory. He had discovered the essential separateness of thrust from lift.

3

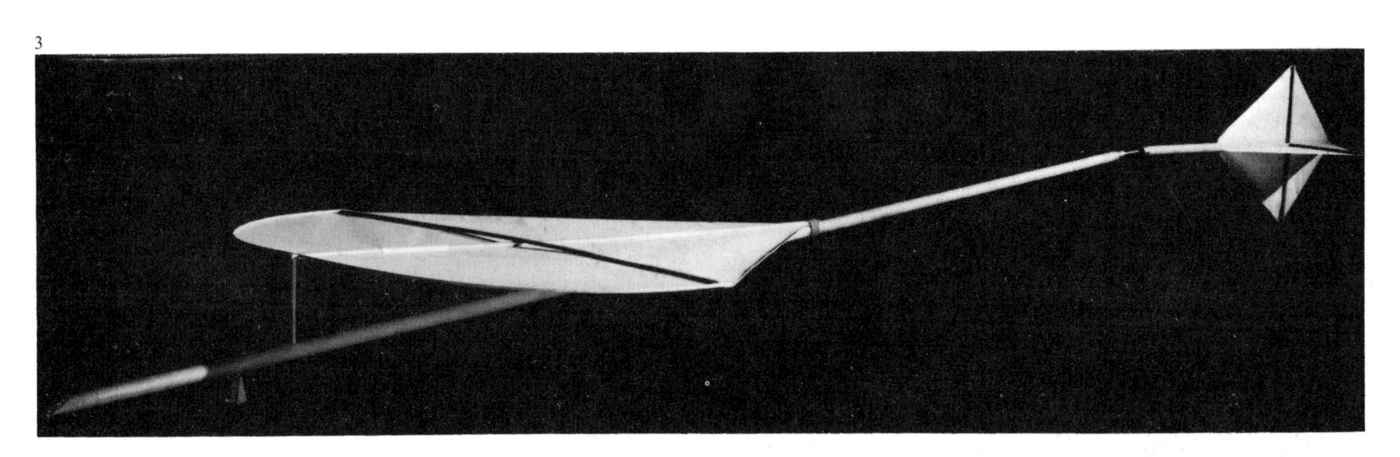

4

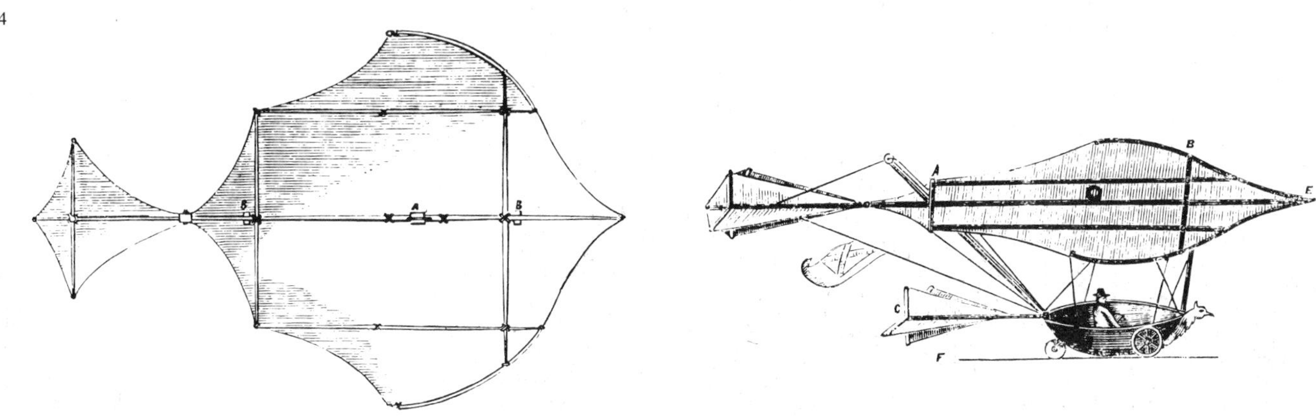

Cayley's first model glider, made in 1804, incorporated an English arch top kite as a wing unit. Had he had an adequate source of power there is little doubt that the aeroplane would have been invented much sooner than it was. Of this kite, or glider, he recorded, 'I have made surfaces of this kind carry down weights as high as 80 or 90 (lb) with perfect steadiness and steerage to either side at pleasure.'[5]

Fourteen years later Cayley designed a model glider incorporating two kites, a large one for the wing unit, and a small one for the tail. The wing unit was set in the form of a dihedral angle, which he discovered gave the glider greater stability. W. A. Eddy made this same discovery seventy-three years later. In 1852 an article appeared in *Mechanics' Magazine* entitled 'Sir George Cayley's Governable Parachutes'. It is likely that this prophetic configuration formed the basis for his so-called 'new flyer' of 1853 in which he flew his coachman across a dale at Brompton. Cayley's grand-daughter, Mrs Thompson, recorded the occasion thus:

'Of course, everyone was out on the high side and saw the start from close to. The coachman went in the machine and landed on the west side at about the same level. I think it came down rather a shorter distance than expected. The coachman got himself clear, and when the watchers had got across, he shouted," Please, Sir George, I wish to give notice. I was hired to drive, and not to fly" . . . That's all I recollect. The machine was put high away in the barn, and I used to sit and hide in it (from Governess) when so inspired.'[6]

5. Gibbs-Smith, C. H., *Sir George Cayley's Aeronautics 1796–1855*, London, 1962, p. 85.

6. Gibbs-Smith, C. H., *Sir George Cayley (1773–1857)*, London, 1968, p. 21.

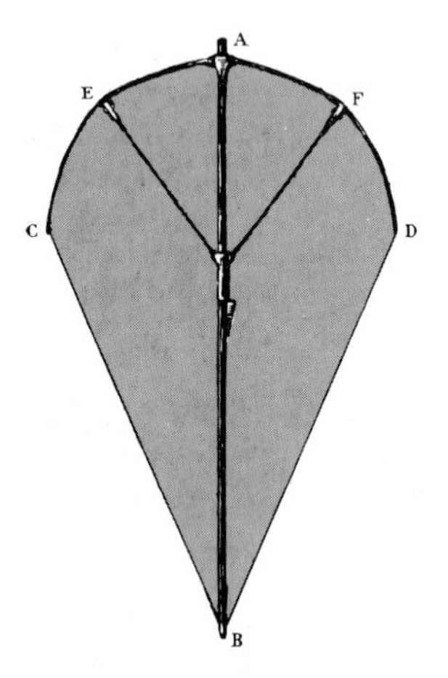

George Pocock's folding kite, 1830, utilizing the umbrella principle.

1

1) Specification drawing for Pocock's *char-volant*.
2) An illustration emphasizing the *char-volant's* capabilities of travelling north, east and west on a single wind direction.
3) Pocock also employed kite traction to propel boats. A boat race is shown in progress.

This was the world's first recorded man-carrying glider flight.

The use of kites as a form of traction dates back to very early times. The Samoans used kites to propel their canoes, and much later Benjamin Franklin recorded how he used a kite to propel himself, whilst floating on his back, across a pond. Probably the most flamboyant use of the kite to provide traction was that devised by the English schoolteacher George Pocock, whose famous *char-volant* was patented in 1826. Drawn by two adapted English arch top kites arranged in tandem, Pocock's lightweight carriage was capable of carrying four or five passengers at speeds of up to thirty-two kilometres per hour (20 m.p.h.). Considerable control was provided by four lines which governed both the lateral and longitudinal angle to the wind, allowing the kites to fly '. . . to the right or the left of the wind's course'. Pocock relates many amusing adventures with his *char-volant*, amongst them how he was exempt from toll-fees as, though the toll-keeper had specified fees for carriages and carts drawn by horses, mules, donkeys and oxen, no such specifications existed for vehicles drawn by kites.

Pocock appears to have been obsessed with the lifting and pulling properties of the kite, and recorded how he combined the two in an amazing experiment that took place about 1826, when

'. . . a large wagon with a considerable load was drawn along, whilst this huge machine at the same time carried an observer aloft in the air, realizing almost the romance of flying.'[7]

7. Pocock, G., *A Treatise of the Aeropleustic Art*, London, 1851, pp. 53–4.

2

3

A little earlier than this Pocock had lofted his daughter Martha to a height of 90 m (say 300 ft), seated in an armchair suspended from the kite line. His son was similarly lofted from a beach to the top of a 60 m (say 200 ft) high cliff. After a safe landing on the bluff, the boy climbed back into the chair and, releasing the necessary tackle, caused the chair and its occupant to slide down the line to the operator on the beach.

Some rather ingenious experiments involving kites were made in Switzerland by Dr Colladon during the first half of the nineteenth century. In one experiment made at his parents' country house near Geneva in 1827 he repeated Newton's famous electric experiment.

In order to establish enough lifting power to support his 'silver strings', he employed three kites attached successively one to the back of the other, apparently discovering for himself the benefits of flying in train. He knew his subject well, and took some rather sophisticated precautions to eliminate risk in his dangerous experiment, which included a winding reel made of glass.

The experiment was spectacularly successful, producing zig-zags of 'thunder' a metre in length, coloured red, white and violet, within a room in his parents' house. Colladon tells us that he ran to fetch his seventy-year-old father in order that he might enjoy the spectacle. However the old man didn't understand electricity, 'and saw with other eyes than mine . . .', begging that the experiment be terminated.

In the summer of 1844 at Cologny, near Geneva, Colladon was amused by his brother-in-law's practice of flying a vast

1

3

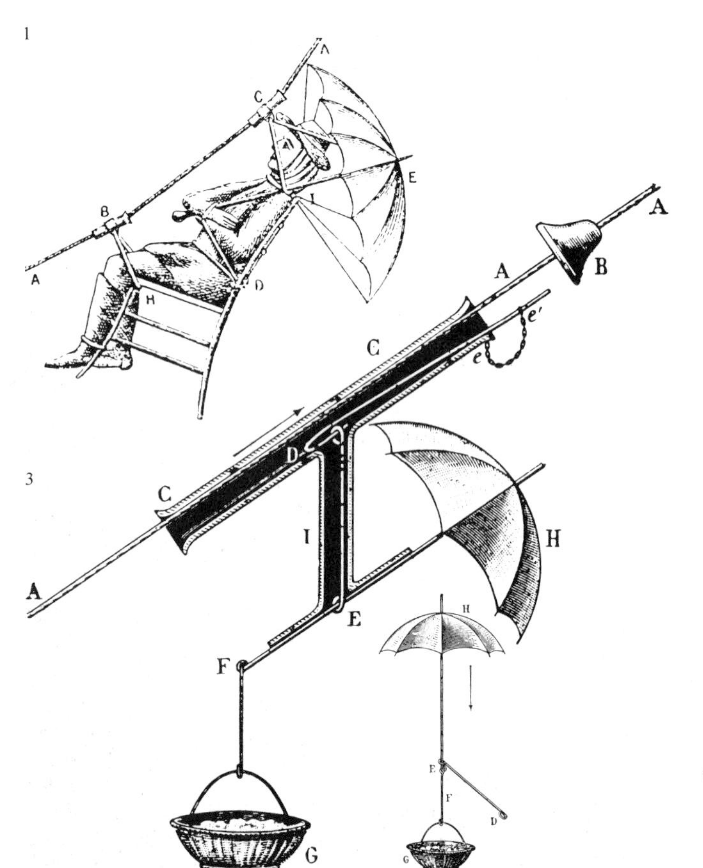

2

1) Colladon's lightweight dummy.
2) An impression of Colladon's dummy aloft, 1844.
3) Colladon's combined messenger-parachute release of 1844. After releasing its payload the carrier's unsupported weight caused it to slide back down the kite line to the handler.
4) Colladon's self-correcting, dirigible kite, capable of automatically tacking into a wind.
5) Pocock's hypothetical nautical rescue operation, employing man-lifting kites.

4

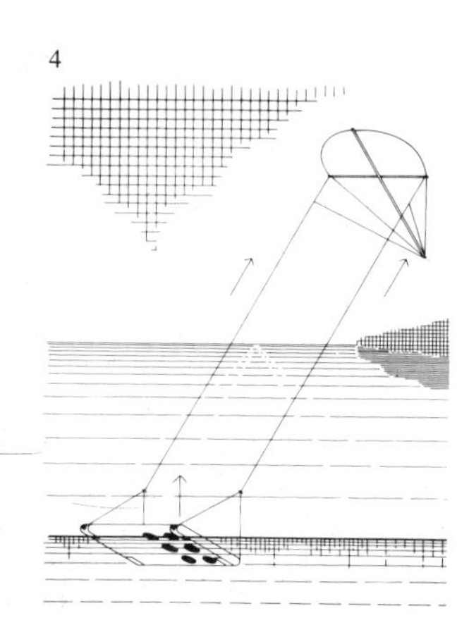

kite, up the line of which he sent an ingenious messenger, bearing flowers or fruit. This was blown up the line by a parachute which detached itself upon hitting a stop on the line, dropping its payload gently into the neighbourhood of friends or relatives. Colladon extended this idea by causing a dummy weighing slightly less than six kilos to be blown up a kite line by means of a huge umbrella. The dummy, seated in a wicker chair, travelled to a height of 200 m (656 ft), much to the amazement of the locals.

About this time Colladon also experimented with double-lined dirigible kites capable of moving through an arc of some 200 m (say 650 ft) across the sky. This technique was later used by an American, J. Woodbridge Davis, who devised a dirigible kite in 1894 with the idea of carrying a rescue line from ship-to-shore in cases of shipwreck.

Cologny being very close to lake Leman, Colladon next experimented with an ingenious arrangement employing the dirigible kite in a crossing of the lake. The ends of each flying line were attached to a board which, by dragging through the water behind the kite, supplied the necessary pull or resistance upon the line essential to keep the kite airborne. By making holes in one side of this board and thus reducing the drag on that side, Colladon found it was possible to make a direct crossing from south to north, despite the fact that a nor'-nor'-easterly was blowing at the time.

During 1847 a competition was arranged between a group of New York children in order to establish the first connection over the Niagara River gorge. An anonymous young boy succeeded in spanning the 240 m (say 800 ft) gorge with his kite line, and a series of heavier lines, and eventually cables,

5

were drawn across, allowing work to commence on the first railway suspension bridge connecting America with Canada.

A dubious contender for the honour of being first man to be raised by a man-carrying kite in the west was Jean-Marie Le Bris, a sea-captain and amateur aviator, who in 1857 constructed a glider based upon the albatross, referring to studies that he had made of the bird during voyages. At Trefeuntec in France he was launched from a horse-drawn cart, kite-style, from the end of a line. His intention was to release the line when enough altitude had been gained, and drift gracefully down to earth. However, the horse bolted, causing a somewhat complicated and long-drawn-out accident. At one stage the flying line broke from the carriage, wrapped itself around the captain's coachman and bore him aloft also. Remarkably, the only injury sustained in the ensuing crash was a broken leg for Le Bris, who, undeterred, went on to build another glider, which he wisely tested with ballast instead of a pilot.

Some two years before the experiments of Jean-Marie Le Bris, a resident of Dijon, Dr Jules Laval, made some interesting and partly successful experiments with load-bearing kites. Using a flat kite measuring 10 m (32·80 ft) by 6 m (19·69 ft) he elevated an eleven-year-old boy named Lieutet to a height of some 10 m (32·80 ft). The boy sat in a wickerwork chair suspended beneath the tail end of the kite. The apparatus was controlled by a team of five men. The attempt almost ended in tragedy. Friction from the line burnt the hands of the aides, who found it necessary to tether the flying line to a tree stump. The continuing friction caused the wood to ignite, severing the line, and the young Lieutet, descending in free flight from a

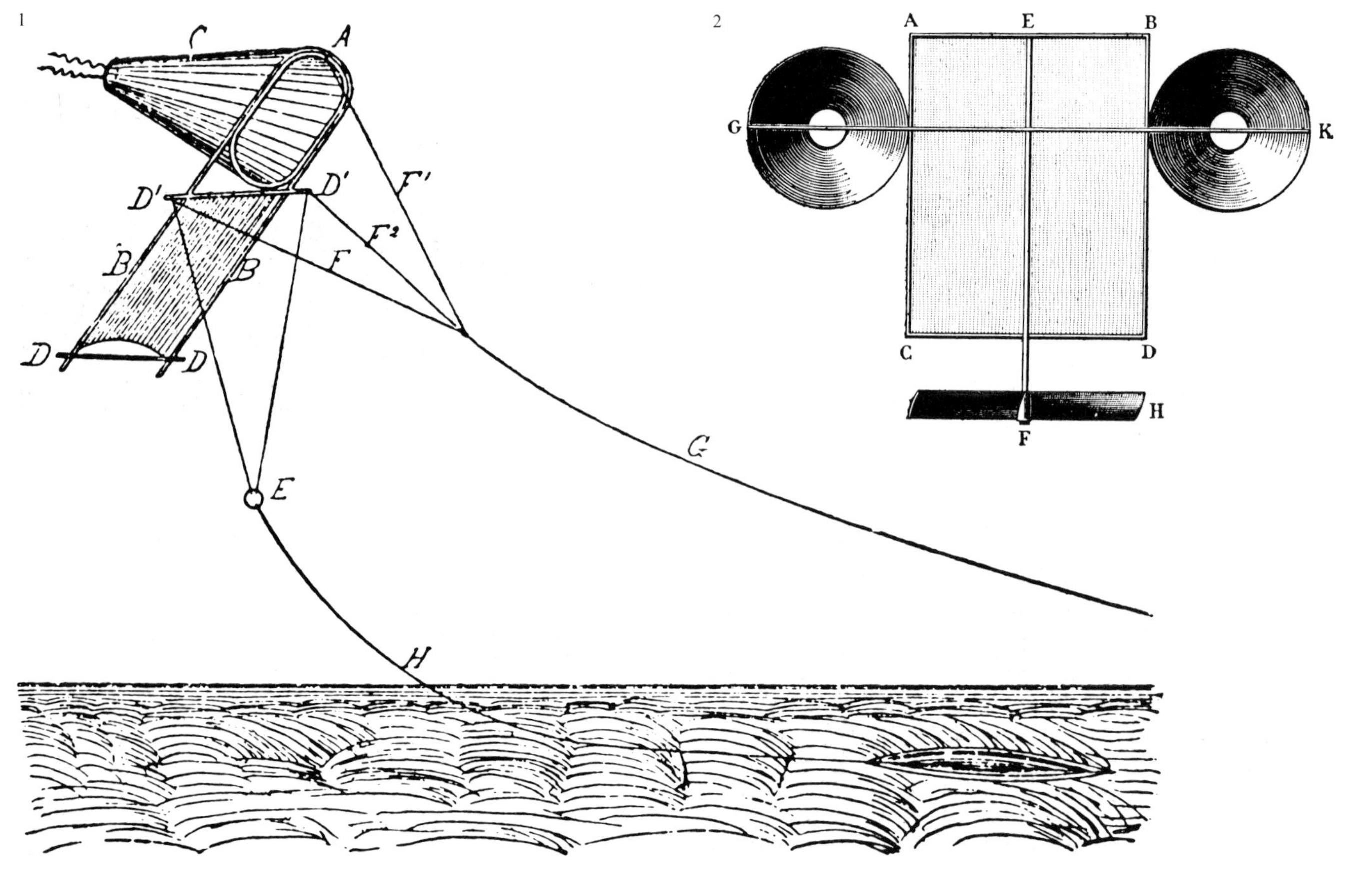

height of 10 m (say 33 ft), luckily escaped unharmed.

The first successful lofting of an adult appears to be that of E. J. Cordner, an Irish priest who, in 1859, designed, built and tested a system of load-bearing kites for ship-to-shore rescue. Although the trials were recorded as being successful, there is no evidence to suppose that Cordner's system was ever put to practical application. The technique used by Cordner incorporated a train of hexagonal kites which were to be raised from the stranded ship. The kites were used to provide traction and additional buoyancy to an extremely light, small boat capable of carrying one or two people. From the stern of this a line was played out from the main vessel. When the survivors were safely ashore the crew of the main vessel simply hauled the boat back, and the process was repeated.

A number of life-saving kites were devised towards the end of the nineteenth century, most of which exploited the fact that a kite could be blown towards a lee shore by the same wind that had caused the vessel to founder in the first place.

In France, in 1887, C. Jobert devised an easily dismantleable life-saving kite capable of carrying a line from a crippled ship to the shore. Successively heavier lines could then be drawn across the water in order that a breeches-buoy system could be erected. Jobert's kite consisted of a cone, or drogue, situated above a plane surface, the whole of which, when set at an angle of thirty degrees, developed considerable pulling power while remaining no more than 40 m or so (say 130 ft) above the surface; though it was also capable of flying at various heights simply by altering the flying angle. The kite was quite stable even in heavy winds, and took out line at a

3

4

5

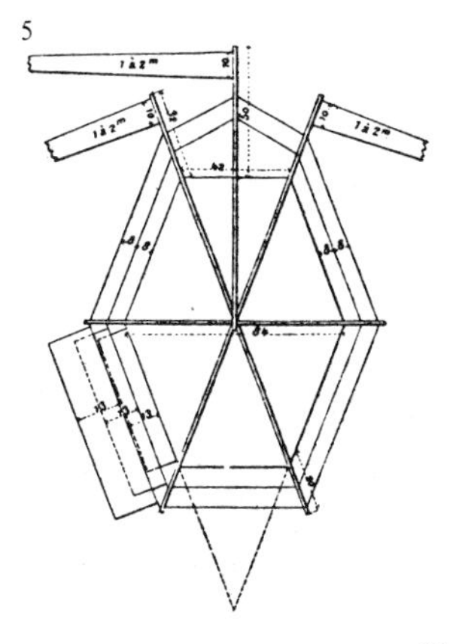

1) Jobert's life-saving kite, 1886.
2) Biot's double-coned rescue kite incorporated a propeller at its aft end, providing stabilizing drag directly proportional to the wind strength, 1888.
3) Dr David Thayer's hypothetical sailing system, using the traction power of a massive steerable kite (late nineteenth century).
4) Le Bris poses in his second glider, built in 1868.
5) A highly decorative American kite of the 1850s, rigged with multiple streamers and buzzers.

good speed while dragging a secondary cable behind it in the water, this latter being within easy reach of the receiving party. To help locate the kite in darkness or in fog, and also to summon help from those on land, Jobert devised signal lamps to attach to his kite, together with a simple but effective siren system. Across the small opening at the back of the cone ran a horizontal bar from which were suspended two metallic leaves. By vibrating in the wind these leaves produced a loud wail capable of being heard a good way off.

A strong supporter of the life-saving kite, Admiral Sir Arthur Cochrane, made numerous trials with kite-drawn torpedoes during the Russian War in 1855 while commanding a frigate. Using kites of 3·65 m (12 ft) to draw simulated torpedoes, heavy logs with percussion caps attached to them, he found that he was able to propel a 'torpedo' over distances of some 3 km (1·9 miles) with considerable accuracy; though careful calculations had to be made prior to launching, taking into account the deflection of the tide and the wind.

J. Lecornu, one-time President of the French League of the Kite, and Émile Wenz also experimented with life-saving kites around 1900, incorporating ingenious line climbers capable of carrying a reel of line, from the end of which was suspended a buoy. When approximately above the wreck the reel of line was triggered, causing the buoy to fall, taking with it line played out by the reel. Retrieval of the buoy allowed the crew to haul down the kite, employing the kite line proper as a link with their rescuers.

The use of the kite as an adjunct to meteorological experiment was first extensively developed by the British meteorologist

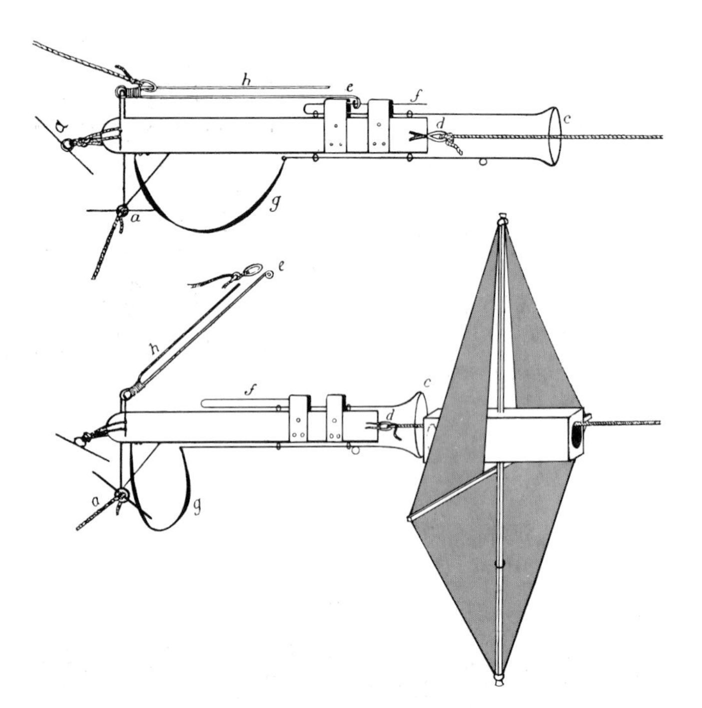

Commandant Brossard de Corbigny's bridle-release bolt, 1905, provided a method of grounding a kite for purposes of ship-to-shore rescue. The flying line was attached at d, while the fore-leg of the bridle was looped over the hook h. When the kite was well situated over land, a messenger with a large sail was released up the flying line. As this depressed the projecting feeler c, the bolt f was released, detaching the bridle fore-leg, upsetting the kite.

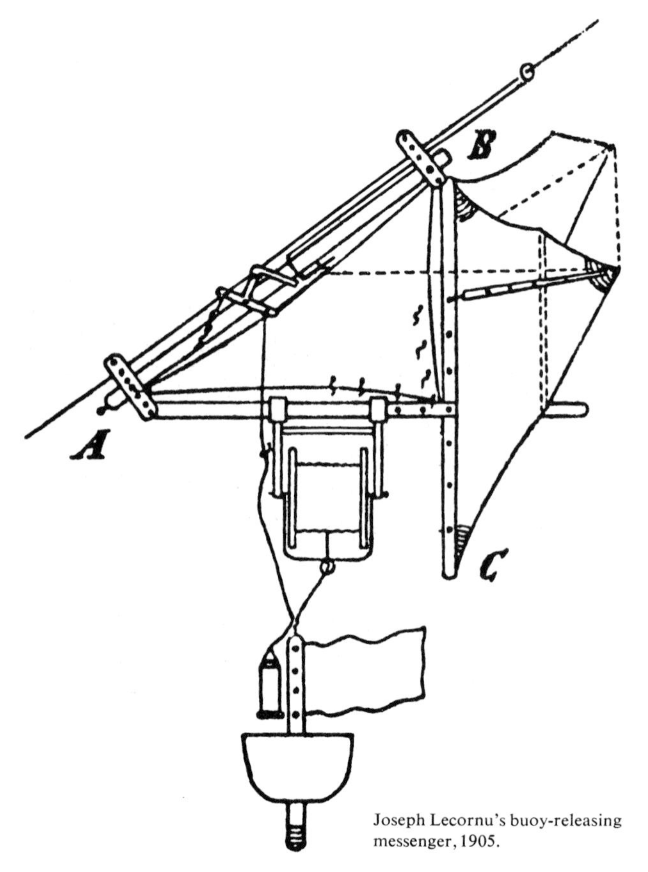

Joseph Lecornu's buoy-releasing messenger, 1905.

E. D. Archibald in 1833. He succeeded in lifting anemometers on kites, measuring wind speeds at various altitudes. As well as reviving the application of the kite as a meteorological tool, Archibald scored a first in 1887 by taking the first aerial photographs from a kite.

Controlled meteorological experiments had also been made in the early 1830s by members of the first formal association of kite flyers ever to be formed; this was the Franklin Kite Club, an American organization set up primarily to experiment, as its name suggests, with electric kites.

At Kew Observatory in 1847, W. R. Birt demonstrated his system for lofting meteorological instruments by way of a tethered hexagonal kite. A large hexagonal kite with a standard tail and bridle was stabilized by means of two lines, additional to the flying line, securing either end of the horizontal strut. These two lines, together with the flying line, were tethered on the ground at the points of a large equilateral triangle, the peg securing the kite line proper obviously being the windward point of the triangle. Having thus established a stable platform in the air, it was Birt's suggestion that measuring instruments might be raised or lowered from the kite at will.

In France, in 1886, Maillot used this same stabilizing technique for his load-bearing kites: though his kite also had a variable angle of incidence which could be adjusted by the 'pilot', who sat on a board like a swing, suspended beneath the kite. At least that was the theory, but in fact control was always applied from the ground. Despite the fact that his kites were consistently stable, Maillot neither made an ascent himself, nor did he ever lift a man.

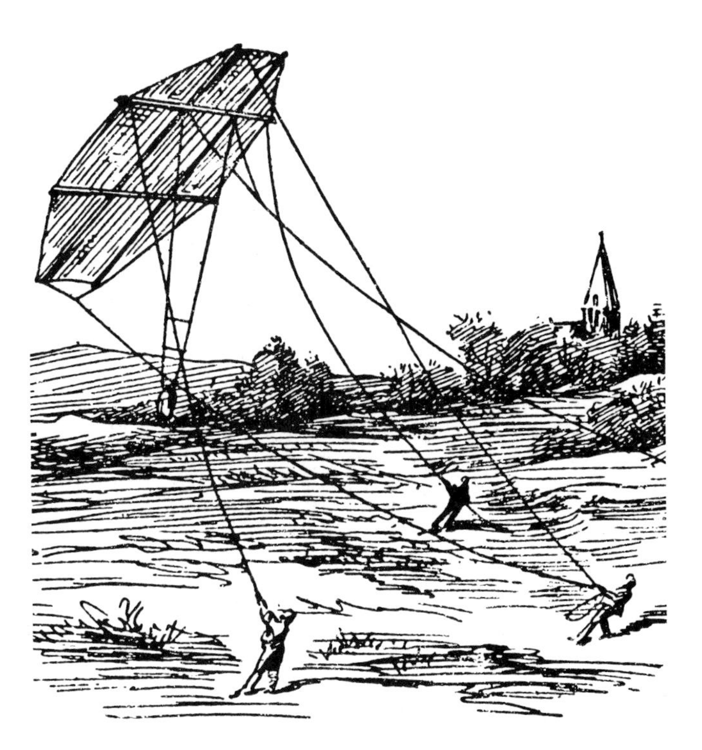

Maillot's man-lifting kite, 1886.

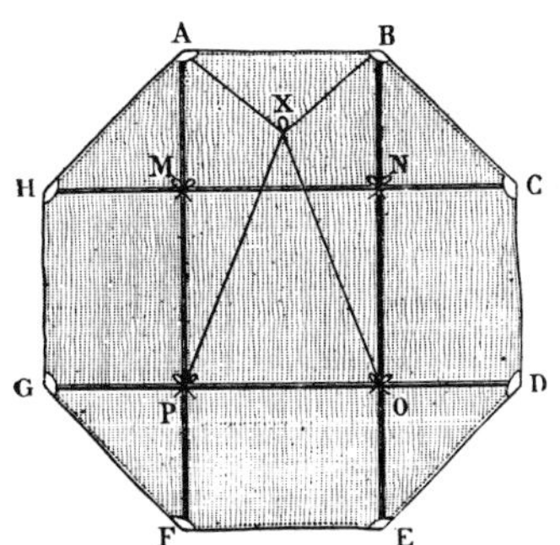

Maillot later rejected octagonal kites in favour of his untrimmed version of Silas J. Conyne's kite.

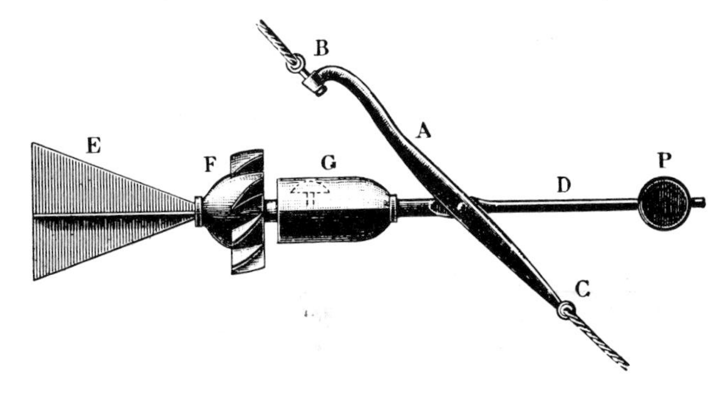

Goupil's kite anemometer, 1886.

While a prisoner in Austria in 1870, Maillot had watched some abortive attempts at raising a military observer in a balloon. Because of the high wind the balloon was constantly blown towards the ground. Maillot realized that, if a suitable kite was used for this purpose, the stronger the wind blew the higher the kite would climb.

On 3 May 1886 Maillot prepared for his famous lifting experiment by raising approximately 65 k (143 lb) on a kite. On the sixteenth of that same month he repeated the experiment in the presence of members of the French Society of Aerial Navigation using a much stronger and larger kite. On this occasion he lifted a sandbag weighing 68 k (say 150 lb) to a height of 10 m (say 33 ft). It appears that during these experiments Maillot had to be dissuaded from raising himself on the kite by members of the society, who felt that further development was needed before lives were risked.
In order to encourage this development the society awarded Maillot 100 francs. He went on to build bigger kites, eventually attaining a lift of 270 k (595 lb), before discontinuing his lifting experiments in favour of developing a lightning conducting system for kites. This lead to further meteorological applications, and during the late 1890s Maillot was associated with the observatory at Trappes before abandoning aeronautical experiments for some years.

With renewed enthusiasm after an outstanding success in the French Society of Aerial Navigation competition of 1905, he again set to work on a system of man-lifting. He now rejected his earlier octagonal kite in favour of a train of compound kites not dissimilar to the Conyne kite which had been patented by an American, Silas J. Conyne, in 1902. It was

Man-lifting Conyne kites, 1910.

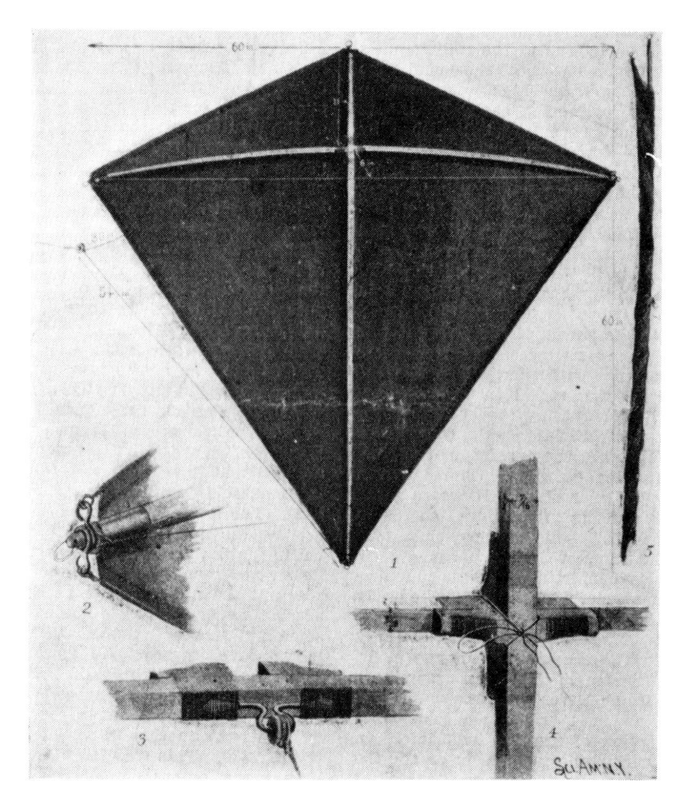

Wardwell's folding Malay kite, 1909.

a form of this kite that was eventually adopted by the French army, and as a consequence has become better known as the French Military box kite. Again Maillot's experiments were confined to the lifting of ballast, and it is said that he died deeply regretting that he had never taken to the air himself.

Throughout the 1890s numerous experiments concerning aerial photography were made on both sides of the Atlantic. Despite Archibald's success in 1887, a number of other claims for this 'first' were still appearing during the following decade. In his remarkable work *Parakites*, Gilbert Totten Woglom states his claim as having made the first aerial photographs to appear in America.

'By the first expedition of the camera, on 21 September 1895, at three o'clock and thirty-five minutes, were secured . . . the first aerial photographs from glass plates taken on the Western Continent; the writer is ready to be corrected if he misclaims conjointly with Mr Henshaw to have taken these the largest kite line photographic views in the world.'[8]

'Parakite' was Woglom's name for his tailless kite, virtually a bowed Malay, similar if not identical to William A. Eddy's bow kite, which Eddy developed in the 1890s. It seems quite likely, however, that Woglom and Eddy rediscovered the virtues of the Javanese bow kite quite independently.

William A. Eddy was a journalist from Bayonne, New Jersey. He contributed a great deal to western kite development, and made extensive experiments in the raising of photographic and meteorological payloads. For this he needed good, steady lift

8. Woglom, G. T., *Parakites*, New York, 1896, p. 43.

William A. Eddy.

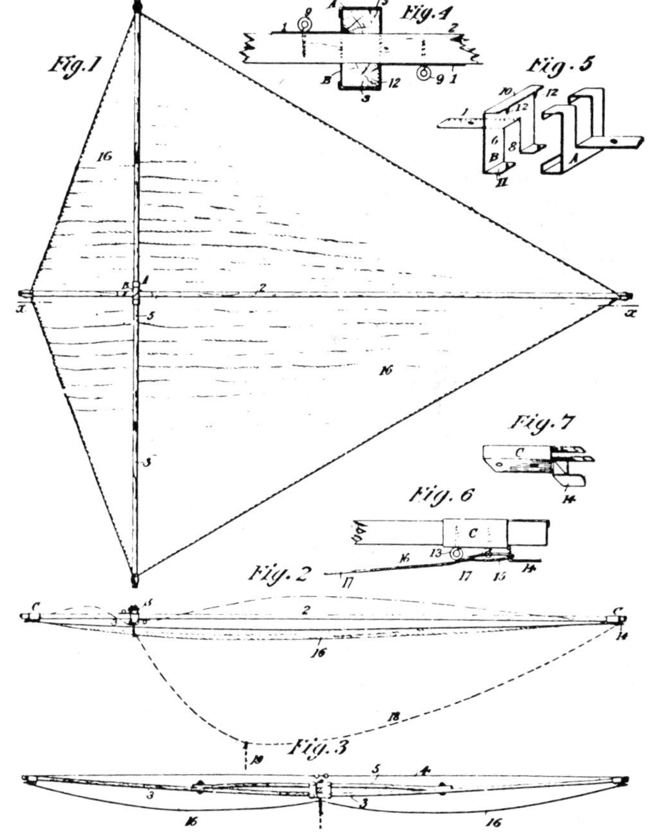

Patent drawings of Eddy's kite, 1900.

to great heights, and turned to the technique of train flying to provide him with the required stability and efficiency. His first experiments with train flying were made with hexagonal kites, sometimes flying as many as eighteen kites on one line. However, the tails of these proved to be unmanageable and inefficient in this application, and in order to combat these disadvantages he set himself the task of developing an efficient, stable kite, able to fly without a tail, resulting in his famous bowed kite. Eddy knew of the existence of the Javanese tailless kite, but could find no information on it. He subsequently 'invented' his own version. He eventually did see an original Javanese kite at the Columbian Exposition of 1893, and was able to confirm his own findings, and with a few modifications arrived at his own version of the Javanese kite which he patented in 1900.

Eddy found that by bowing the spar to form a dihedral angle, and by using a looser cover than usual, the kite took on something of the character of a ship in water, giving good fore-and-aft stability by virtue of a keel being formed by the spine, with good lateral stability by way of the standard compensatory qualities of the dihedral set of the wings. Furthermore, when set into the wind, the loose cover over the bottom area of the kite billowed upwards, acting to some extent as an aerofoil, giving the kite increased lift.

Eddy bows were used at the Blue Hill Observatory, Massachusetts, and by the U.S. Weather Bureau during 1894–5, but were soon ousted by the introduction of Lawrence Hargrave's box kite, the stability and great lifting powers of which were to win it a place in meteorological survey continuously through to the mid nineteen twenties.

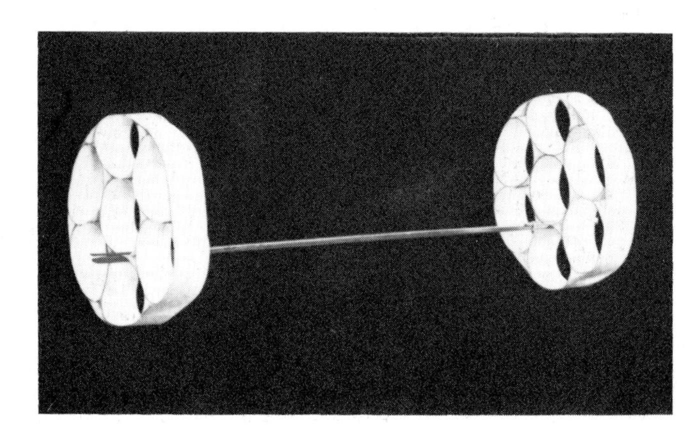

As was the case with Cayley, Hargrave's experiments with the kite form were a by-product of his ambitions towards powered flight. Born in Greenwich, England, on 29 January 1850, Lawrence Hargrave emigrated to New South Wales in 1866. A scrupulous and remarkable man, he refused to patent any of his findings, preferring that they should be made common knowledge, in order that they might benefit anybody who could make use of them. He invented his box kite in 1893. In order to further his experiments in powered flight Hargrave built a great variety of model aeroplanes and kites during that year, resulting in various forms of plane-surface, dihedral and box kites. He also made copious notes on all his trials, including his one and only kite flight, beneath a train of box kites, to a height of some 5 m (16 ft). A further contribution to aerodynamics stemmed from Hargrave's experiments towards the development of the cambered aerofoil, that is the curved wing section for greater lift. While Cayley had guessed at the advantages of a cambered wing it was Horatio F. Phillips who, around 1880, discovered and developed the principles of a double-surfaced aerofoil capable of producing a lower pressure above the wing surface than below. Hargrave was quick to experiment with Phillips's findings, and greatly increased the efficiency of his box kite, or 'cellular' kite as he preferred to call it. The following year, after repeated failures in his attempts at powered flight, Hargrave retired from full time experimentation.

During his early forties Lawrence Hargrave (opposite) made extensive experiments with both dihedral and cellular configurations. Materials used ranged from tin sheet to redwood veneer, 1893.
Royal Aeronautical Society.

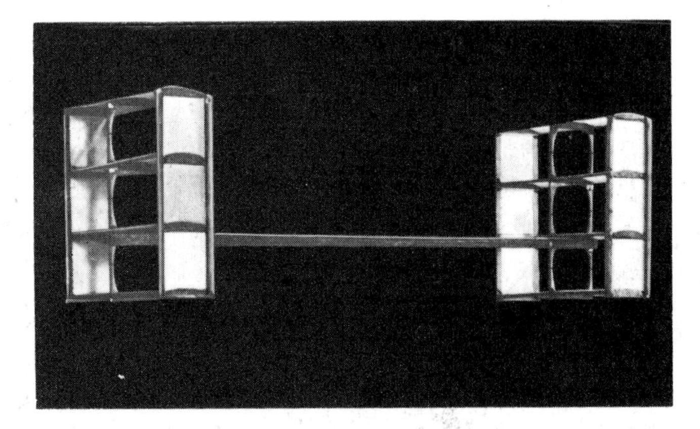

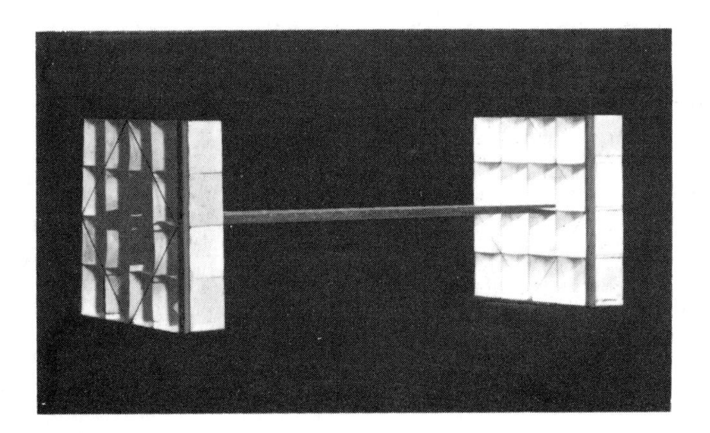

1

2

3

4

1–2) Hargrave experimenting in New South Wales with some cellular permutations.
3) Assisted by James Swann, Hargrave tests a lightweight alternative to the usual nacelle, suspended beneath a well ballasted box kite.
4) Hargrave with a model of his box kite aeroplane, incorporating his single-celled, reflex-curved aerofoil kite.
5) A typical page from Hargrave's voluminous and meticulous note-books. *Royal Aeronautical Society.*
6) Single-celled, reflex-curved aerofoil kite by Lawrence Hargrave. *Lent to the Science Museum, London, by the Royal Aeronautical Society.*
7–8) Two of numerous soaring kites produced by Hargrave during 1898. *Royal Aeronautical Society.*

5

April. 20th 1896.
I am thinking that the very best method of trying my flying machine will be to start from calm water & if possible, with a strong current running in the direction I am going: wheels, truck or track would be dispensed with, & 3 or 4 wager boat or spindle shaped (wood or paper) floats, totaling 300 lb displacement substituted every increase of speed would increase the lift of the silk surfaces & decrease the skin resistance of the water on the floats: the current running with the machine & a light air meeting it would also assist.

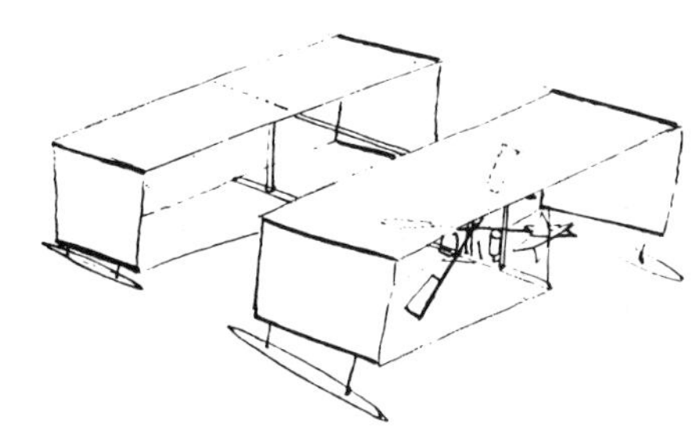

April: 22nd 1896 Tried No 2 boiler & burner; with hand pump. Kerosene spilt & took fire on air pump delivery pipe. melted solder spoilt trial. blanket (double) over asbestos boiler casing charred: at top.
April 23rd Made an outer asbestos boiler casing about 3/4" air space between the two casings. repaired damaged pipe. & tried again.

	h	m
Lamp lit	3	35 1/2
Fire lit	3	43 1/2
began to pump	3	43 3/4
Kerosene done	3 -	48

4 1/4 minutes.
1 pint of Kerosene used: much slopped about. 4 1/2 pints of water pumped.
Steam discharged into a tilted bucket. Some water carried over, not measured as force of steam drove the water over the edge of the bucket: pumping & fire irregular, the Kerosene cock is stiff & very easily turned on too much: The water pump (.636" dia area 1.44" stroke double acting) was hard to work by hand, there was about 15 lbs force on the rod i.e. 23.6 lbs per sq in boiler pressure due to the resistance of the long pipe to the passage of the steam;
no flame visible at the chimney: outer asbestos casing quite cool.
I think this rather good, as it approaches the required quantity of water to be evaporated. 13 pints in ten minutes: 4 1/2 pints in 4 1/4 mins
= 10.6 — 10 mins.

April. 26. 1896 on taking out the coil I find a deposit of soot evenly distributed all over the inside of casing (except the bottom) coil, & funnel. There was no soot on March 24.
April 27. The soot will be due to the pressure on the Kerosene being too high & forcing it into the furnace too quickly so that it is not burnt properly.
Bored the sparkers; hole to 1/7 in

6

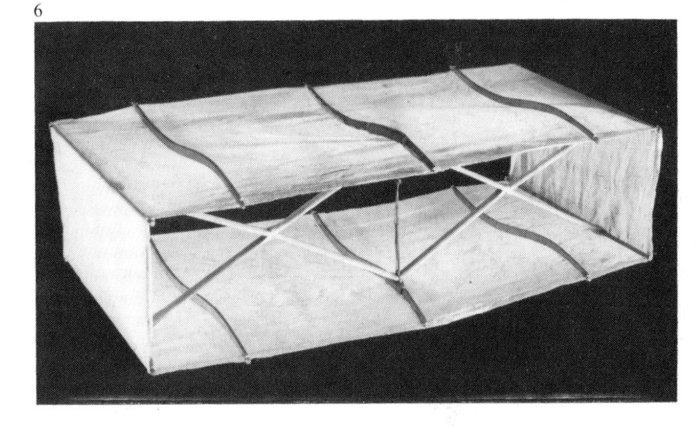

7 8

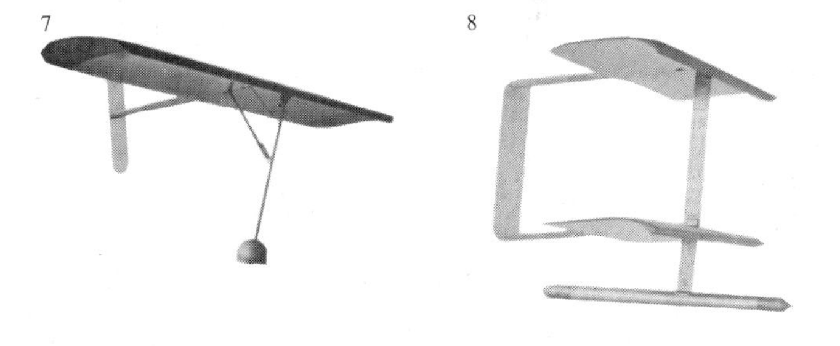

A modification of Hargrave's box kite, the Blue Hill meteorological kite, 1896.

Steam-driven capstan used at Blue Hill Observatory in conjunction with the Blue Hill box kite.

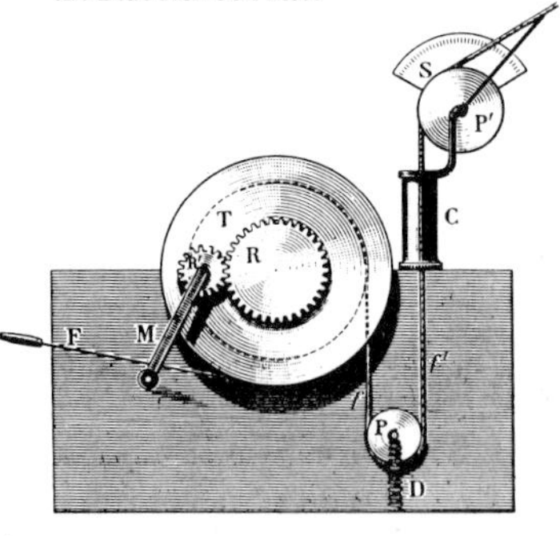

The final perfected version of Hargrave's box kite, 1893.
Lent to the Science Museum, London, by Sir Richard Threlfall.

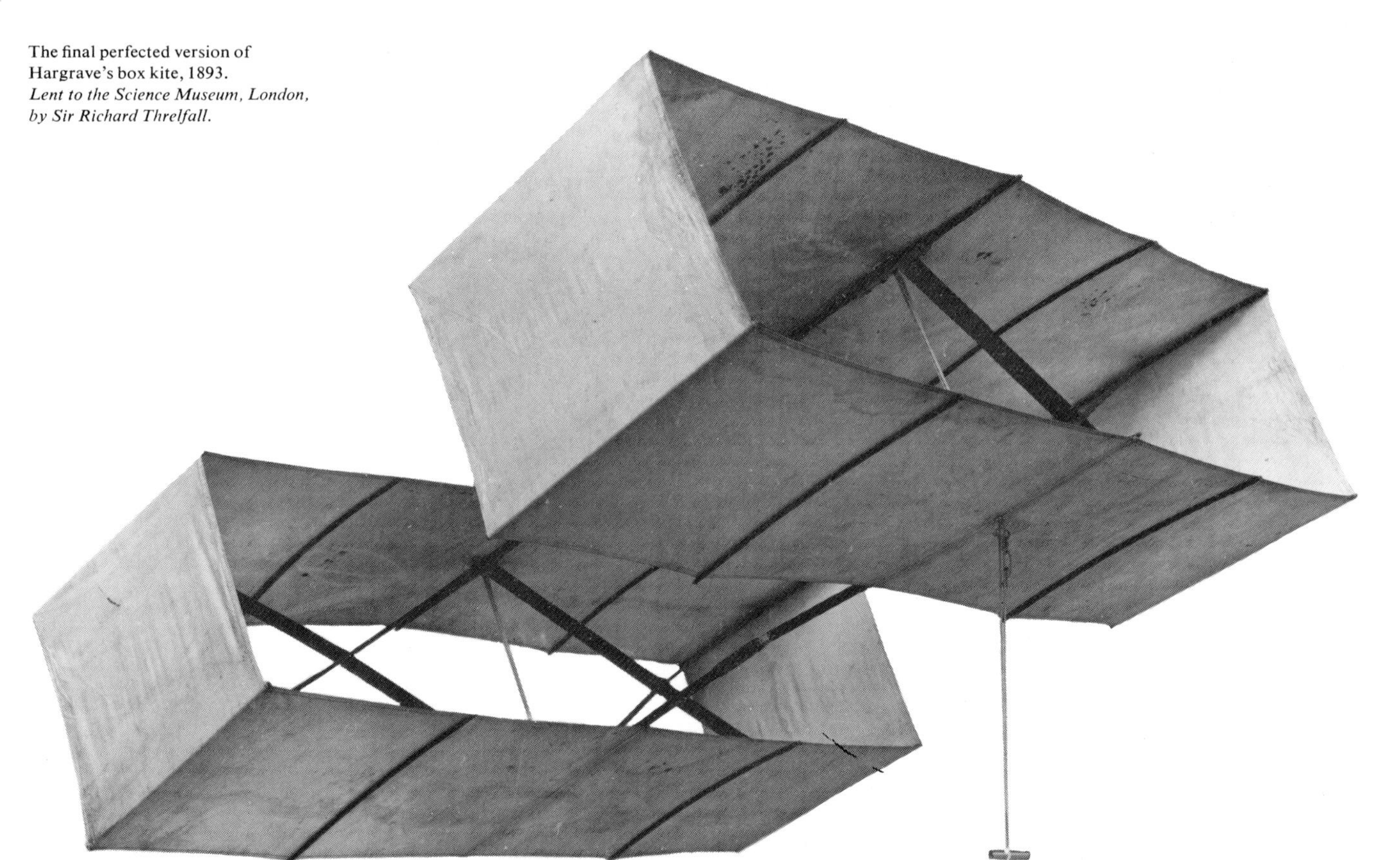

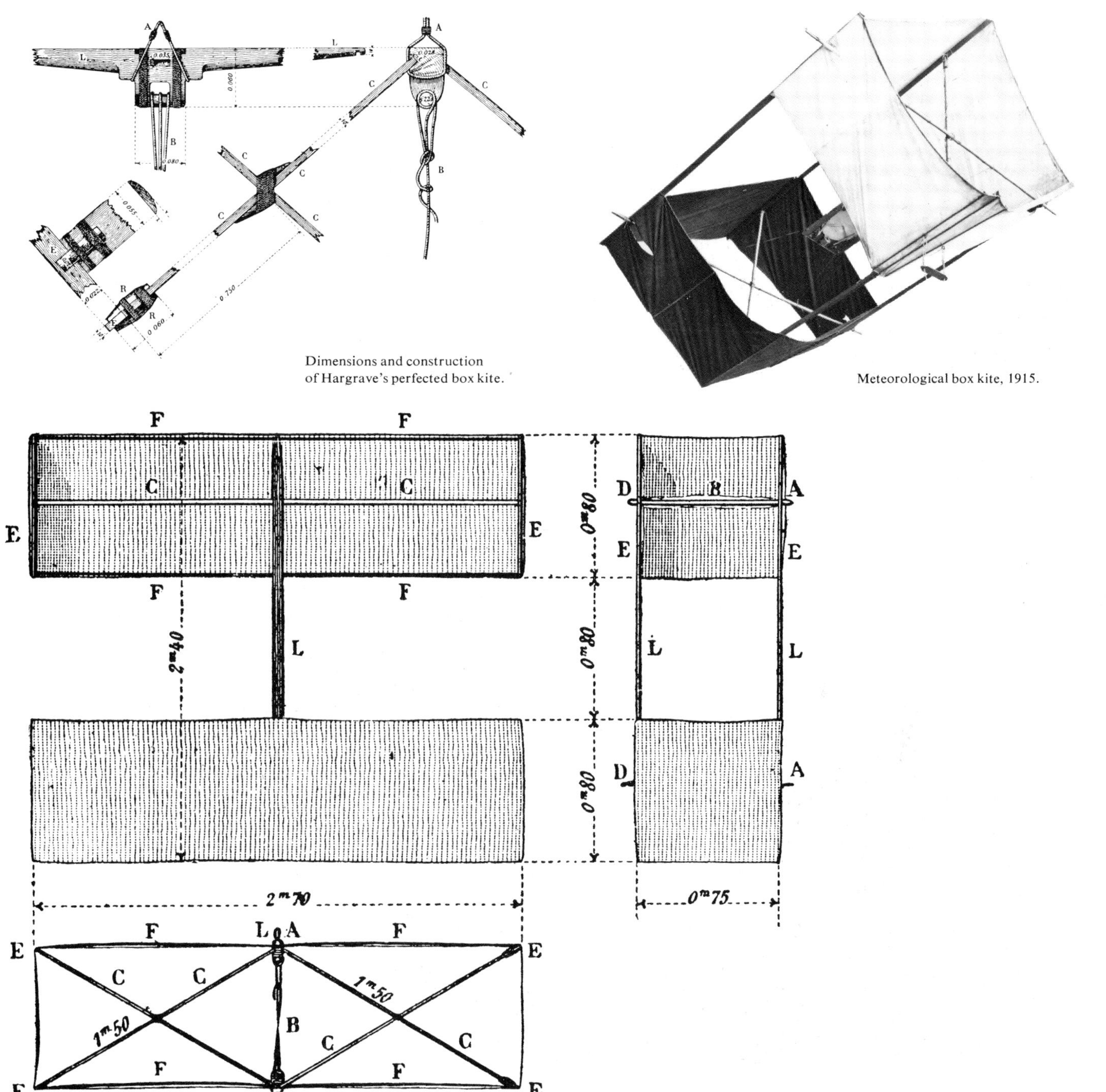

Dimensions and construction of Hargrave's perfected box kite.

Meteorological box kite, 1915.

An important pioneer of man-lifting techniques was B. F. S. Baden-Powell, of the Scots Guards. He was a well-known balloonist, and brother of the founder of the Boy Scout movement. He first gained recognition with his kites on 27 January 1894, at Pirbright Camp, England, when he lifted a man with a single kite, with the idea of providing the army with a means of aerial observation.

Working at a time when aerodynamic knowledge was in its infancy, Baden-Powell placed great store on plane-surface hexagonal kites, apparently refusing to acknowledge that the Hargrave kite had any theoretical advantage. This first success was with a giant kite, 11 m (36 ft) high, made of bamboo with a cambric cover. It was not unlike the traditional Japanese Rokkaku, though its spars were flexible enough to allow it to develop its own dihedral when set into a reasonable wind, giving the kite fairly good stability without recourse to a tail. With this kite, flown from twin lines for greater stability, he raised men to 3 m (say 10 ft) or so, as any greater height was considered too dangerous for such crude equipment. Baden-Powell's faith in his apparatus can to some degree be measured by the fact that he generally made his ascents with an open parachute over his head. He consequently developed a system of flying in train, using smaller kites of approximately 10 m² (110 ft²) in area, varying the number of kites between four and seven at a time, depending upon the wind conditions. This system proved to be far more reliable, and Baden-Powell patented the design in 1895, calling the kite the Levitor. That same year he demonstrated the system to the British Association, lifting himself and others to heights of about 30 m (say 100 ft). Again, however, because of his kite's basic instability, he adopted a two line system of bridling, separate

1

2

1) Man-lifting trials with a train of Baden-Powell Levitors.
2) One of the first ascents made with a single Levitor kite, 1894. *Royal Aeronautical Society*.
3) Baden-Powell's 11 m (36 ft) man-lifting giant, 1894.
4) Marconi's assistants raising a kite-aerial for transatlantic reception tests at St John's, Newfoundland, in December 1901. Marconi is on the extreme left. *G.E.C. Marconi Electronics Ltd*.
5) Marconi's assistant G. S. Kemp (in later life) with one of the Levitor kites used for aerial elevation in Marconi's early experiments. *G.E.C. Marconi Electronics Ltd*.

lines being connected at points on the ground some distance apart, in order to hold the kite firmly into the wind.

On 12 December 1901 Guglielmo Marconi made his first successful transatlantic wireless reception tests from Poldhu in Cornwall to St John's, Newfoundland. The receiving aerial was raised 122 m (400 ft) or so by means of the Baden-Powell Levitor kite. A strong wind was blowing, and the first attempt to raise the aerial resulted in the loss of a kite. Even though the second kite fared more successfully, its basic instability caused such violent movement in the aerial that Marconi was forced to make some technical compromises to his receiving equipment in order to compensate for the kite's misbehaviour.

3

4

5

It was with the aid of a double train of Hargrave's box kites that Lieutenant Hugh Wise of the U.S. Army succeeded in lifting himself in 1897. Wise had made preliminary tests with a dummy weighing some 68 k (150 lb). This was raised on a single train of three box kites. A pulley was attached at the point at which the two upper kites joined the main line. Through this pulley a line supporting a boatswain's chair was passed, and when sufficient height had been attained the dummy was hoisted up in the chair. The main line was then run out for some distance before a squall upset the whole arrangement, depositing 'Jimmy', Wise's name for his dummy, and all three kites, somewhat unceremoniously into New York Harbour. Benefiting from the accident, Wise evolved a different arrangement of setting the kites. Two separate trains were used, each made up of a pilot kite, attached to a much larger lifter kite. The two flying lines were then gathered at the pulley point, and on this apparatus Wise duly ascended to a height of 12 m (say 40 ft) – and eventually descended five minutes later – with considerably more success than Jimmy had had just two days before.

Up to this point all recorded man-lifting attempts had been made with the aviator being suspended from the kite line at a point considerably below the kite itself. It was an American, Charles J. Lamson, possibly the finest kite designer of all time, who first succeeded in flying virtually within a kite. In August 1896 Lamson began a series of experiments, attempting to lift an observer with the help of a modified Hargrave box kite, flying from piano wire. The kite was fitted with a movable back cell, which allowed the rear of the kite to be raised or lowered by the pilot, thus controlling the angle of incidence. Further control was gained by the pilot,

1

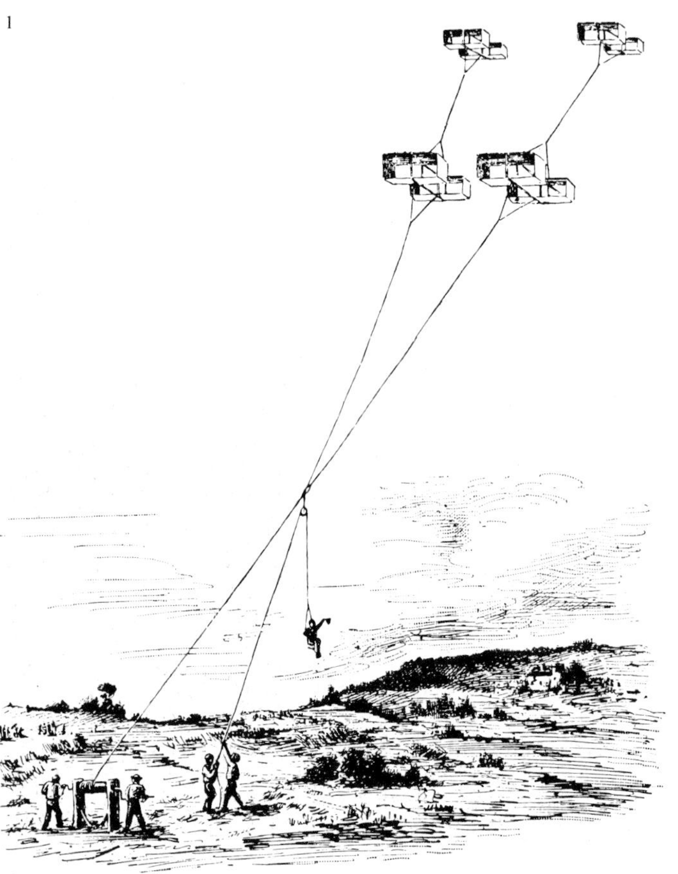

2

3

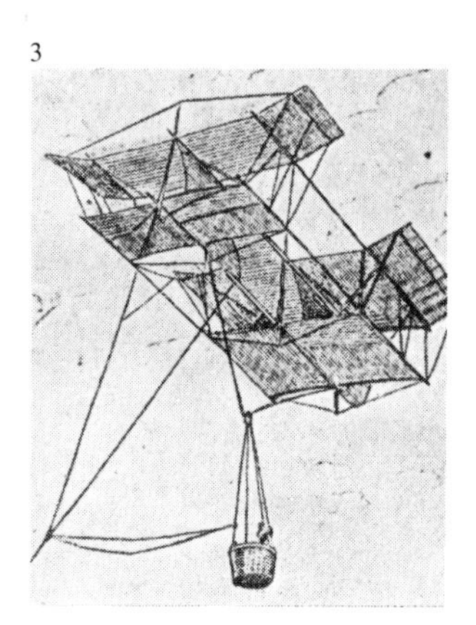

1) Wise's successful man-lifting experiment, 1897.
2) Lamson's biplane Aerocurve kite, built for A. Lawrence Rotch of Blue Hill Observatory, 1897.
Royal Aeronautical Society.
3) Man-lifter by Lamson, 1896.

suspended immediately below the kite in a nacelle, shifting his weight to right or left. During early tests with a dummy weighing 68 k (150 lb), weakness in the struts separating the biplane wings caused an accident which resulted in a fall of 180 m (590 ft), though in Lamson's words '. . . a man would not have been hurt, for the fall was as gentle as a dove's lighting on the ground.'[9]

Encouraged by his experiments, Lamson went on to build other man-lifters. These took the form of two pairs of biplane surfaces made of canvas, stretched over a framework of deal. At the end of each pair of upper wings, vertical direction planes were placed to help lateral stability. The efficiency of his final apparatus was proven in June 1897 when he soared at a height of 15 m (say 50 ft) for half an hour or so, repeating the experiment several times with complete success. Lamson gradually modified his kites until they took on quite their own character. His fine Aerocurve kite, so-called because of its pronounced use of the aerofoil in its wing structure, was designed and made in 1897 in both biplane and triplane versions, its form anticipating remarkably the shape that the aeroplane was subsequently to take.

9. Mullane, W. H., *Eddy Current* (Newspaper), Eddy, New Mexico, 1897, issue of 28 August.

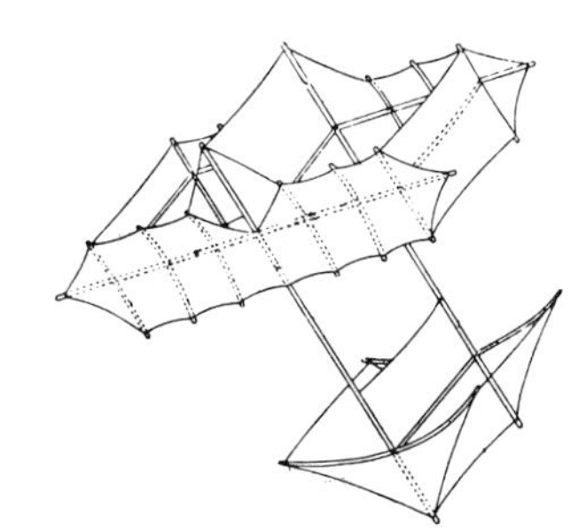

Lamson and aide display the biplane version of the Aerocurve kite.

Meanwhile in Germany, the great gliding pioneer Otto Lilienthal had already published his classic work *Der Vogel Flug als Grundlage der Fliegekunst* (Birdflight as the basis of the Flying Art) some eight years before. In this work he examined in meticulous detail the aerodynamic properties of birds' wings as applied to the problems of human flight. In effect, Lilienthal accumulated all aeronautical theory known at that time, propounding it in his own terms, substantiating it by his own conclusions, pointing the way for subsequent aeronautical development.

A distinguished engineer, inventor and manufacturer of a wide range of marine components, Lilienthal became attracted to the soaring flight of seagulls, whilst working on the installation of a fog horn of his invention that was adopted for German lighthouses. From early experiments with 'aeroplane' kites during the 1870s he made and flew a series of fixed-wing gliders from a specially constructed hill at Gross Lichterfelde near Berlin. The hill, some 15 m (50 ft) high, had a hangar for his gliders built into its summit, and was conical in shape in order that flights could be made into the wind regardless of its direction. Lilienthal became the first man to achieve sustained controlled flight, often soaring for 230 m (say 750 ft), controlling his flight by shifting his weight in true hang glider style. He was fatally injured when one of his most trusted and stable machines, his 'standard sailing machine' designed in 1894, stalled and crashed at Gollenberg on 9 August 1896.

Another outstanding pioneer aviator, Octave Chanute, continued to develop Lilienthal's findings, building a highly sophisticated biplane hang glider incorporating a great many

Percy Pilcher, a young Scottish engineer, was quick to follow Lilienthal's lead in soaring flight. Undeterred by the death of the German pioneer, Pilcher was himself fatally injured when the tail-boom of his Hawk (above) gave way while the hang glider was being towed into the air, kite style, by horses in 1899.

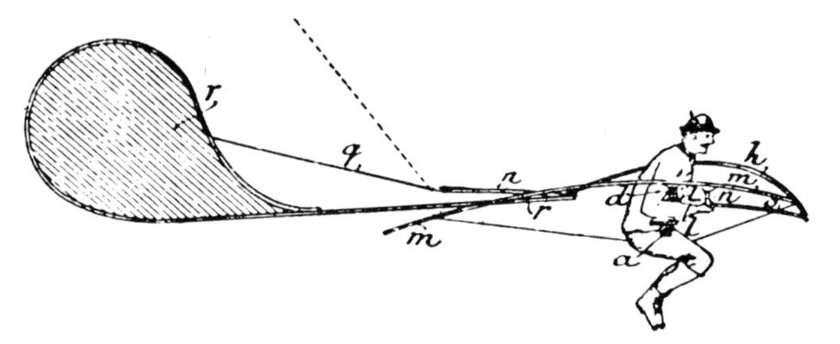

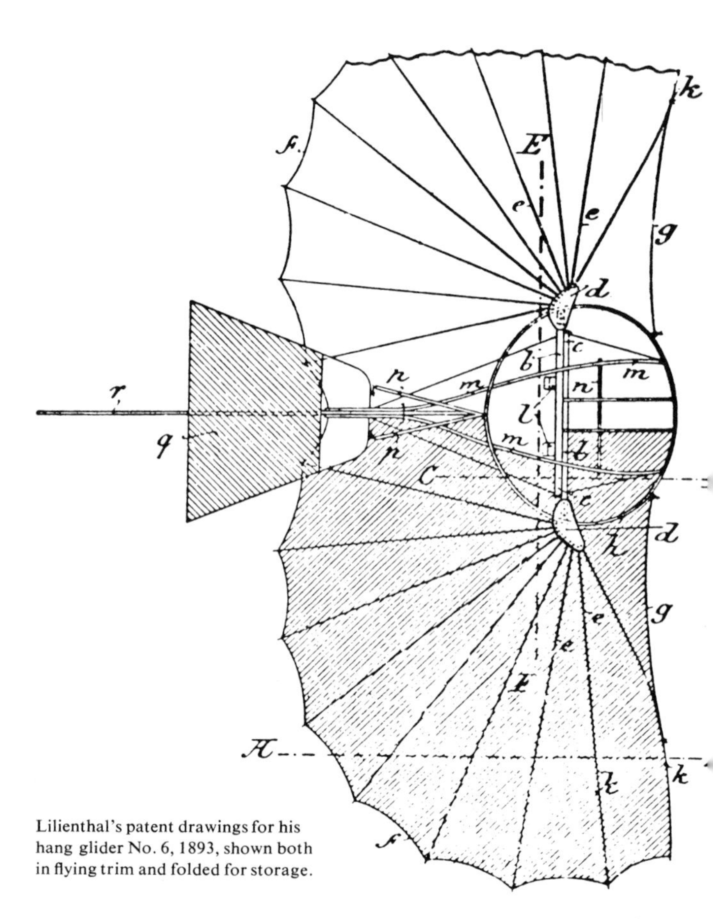

Lilienthal's patent drawings for his hang glider No. 6, 1893, shown both in flying trim and folded for storage.

1

2

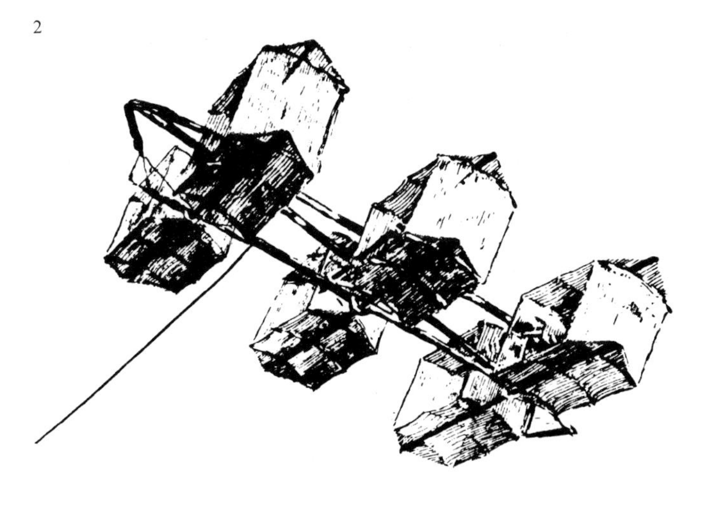

1) Lilienthal, gliding from his artificial hill near Berlin, 1894.
2) Octave Chanute's Ladder kite, 1897. This kite was essentially a prototype of his subsequent hang gliders.
3) Lilienthal, gliding on the biplane version of his hang glider No. 6, 1894. *Science Museum, London.*

3

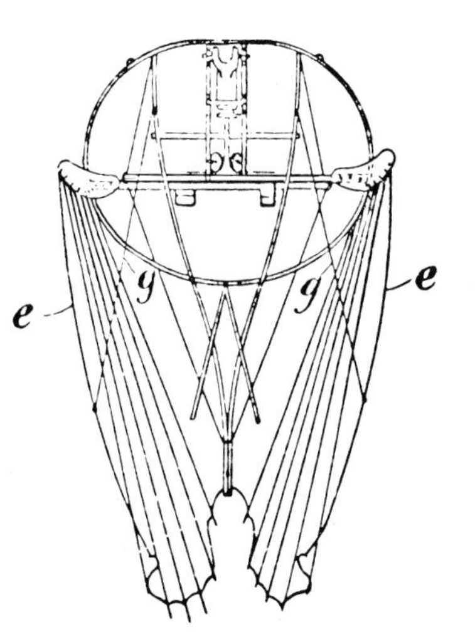

Lilienthal features. Chanute's glider later made a substantial contribution to the experiments being carried out on the other side of the Atlantic by Chanute's friends and fellow pioneers, the Wright brothers.

The Wright brothers' first glider, built in 1900, was virtually a biplane kite. Having built it mainly to confirm their theories of control by wing-warping, the Wrights in the main flew it as a tethered glider, or kite. The controls were operated either from the ground or, on the few occasions when there was enough wind to permit manned flights, from the machine itself.

Because of its remarkable inherent stability, the Hargrave box kite formed the basis of a number of successful power-driven aeroplanes developed in the first decade of the twentieth century. Its influence is obvious in the design of Santos-Dumont's *14bis* which was very little more than a huge pair of motor-driven Hargrave box kites set dihedrally. As the first public powered flight in Europe it aroused a great deal of enthusiasm for flying, and the race to develop ever more sophisticated flying machines on this side of the Atlantic had started in earnest.

The predecessors of the Santos-Dumont *14bis* were the float-borne gliders of Gabriel Voisin, in co-operation with Ernest Archdeacon and Louis Blériot. These two gliders had colourful careers, and were flown, in the main unsuccessfully, from a variety of destinations around Europe. They were basically a combination of Wright and Hargrave features, again closely resembling the Hargrave cellular kite, incorporating refinements of control and stability from the Wright experiments.

1

2

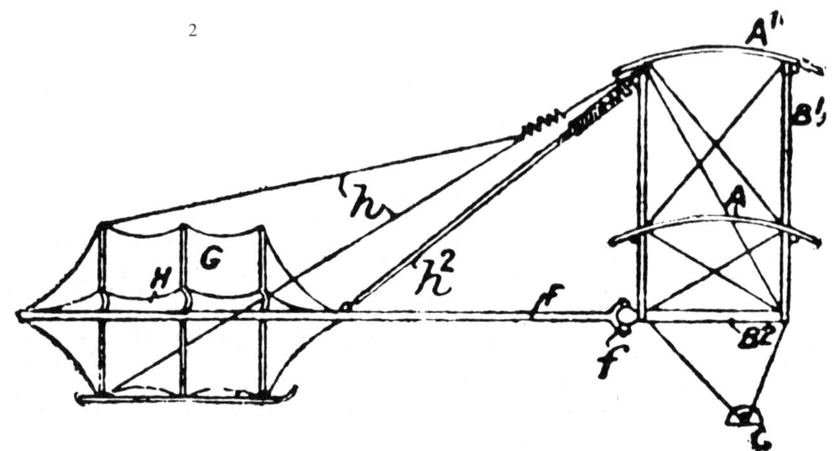

1) *Planeur* Chanute about to take to the air, 1897.
2) Patent drawing for Chanute's classic biplane hang glider, 1896.
3) The Wright brothers tested their early gliders by flying them as kites. The glider shown is the early 1902 model, with the fixed double tail, before it was converted into a rudder.
4) One of the Voisin-Archdeacon float-borne gliders of 1905 during trials on the Seine.
5) Model of the Santos-Dumont tail-first biplane *14bis*, 1906, showing the obvious influence of the Hargrave box kite.
Science Museum, London.

Just how closely related to the kite these craft were becomes very clear from the following contemporary accounts of flights from both land and water. At the military drill ground at Issy-les-Moulineaux in 1905 . . .

'The method of operation was to place the aeroplane, without motor, but with a pilot on board, on suitable rails, attach it by means of a towrope to the motorcar, and pull it until it rose in the air in the same way as a kite.'[10]

And on the Lake of Geneva that same year . . .

'. . . the only practical result of the visit was a little experiment made by Gabriel Voisin when the aeroplane was lying at anchor on the lake. In a very strong wind Voisin discovered that he could cause the aeroplane to rise from the surface of the water merely by operating the elevation rudder, and remain in the air, struggling at its cable until a lull in the wind, or the manipulation of the rudder, caused it to descend.'[11]

10. The *Aero Manual*, London, 1910, p. 64.
11. *ibid.*, p. 65.

3

4

5

The fact that Baden-Powell's military man-lifting work was never put to any practical use proved to be a stumbling block to Samuel Franklin Cody when he first put forward his more sophisticated system of man-lifting to the army in 1901.

Among all the pioneers of early aviation, probably the most remarkable was the flamboyant Samuel Franklin Cody. Born in Birdville, Texas, in 1861, from boyhood he lived the typical prairie life of a cowboy, catching and training wild horses in true bronco-buster style. He was also a highly skilled buffalo hunter, and became an expert with the rifle and lasso. During 1883–4 he was gold prospecting around the junction of the Klondyke and Yukon Rivers, living in great hardship in a location which thirteen years later grew into Dawson City, centre of the Alaskan Gold Rush, the biggest gold rush of all time. Cody, however, made no strike, and after a few years spent touring America with a Wild West show, where he was billed as 'Captain Cody, King of the Cowboys', he eventually settled in England in 1890.

He soon became a showman, forming his own company of entertainers, largely made up of his immediate family and close relations. With this company he toured the music halls, giving demonstrations of his exceptional skills in riding, lassoing and shooting. As a professional showman he adopted the extravagant form of dress for which he was to become so famous from his compatriot, namesake and friend, Colonel William Fredrick Cody, alias 'Buffalo Bill', whose hugely successful Wild West show he had seen and admired greatly. Apparently, with the help of the coincidence of their names, close physical resemblance, and Cody's affectation of shoulder-length hair, beard, moustache, stetson, fringed

1

2

3

1) Portrait of Samuel Franklin Cody, from a self-promotional poster, 1904. *R.A.F. Museum.*
2) An early version of the War kite displayed by Cody and assistant. *Royal Aeronautical Society.*
3) Cody dwarfed by one of his very early creations, 1900.
4–5) Cody prepares his kite and tends his winding gear at the Aeronautical Society's 1903 kite competition held at Worthing. *Royal Aeronautical Society.*

4

buckskins and cowboy boots, Samuel Cody quite deliberately nurtured confusion in the minds of the public, some of them genuinely believing that they were watching Cody's archetype 'Buffalo Bill' himself, or at least the son or brother of the famous cowboy.

In 1898 the turning point in Cody's life occurred when the family's latest production, a gory melodrama called *The Klondyke Nugget* became wildly successful. Based largely upon Cody's experiences in the Yukon, it was an extravagant, somewhat piecemeal affair, which was basically a vehicle for the various skills of the Codys. Cody's son Leon was a keen kite flyer about this time, and father and son competed with ever larger kites, capable of ever increasing heights. By 1900 Cody's enthusiasm for the pastime was eclipsing his other interests, while *The Klondyke Nugget* continued to play to

5

packed houses, financing his exhaustive experiments with a series of kite configurations. He finally settled for a winged variation of Hargrave's double-cell box kite, which he patented in 1901. With this kite he devised his remarkable system of man-lifting, and gave a demonstration of the apparatus to the War Office in December of that year, with a view to its military application.

Cody's man-lifting system involved first flying a small steadying pilot kite, then a team of lifter kites, the number used depending on the condition of the wind. These lifter kites were attached to the main flying cable by two towing rings, one at the head of the kite, the other at the towing point of a four-legged bridle. Upon being released the kite would be blown up the flying cable, which was provided with a number of conical stops at predetermined mooring points along the length of the cable. The conical stops were progressively larger towards the top of the cable, corresponding to a variation in size of the towing rings. Consequently, as the first lifter kite travelled up the cable, its large towing ring would pass over the smaller cones, and its free travel would only be halted when the kite reached its prescribed mooring point. And so the next lifter would be released with a slightly smaller towing ring, which in turn passed over the smaller cones until halted against the penultimate mooring point. Finally the carrier kite was attached to a trolley, the wheels of which ran against the top of the cable. From this trolley was suspended the basket-work car in which the passenger travelled. The carrier and its load were released up the cable towards the lower lifter kite. The passenger was able to control the ascent and descent by working a complex system of lines and brakes. The lines adjusted the inclination of the kite to the horizontal, in order

1

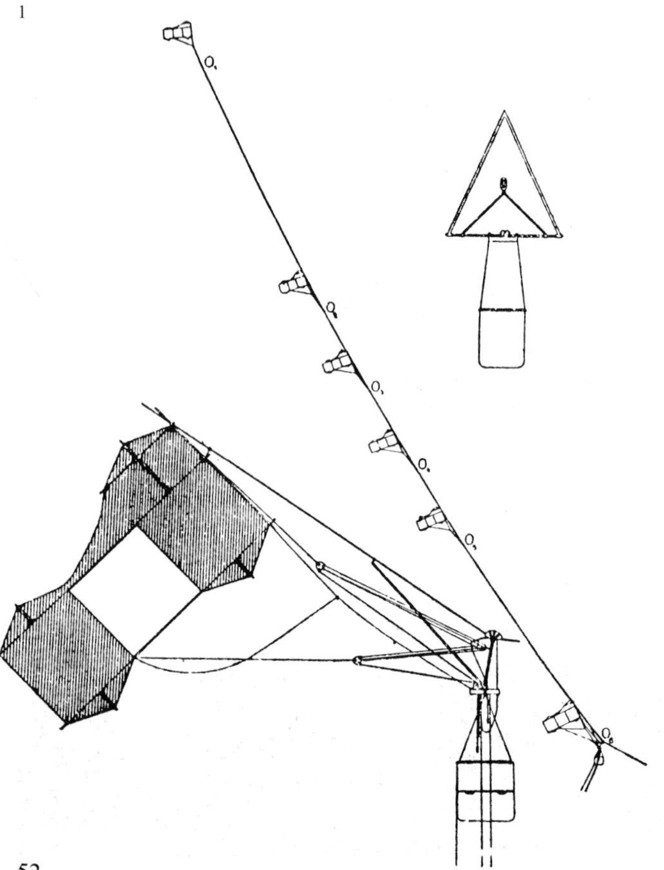

2

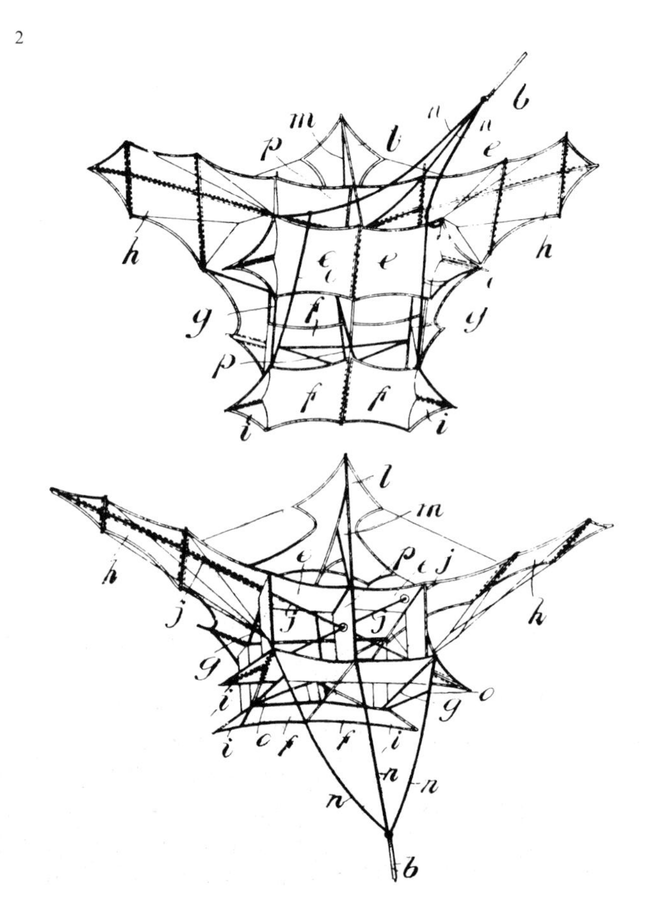

3

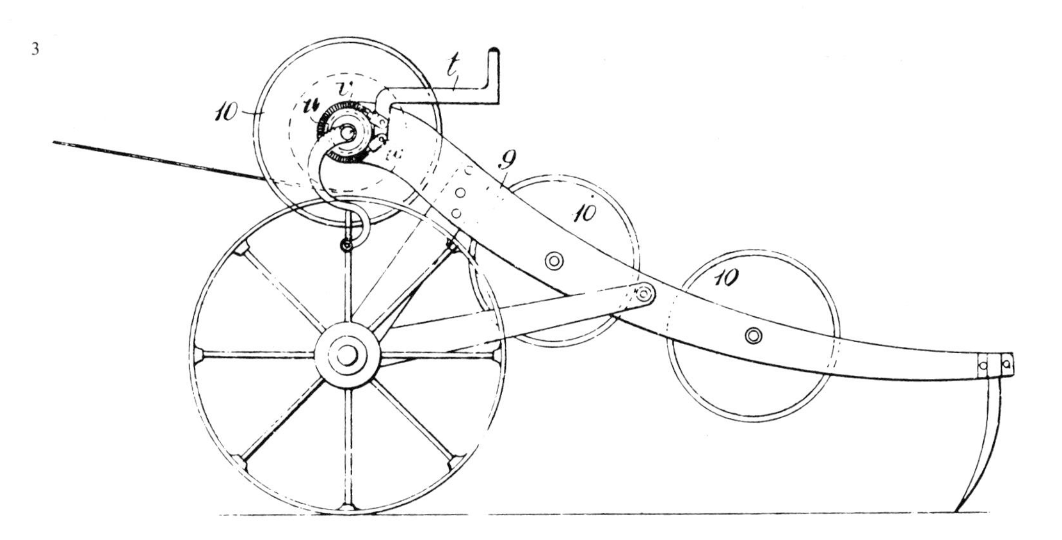

1) Cody's method of securing a line in the air, up which his man-lifter could ascend.
2) Patent drawings for Cody's War kite, popularly known as the Bat.
3) Patent drawing for Cody's field winch with interchangeable drums.
4) Cody, in characteristic pose, gives kite instruction at Aldershot, 1904.
Royal Aircraft Establishment.

4

to give the kite greater or lesser lift.

In a military situation it was proposed that the passenger should be equipped with a telescope, telephone, camera and firearm. If a telephone system was impractical a system of messengers was used. Communications were blown up the cable by the wind, and returned in a weighted bag which was allowed to simply slide down the cable.

Despite his flamboyant exterior, and the fact that he was said to be illiterate, Cody was a man of great intelligence, with an extremely practical outlook which was supported by apparently unlimited reserves of courage, strength and perseverance. Nevertheless his image was against him at the outset of his aeronautical career, and initially there was a general reluctance to regard his achievements in the air as anything

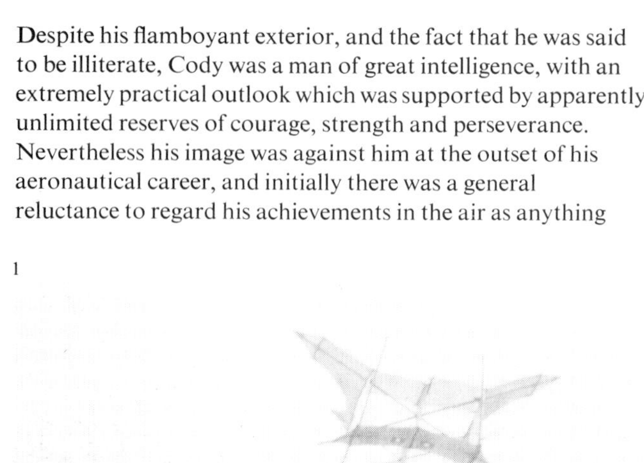

1

2

3

4

5

more than an extension of his show-business activities. Consequently nothing came of his first approaches to the British military authorities, though they were so impressed with his skill as a marksman that they offered him the post of Shooting Instructor at Aldershot, which Cody declined.

In an attempt to publicize the traction potential of his system Cody successfully crossed the English Channel in November 1903 in a collapsible boat, drawn by kites. The boat, Cody's own modification of an existing collapsible dinghy, was approximately 4 m (13 ft) long, had its deck covered with cork for maximum buoyancy, and its keel well ballasted. A drogue anchor was towed behind the boat, providing resistance to the pull of the kites in order to keep the kite line taut. This attempt, which was made from Calais to Dover, had been preceded by several unsuccessful attempts from Dover, all of

6

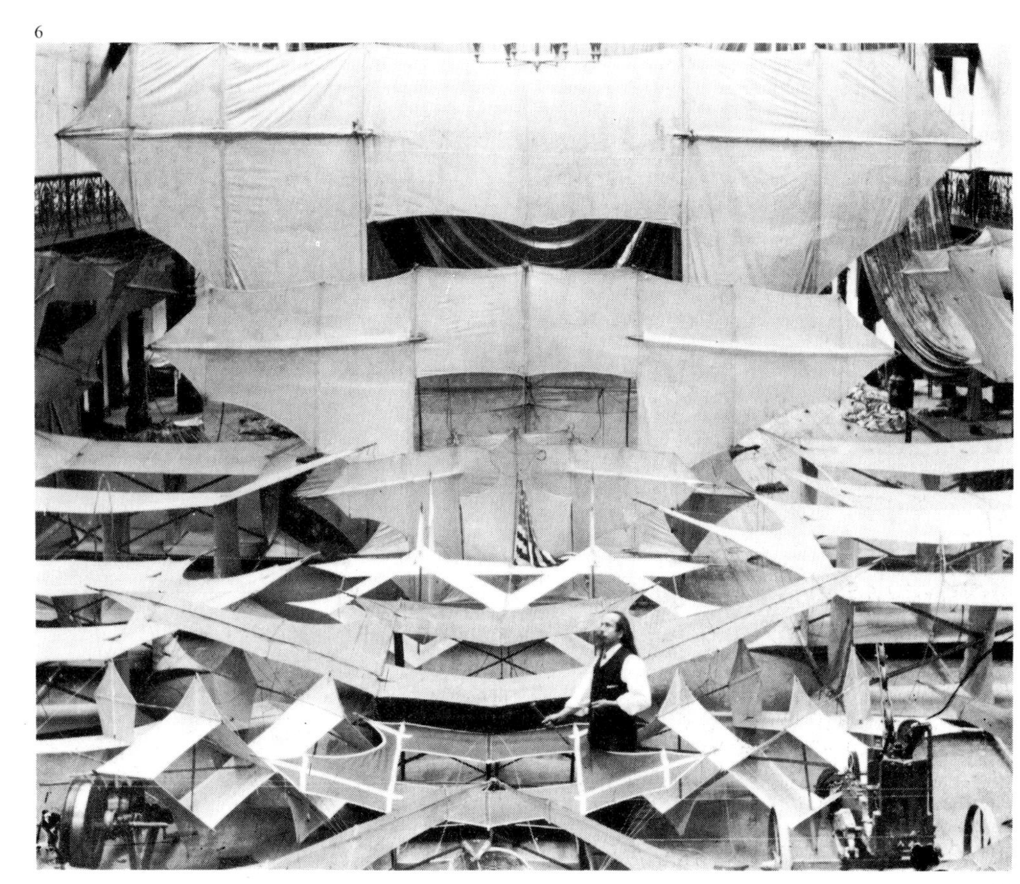

1) Cody makes an ascent during Admiralty trials, Spithead, 1903.
2) A convincing demonstration of the lifting properties of Cody's system.
3) Cody makes last minute adjustments to his motor-kite, 1907.
4) Cody's biggest kite had a wingspan of 11 m (36 ft).
5) Members of Cody's Kite Corps manoeuvring a lifter kite at launch.
6) Cody exhibits a selection of his kites at Alexandra Palace, 1905.
Royal Aircraft Establishment.

which had been thwarted by adverse wind conditions. The triumph pleased Cody, and the resulting publicity, which included a number of public demonstrations of his invention seems to have had the required effect.

Despite the War Office's earlier reluctance to adopt Cody's invention, they eventually expressed interest. Extensive trials were carried out in 1904–5 on both land and water, the Admiralty having put some warships at Cody's disposal. During these trials Sapper Moreton reached the possibly record height of 792·6 m (2,600 ft) on the end of a cable 1219 m (4,000 ft) long. The War Office finally adopted the system in 1906 for Army observation, and Cody was given Officer status with the post of Chief Kite Instructor at Farnborough, where his basic responsibilities were for the design and manufacture of kites, together with providing

S. H. R. Salmon's multiple-celled rhomboidal kite, at the Aeronautical Society's kite competition, June 1903. In 1906 Salmon released three such kites from Brighton in an experimental Channel crossing. One kite successfully reached Vierville eleven-and-a-half hours after launching. *Royal Aeronautical Society.*

A heroic portrait of Cody at the controls of his British Army Aeroplane, at Laffan's Plain, 1909. *Royal Aircraft Establishment.*

instruction in their operation. For this he received a salary of £1,000 per annum, together with free fodder for his white stallion, his favourite and famous means of transport. Cody's War Kites, as he called them, were to remain a part of military equipment for some years, until they were overtaken by the rapid advance of the aeroplane. Cody's courage and enthusiasm led him on to experiment with powered flight, and in October 1908 he became the first man to build and fly an aeroplane in Britain. The slang term 'kite' for aeroplane is said to have been derived from this period when aeroplanes were virtually power-driven kites. On 7 August 1913 Cody and his passenger were killed when his last creation, the Waterplane, broke up in the air over Laffan's Plain, Aldershot.

Charles Brogden displays his prize-winning dihedral kite, 1908.
Royal Aeronautical Society.

Cody's man-carrying biplane glider-kite, so called because it was winch launched in the manner of a kite, or modern glider. Its towing line was released when sufficient altitude had been gained for it to operate as a glider. While an innovation in itself, its rudimentary ailerons, situated beneath the lower wings, are believed to be the first successful application of this device, 1905.
Courtesy, Percy B. Walker.

Not all of Cody's kite experiments were directed towards military ends however. During a kite display held at Cobham Common in 1907 he gave a demonstration of an instrument developed by the Meteorological Office, the meteorograph, capable of registering height, temperature, humidity and wind velocity. Cody had already been made a Fellow of the Royal Meteorological Society for his valuable contributions to weather research, having on one occasion lofted instruments to the then record altitude of 4,268 m (say 14,000 ft).

A considerable number of kite competitions were being held throughout Europe during the first decade of this century, the more significant English meetings being organized by the Aeronautical Society of Great Britain. Though the competitors' lists invariably included Cody, his son Leon, and Major Baden-Powell, it was usually Charles Brogden, possessor of a six-winged lightweight giant, who took first prize for altitude.

Lieutenant Schreiber of the Imperial Russian Navy was also experimenting with a man-lifting system similar to Cody's during 1903. Schreiber had adopted a kite that was virtually a Hargrave original double box, incorporating a spring bridle which automatically adjusted the angle of incidence to the prevailing wind conditions. Schreiber's apparatus proved to be highly dangerous however, and after a number of fatal accidents the system was abandoned in favour of the more reliable methods developed by a Russian army officer, Captain Ulyanin, who achieved lift with a train of double Conyne kites.

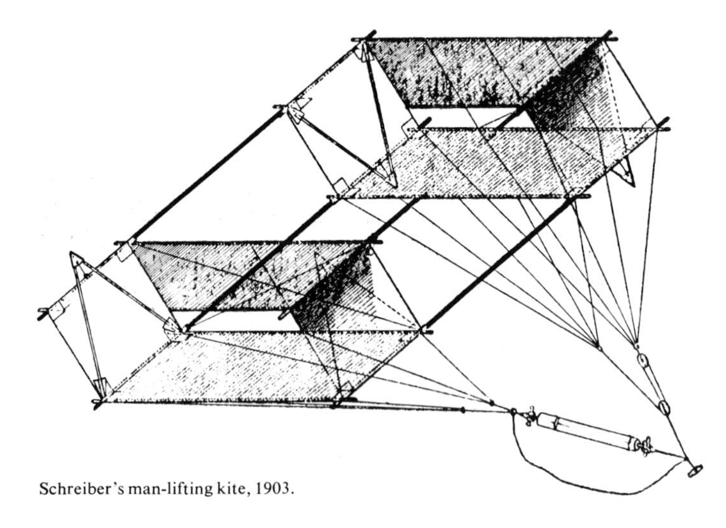

Schreiber's man-lifting kite, 1903.

A train of Captain Madiot's man-lifters on trials, 1909.
Radio Times Hulton Picture Library.

Cody's flamboyant character had done a great deal to popularize the work of the aeronautical pioneers in general, and as a result of the interest that his experiments caused in France, Charles Dollfus held a competition in 1909, to establish the most successful man-lifting techniques, so that they might be considered by the French Military Authorities. Captain Madiot took the prize with a system similar to that of Cody, but he died in a flying accident before the system could be fully developed. Consequently the French army adopted the system proposed by Captain Saconney, which again was very similar to the Cody original.

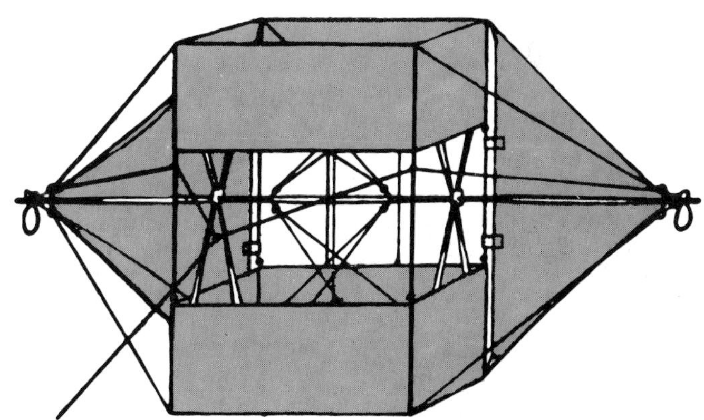

Madiot's kite, showing its unique construction method. Barrelled spars were force-fitted into a central boss, and the whole unit was held together under tension.

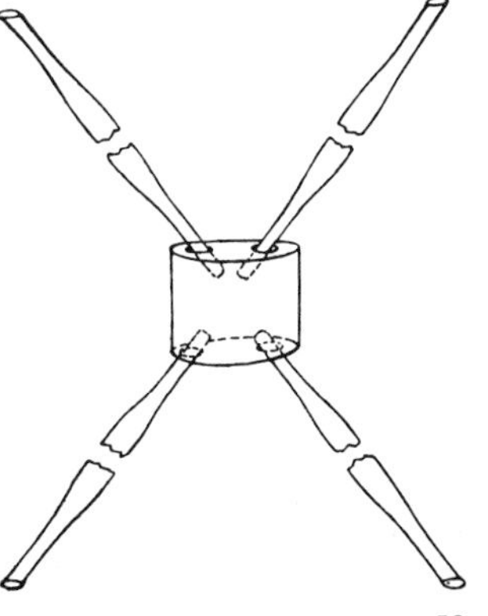

Captain Saconney's man-lifting system, undergoing trials in 1910. *Musée de l'Air.*

1

2

3

1) Captain Génie Saconney (out of uniform) inspects a field winch, 1910.
2) French military winching vehicle.
3) Departing on a high altitude attempt under a train of Saconneys.
4) French military, setting out on a man-lifting attempt.
5) The Saconney basket nacelle of 1909, showing the trolley suspension system.
6) Saconney's man-lifting kite.
Service Historique de l'Armée de l'Air.

4

5

6

In the meantime, on the other side of the Atlantic, a far less warlike attitude towards man lifting was being developed by Dr Alexander Graham Bell, whose first aeronautical experiments were undertaken purely for entertainment and amusement. Gradually Dr Bell's experiments assumed a more serious character as he realized the potential of their contribution to man's conquest of the air.

1

Like so many of the early pioneers of flight, Bell made many observations and notes on the flight of birds, and was initially preoccupied with the safe vertical ascent and descent of a craft, seeing these characteristics as being somewhat divorced from forward velocity. In consequence a great many of his early experiments involved rotors and winged fly-wheels, sometimes propelled with rockets at the rotor tips, capable of achieving heights of 45 m (say 150 ft) or so.

2

PHOTOS: DAVID GEORGE MCCURDY

Bell was born in Edinburgh in 1847, into a family prominent in the science of speech. In 1870, after the death of his two brothers, he moved to Canada in search of a more healthy climate. His passionate interest in speech, and his knowledge of the properties of sound, led him to a series of experiments which climaxed, but by no means culminated, in his invention of the telephone in 1876. With this success came moderate wealth, and a move to Washington D.C. where he soon adopted U.S. citizenship. From Washington he continued his researches, achieving further success with his contribution to the development of the gramophone.

In 1893 the Bells moved back to Canada, buying a peninsula near Baddeck, which they named Beinn Bhreagh, which is Gaelic for Beautiful Mountain. Three years later Bell attended a demonstration flight of a large propeller-driven

4

1) Hexagonal kite with six radial wings, loaded in the middle with an adjustable weight, 1902.
2) A Bell kite comprising two tetrahedral structures, connected by a system of tetrahedral frames. This kite was subsequently developed into a winged boat in anticipation of a manned landing on water, 1902.
3) Twelve-sided giant radial-winged kite. The helper is controlling the angle of attack by means of a tail- or landing-line.
4) By shifting the cellular superstructure to different parts of the body frame, Bell determined the relationship of centre of gravity to centre of lift in flying structures.
© *The Bell Family: courtesy of National Geographic Society.*

model aircraft given by his friend Samuel Pierpont Langley, and became determined to construct a flying machine.

Bell was a very gentle and humane man, whose concern for the safety of the aeronaut is amply illustrated by his choosing to make his first man-carrying attempts over the waters of Baddeck Bay in craft that would float, piloted by men who could swim. He advocated that flights should be first made at moderate elevation in order to allow the pilot to develop skill in the control of his apparatus.

He embarked upon an exhaustive programme of kite tests directed towards establishing the most reliable form capable of carrying a man and an engine with maximum stability and lift. Carrying out experiments with a great variety of kite configurations he eventually decided upon the tetrahedral cell, or regular tetrahedron, covered on two of its four sides in silk. This structure he found to possess an extraordinary ratio of lightness to strength.

Having established his norm, he proceeded to make further comprehensive tests with various combinations of these cells. His earlier findings that kites so constructed possessed remarkable stability in varying wind conditions were confirmed, and in 1905 a combination kite made up of 1,300 such cells, and known as the Frost King accidentally lifted one of its handlers approximately 10 m (say 30 ft) off the ground. The kite, including its tackle, weighed some 57 k (125 lb). The weight of the handler was 75 k (165 lb), and a 17 km per h (10 m.p.h.) wind was recorded. Bell concluded that a larger structure, carrying an engine capable of imparting a 10 m.p.h. thrust, would certainly carry a man.

1

Four-celled Bell tetrahedral.

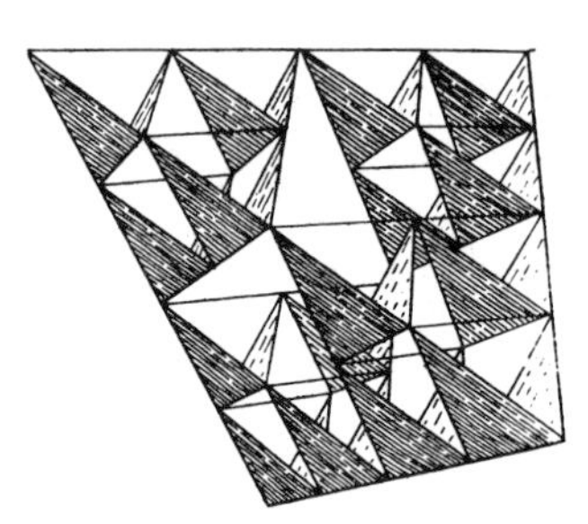

Sixteen-celled Bell tetrahedral.

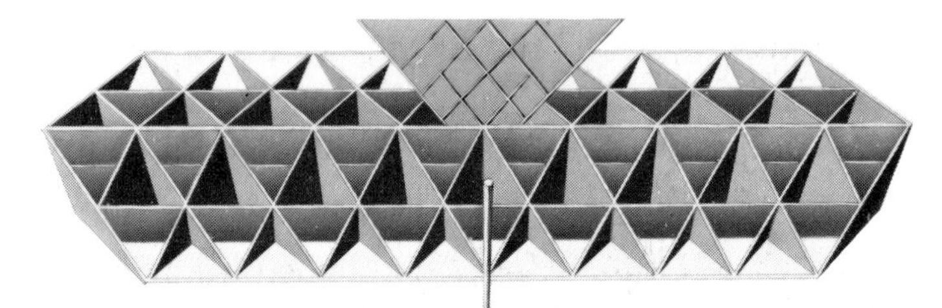

The later, two-tiered Oionos kite, showing the adjustable tail. Developments of this kite involved a movable tail unit, capable of being controlled in flight by the action of a lead weight. As the head of the kite fell forward, the weight also slid forward, causing the tail to be elevated automatically, correcting the dive.

2

1) Mrs Mabel Hubbard Bell measures the pull of one of her husband's kites by means of a spring scale.
2) Bell's floating kite was designed to support itself equally well on air or water, 1902.
3) Launching the Oionos kite. Red silk was tied to the flying line in order to record photographically the relationship of the line to the kite when in flight.
© The Bell Family: Courtesy of National Geographic Society.

3

PHOTOS: DAVID GEORGE MCCURDY

His first controlled man-carrying project took place in December 1907, when the Cygnet, a larger version of the Frost King, made up of 3,393 cells and equipped with floats, ascended to a height of 51·2 m (168 ft) whilst towed behind a steamer across Baddeck Bay, carrying Lieutenant Thomas E. Selfridge of the United States Army as volunteer passenger. The flight lasted for seven minutes, during which time the Cygnet displayed admirable stability and lift.

As the steamer played out slack line the kite descended slowly and evenly, settling so gently upon the water that Lieutenant Selfridge was not aware that contact had been made. Unfortunately though, the winding crew aboard the steamer were not quick enough in releasing the kite's towing line, and the beautiful craft quickly broke up as it was dragged behind the steamer. Selfridge suffered no more than a ducking, though only nine months later he was killed while flying as passenger with Orville Wright. Wright crashed on what was only his third passenger-carrying flight, and Lieutenant Selfridge became the first fatality in the history of powered flight, while Wright sustained no more than a few broken bones.

Fired with the success of the Cygnet, Bell's next step was to build Cygnet II, a modified version of its predecessor capable of carrying a man and an engine. In the same year of Cygnet's success Bell founded the Aerial Experiment Association, whose sole purpose was 'to get into the air'. The other founder members of the association were two Canadian engineers, John McCurdy and F. W. 'Casey' Baldwin, the famous American aeroplane manufacturer and aviator Glen Curtiss, and Lieutenant Selfridge.

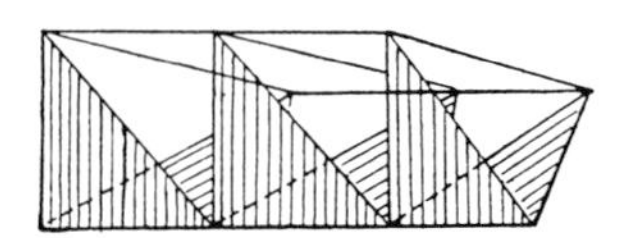

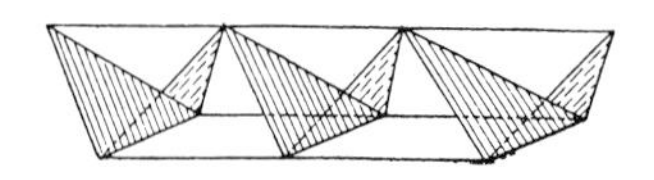

Tetrahedral cells, compounded perpendicularly and horizontally, formed the structural basis of all Bell's later configurations.

One of Dr Bell's early multi-cellular giants at launch. Moments after this picture was taken the strong body frame broke up in the air while the fragile superstructure remained intact, at least until contact with the ground, 1902.

Emphasis now turned to the construction of a suitable engine, and during the course of its development the members of the A.E.A. decided that it should be housed in a more conventional aeroplane configuration. The group developed and built four aeroplanes in all, the last of which was Curtiss's June Bug, which won the *Scientific American* trophy in 1908, for the first public flight in America to reach a kilometre in distance.

Cygnet II was the culmination of Bell's kite programme. Unfortunately the engine that was eventually fitted was incapable of developing sufficient thrust to lift the kite. Nevertheless, the objectives of the A.E.A. had been achieved, and the association was disbanded in 1909. A number of Dr Bell's kites, along with many other relics of his remarkable imagination, can still be seen at the Alexander Graham Bell Museum at Baddeck, Nova Scotia.

Bell's potential man-carrier Siamese Twins, so called because it consisted primarily of two huge multi-celled tetrahedral kites connected by a bridge of strongly braced cells for supporting the weight of a man, 1905.
© *The Bell Family: courtesy of National Geographic Society.*

Joseph Lecornu with two of his highly original cellular kites. Though his construction methods have been superseded by modern techniques, they serve as a reminder of the degree of finish that went into such kites.

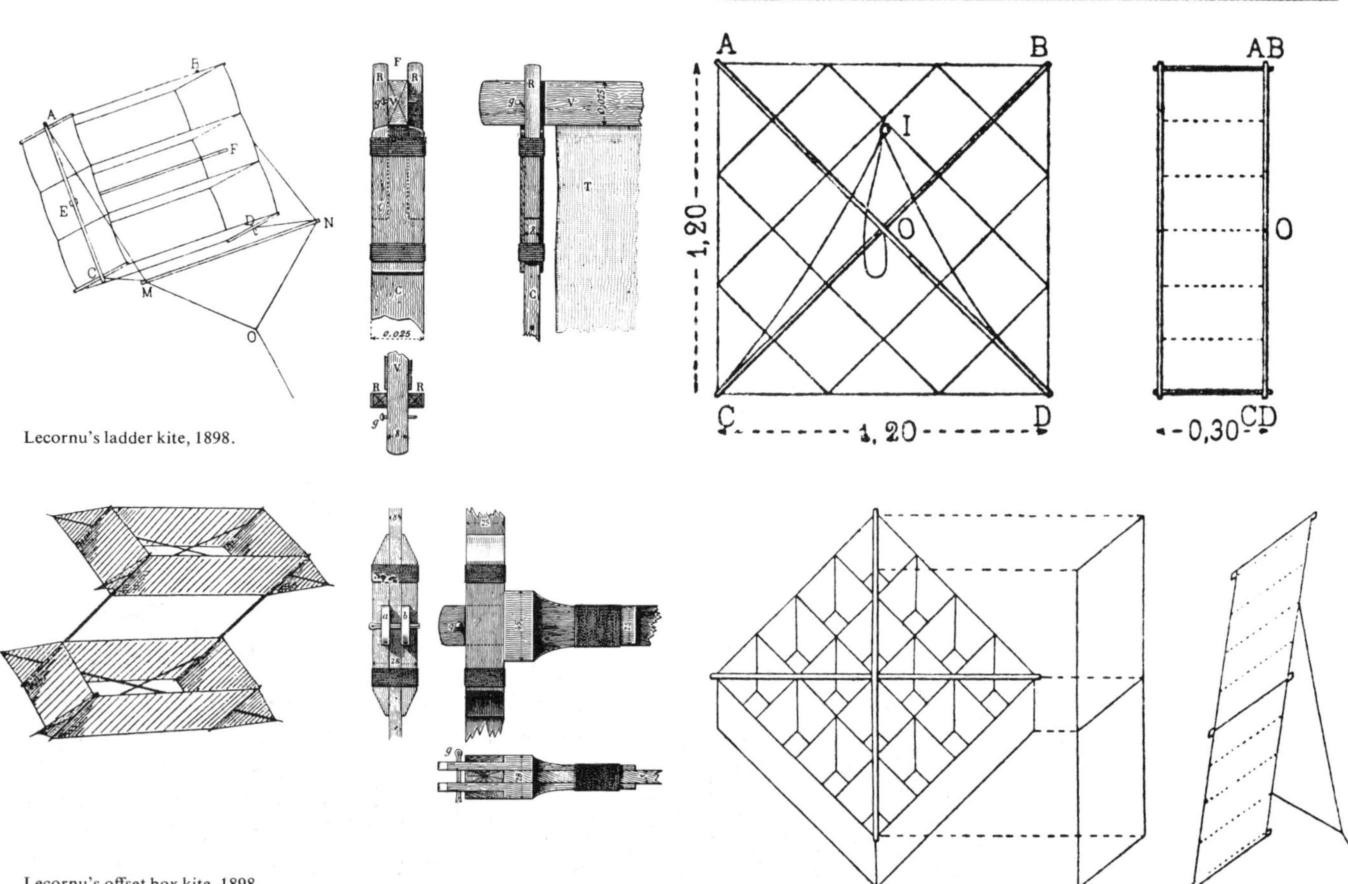

Lecornu's ladder kite, 1898.

Lecornu's offset box kite, 1898.

Hugo Nikel's registering kite of 1899 was designed to provide a steady and safe lift for self-registering meteorological instruments. The kite measured 8 m (26 ft) × 4 m (13 ft) and proved highly successful at its trials.

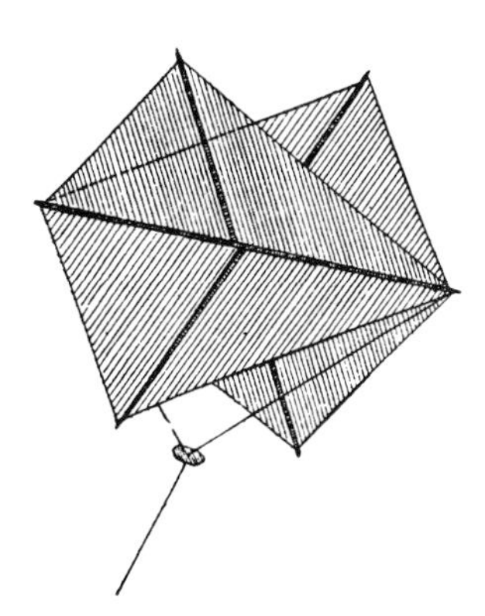

Flaix's kite, 1900.

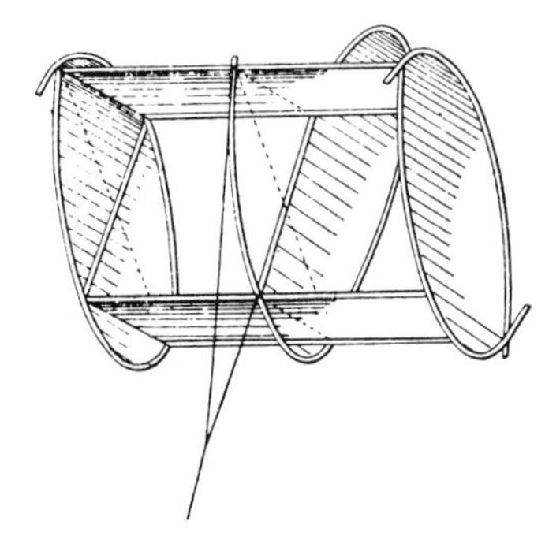

The Köppen kite was adopted by the Maritime Observatory of Hamburg, during the 1890s.

PHOTO: J. H. LARTIGUE

A very good-looking winged box kite being launched at Château de Rouzat, 1905.

Kite flying on the beach
at Biarritz, 1904.

PHOTO: J. H. LARTIGUE

Considering the pace at which aviation technology accelerated into the second decade of the twentieth century, it seems hardly surprising that the kite was virtually forgotten for a period of thirty years or so. Apart from isolated military, meteorological and advertising applications during and between the two World Wars it was to lie, in the main, neglected by all except children. It was only in the mid fifties, through the work of Francis Rogallo of the National Aeronautical and Space Administration that the simple kite was once again reinstated as a potentially important tool of science.

2

1

1) Patrick Alexander's man-carrying kite, constructed entirely from broom sticks, canvas and wire, 1909.
Royal Aeronautical Society.
2) Boy with kite made from German banknotes, during inflation in Germany, following the First World War. Early 1920s.
3) Amateur aviator realizes his dreams at Château de Rouzat, 1907.

3

PHOTO: J. H. LARTIGUE

A selection of kites manufactured by Brookite in the mid 1920s.
1) Man-lifter, as supplied to the British Admiralty.
2) The Vampire, apparently influenced by Cody's Bat.
3) The well-known Pilot or Signal kite, derived from the earlier French rescue kites.
4) One of a wide range of bird kites.

1

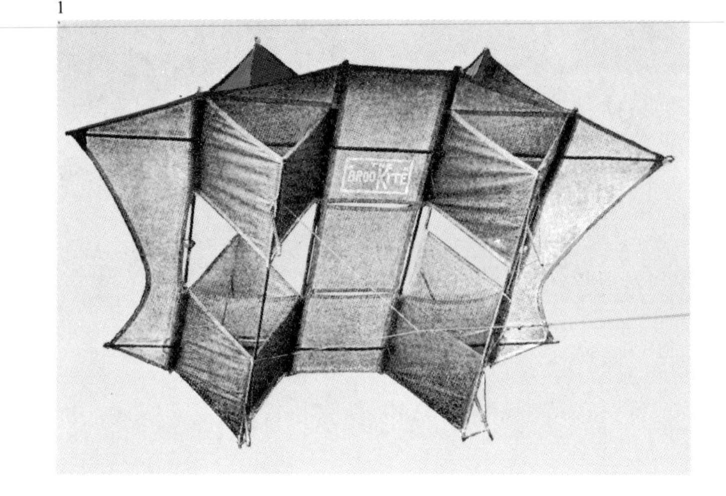

Walter Brook, holding a jibbed box kite. Brook, with his brother Thomas, was making kites for pleasure and profit in the early 1900s.
They began in the toy trade and were very soon handling contracts for the British government.
Marconi was also a good customer.
Today Brookite export thousands of kites annually throughout the world.

2

3

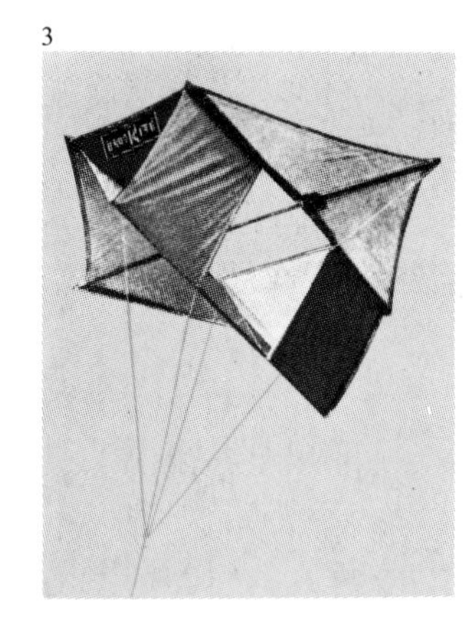

4

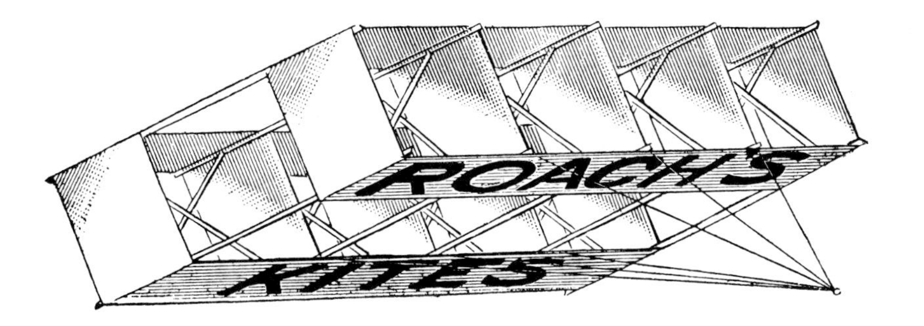

A selection of English box, keel and compound kites of the mid 1920s. The large multi-cellular box kites were specifically designed to carry advertising banners.
Courtesy, Brookite Limited.

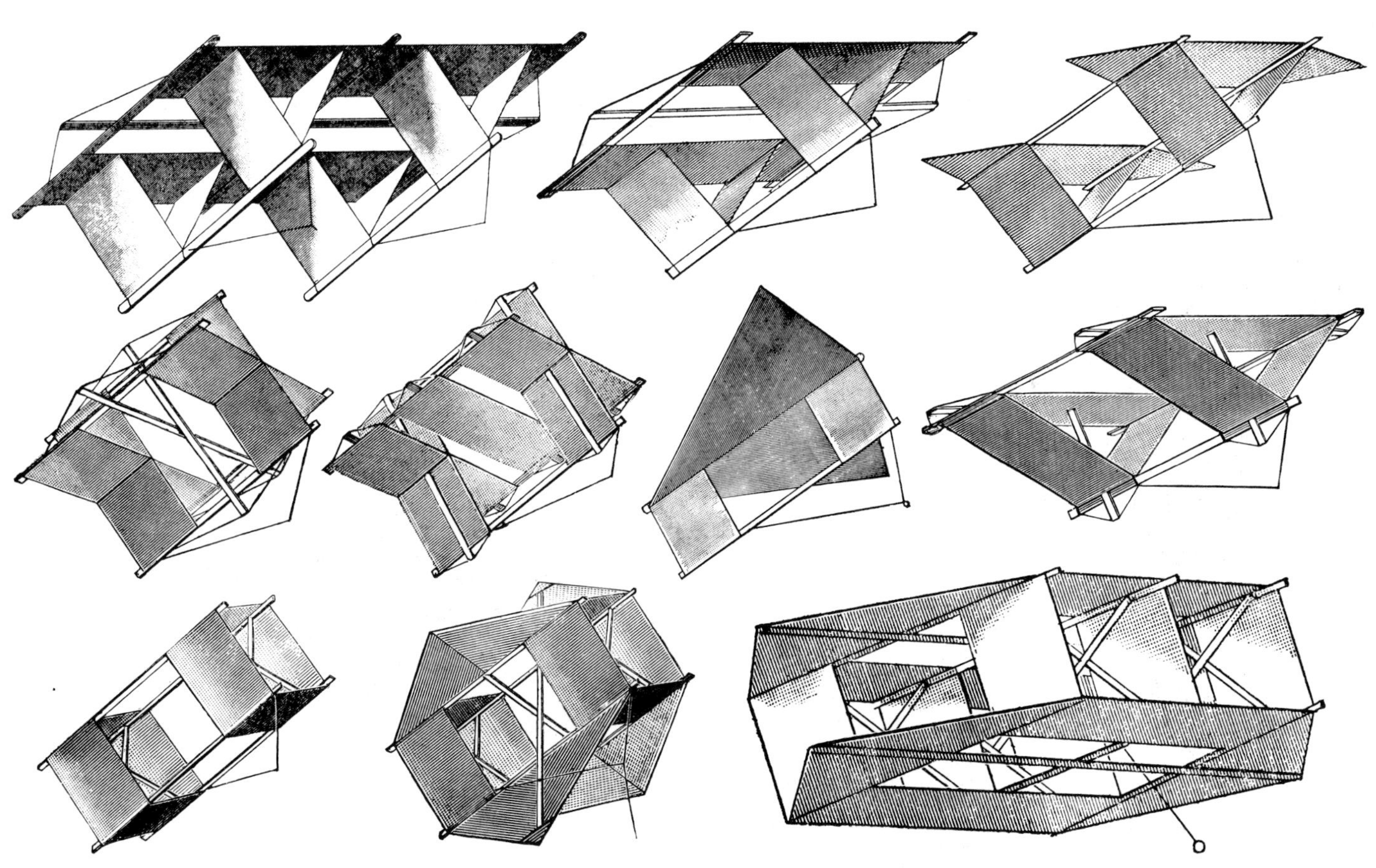

In 1911 the U.S. Navy carried out target practice at kites 'with the object of determining the chances of repelling aerial craft'.[12] Again in the Second World War a highly manoeuvrable target kite was developed by Commander Paul Garber, also for American naval gunnery practice.

In order to increase their range of observation at sea, the Germans used man-lifting kites flying from their submarines while surface cruising in both the First and Second World Wars. The 8 km (5 miles) visibility at sea level was increased to approximately 40 km (25 miles) at an altitude of 120 m (say 400 ft) or so. Huge box kites were used in the First World War. These were towed behind the submarine, and consequently were not dependent upon a favourable wind. The observer was hoisted up the kite line in a nacelle, when sufficient height and stability had been attained. The kite was box in form, similar to the more familiar British survival kite used in sea rescue in the Second World War, though very many times larger. The British kite was designed to be flown from a fine aerial, acting as a beacon capable of transmitting a distress signal. The signalling properties of kites were also exploited in other ways during the Second World War, as was recorded in an article that appeared in the London *Daily Sketch* in 1939. Under the gripping headline 'Kite flying spy caught at work – East Coast arrest in Christmas round-up' we learn how counter-espionage agents arrested a spy while transmitting coded messages to the Nazis by means of a kite bearing automatic signalling equipment.

12. *Aeronautics*, London, Vol. 4, No. 1, October 1911, p. 201.

1

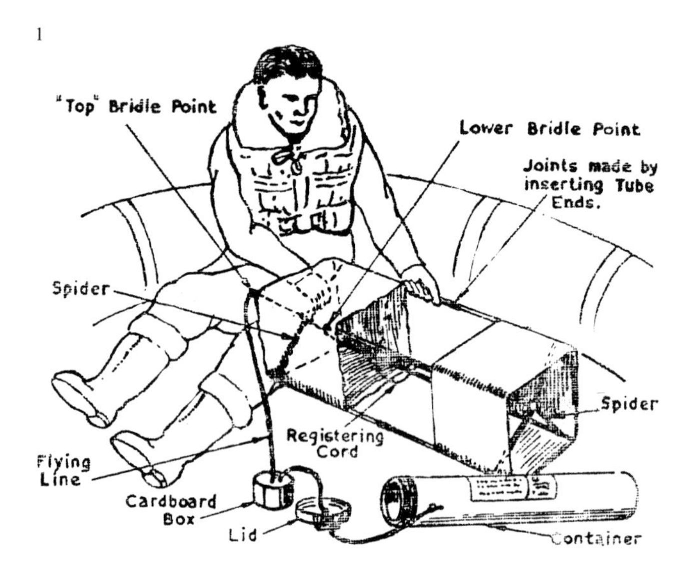

2

PHOTO: PAUL HILDER

1) Illustration from launching instructions of the Gibson-Girl survival kite used in sea rescue in the Second World War.
2) Gibson-Girl box kite with assembly instructions printed upon forward cell. Flown without a bridle, the kite had three alternative towing points for a variety of wind-speeds.

3

3) Insulated winch used in conjunction with the Gibson-Girl kite. Total depth 28 cm (11 ins.), drum diameter 12·7 cm (5 ins.).
Courtesy, L. Pradier Esq.
4) German Focke-Achgelis gyroplane observation kite, 1943.
Smithsonian Institution.

4

The Germans devised a far more sophisticated method of lofting an observer during the Second World War. In 1943 they put into service the Focke-Achgelis F.A.330 rotating wing, or gyroplane kite. This was a highly manoeuvrable autogyro, again achieving lift by means of the traction supplied by a submarine. Directional control was provided by a rudder, operated by a conventional rudder-bar, and its rotors were capable of being jettisoned in an emergency, the pilot descending by parachute. The whole apparatus could be quickly dismantled and stowed by virtue of a series of quick-release pins. Gyro-gliding with modified versions of the Focke-Achgelis is currently a growing sport in the U.S.A.

Another war-time application of the kite was as a barrage protection for U.S. convoys in 1941. The kite used was that developed by Harry C. Sauls of the U.S. War Shipping

2

1

Administration over a period of twelve years. Sauls extensively adapted an existing kite hitherto used for advertising purposes. Some 6 m (say 20 ft) wide and basically double box in form, Sauls's huge kites were flown on wire lines 609 m (2,000 ft) long from which further wire lines were suspended. Capable of shearing wings and fouling propellers, they provided a formidable deterrent to enemy pilots bent upon strafing the merchant vessels below.

The Admiralty had also introduced an ingenious lethal barrage kite for protecting destroyers from aerial attack in 1940. The object of this kite, a modified Hargrave double box, was to suspend a wire on the end of which was a bomb. The impact of an attacking aircraft upon the wire caused a chisel, fired by a 0·22 cartridge, to sever the flying line below the bomb assembly, thus releasing the kite wire, allowing it to slide over the wing of the aircraft. Assisted by the drag of the kite, and the forward velocity of the enemy machine, the bomb was drawn quickly up to the aircraft, exploding upon impact. Even when flown without its lethal assembly the Admiralty regarded the kite as a valuable deterrent to aerial attack.

3

4

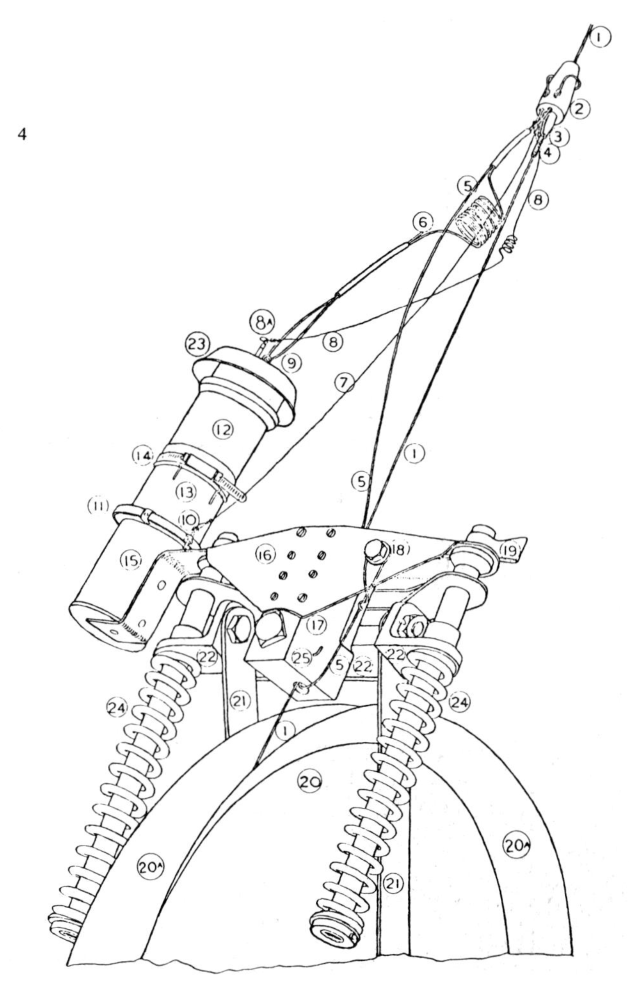

1–2) Sauls' barrage kite.
3) David Williams of Kentucky tests the scoop-lines of his 9 m (30 ft) modified parachute. Parachute kites are capable of developing a frightening degree of drag and tend to be inefficient. Any virtues that such kites may have appear to be far out-weighed by the dangers involved in flying them.
American Kiteflyers Association.

4) The 'lethal assembly' of the British Admiralty's barrage kite. Impact from an enemy aircraft, absorbed in part by the springs (24), caused the kite line (1) to be severed by an inertia cutter (17) causing the bomb (12) to be drawn up towards the aircraft. Immediately before release a system of lines of varying lengths sequentially withdrew the bomb release pin (10) and the bomb arming pin (8a). The mushroom head of the bomb (23) operated the bomb striker, as it made contact with the aircraft.

One of the most significant contributions to the development of a truly modern kite was that of Francis Rogallo of the U.S.A. The invention and subsequent development of his Flexible kite, which was filed for patent in 1948, resulted in the famous delta wing kite, making Rogallo the father of hang gliding as we know it today. With this invention he realized the dreams of countless brave and forgotten men, who died as a result of their conviction that men could fly like birds. Passing over countless failures, the 'tower jumpers' of the eleventh century and even Leonardo da Vinci amongst them, truly significant results were not achieved until 1853 with Cayley's New Flyer. Hang gliding enthusiasts often mistakenly revere the pioneering work of John J. Montgomery of Santa Clara College, California, whose gliding experiments made between 1883 and 1886, and subsequent experiments of the first decade of the twentieth century, made no significant contribution to man's conquest of the air. Montgomery died as the result of a crash in 1911. It is undoubtably Otto Lilienthal who is the doyen of today's hang gliding revival.

Rogallo, an aeronautical engineer associated with the National Aeronautics and Space Administration, Virginia, advocated that flexible wings provided potentially greater stability than fixed surfaces, and that the aircraft should conform to the flow of the wind, as opposed to the wind conforming to the form of the aircraft, or kite. Installing a large electric fan into his home, Rogallo, with the help of his wife Gertrude, made extensive tests and experiments on kite structures, eventually achieving success with his Flexible kite of 1948. This was marketed at a time when little interest was being given to kites, and the project was abandoned. Nevertheless, the potential of Rogallo's theories proved of

1

2

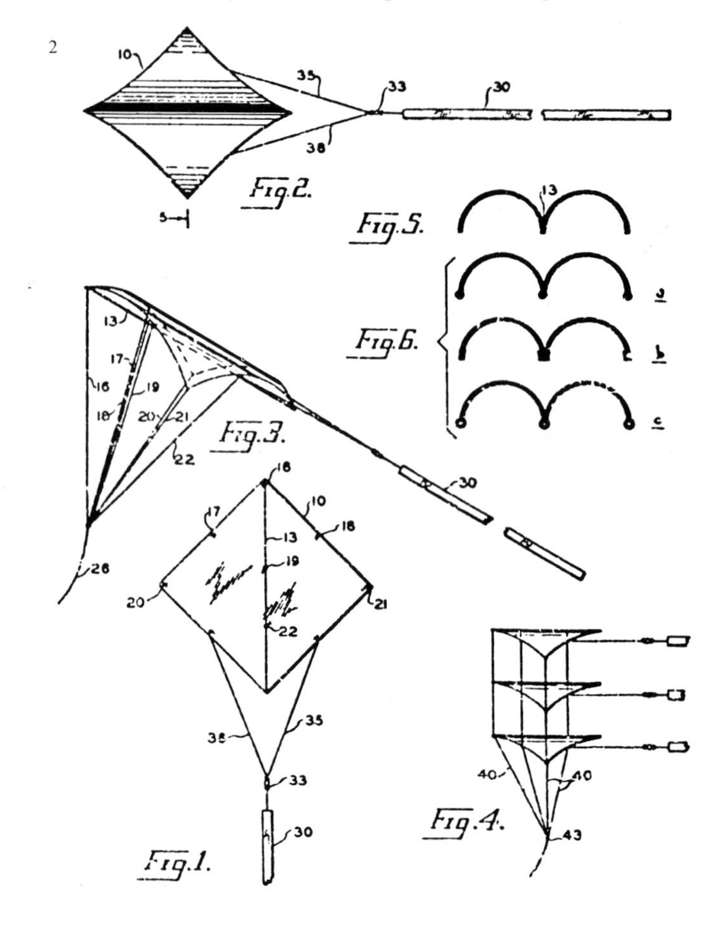

1) Francis M. Rogallo flies a dirigible version of his Flexible kite.
Popular Science Publishing Co.
2) Rogallo's patent drawings show a multiple version of his Flexible kite.

3) Rogallo displays models of his flexible wing at the Langley Research Centre, Hampton, Virginia.

great interest to the U.S. space programme, and he was soon involved in extensive research at the vast wind tunnel at Langley, Virginia, developing a series of highly sophisticated parawings, capable of being deployed and controlled with great accuracy for the landing of returning space capsules. In his efforts to achieve minimum supporting area with maximum lift, Rogallo worked towards the total elimination of rigid spars. Via a series of wings held in configuration by inflatable spars his experiments led him to the invention of the limp wing, a totally unsupported sail area, capable of holding its shape solely by means of the distribution of the air load on the kite surface, counterbalanced by the tension of the shroud lines. In effect, the shroud lines form the central spine or keel of the kite, without recourse to rigid supports, the keel deflecting the wind into the supporting wing areas, giving the kite both form and lift with maximum economy.

PHOTO: TREVOR WOOD

3

PHOTO: ALFRED EISENSTAEDT/TIME-LIFE BOOKS © TIME INC 1975

The characteristics of the limp wing, basically an extremely manoeuvrable parachute with a high glide ratio, quickly established it as a favourite with skydivers, who use the wing as a high-performance hang glider, descending in an extended glide rather than a drop. Developed at a time when man's concern for squandered resources is nearing neurosis, Rogallo's concepts have been embraced as classic examples of purity and efficiency. The simple construction and high stability of his aircraft have ensured their place in the low-energy, low-cost technology of the future.

2

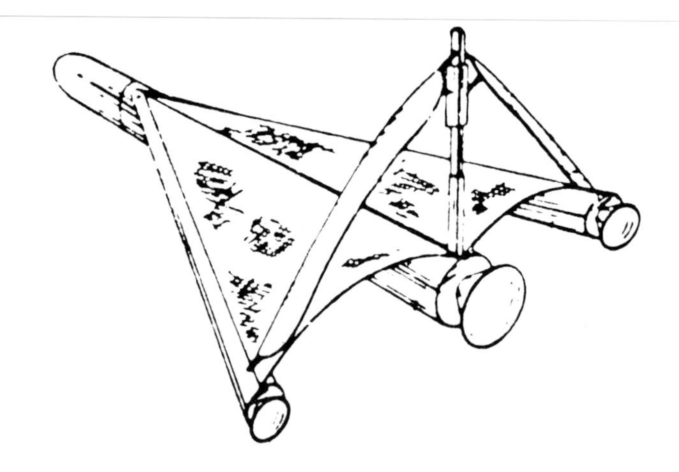

1

3

1) A Rogallo inflatable wing, undergoing wind-tunnel tests at the Langley Research Centre, Virginia.
2) Configuration for a flexible-wing re-entry vehicle, primarily for the recovery of rocket boosters. Signals controlling re-entry and return were transmitted by telemetry, 1963.
3) Rogallo limp wing during tests with a space capsule payload.
American Kiteflyers Association.

4

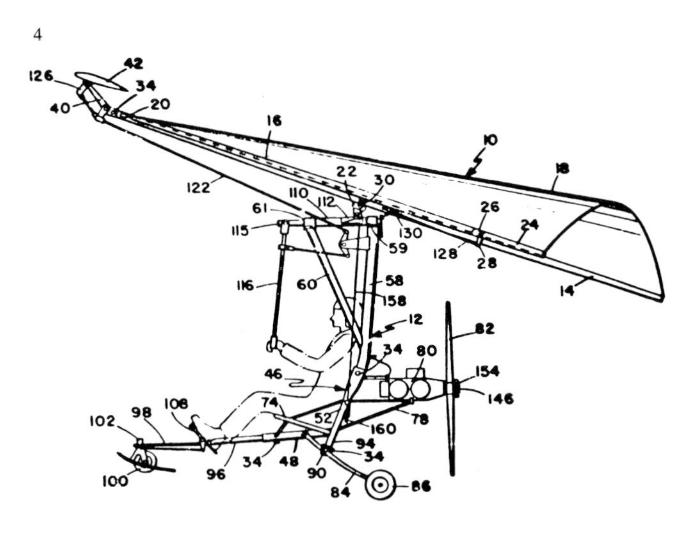

5

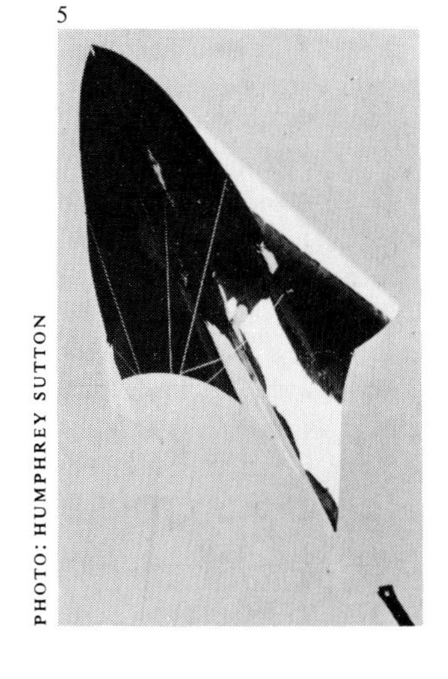

4) Demountable aircraft with flexible wing, by Girard, La Mesa and Landgraf for the Ryan Aeronautical Company, 1966.
5) Rogallo's Flexible kite, 1948.
6) Russell Hall's kite, 1966.
7) An impression of the Bell Aerospace Company's rocket-propelled high-ejection delta wing.
Popular Science Publishing Co.

6

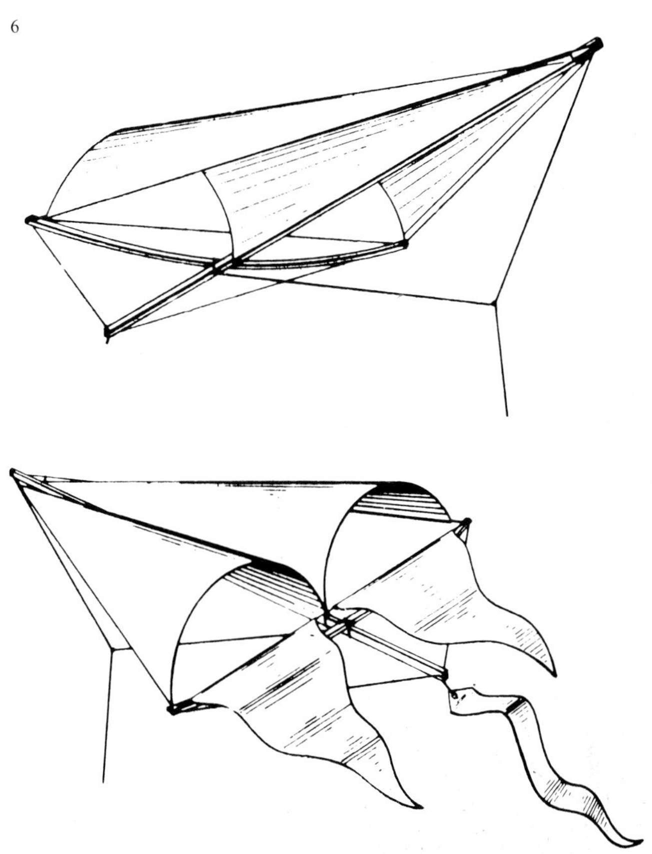

7

Another entirely new genre of kite emerged with the filing of a patent in 1950 for what has become known as the Allison or Scott sled. The conception of this kite was the work of William M. Allison of Dayton, Ohio, whose patent, because of possible conflict with the pending patent for the Rogallo Flexible kite, was not issued until 1956. Basically Allison's invention was a semi-rigid canopy kite, supported only in its longitudinal plane, relying upon the wind to give lateral support to the structure by holding its canopy open. The bridle, being attached to the lateral extremities, holds these down to form keels, lending the kite its remarkable lateral stability. Allison's patent specification shows this early model, classified also as a flexible kite, as having three spines supporting a tapering non-vented cover.

1

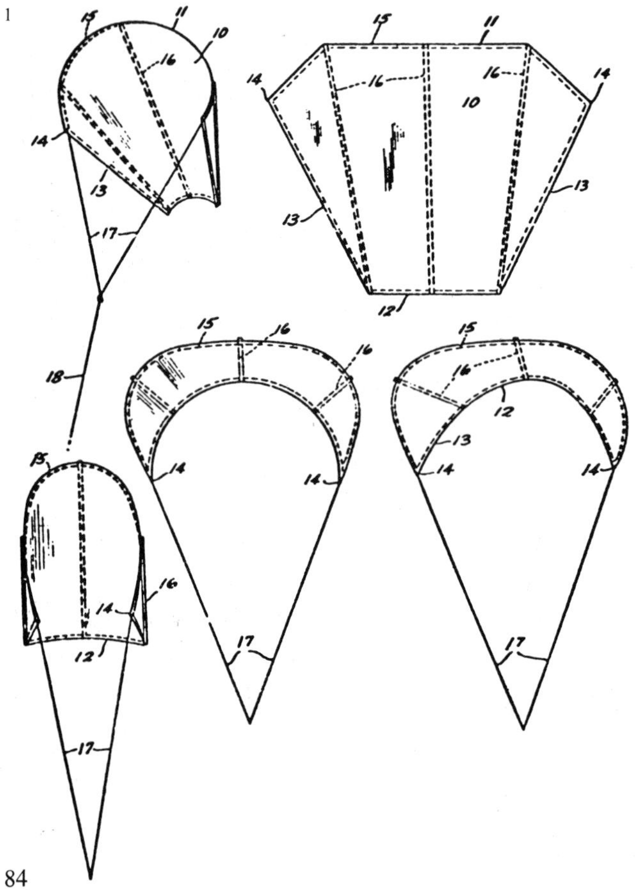

2

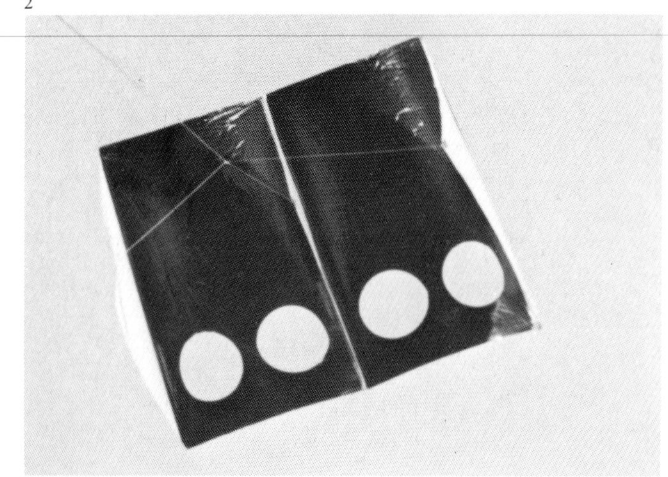

3

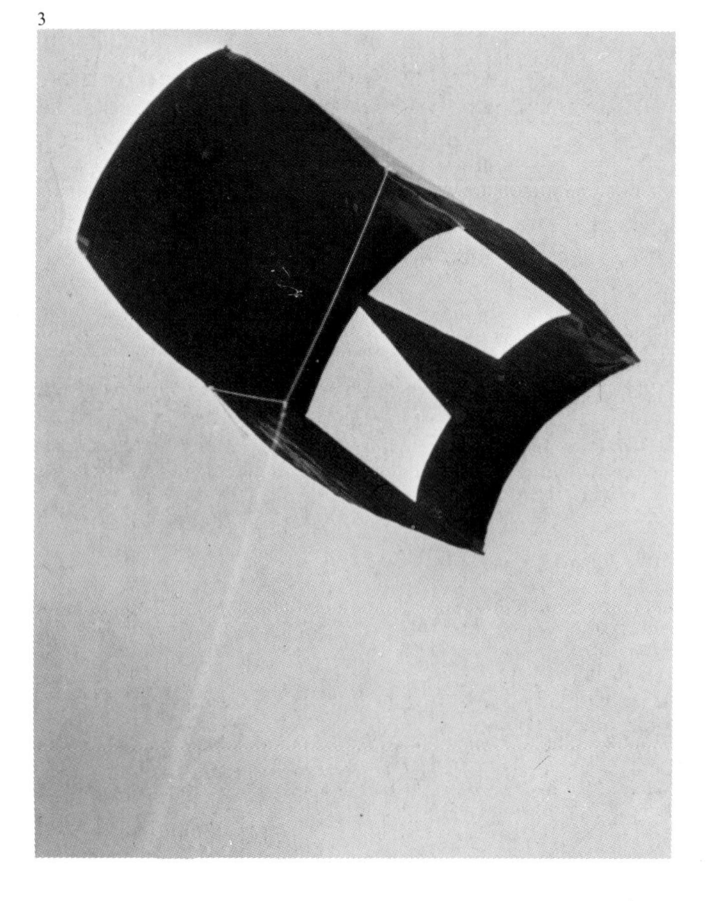

4

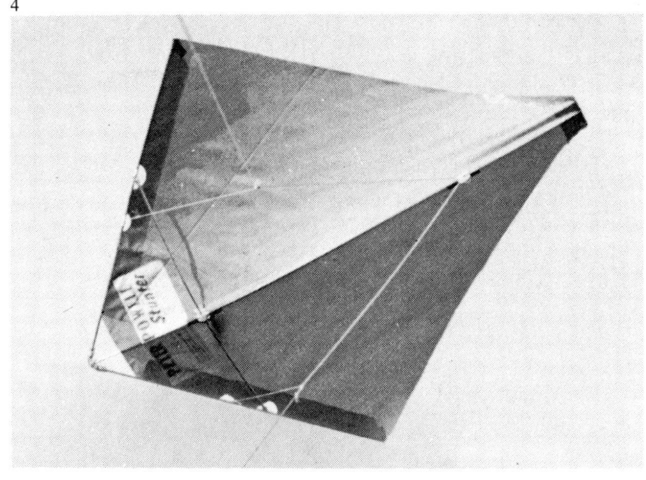

The Allison sled appears to have languished in this form until 1964, when Frank Scott, also of Dayton, introduced a modified version of the original, sporting a vent in its lower half, with its sides no longer tapering towards the trailing edge, but parallel. In this form it is an extremely efficient and lively flyer, capable of thermal soaring at a high angle, but also prone to losing its shape and folding up when either the wind drops, or it is struck by a sharp side wind. Because of this characteristic, it becomes particularly necessary to fly the sled on a taut line, in order that its form can quickly be restored by working the line.

5

PHOTO: MARK ELLIDGE: TOPIX

6

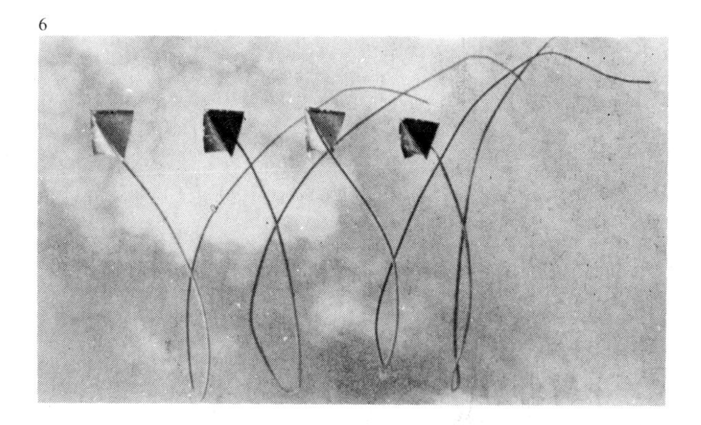

1) Patent drawings for William Allison's flexible kite, 1950.
2) A polythene double sled. It is an extremely efficient kite in stable winds, and is inexpensive and quick to build.
3) Ed Grauel's modification of the Scott sled employs the most efficient vents yet devised for this type of kite. Collapsing is virtually eliminated. It has a fast climb rate and a high and stable flight angle.
4) The Peter Powell Stunter is a high-performance dirigible kite. It is highly sensitive to line control, and is capable of complex aerial manoeuvres including dives, lateral loops and hedge hopping at speeds in excess of 60 m.p.h. in strong winds.
5) Powell and Stunters. 23 m (75 ft) sky-writing streamers show where the kite has been. The picture shows three Stunters flown 'stacked' one behind the other.
6) Flown stacked in multiples, Powell's Stunters make an impressive spectacle for onlookers, though the handler sees only the lower kite.

The most recent innovation in the history of the form of the kite is the parafoil, a totally original concept in kite design invented by Domina C. Jalbert of Boca Raton, Florida.

Jalbert has spent a lifetime dedicated to employing the resources of the wind, either adapting and developing existing methods or inventing new ones. Like Rogallo, Jalbert feels that form should follow wind flow, and one of his earlier inventions, a multi-cellular parachute featuring a multiplication of centre-of-efforts, utilized wind force to a considerably greater degree than the standard canopy configuration, with its single centre-of-effort. Jalbert, finding the general shape of the conventional parachute to be inefficient, owing to its considerable air spillage, set about designing one capable of retaining a greater volume of air, giving more buoyancy and a generally more stable and softer descent. In addition to this, the parachute was fitted with a double keel for increased manoeuvrability and stability. Jalbert devised various ingenious inventions, through his remarkable ability to apply the forces of the wind, and his love of sailing brought about a highly efficient nautical ventilator capable of 'finding' a breeze, regardless of its direction, and deflecting it below decks. His use of multi-cellular surfaces also helped him develop a highly reinforced spinnaker for racing yachts, each cell working virtually independently from the others, gaining its strength, as Jalbert explains, in much the same way that a multi-paned window is stronger than a large uninterrupted sheet of glass. Known as the Super-Chute, Jalbert's spinnaker also gives extra buoyancy to the bows of the yacht, considerably reducing the drag factor of the hull. For Byrd's Antarctic expeditions he designed a 'blimp' for lofting aerials. Being

1

2

1) Checking the steering lines of the Jalbert multi-celled parachute. *Courtesy, Florida Life.*
2) The Bede Wing, named after its inventor, the famous U.S. aviation designer Jim Bede. A safer alternative to the usual hang glider configuration, the Bede Wing is inflated with helium before launching.

3

something of a cross between a kite and a balloon it was named the Kytoon, and was basically an aeroform balloon, bearing rigid lifting and stabilizing surfaces. While the stabilizers were capable of keeping the Kytoon headed into the wind, the wing surfaces ensured a good lift, enabling it to be accurately moored over its anchorage, rising into the wind rather than being blown towards the ground as a normal balloon might. Because of its comparatively high degree of controllability, large versions of Jalbert's original Kytoon are still used in the Canadian timber industry, where they are employed to lift logs from otherwise inaccessible areas.

In 1963, inspired by the wing section of his aeroplane, Jalbert hit upon the idea of making a lifting surface in the shape of a rigid low-speed wing, made entirely from fabric, maintaining its form not with weighty rigid structures but entirely by the

4

5

3) Jalbert with small Kytoon.
4) The Jalbert J-15 demonstrates high-performance flight angle of the parafoil.
5) J-30 parafoil weighs only two and a half lb. Jalbert parafoils took first place in the U.S. National Sky Diving competitions of 1975.
Jalbert Aerology Laboratory, Inc.

action of the wind entering openings in its leading edge, setting up internal pressure. The wing is divided by a series of fabric aerofoil-shaped formers called ribs, or risers, which retain its critical aerofoil shape in flight. Lateral stability is achieved by a system of triangular ventral fins, or flares, sewn to the face, or bottom surface of the kite. These ventrals are held in shape by a system of shroud lines, basically a multi-legged bridle, from which the parafoil is flown.

A truly generic kite, the parafoil is the product of an amalgamation of Jalbert's prime preoccupations. Incorporating balloon, parachute, aerofoil and kite features, it is the lightest, most efficient and economical non-mechanized lifting surface yet devised. Employing the principle known as ram-air inflation the parafoil is the realization of the proverbial sky hook.

2

1

3

1) Typical Indian fighting-kite reel.
2) Hand-held 'deep sky' reels.
3) Will Yolen, veteran U.S. kite flyer, with adapted tuna-fishing reel for flying trains of kites.
American Kiteflyers Association.
4) 'Deep sky' reel on monopod stand.
5) Record breaker Vincent Tuzo surveys a wind-worn Bermudan octagonal kite, similar to that with which he made his duration record flight of 49 hrs 40 mins.
Courtesy, Bermuda News Bureau.
6) Launching a Bermudan giant.

4

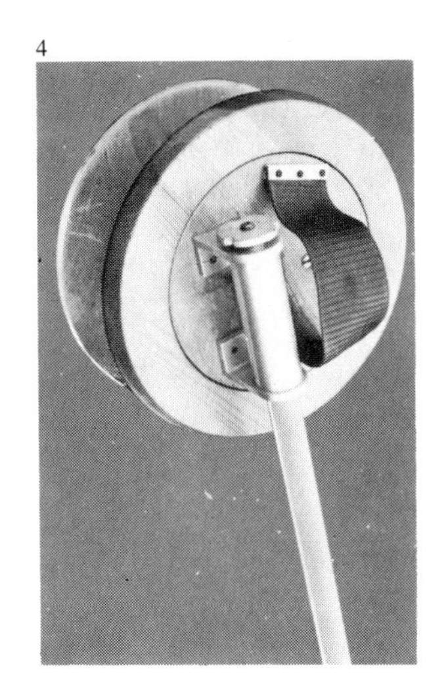

A further refinement of this basic idea was the inclusion of an automatic ventilator, or flutter valve, sewn into the face of the centre cells. This ensures that the pressure within the cells is never great enough to distort their shape, adversely affecting the efficiency of the kite. The valve is simply a rectangle of nylon mesh, set into the belly of the kite. A corresponding air-opaque flap is fitted inside the cell, being sewn at the leading edge only. Consequently as the air pressure within the cell builds up to a point where it is greater than that of the surrounding air, so the flap is blown forward, releasing the excess pressure, restoring the cell to its maximum operational form. The flutter valve principle is further extended in the parasled – a close relative of the parafoil – which also incorporates the valve into the leading edge intakes of the wing, ensuring that, in the event of a drop in wind velocity, the pressure within the cell is retained, and thus preventing

5

6

the kite from losing its essential form.

The military application of the parafoil is considerable. As a means of lifting payloads its full potential has not yet been realized, while used as a parachute it enables a pilot or paratrooper to fly distances of up to five times his ejection altitude, while performing remarkable evasion tactics far beyond the limits of a conventional parachute. The flyer is also capable of soft, controlled landings in far stronger winds than is normally considered possible, simply by turning his 'chute into the wind immediately prior to contact.

J. G. Hagedoorn, professor of geophysics at the University of Leiden, is currently developing a further application of the parafoil. Working towards a more efficient – and probably ultimate – means of sailing, it is Hagedoorn's eventual goal to dispense with the hull of the yacht altogether, seeing it as an inefficient and drag-producing impediment. Basically the 'aquaviator' is suspended above the sea from a vast parafoil, while from his harness is suspended a highly developed version of the paravane, the under-water kite used in mine-sweeping. By judicious control of both his air and his water kite, he will skim across the surface of the water, taking advantage of absolute minimal drag and maximal efficiency in both elements.

1

2

PHOTO: PAUL HILDER

3

PHOTO: PAUL HILDER

1) Sixteen-celled tetrahedral, by Synestructics, Inc.
Courtesy, Go Fly a Kite Store, Inc.
2) Hexagonal roller with fin and rudder, designed by the author.
3) Soaring Bird kite with rudder.
4) Multicoloured double box, or double Conyne kite, with detachable panels for high-wind flight.
5) Standard Eddy bow kite.
6) Jalbert's J-7·5 parafoil with drogue. This type, measuring only 91·5 cm (3 ft), is marketed as a toy.

4

5

6

PHOTOS: HARRI PECCINOTTI

1

2

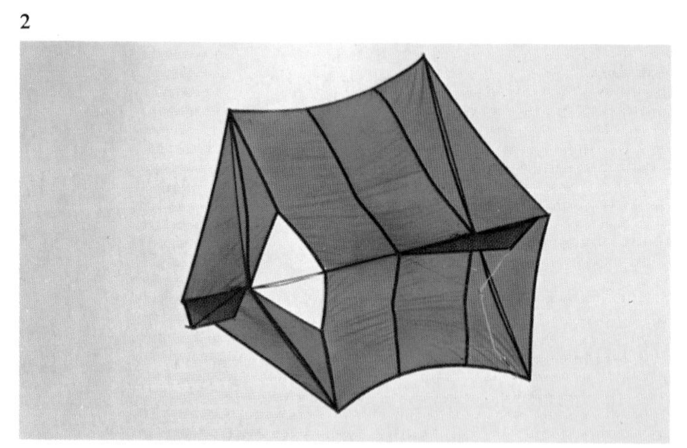

3

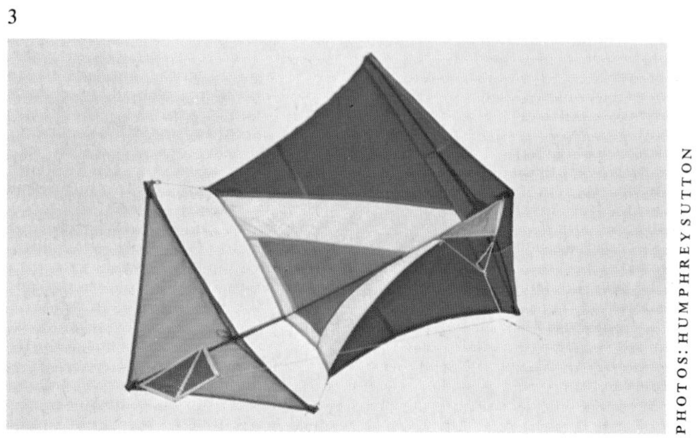

PHOTOS: HUMPHREY SUTTON

4

PHOTO: HARRI PECCINOTTI

5

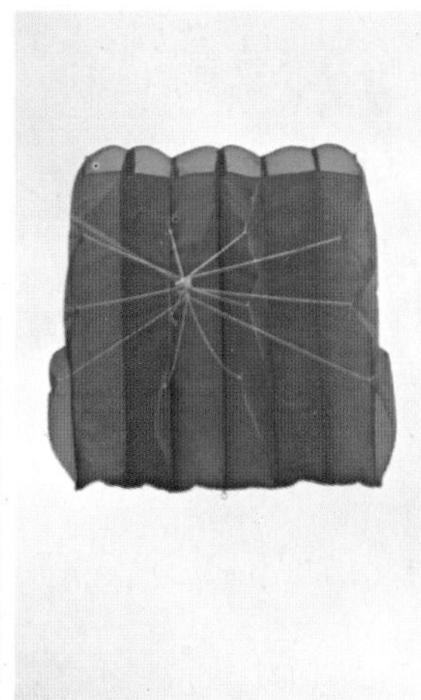

PHOTO: HUMPHREY SUTTON

6

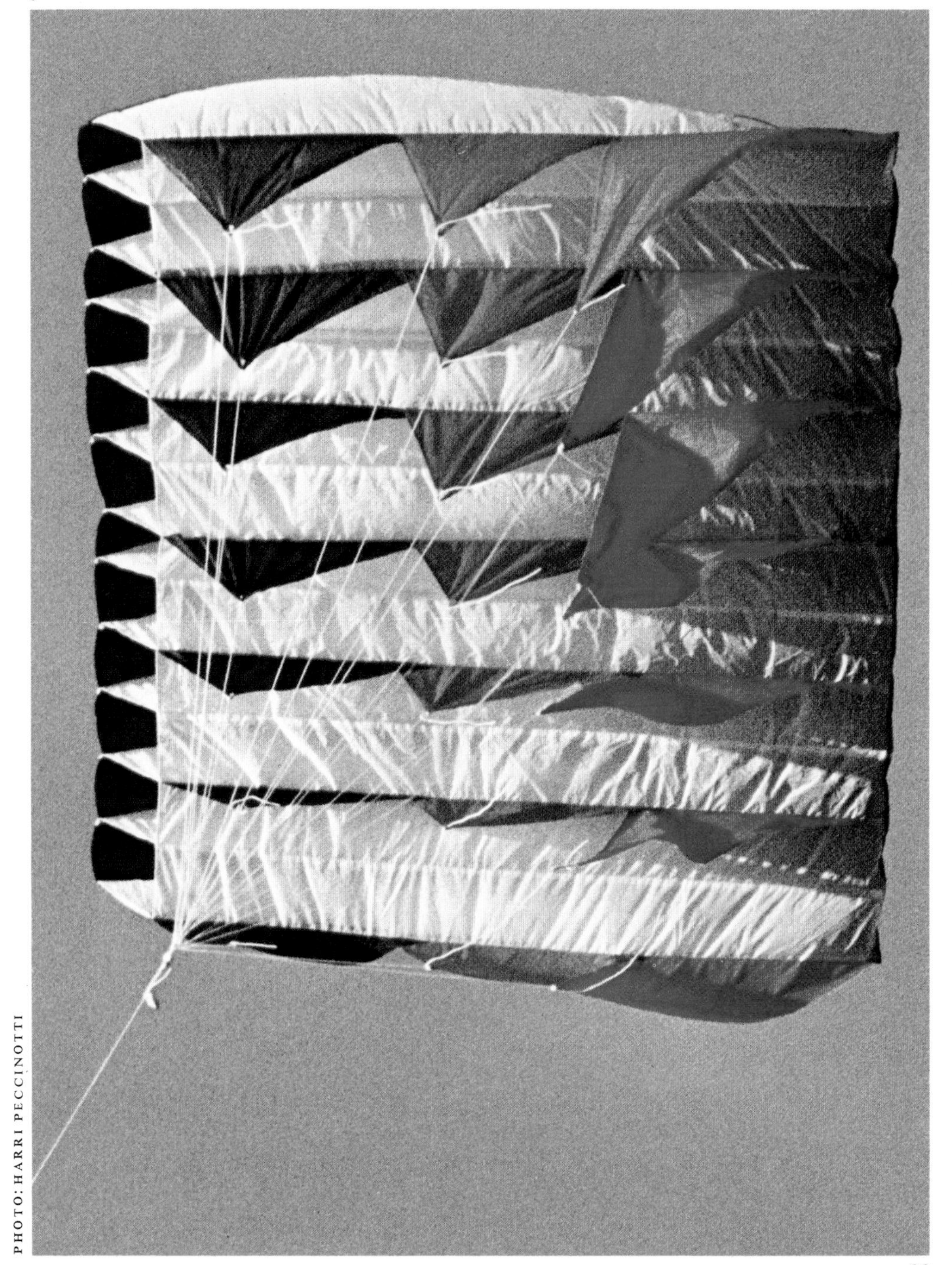

PHOTO: HARRI PECCINOTTI

1) Lightweight Multi-flare kite for ultra-light wind-speeds, designed by the author.
2) Aluminium-framed hexagonal roller with fin, rudder and vent, designed by the author.
3) Aluminium-framed light-wind double-sailed roller.
4) Ultra lightweight Flare kite, flown drogued in all but the very lightest wind-speeds.
Designed by the author.
5) Six-celled parafoil.
6) Giant parafoil, being test flown during trimming of shroud lines.

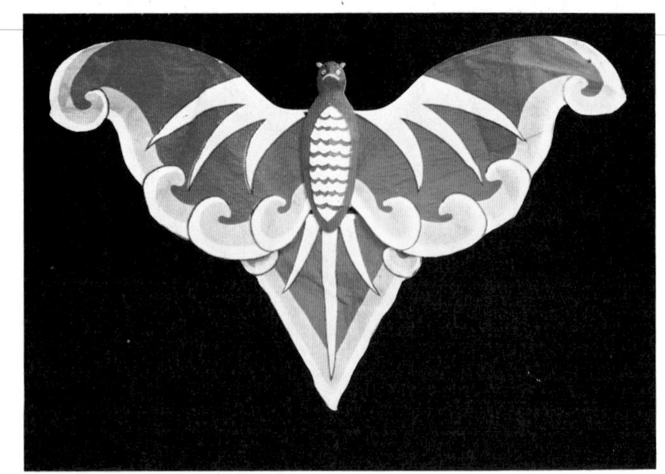

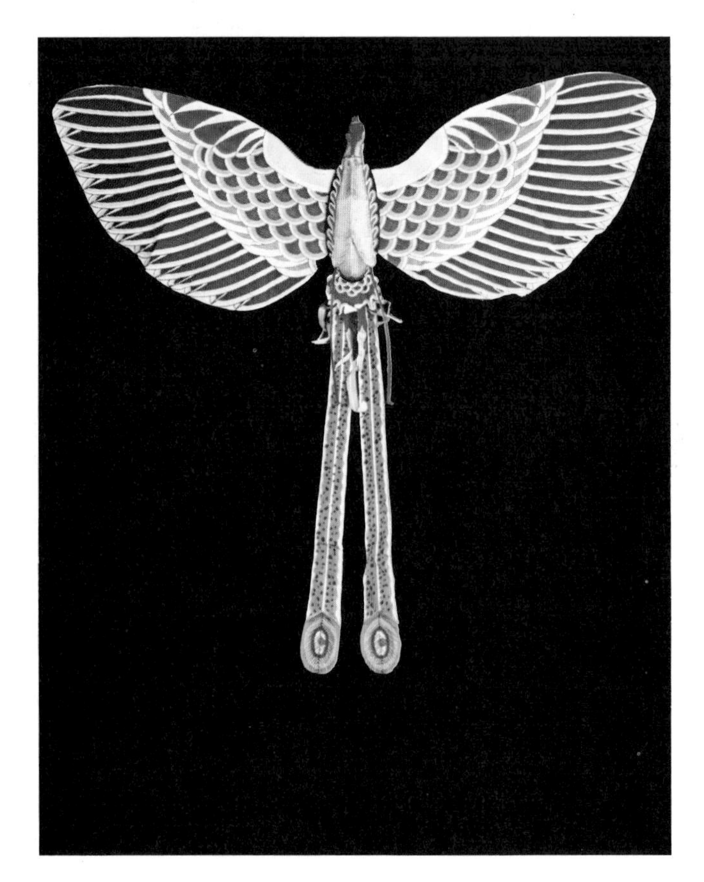

A selection of modern paper kites from the People's Republic of China.

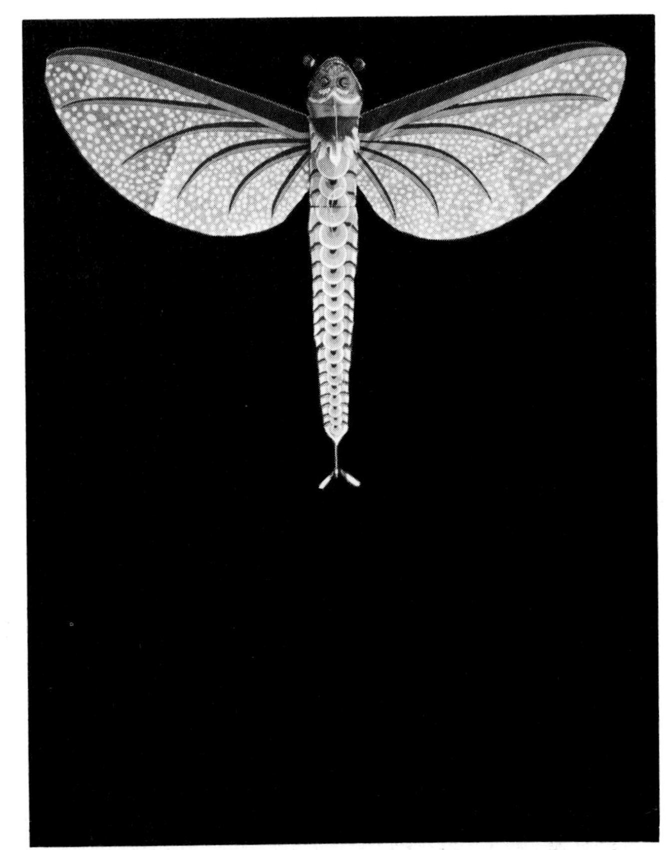

It is somewhat comforting to find that, while so many advancements in kite design have been motivated by either martial or scientific needs, the kite, seen simply as an aesthetic object, still provides inspiration to artists even today.

While the long tradition of kite painting – which itself helps to keep alive the dreams and legends of old Japan – is still continued by such modern masters as Teizo Hashimoto, Toranosuke Watanabe, Tatsusaburo Kato and Tsuzan Yoshitani, a number of dedicated artists and craftsmen, both eastern and western, still respond to the concept of the kite itself as a means of conveying their creative impulses.

The remarkable work of the well-known American sculptor Tal Streeter is of particular interest in as much as it embodies traditional Japanese kite making techniques with an essentially western attitude to fine art. Having worked in welded steel for some years, and being preoccupied with creating objects that lead the eye, via the sculpture, to the surrounding landscape and sky, Streeter defied the established maxim of drawing the attention of the observer into the work itself. It was while erecting his 21 m (70 ft) high zig-zag form *Endless Column* in Central Park, New York City, that he realized that, as the piece was expressly designed to lead the eye ever upwards, the inevitable extension of his work was in the sky itself. Subsequently he moved to Japan solely to study the ancient art of kite making, meeting and talking with many kite makers, collectors and enthusiasts, completely immersing himself in Japanese culture, learning everything he could of their skills, their attitudes, and occasionally their secrets. Building kites for himself in Japan, Streeter had a one-man exhibition in Tokyo's prestigious Minami Gallery before

1

2

returning to New York, where he continues to build his fine kites, displaying not only an extraordinary degree of craftsmanship but also a deep appreciation of Japanese attitudes and sensibilities.

3

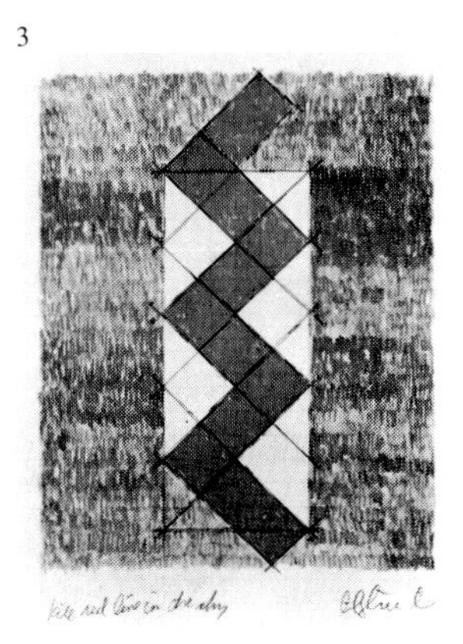

4

PHOTO: JIM ENYEART

1) Tal Streeter at work on a square kite, using traditional Japanese methods and materials.
Courtesy, Tal Streeter.
2) An exhibition of Streeter's Flying Red Lines, 1972.
Courtesy, A. M. Sachs Gallery.
3) 'Kite, Red Line in the Sky', 1970. Coloured pencil on graph paper by Tal Streeter.
Museum of Modern Art, New York.
4) Streeter receives assistance in preparing a 4·6 m (15 ft) Flying Red Line for launching.
Courtesy, Tal Streeter.

Kite flying in the east has continued to be a regular social activity for hundreds of years, and a single fighting kite seen in the sky is taken to be an invitation to a contest. Frequently whole villages in Japan will collectively construct and fly huge kites simply for the fun of it, considering kites of such size as being too dangerous for fighting. The annual two-day festival at Hoshubana, though in many ways typical, is exceptional in as much as the Hoshubana kites are said to be the largest built in Japan today. Measuring some 14·5 m (48 ft) by 11 m (36 ft) with bridle lines 30 m (100 ft) long, it takes fifty members of the O-dako Association of Hoshubana, suitably uniformed to match their giant creation, to manoeuvre it into the sky, to the delight of the 70,000 spectators.

Formal pre-flight photograph of the Hoshubana flying team. *Courtesy, Tal Streeter, from The Art of the Japanese Kite.*

An outstanding kite maker of Yokosuka, Matsutaro Yanase, employs his fine craftsmanship to build a dazzling variety of kites that delight the eyes and minds of children and adults alike. His colourful creations flying in the skies high above Japan are fragile reminders of a slower, gentler and altogether more pleasurable way of life.

In the west the central core of kite flying is the ten-year-old American Kiteflyers Association. With members in every American state and twenty-six different countries, its ever growing activities, together with kite designs, news and views, are recorded in the association's quarterly magazine *Kite Tales*. The existence of highly successful shops, such as the *Go Fly a Kite Store* in New York, and its close cousin *Come Fly a Kite* in San Francisco, catering purely for kite enthusiasts, gives some measure of the extent of the current revival.

With its important development, and its application to modern man's technological, aesthetic and recreational needs, it does not seem beyond the realms of probability to suppose that the future of the humble kite may well be as rich as its past.

Master kite maker Matsutaro Yanase amongst the organized clutter of his ancient craft. *Courtesy, Tal Streeter.*

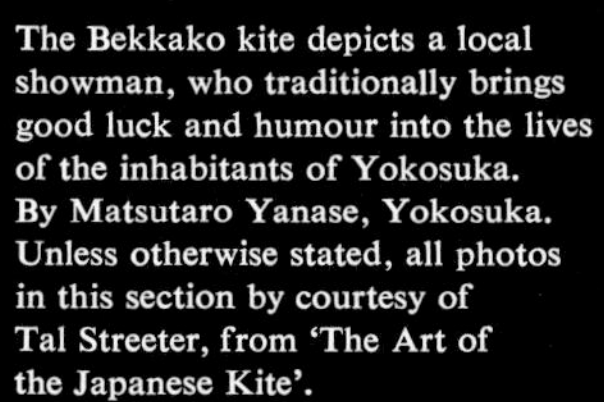

The Bekkako kite depicts a local showman, who traditionally brings good luck and humour into the lives of the inhabitants of Yokosuka. By Matsutaro Yanase, Yokosuka. Unless otherwise stated, all photos in this section by courtesy of Tal Streeter, from 'The Art of the Japanese Kite'.

The Semi, one of the many popular insect kites, represents the cicada. By Matsutaro Yanase, Yokosuka.

The Tsugaru kite is singular among
Japanese kites in that its frame
is built from a type of cypress,
as opposed to the inevitable bamboo.
By Tsuzan Yoshitani, Hirosaki.

The paintings that appear upon the face of the Tsugaru kites are among the finest to be found in Japan. By Tsuzan Yoshitani, Hirosaki.

A hexagonal Sanjo kite, depicting a Kabuki actor as Oishi Yoshio. By Toranosuke Watanabe, Shirone.

An antique Sanjo kite, bearing a portrait of the Samurai warrior, Yoshitsune. Author's collection.

A fine example of the Edo kite. Edo was the old name for Tokyo. By Teizo Hashimoto, Tokyo.

A Suruga kite, bearing the traditional warrior motif. By Tatsusaburo Kato, Shizuoka.

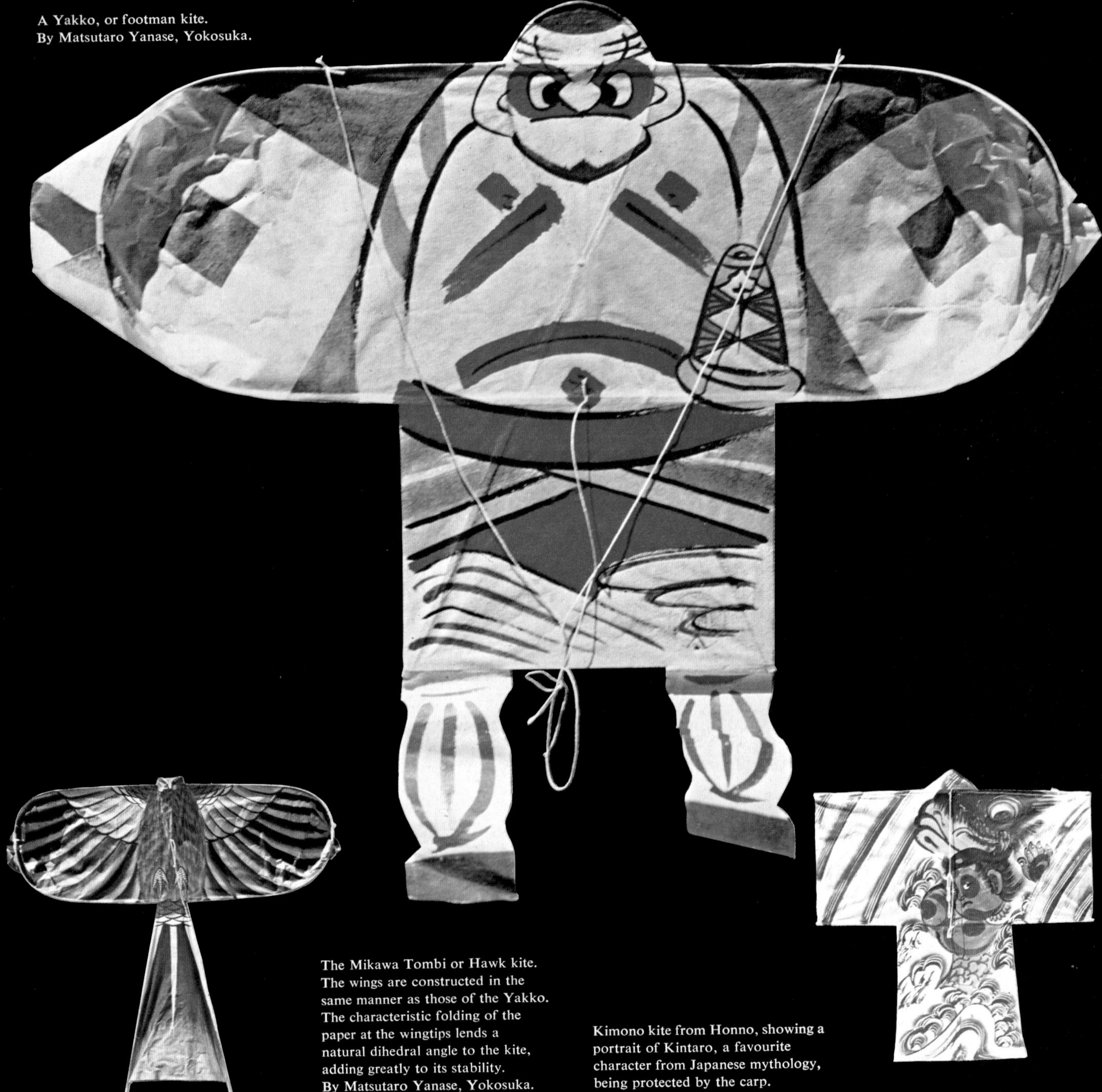

A Yakko, or footman kite.
By Matsutaro Yanase, Yokosuka.

The Mikawa Tombi or Hawk kite. The wings are constructed in the same manner as those of the Yakko. The characteristic folding of the paper at the wingtips lends a natural dihedral angle to the kite, adding greatly to its stability.
By Matsutaro Yanase, Yokosuka.

Kimono kite from Honno, showing a portrait of Kintaro, a favourite character from Japanese mythology, being protected by the carp.

A magnificent Mori Buka kite, showing the hardy carp struggling upstream. The 'Buka' of its title refers to the sound that the kite makes as it rises into the sky.

The Hirado Oniyocho kite represents the masked helmets once worn by Samurai warriors, in order that their comrades might easily recognize them in battle. The framework of the Oniyocho kite is among the most complex to be found in Japan.

The Izumo Iwai kite relies upon the bold use of an ideograph for both its decoration and configuration. The symbol represents the tortoise, traditionally associated with longevity.

Probably the best methods and materials for constructing paper kites are those which have been used since ancient times. Woods such as bamboo, cypress and spruce combine strength with lightness, and are comparatively easy to work. The frame must be light, strong, and as symmetrical as possible, and spars must be tested for balance before assembly. This is done by marking the centre point of the spar and balancing it upon a knife edge. Any discrepancy should be either sandpapered or whittled away until a good balance has been achieved. Though bamboo has many excellent features, such as lightness, strength, flexibility and durability, a bamboo strut or bow requires a great deal of careful preparation before it can be used successfully on small- to medium-sized kites. The weight of an average bamboo strip is distributed rather unevenly through its length, and the nodes need particular attention before any degree of balance can be attained. For the more intricately shaped oriental kites split bamboo or rattan cane is used, as these are easily bent into even the most complex shapes by either soaking in water, or heating over a gas jet or candle while being formed. It is advisable to practise this technique on a few scraps before beginning in earnest, however. The bowed head, or 'bender' of the French pear-top kite is traditionally made from hardwood strip, or dowel, as is the spine; though children in eighteenth-century France utilized wooden barrel loops, as shaping the bender can be rather time-consuming and not particularly easy. It is essential to start with a piece of dowel that is straight-grained and knot free. This should be well soaked in warm water. When it is saturated examine it again for knots, as the water will bring up the grain, and any imperfections will be more apparent.

Whether bamboo or dowelling, stick ends should be lashed or taped.

A saw cut produces a good clean notch. Lashing prevents splitting.

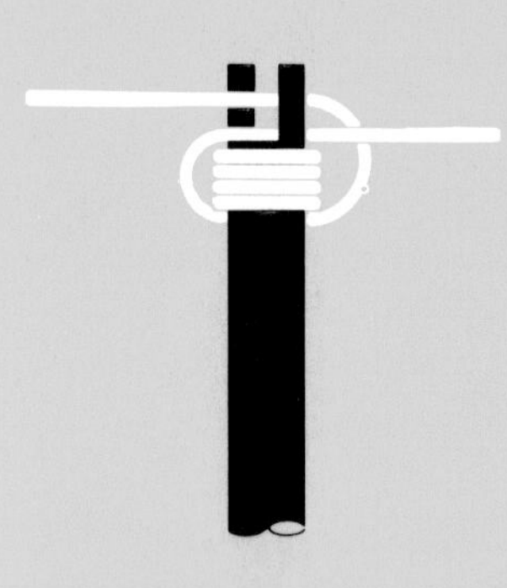

The framing line is looped through stick ends, defining kite's perimeter.

Intersections should be firmly lashed and liberally painted with glue.

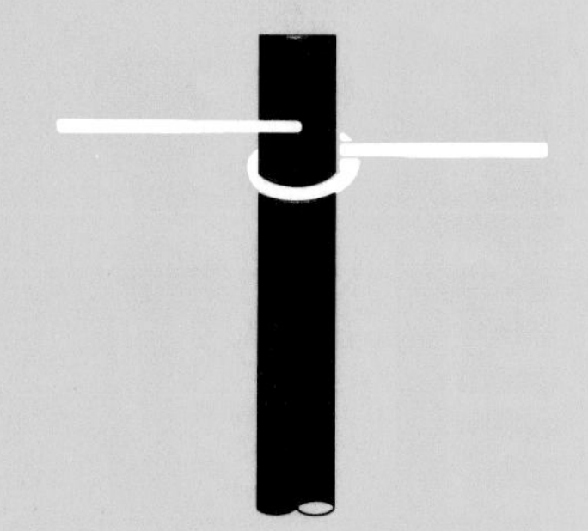

The framing line may also be secured by drilling holes in the stick ends.

Another method of securing framing lines to stick ends is a simple hitch.

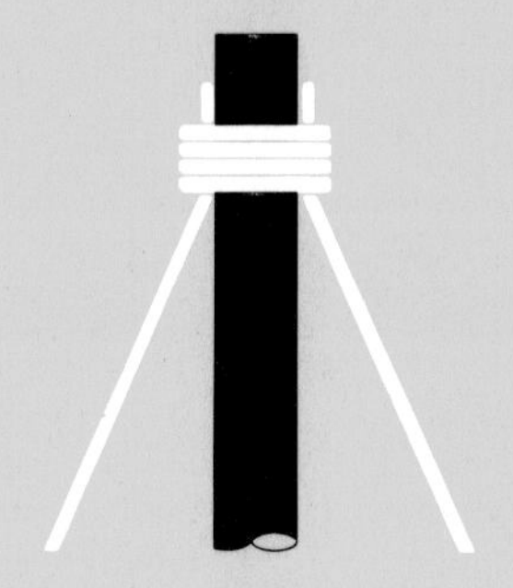

The tension of a framing line is increased by lashing stick ends after stringing.

Intersections provide strong bridling points. Bridles pass through the cover.

Apply the dowel to a source of steam until it is pliable, and very slowly begin to form the curve. When the wood begins to resist further forming, secure the ends with a piece of line, holding the curve in place. Now saturate it again, and repeat the operation. This process may have to be repeated several times in order to achieve the required shape. When sufficiently curved, retain it with the bowstring and allow to dry. Now cut the spine, carving small notches at either end to accept the framing line after the bender and the spine have been assembled. The best, and again the oldest, technique of joining two cross sticks is by lashing with strong cotton or linen thread. Never make a joint by cutting into the wood; this creates weak spots which cannot be afforded in kite construction. After crossing and recrossing the binding, tie the ends and coat the whole joint with a thin resin glue, applying enough to penetrate between the threads, as this not only substantially reinforces the joints, but also makes them waterproof. Moisture can cause the thread to stretch, allowing the kite frame – which when finished will be under considerable tension – to lose its essential form under the stresses that it will be exposed to in the air. It pays to check and re-check measurements and symmetry constantly as work proceeds, as once the cover has been applied a basic fault cannot be made good. Starting at the tail end of the spine, secure the framing line, lead it to the tip of the bender, and again secure; then take the line up through the notch at the head of the kite, eventually ending up back at the tail end of the spine via the opposite tip of the bender. After securing the framing line, make a small loop to take the tail later on. The framing line should be firm and taut, though if natural fibre line has been used additional rigidity can be given to the structure by dampening the line and allowing it to dry quickly.

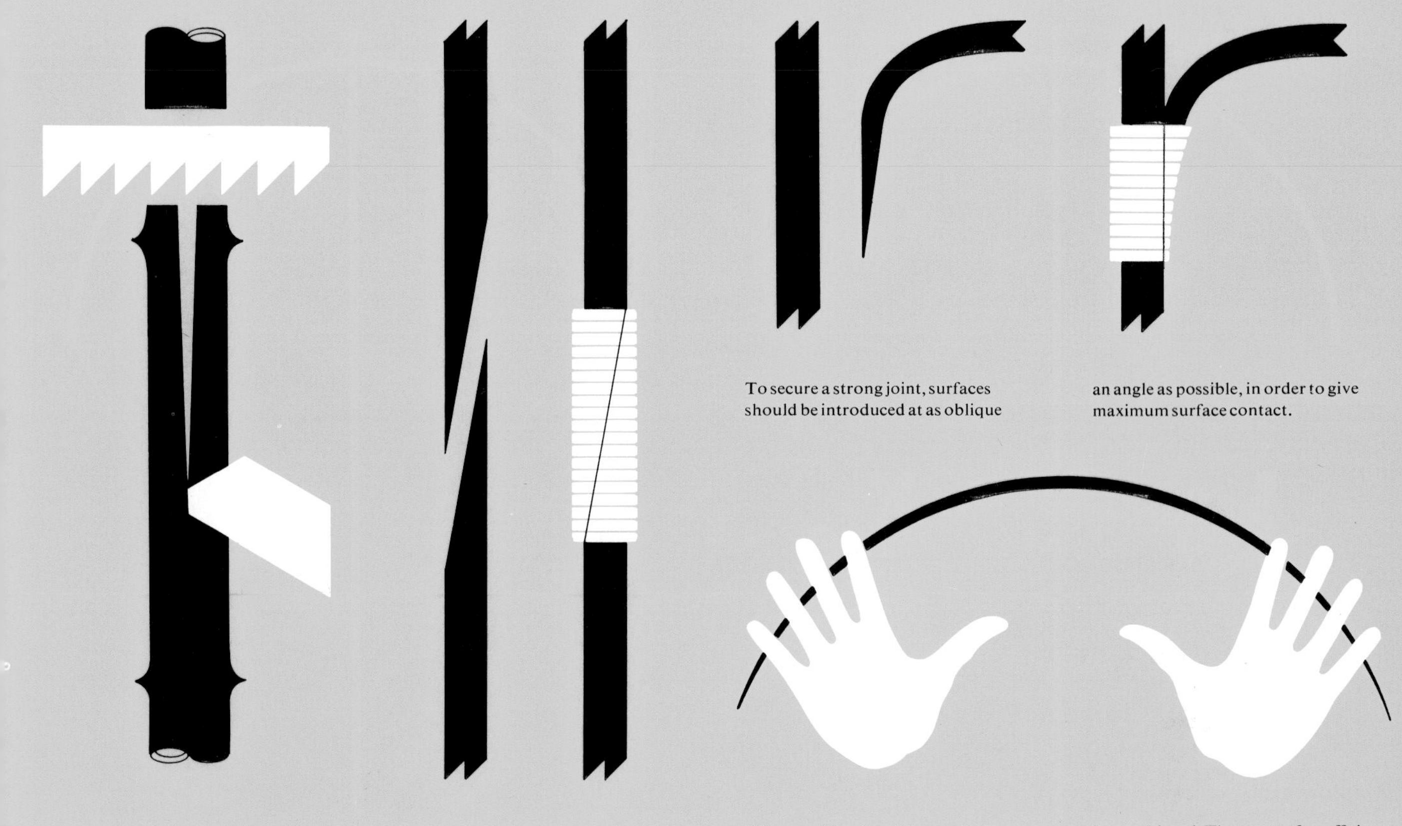

To secure a strong joint, surfaces should be introduced at as oblique an angle as possible, in order to give maximum surface contact.

Bamboo should be sawn through its breadth and split through its length.

Bamboo and rattan cane can be joined by glueing and lashing.

All bow sticks should be carefully worked until maximum symmetry has been achieved. The secret of an efficient fighting kite lies in a well made bow.

Now trim off all loose ends of line and the frame is complete.

Probably the best definition of an ideal cover paper is that given by Woglom in his book *Parakites.*

'It was found – after a sufficient area of tough paper had been prepared for one covering – that, by crushing it all together in a mass, gently rubbing it against itself as a laundress when hand-washing a piece of cloth, and thereafter smoothing it out, a much improved quality was imparted to it – a softness, elasticity, pliability, as of an old bank note, was effected. Paper which will not withstand such rubbing and crinkling has not sufficient durability for covers. Smooth paper imparts a quick, nervous action, while the crumpled paper produces the graceful, easy flight and movements characteristic of textile fabrics.'

However, Woglom was motivated by purely practical considerations, and did not take into account those kite enthusiasts who particularly like flying a lively, skittish kite. If this is more the type of flight required, then the old English method of stretching paper is ideal. This technique, traditional to the old arch tops, involves laying the cover paper between two sheets of damp cloth prior to applying it to the frame. The paper must be left to dry slowly and evenly, and results in an extremely smooth and attractive surface.

Papers used for kite covers range from sturdy brown craft papers, for large practical kites, right through the range to the finest tissue papers traditionally used for the tiny Indian fighting kites, while Bermudan kites are beautifully decorated with panels of fragile multi-coloured tissue. Having decided upon the type of cover required, spread the paper out flat and

Wing-tip tassels are not simply for decoration. By laying spine line of finished kite along the edge of a yardstick, tassels can be trimmed until perfect balance is achieved.

The frame and framing lines ready for covering.

lay the frame upon it. Cut around the outline of the frame, either with a scalpel blade or scissors, leaving a 3 cm (say 1 in.) margin for turning over. Cut notches against the curved edges to give a good close fit, then simply turn all flaps over the framing lines and paste down to the kite cover. Although plenty of good commercial adhesives are available, traditional flour paste does a perfectly good job, particularly if it has been lightly boiled first, as this gives it better penetration, makes it easier to work, and causes it to dry to an almost transparent finish.

As a general rule any lines within the framework of the kite should be pasted flat against the kite cover with paper strips in order to hold the surface flat to the frame. A couple of squares of tough paper should also be pasted onto the back as reinforcement for the bridling points. These should be pierced between the cover and the spine in order to accept the bridle. The ends of the bridle need to be tightly secured to the spine, as should they work loose there is a danger that they may slide up or down the spine in a high wind, ripping through the cover as they go.

After attaching the tassels and a paper-bow tail – which should be approximately seven times the length of the spine – the kite is ready to take to the air.

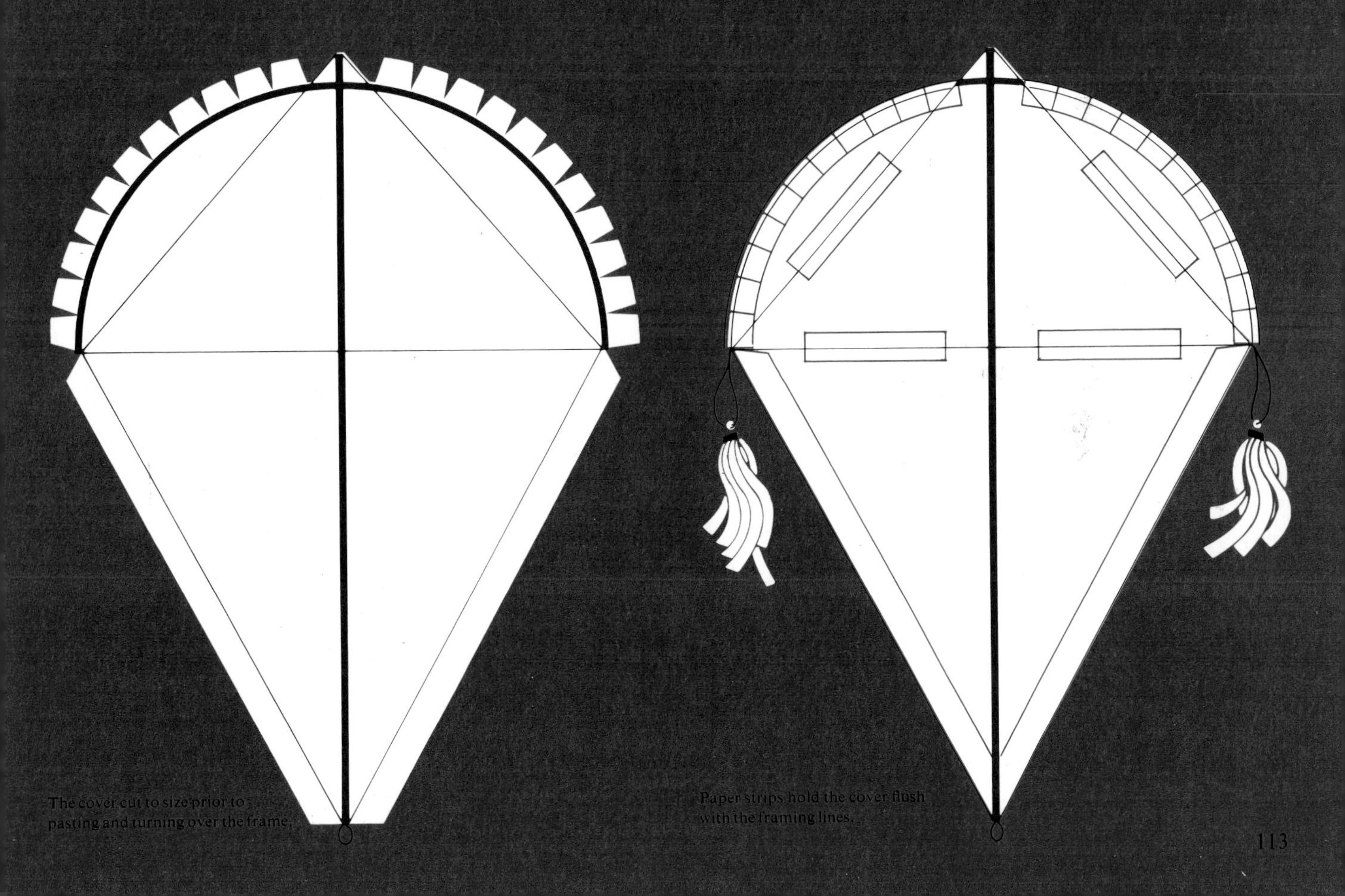

The cover cut to size prior to pasting and turning over the frame.

Paper strips hold the cover flush with the framing lines.

The main advantages of cloth-covered kites is that they are strong, rigid, produce an easy fluid movement through the air, and are collapsible. Kites are designed to fly, and they can be as ungainly on the ground as they are graceful in the air; consequently, the construction methods outlined here are for building kites that are quickly collapsible for easy transport and storage.

Having selected both pattern and fabric, draw a template of one half of the kite on heavy paper or a large sheet of card. Assuming that a fabric cover has been chosen, there is no need to leave any excess material at the edges, as with paper and plastic kites. Lay the fabric on a flat surface and press it with a moderate iron. Weights should now be placed around the outside edges of the fabric, holding it as flat as possible, and the vertical centre should be marked through the vertical grain of the fabric. After laying the template against the spine line, the template, too, should be weighted in place before the pattern is marked out. When both sides of the kite have been defined – tailors' chalk is best for this – fold the fabric along the spine line and check the symmetry. Having again weighted the fabric flat, apply 12 mm ($\frac{1}{2}$ in.) cellulose tape around the surrounding edge of the pattern, carefully positioning it so that it centres on the pattern line. Four hands are best for this job, and, if the tape is held taut above the pattern line, then placed directly down on top of it, the operation is simplified. Next, trim the fabric against the outside edge of the cellulose tape, preferably with pinking shears, though ordinary scissors or a blade and a straight edge may be better suited for the choice of fabric.

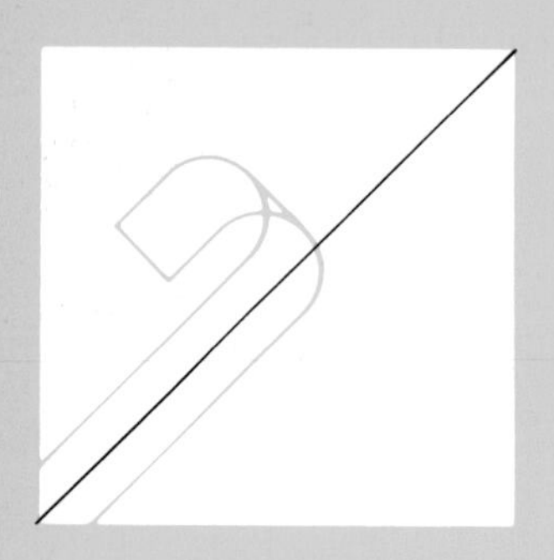

Lay lengths of cellulose tape over the perimeter pattern lines.

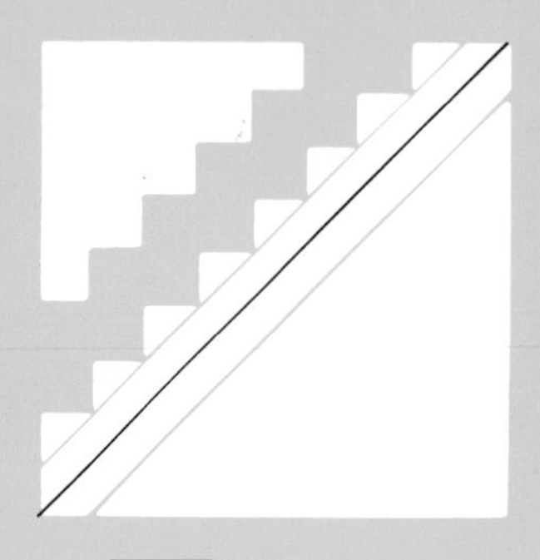

Trim flush against the outside edge of the cellulose tape.

Fold all edges over accurately on the perimeter pattern line.

Sew on the binding tape with two rows of stitching to finish edges.

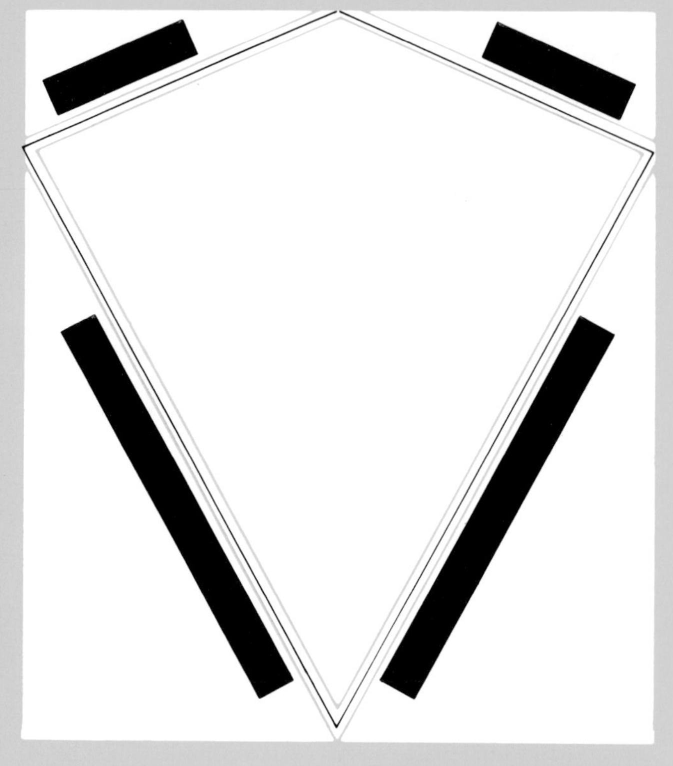

The fabric is weighted so that it holds its shape during marking.

The cellulose tape ensures that the shape is retained during further work.

The cellulose tape should now be folded in half – which, if it is accurately placed, will be along the original pattern line. This fold should now be pressed in with a moderate iron, and the sewing stage has been reached. With a sewing machine, stitch 12 mm (½ in.) binding tape – preferably not bias binding, as it is prone to stretch – as closely as possible to the edge of the kite cover, being sure that the trimmed (and turned) edge of the kite cover is contained within the width of the binding tape. The spine and spar spans of the kite should also be reinforced with binding tape. Any tying tapes that are considered necessary should now be securely sewn in place. Next, insert eyelets through the spine tape at the kite's bridle points, and sew on the necessary fastenings fore and aft of the spine and at the wing tips.

Spine dowelling of the appropriate diameter should now be cut to length, sandpapered, and – by being carefully bent – should be inserted into the fore and aft fastenings of the spine. Check that this dowel is of the correct length, holding the fabric under reasonable tension through its length, while at the same time lying flush to the surface, and not bowing in any way. After preparing the spar, insert this into the wing fastenings, and secure any tying tapes around the spar by means of a bow. Now check the fit of the cover. If the edges of the kite are not taut to the point of tightness, then either the spine or the spar is too short. If horizontal crinkling occurs on the cover then the spine should be replaced by a longer one. If vertical crinkling occurs, then a longer spar is needed. When satisfied that the cover is even and taut throughout the length and breadth of the kite, make two bridle fastenings by cutting two lengths of nylon line approximately 15 cm

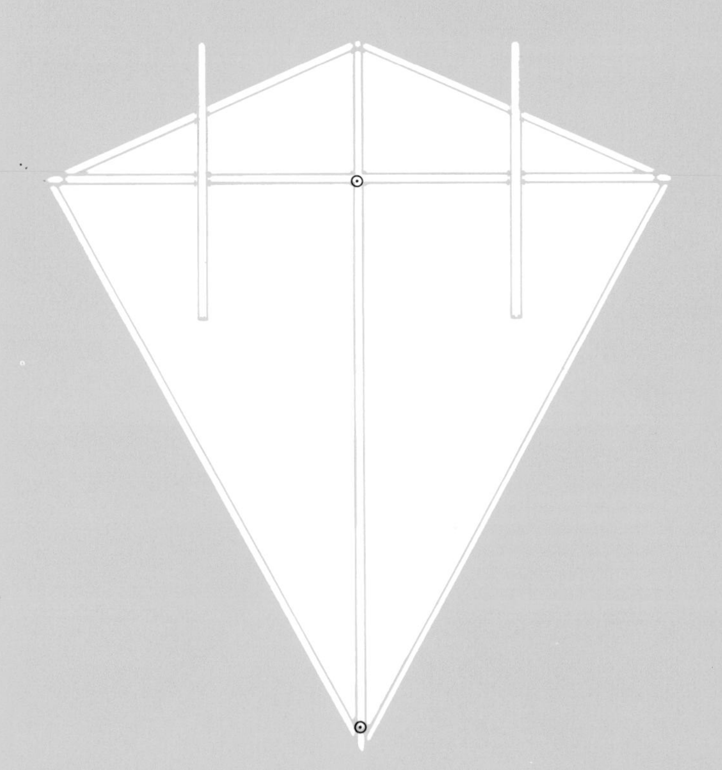

Binding tape sewn against all edges, and the spans of spine and spar, ensure an even tension through the cover. Insert eyelets. Sew on the fastenings and ties.

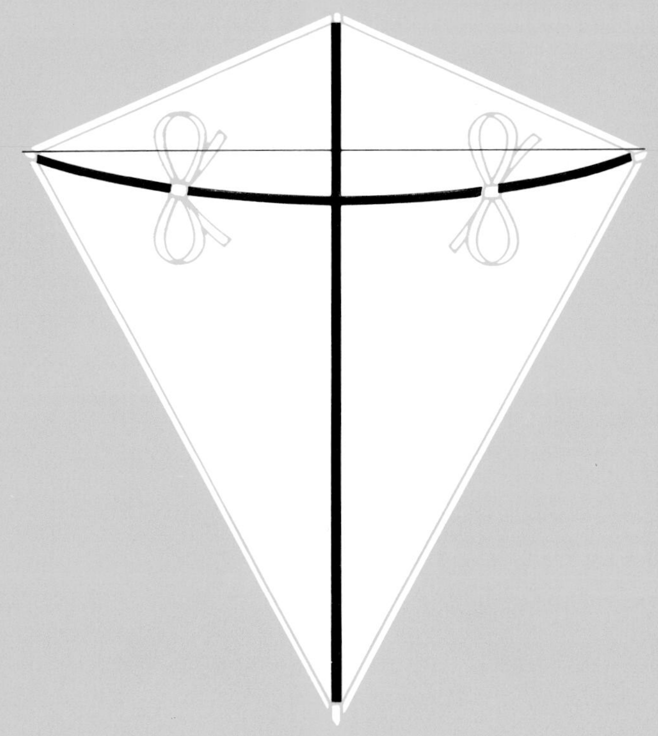

Cut dowel to length for the spar and spine and test them for fit.

Sharp edges of dowel ends are removed with a few turns of a pencil sharpener.

(12 ins.) long. Double these over and thread each of them onto a metal curtain ring by using a lark's head hitch. Take one of them, and pass both ends of the nylon line through one of the eyelet holes, from front to back of the kite cover. Now pass the line ends around the spine and secure them at the back with a surgeon's knot, being sure to trim and burn the ends close to the knot to avoid slip. Do the same with the other bridle fastening and attach a nylon line bridle to the fastenings. An adjustable towing ring should now be slipped onto the bridle, again with a lark's head hitch.

Lastly, either bow the spar or attach a tail, or try both for maximum stability. Apart from a few preliminary tests to establish the best angle of attack and the correct set of the bow, it should fly very well.

Construction Fastenings

In kite making everything depends upon everything. A large kite with a high-porosity cover that lets through a lot of air will give a light lift, putting little pressure upon the spars, whereas a kite of the same size, covered with a low-porosity fabric which is much more air opaque, will give a considerably stronger lift, while putting very much greater pressure upon the spars. A little experimenting with the permutations will quickly develop into a sense for the ratio of porosity to frame strength.

Many ingenious methods of fastening spars to fabric have been developed over the last few years. These points tend to be very vulnerable, as the fabric is usually under considerable stress, and they should be suitably reinforced with fabric tape, if the kite is to survive high wind-speeds and the occasional

Ring fastening with additional ring to take the bow string.

Fabric pocket fastening with ring for the bow string.

Tubular fastening. Fastenings may quickly be made from aluminium or thermoplastic tubing by cutting the tube into small lengths and flattening and drilling one end of each section. These can then be sewn to cover with nylon thread.

Button fastening. A small metal button may be sewn onto the cover with nylon thread, leaving enough space to allow the stick to be inserted between button and cover.

crash. The standard method of fastening wood to fabric is by means of pockets; these can be made from fabric tape, or either aluminium or thermoplastic receivers which have to be pressed at one end, drilled, and sewn to the cover with nylon thread. A practical alternative to this is the use of rings capable of accepting notched spar ends. The tying tapes sewn to appropriate points on the back of the kite cover stop spars and spines from whipping, and also help to distribute stress throughout the length and breadth of the cover.

Some of the more complex box and compound kites often call for intricate joints and spar fastenings. Both enthusiasts and professional kite makers have been quick to adapt new materials to suit their needs.

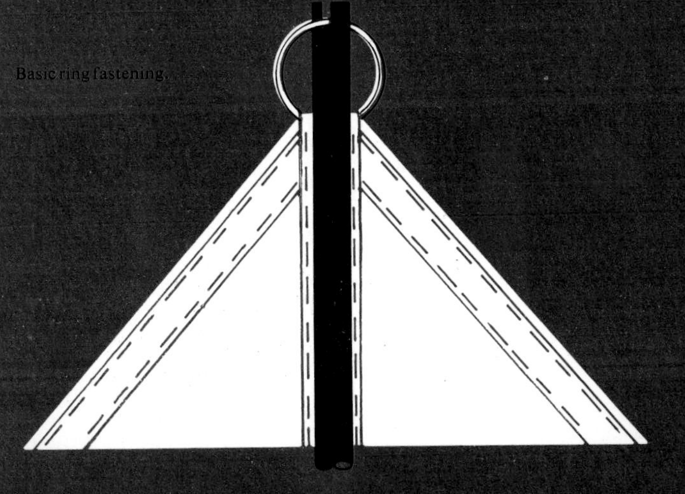

Basic ring fastening.

Plastic fastening. A quick, efficient fastening method for plastic kites employs a short length of polyethylene tube, pierced to accept a stick. The cover is cut with extension tabs, which are also pierced.

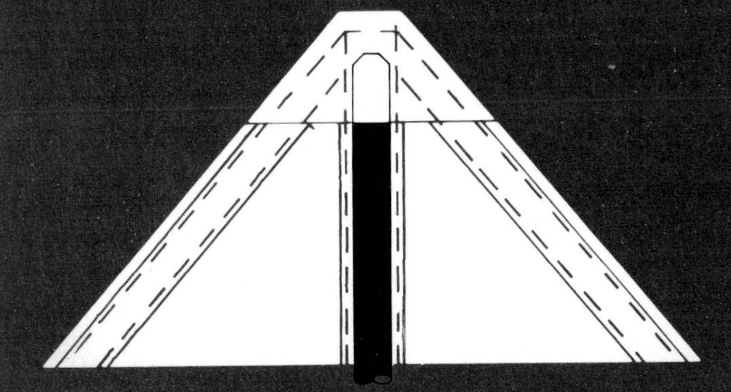

Triangular pocket fastening.

By simply registering the two holes and rolling the tab end under, a secure fastening is made.

Extremely positive and quickly formed joints and fastenings can be made from synthetic tubing, both flexible and rigid. Flexible polyethylene tubing can be cut and bent into an almost unlimited number of configurations which make for quick assembly at the flying site. Thermoplastic tubing softens when heated but hardens again when cooled, and this allows it to be shaped very easily. Softening and rehardening thermoplastic does not significantly alter its properties, and it is therefore a very useful material for forming rigid joints. It is considerably more versatile and lightweight than aluminium, which for years has occupied a pride of place in the kitemakers' compendium.

The most common wood used in the frames of cloth kites is white-wood dowel or flat strip. For the smaller spans, or spans of light stress, 6 mm ($\frac{1}{4}$ in.) dowelling or 10×6 mm ($\frac{3}{8} \times \frac{1}{4}$ in.) flat strip is ample. For the larger spans, or spans of high stress, 8 mm ($\frac{5}{16}$ in.) dowelling or 13×6 mm ($\frac{1}{2} \times \frac{1}{4}$ in.) flat strip should be used. Where dowelling is used for a span of over 1·25 m (say 4 ft) it is usual to sleeve it at the centre with an aluminium ferrule approximately 15 cm (6 ins.) long in order to distribute the stress more evenly through the length of the dowel. For very large high performance kites, young spruce has traditionally been used in the west, together with bamboo. Aluminium rod is also a good material for bracing larger kites, while the most recent development is fibre-glass rod, which, because of its remarkable strength to weight ratio, offers a whole new potential in kite design.

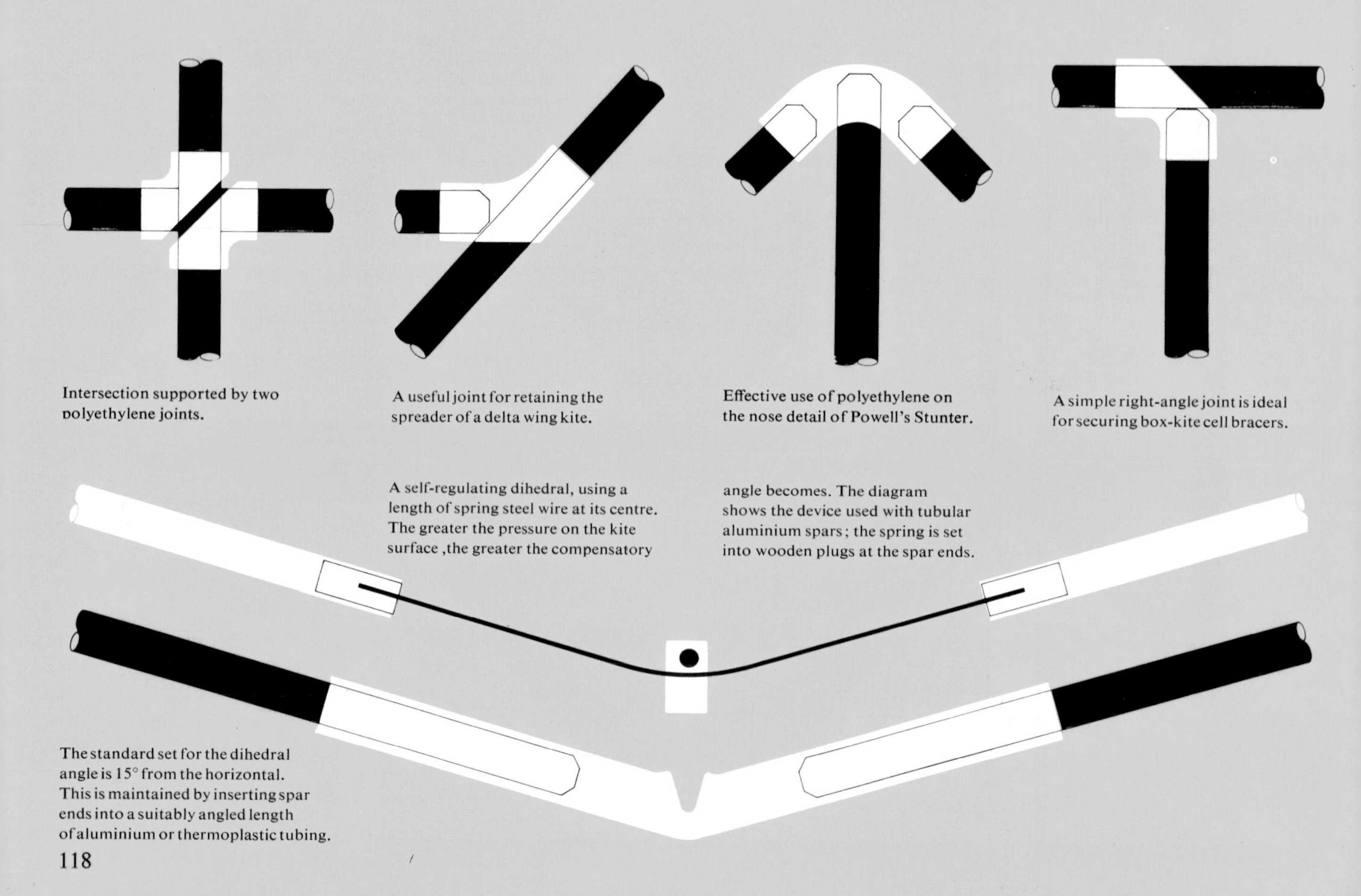

Intersection supported by two polyethylene joints.

A useful joint for retaining the spreader of a delta wing kite.

Effective use of polyethylene on the nose detail of Powell's Stunter.

A simple right-angle joint is ideal for securing box-kite cell bracers.

A self-regulating dihedral, using a length of spring steel wire at its centre. The greater the pressure on the kite surface ,the greater the compensatory angle becomes. The diagram shows the device used with tubular aluminium spars; the spring is set into wooden plugs at the spar ends.

The standard set for the dihedral angle is 15° from the horizontal. This is maintained by inserting spar ends into a suitably angled length of aluminium or thermoplastic tubing.

The keyword in kite building is accuracy. Accuracy in the construction and balancing of the frame, the drawing and cutting of the pattern, and the sewing or joining of the cover is essential for a strong even lift. To help achieve this accuracy it is advisable to build a kite that measures a minimum of 1 m (about 3 ft) in either height or width. Although it is possible to reach a point of diminishing returns, a general rule is that the larger the kite the more stable is its flight. Anything under 1 m in either span is considered to be a small kite, and small kites tend to be erratic in flight unless made with almost microscopic accuracy. However, this rule doesn't deter Fumio Yoshimura from making kites which are no longer than the nail of the little finger, flown in a suitable draught indoors, from a line of human hair.

A degree of pride in the workmanship of a kite provides its own rewards. Careful attention to finish and detail, such as sandpapering dowels, and even making a drawstring bag to contain the kite when dismantled, all make for an attitude which results in more efficient and impressive kite flying.

With a few notable exceptions, such as fighting kites, the main aim in kite flying is towards a good steady lift, maintaining a virtually stationary aspect in the sky.

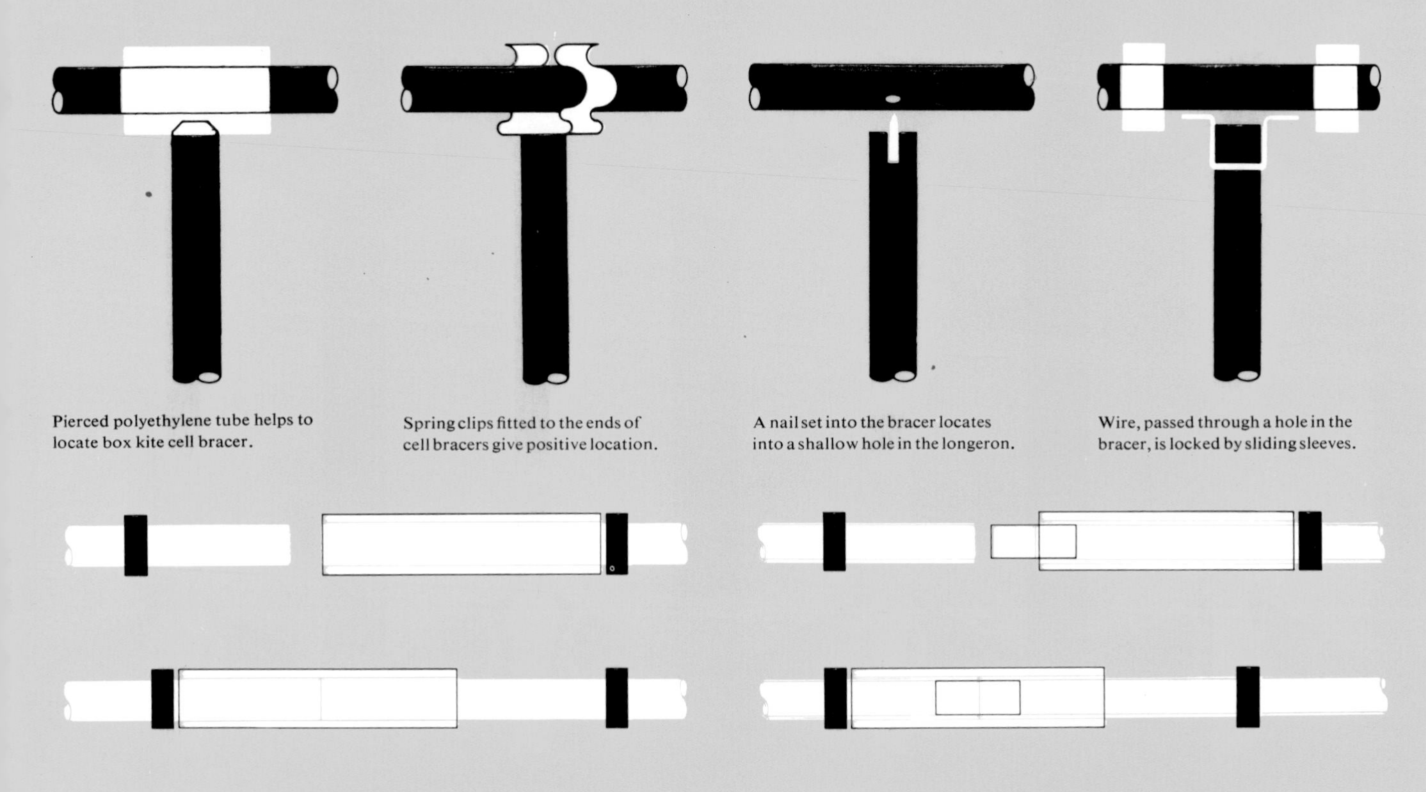

Pierced polyethylene tube helps to locate box kite cell bracer.

Spring clips fitted to the ends of cell bracers give positive location.

A nail set into the bracer locates into a shallow hole in the longeron.

Wire, passed through a hole in the bracer, is locked by sliding sleeves.

For greater collapsibility a length of sliding tube securely locks two halves of an extra long spine. Binding tape fore and aft of the joint checks the travel of the sleeve.

When this technique is used for a tubular aluminium spine, it is necessary to support the joint with a short projecting core of aluminium rod.

After 2,000 years or so, silk remains an ideal cover fabric. Its lightness and pliancy is so far unmatched in lending a remarkably buoyant and graceful movement to a kite. However, silk has only a moderate tear strength, it is difficult to work, and is expensive. Consequently a silk kite is very special, and usually takes pride of place in a collection. The other natural fibre most favoured by kite makers is cotton. Most of the early man-lifters were covered with either linen or cotton cambric.

Most western kite-makers favour modern synthetic fabrics of the industrial nylon variety, including ripstop, or spinnaker nylon, and plastic film, or sheet, such as polyethylene and Mylar. A number of synthetic fabrics, woven from artificial silk yarn include rayon, nylon, Terylene or Dacron, and are available in many grades of weight and porosity. In their lighter, more closely woven grades, these man-made fabrics are ideal for kite covers, being strong and supple, easily workable and relatively inexpensive. Ripstop, or spinnaker nylon, a high-performance fabric reinforced with a mono-filament grid, was originally developed for the sails of racing yachts. It is one of the best cover fabrics available. If properly used it is virtually indestructible, and is manufactured in a wide range of weights, porosity ratings, and colours. Polyethylene, or polythene, is a tough thermoplastic of high flexibility and considerable strength. In sheet or film form it has zero porosity, comes in all weights and is ideal for all plastic-covered kites. It is quick and easy to work, and can be joined either by cellulose tape or polythene cement; though being thermoplastic it can also be heat-sealed. While

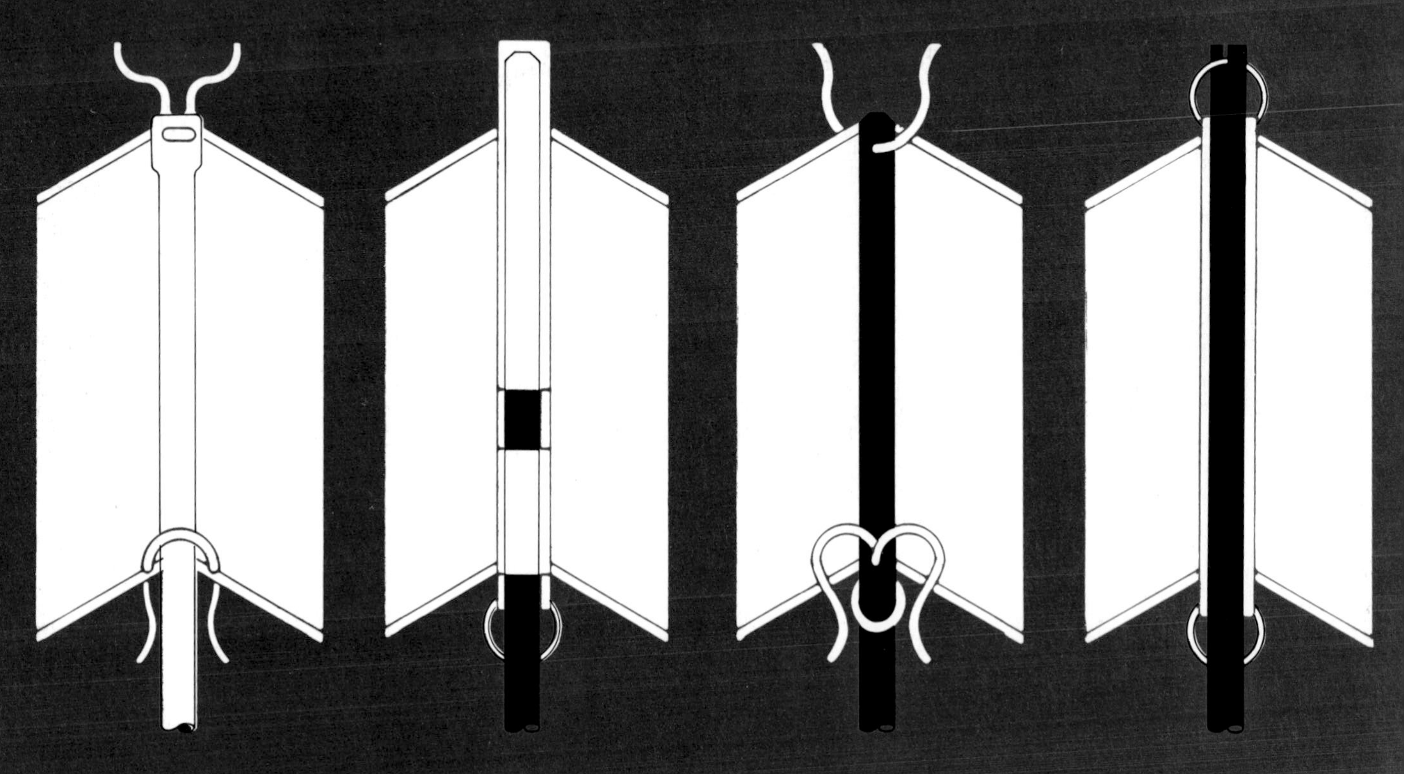

Alternative methods of attaching longerons to box-kite cells. The diagram shows how an aluminium longeron may be flattened, drilled and tied to the top edge of the cell.

A sleeve of tape is broken at one point to accept a bracer. A line, or tape, is passed through the ring at the bottom edge and secured to its counterpart on the cell below.

Holes may be drilled through the relevant points of a longeron, which is then tied to the cell. Line ends from the bottom edge are secured to their counterparts on the cell below.

Reinforcing tape is ringed at either end of the cell. Again line, or tape, secures the bottom ring to its counterpart on the top edge of the cell below. See diagram opposite right.

inexpensive heat-sealing styluses are sometimes available from good model-making shops, polyethylene can be welded quite successfully with a skilfully operated soldering iron; though a certain amount of practice is to be recommended beforehand.

A comparatively new product, Tyvek, is made up of 100 per cent high density polyethylene, and in its softer structures it is as good a cover material as one could wish for. Spun-bonded from continuous filaments of polyethylene, it is inexpensive, has an extremely high tear strength, and comes in a number of finishes and weights. Tyvek can be cut without fraying, and can be sewn, glued, coloured and generally mistreated with no adverse effects to its structure, it is available in a micro-perforated form as well as its normal zero porosity.

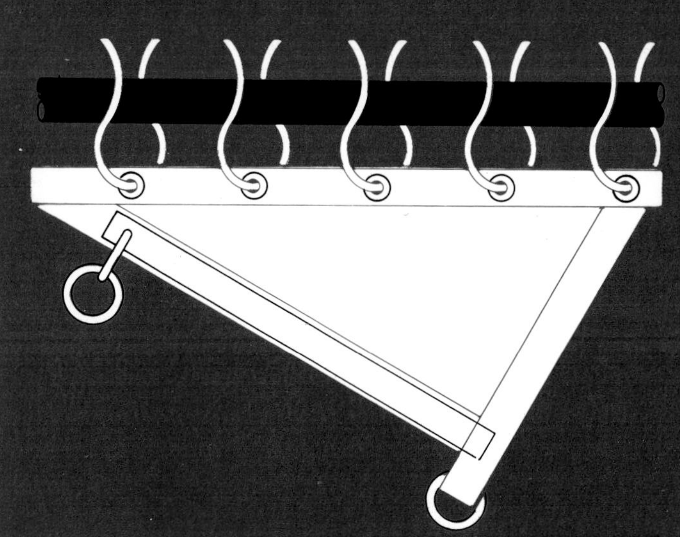

Method of attaching a stabilizing fin or rudder to the kite spine with lengths of nylon line. For reasons of clarity the kite cover has been omitted. The cover is in fact situated between the spine and the fin, the lines being passed through eyelets correspondingly placed in the cover.

The fin edge to which the bridle is attached is supported by a length of dowelling enclosed between tape and fabric. A slip-bridle (see page 135) ensures an even downward pressure throughout the length of the fin.

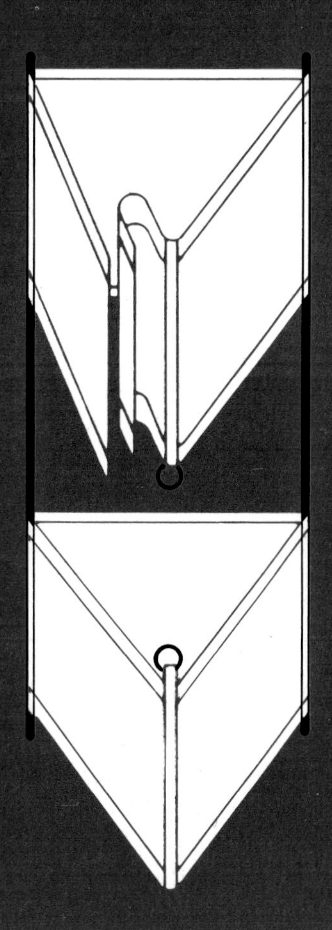

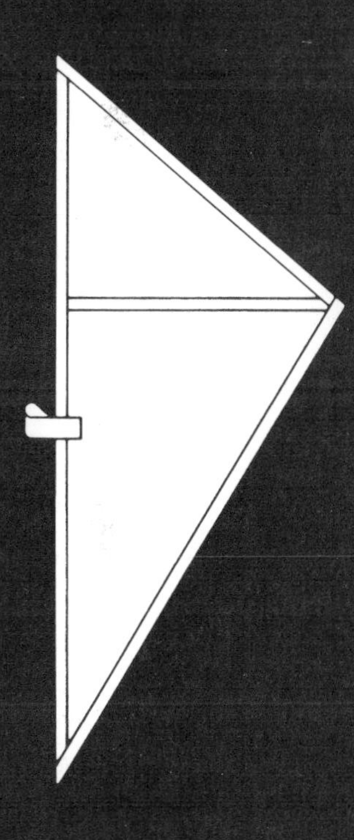

Assembling a Conyne kite. Cells and wings are finished separately. The loop on the wing's inside edge secures this edge to the longeron. Longerons are indicated for clarity only in the diagram, as they are not fitted until all sewing has been completed.

During both the making and the flying process a good deal of knots will have to be tied. These are usually under considerable stress, and a poorly tied knot can easily lead to a kite being damaged or lost. Synthetic line, such as nylon, Dacron and plastic is particularly difficult to secure unless the appropriate knot or hitch is used, and a little time spent practising with an odd piece of line may well save frustration at the flying site, especially when more ambitious projects such as train flying, and weight lifting are being attempted. A lack of confidence in the many fastenings used can mar an otherwise exciting experiment, particularly when an expensive payload such as a camera is involved.

One thing that should be remembered is that *any* knot in the flying line, however well tied, tends to cut into the line under stress, and will always be a vulnerable point. Consequently, joining flying lines should be avoided, and is particularly risky with large kites capable of developing a heavy pull. If two lengths of flying line *must* be joined, however, the following methods have proved to be the most satisfactory. When joining two lengths of natural line, such as thread, string or twine, the fisherman's knot is a good choice inasmuch as it doesn't involve any sharp bending of the line; it is quick and simple to tie, and doesn't slip under any conditions. This knot is also good for joining lines of different thicknesses, though is quite unsuitable for synthetic line, which should be joined with a blood knot.

The lark's head is a quick and easy hitch, ideal for securing the towing ring to the bridle. The finished hitch is shown below.

The toggle hitch gives easy curves which are less prone to breakage than most. It is ideal for securing secondary lines for train flying.

The tiller hitch is secure and quickly untied, and is good for attaching a secondary flying line to a toggle hitch when flying in train.

The surgeon's knot is useful for quickly and easily joining two lines bearing light stress. Its main application is in kite making.

The lark's head hitch can be used for attaching secondary lines to the main flying line for train flying in light winds.

A round turn with two half hitches forms an excellent running noose for tethering a kite line. Always tether kites to a smooth surface.

The half blood knot is particularly well suited to securing nylon and mono-filament line. It is equally useful in kite making and flying.

The bowline is an extremely secure and reliable knot. Giving a high knot strength it has many applications in both kite making and flying.

The safest way of joining synthetic and natural line is to tie both ends to a small brass or aluminium ring with a round cross-section, such as a curtain ring. The synthetic line should be secured with a half blood knot while a bowline is best for the natural line. To make absolutely sure that no slipping occurs, professional kite makers tend to tie a simple overhand knot at every protruding end of line or, if synthetics are used, a slight burning of the line end produces a knurl which has the same effect.

The double sheet bend is a good knot for joining lines of varying diameters. Joins involving synthetic and natural lines should be tested.

The blood knot is the standard knot for joining both nylon and mono-filament lines of equal diameter. No other knot should be used for this.

The fisherman's knot provides as secure a tie as any, when two lengths of natural fibre of equal or varying diameter are to be joined.

The traditional method of stowing a multiple bridle to avoid tangling. By simply pulling the towing loop the lines neatly unravel.

Of all the equipment used in kite flying, the most temperamental and frustrating piece of apparatus is the winding device. Ranging from the traditional piece of stick to highly sophisticated power-operated and geared winches, winders tend to be as many and varied as kites themselves. The enjoyment of flying a kite of *any* size is considerably reduced if an unsuitable retrieval system is used. The larger the kite, and also the higher the altitude to be reached, the more critical the need to use an efficient winding device. While there is nothing wrong with the sticks, bottles and tin-cans so favoured by small boys, winding in from great altitudes becomes difficult and tedious without the right equipment.

Light to medium kites can be flown very successfully from a fishing rod and reel, using mono-filament nylon line for best results. Will Yolen, a colourful and well-known character of the American kite flying fraternity, flies trains of 200 or so kites from an adapted deep-sea fishing rod, complete with a massive tuna-fishing reel.

An important aspect of the kite-reel is its central core, or drum. The amount of line taken in at each revolution depends upon the diameter of the core. An extremely large core of 30 cm (say 1 ft) diameter is capable of taking in close to 1 m of line with every revolution, while a core of 5 cm (2 ins.) diameter would need almost six revolutions to take in the same amount. However, the larger the diameter of the core the more difficult the reel is to turn. Large core reels often have an extended crank handle to provide greater leverage.

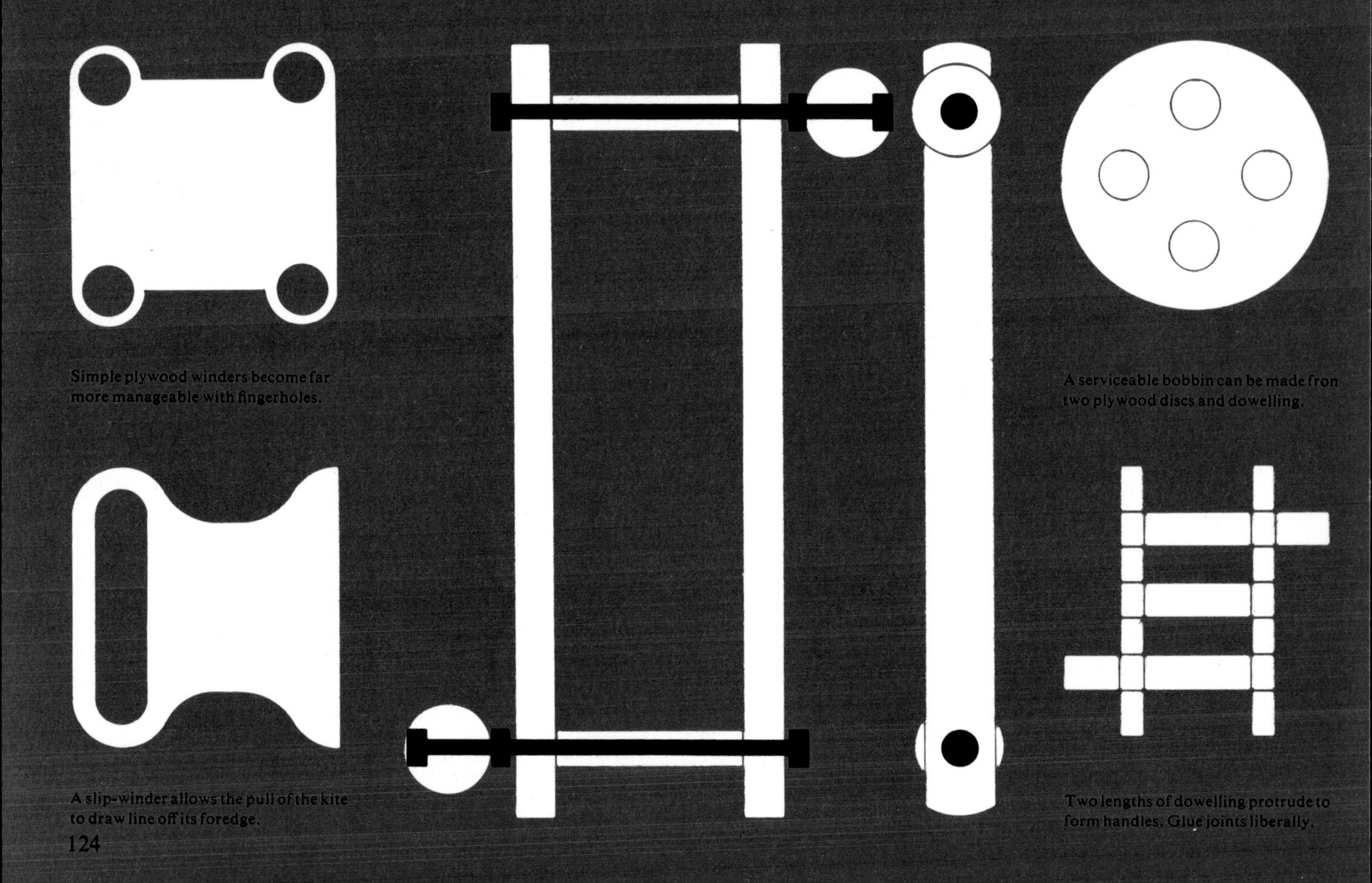

Simple plywood winders become far more manageable with fingerholes.

A serviceable bobbin can be made from two plywood discs and dowelling.

A slip-winder allows the pull of the kite to draw line off its foredge.

Two lengths of dowelling protrude to form handles. Glue joints liberally.

Large cores are usually used in conjunction with light wind kites when flown to great altitudes, though an excellent alternative to this is a shortened fishing rod with a geared reel.

The reel, particularly those to be used for heavy wind kites, should be sturdily constructed, as reeling in an already stretched line while under tension brings quite extraordinary pressure to bear upon the core of the reel, and to a lesser extent upon its sides. Occasionally, seemingly well constructed reels are quite literally pulverized under this pressure, being reduced to a tangle of line and splinters in a matter of seconds. Even so, line should never be taken onto the reel when slack, as this inevitably leads to tangling. The ideal is to have a little tension on the line when winding in.

The more sophisticated hand-held reels are occasionally equipped with gears and a disc or clutch brake. Though these are capable of handling considerable lengths of line extremely efficiently, they tend to be heavy and difficult to manage unless mounted upon some kind of support. Nevertheless, all reels are supported to some extent by the pull of the kite line. Projects involving a really heavy lift should never be attempted without adequate man-power standing by for line retrieval, and a well secured field-winch – either hand or power-operated – is essential. The latter is seldom used outside highly specialized scientific applications, though they are occasionally seen at kite festivals. Power-operated winches tend to take all of the hard work – and possibly a lot of the fun – out of kite flying.

When making a kite line winder the extra trouble of using coach bolts and revolving handles is well rewarded. The coach bolts are best sleeved with aluminium tube for greater strength. The four-handled winder has advantages over the more common two-handled version shown opposite. Not only does its better balance make it more comfortable to use, but also the operator has twice the chance of 'finding' a handle quickly in an emergency.

An excellent revolving handle is made by drilling through a wooden ball – easily obtainable from timber merchants – and securing it with a coach bolt, a washer and two sets of locknuts as shown in the diagram above. The handle should be positioned as close to the outer edge of the reel as possible for maximum leverage. The locknuts at the end of the coachbolt should be countersunk into the handle for greater comfort, and the end of the bolt domed over the locknuts to avoid slip.

A sturdy and efficient 'deep sky' reel can be made by using a bicycle wheel spindle as an axle. This gives an extremely easy movement, which is essential for high altitude flying. The reel can be made in either wood or aluminium, and though the hand-held version is shown, it can be secured to posts etc.

Abbreviations O.D. and I.D. refer to outside and inside diameter.

- A Seven-ply wooden disc 20·5 cm (8 ins.) diameter
- B Plastic pipe 11 cm (4 $\frac{5}{16}$ ins.) O.D. × 10·3 cm (4 $\frac{1}{32}$ ins.) I.D.
- C Three-ply wooden ring 10·2 cm (4 ins.) O.D. × 5 cm (2 ins.) I.D.
- D Standard bicycle spindle
- E Three-ply wooden ring 10·2 cm (4 ins.) O.D. × 2·5 cm (1 in.) I.D.
- F Seven-ply wooden ring 20·5 cm (8 ins.) O.D. × 17·5 cm (6$\frac{7}{8}$ ins.) I.D.
- G Three-ply wooden ring 17 cm (6$\frac{3}{4}$ ins.) O.D. × 12 cm (4$\frac{3}{4}$ ins.) I.D.
- H Seven-ply wooden disc 15 cm (6 ins.) diameter
- I Leather or webbing hand loop
- J Rectangular aluminium washers

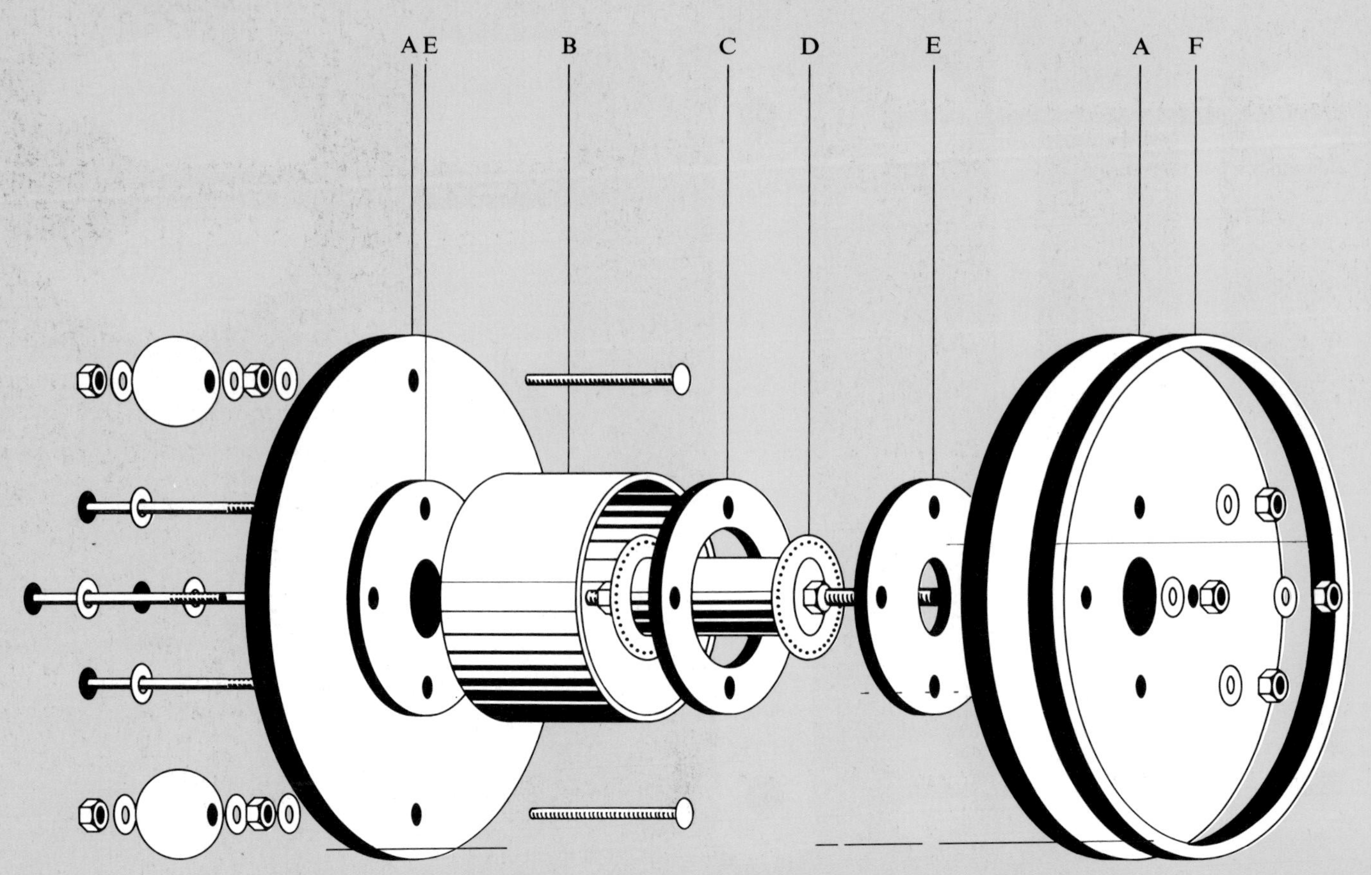

Construction   Line

The choice of flying line can greatly influence the performance of a kite, as the line itself is every bit as susceptible to drag as is the kite itself. Too heavy a gauge tends to draw a kite backwards and downwards towards the horizon, while too light a gauge will result in a line break. In order to avoid unwanted wind friction the smallest gauge of line possible should be used, though this of course should be consistent with the anticipated strain. Determining the anticipated strain only comes with experience, though even then it is a somewhat hit and miss affair. Different wind-speeds and bridle settings can vary the pull enormously, therefore lines should never be subjected to stresses beyond one third of their break strength. As an experienced sailor knows when to reduce sail, so a good kite flyer should be able to judge in good time when wind pressure is about to threaten the reserve strength of his line. In order to avoid losing too many kites while gaining this experience an arbitrary, though quite dependable, rule for determining what gauge of line to use, is to measure the surface of the kite in square feet, then choose a line with a break strength at least three times greater – in pounds – to the total area. For example, when flying a surface of, say, 5 sq. ft, a line of certainly no less than 15 lb break strength should be used. Normally the strength of the line is printed on the reel or spool by the manufacturer, but, if in any doubt, a simple spring scale and a little ingenuity should establish the break strength of at least the lighter gauge lines. Heavier kites tend to be flown on lines of twine, string, cord, upholsterers' linen thread, Dacron or nylon line – either braided or twisted – and shark-line; depending upon the size of kite and what is available, or within one's budget.

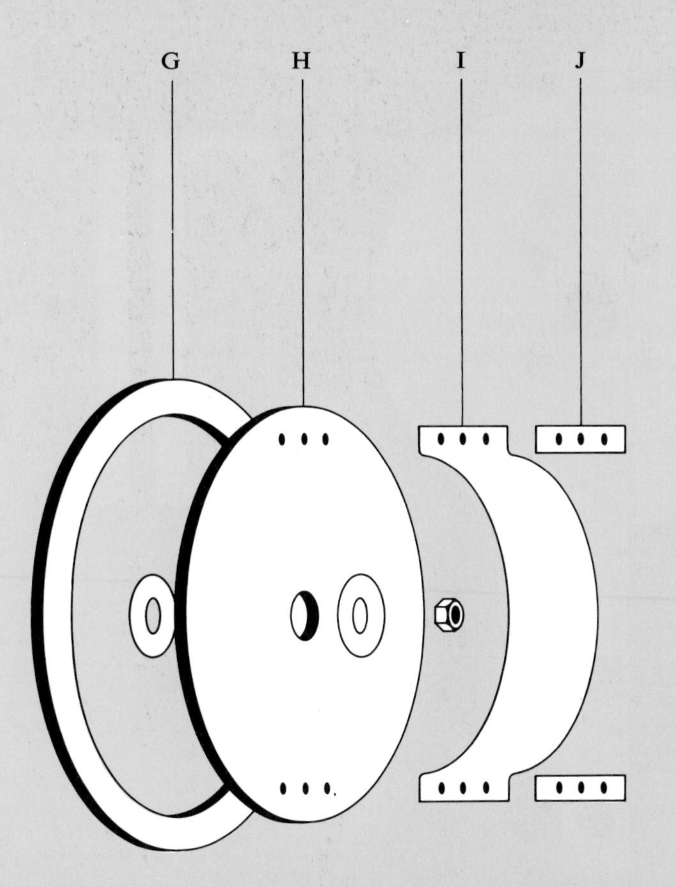

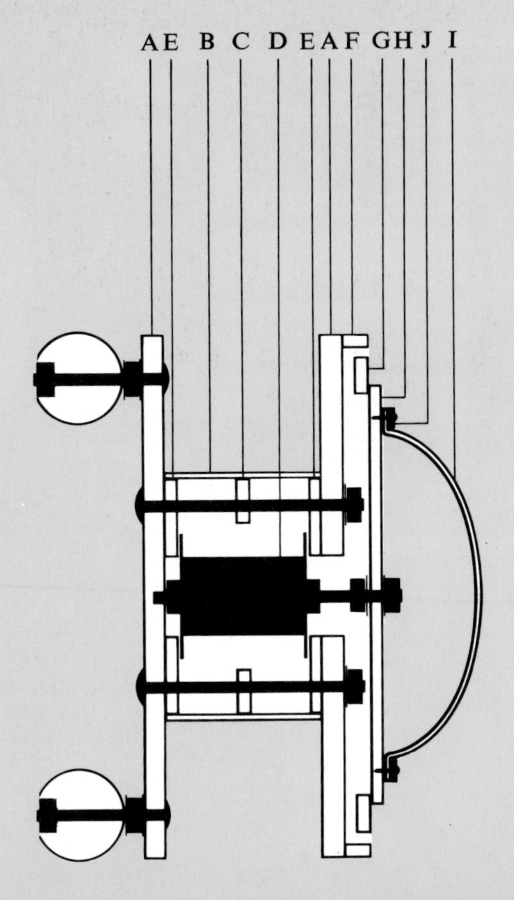

Braided nylon line comes in two types; with or without a central core. Simply a braided sleeve of finely woven nylon, the stronger type has an inner core of twisted nylon, Dacron or cotton. Both types are very pleasant to use, being smooth and easy to handle, not being prone to twirl under pressure as does twisted line. Usually made from three strands of spun flax or synthetic fibre, twisted line holds together by the inertia provided by the spinning of the individual strands. When played out into the air at considerable lengths the stress it is put to has the effect of unravelling these three main strands, increasing its elasticity. Though this is good from a load-bearing aspect, when the line is ultimately wound back onto its reel in its stretched state it puts great pressure onto the reel drum.

A favourite line for flying light wind kites is mono-filament nylon fishing line, though sailmakers' thread or even button thread is sometimes used. Although mono-filament is prone to stretch, it is a fine hard line, capable of cutting the wind like no other, and is much to be preferred to fibrous, loosely woven cord which induces drag. Should this be all that is available, however, the old technique of waxing a fibrous or 'hairy' line with a candle as it is taken out by the kite certainly improves its efficiency remarkably.

Ideally the line should be either straight out in the air or securely wound round the reel. Line should be handled with care, as even treading on it causes damage to fibres which may well take effect at great altitude. Occasionally, a high start launch or a severe drop in wind velocity can justify the need to spread the line on the ground, as it will have to be

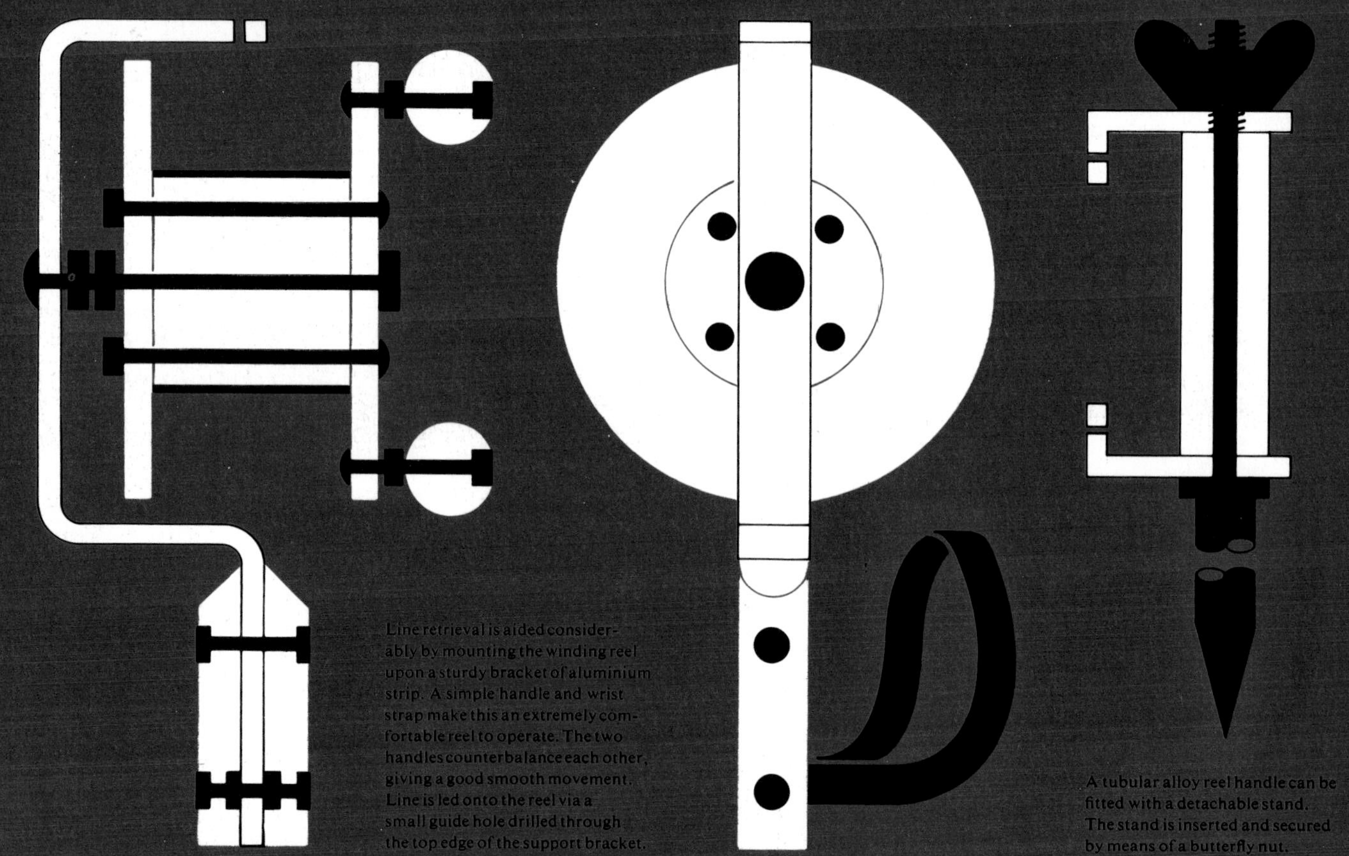

Line retrieval is aided considerably by mounting the winding reel upon a sturdy bracket of aluminium strip. A simple handle and wrist strap make this an extremely comfortable reel to operate. The two handles counterbalance each other, giving a good smooth movement. Line is led onto the reel via a small guide hole drilled through the top edge of the support bracket.

A tubular alloy reel handle can be fitted with a detachable stand. The stand is inserted and secured by means of a butterfly nut.

taken in as quickly as possible – which means hand-over-hand. Even this can be done badly. In these circumstances line should be taken in with a consistent movement while occasionally taking a backward step, leaving the line evenly distributed, untangled and clearly visible along the ground. This line should be wound back onto the reel, under slight tension, as soon as possible.

As well as being the first man to loft a camera, the English meteorologist Archibald scored another first by using flying lines of steel wire, or piano wire. Though it was, and possibly still is, held to be stronger, finer and lighter than any alternative, as a flying line it's not without its hazards.

The indefatigable Woglom had this to say on the subject:

'Piano wire presents its merits . . . But as there is only one of each of us kite flyers, and we may be useful on the earth, it is unwise to risk an untimely entrance into the great hereafter; the volume of atmospheric electricity which may be accumulated during, and discharged at its lower end by, an exposure of several thousand feet of steel wire in the atmosphere – which is one vast generator – is too dangerous an elemental force to be trifled with, in comparison with the innocuous, non-conducting flax twine.'

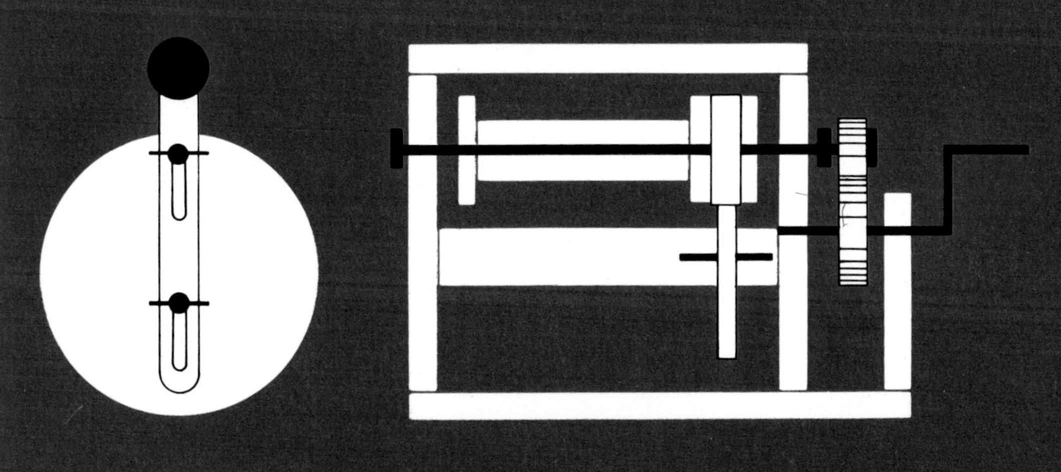

A basic field winch, incorporating a geared crank handle and a belt brake working against the brake drum to the right of the reel core.

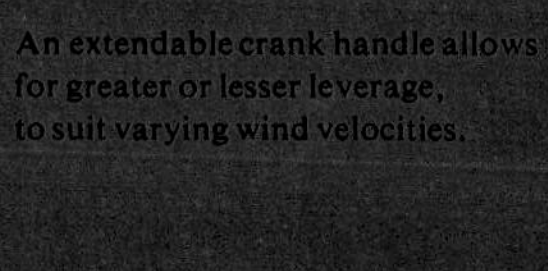

An extendable crank handle allows for greater or lesser leverage, to suit varying wind velocities.

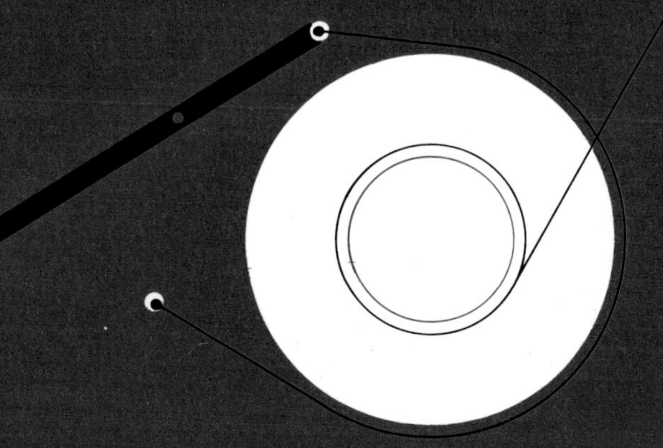

Because of its efficient simplicity the belt brake system is still used on some modern field winches.

A number of kite enthusiasts obtain as much pleasure from designing and building their kites as they do from flying them; and a great deal of time and effort often goes into highly imaginative and well-finished creations. Unfortunately imagination and craftsmanship alone don't produce lift and stability, so before proceeding with an original configuration it is as well to have a grasp of the roots of aerodynamic theory as applied to kites, for, as in any other field of design, the measure of good design is directly proportional to the amount of information that one has on the problem.

A kite is a tethered aircraft flying in a stalled state. As it is heavier than air, in order to stay aloft the weight of the kite must be counteracted by an upward supporting force. This is produced by positioning the kite surface – by means of the bridle – at a suitable angle to the wind, causing the wind to exert pressure upon it. Lift results from this pressure being deflected along the kite face. The kite is not only pushed upwards in this manner; to a lesser degree it is also pulled, or sucked by a corresponding area of low pressure, or partial vacuum built up at the back of the kite in much the same way that an area of low pressure builds up on the top surface of a cambered aerofoil. As the aerofoil is dependent upon forward momentum in order to maintain lift, so the kite in its captive state depends upon the resistance of the flying line, or tether, to provide its 'momentum'. Normally, a kite is so light in proportion to its surface area that lift is not a problem.

Three main forces are at work on a kite in flight; lift, gravity and drag. For the sake of clarity each one of these forces is

An aerofoil at a low attack angle causes air to accelerate over its top surface, decreasing pressure and causing lift.

An aerofoil at an extreme angle causes the airflow over its top surface to break up into turbulence, and lift is decreased.

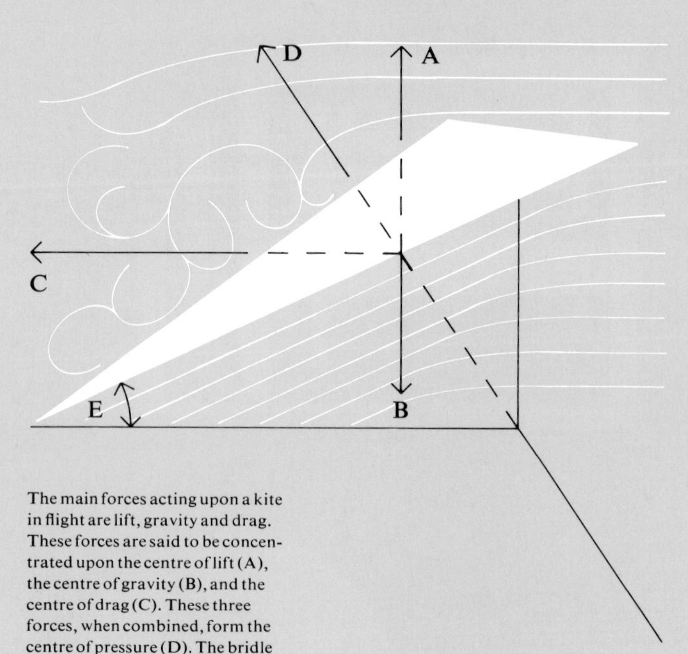

The main forces acting upon a kite in flight are lift, gravity and drag. These forces are said to be concentrated upon the centre of lift (A), the centre of gravity (B), and the centre of drag (C). These three forces, when combined, form the centre of pressure (D). The bridle should be adjusted to coincide the angle of attack (E) with the centre of pressure.

Longitudinal stability concerns motion within the plane of symmetry, such as rising, falling and pitching. Lateral stability concerns motion out of the plane of symmetry, such as side slipping, rolling and yawing.

The three axes of the kite are longitudinal (roll), lateral (pitch) and vertical (yaw).

said to be concentrated upon a single point of balance upon the kite surface. The centre of lift is the point at which the air pressure against the entire surface is concentrated; the centre of gravity is the point where all weight forces of the kite are concentrated, and the centre of drag is the point where all resistant forces exerted by the air upon the kite are concentrated. All three forces are balanced at the centre of pressure, the point where *all* pressure forces may be said to act. Consequently, if the kite is well balanced structurally, and the bridle is well set for the anticipated angle of attack that the kite is designed to adopt, then a good lift to drag ratio has been achieved. A low lift to drag ratio on even the lightest kite will cause it to fly at a low angle to the horizon, whereas a more streamlined surface with a high lift to drag ratio will cut through the wind, climbing steadily along its arc, well up towards its zenith.

The dihedral angle automatically restores equilibrium in a roll. The lower wing presents a greater area to vertical pressure than does the higher wing. Consequently the greater pressure acting upon the lower wing causes it to return to its normal attitude.

Another tool in the hands of the practised kite designer is the aspect ratio. This is the relationship of the span, or width of the kite to the chord, or length of the kite. A kite of high aspect ratio is considerably wider than it is long, and while it is capable of extremely buoyant flight, it is difficult to stabilize. Conversely, a kite of low aspect ratio is considerably longer than it is wide, and though remarkably stable, it has a high sink rate.

Maximum lift can only be achieved when the kite is directly opposed to the wind direction, and in order to remain headed into the wind it requires lateral, or directional, stability.

There are numerous methods of providing a kite with lateral stability; the most basic being the tail, which is essential for plane-surface kites. Tailless kites obviously rely upon alternate

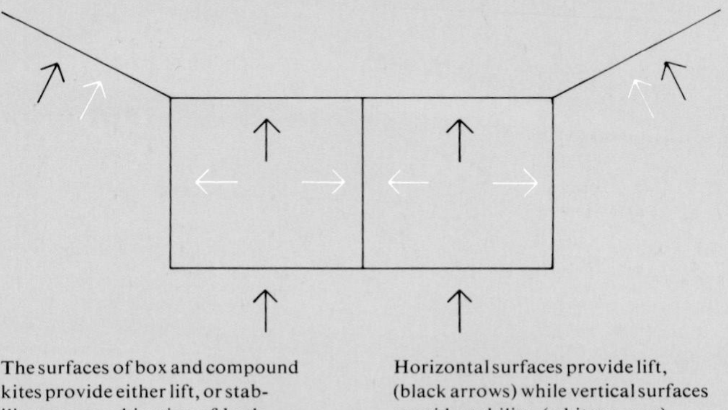

The surfaces of box and compound kites provide either lift, or stability, or a combination of both, depending upon their surface angle. Horizontal surfaces provide lift, (black arrows) while vertical surfaces provide stability, (white arrows).

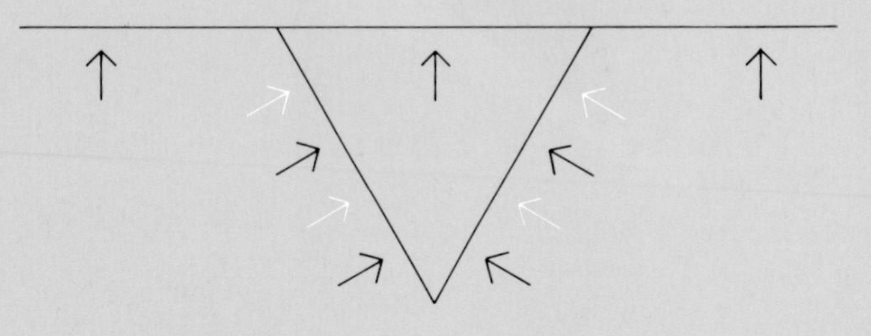

When designing an original configuration which is intended to be flown without a tail, it is important to consider the ratio of lift to stability required. The wind velocity for which the kite is intended will largely govern this ratio.

methods, the most common being the bowed spar as used on the Eddy kite, which provides stability in roll in much the same way as do dihedrally mounted spars. Another tail-less classic is the box kite, which depends upon its vertical sides for stability. Keels and rudders mounted on either the face (ventral) or back (dorsal) of the kite also provide excellent directional stability, particularly when used in conjunction with a dihedral lifting surface. The use of skilfully placed and proportioned vents, such as those used in the Grauel sled, show very clearly how this technique can also lend stability to an otherwise temperamental kite.

Flying Bridles, keels and rudders

The bridle is the line which runs fore to aft of the kite, to which the flying line is attached. The point at which the flying line is attached to the bridle is called the towing point. The towing point is probably the most critical part of the entire kite inasmuch as, if it is wrongly situated, even the most perfectly designed and constructed airframe won't get off the ground. The towing point and bridle perform the important function of establishing the kite's correct flight attitude, or angle of attack.

Without exception Hargrave flew his box kites without bridles, the flying line always being attached directly to the face of the kite. The normal fore to aft bridle is referred to as a two-legged bridle, and there are no rules concerning how

The bridle allows the kite's angle of attack to be adjusted. In exactly the same way that an aeroplane's thrust and angle of attack are co-ordinated, adopting a high angle at low speeds, and a low angle at high speeds, so the kite must be adjusted to suit different wind velocities.

The action of the bridle is more easily understood by imagining a rod being suspended by a single string tied to its centre point. If a weight is hooked to the rod it immediately tips. However, if a bridle is attached to the rod, a weight can be hooked on at any point between the strings without the rod tipping to any great extent. Only when the weight – or more accurately the centre of gravity of the whole – hangs directly below the point of suspension, will the rod be horizontal.

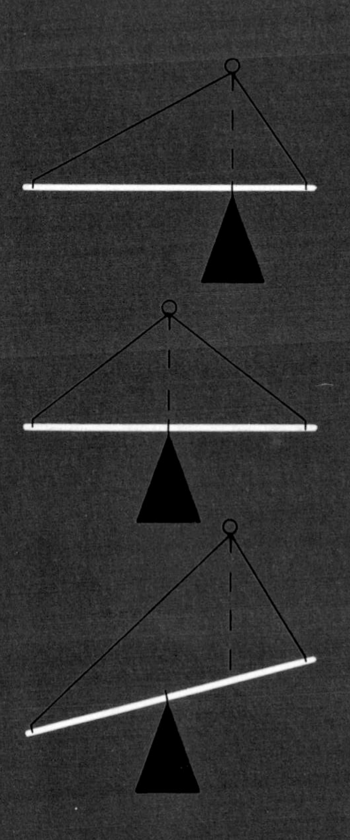

A kite is flying at optimum angle when the pull of the flying line corresponds with the centre of pressure.

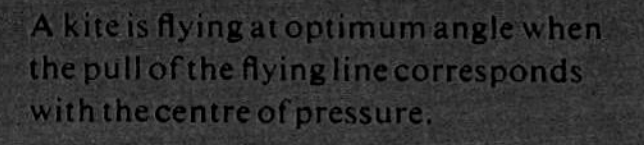

The use of a strong swivel clip for attaching line to bridle eliminates the bridle's tendency to twist in the air.

many legs a bridle need have. Usually the configuration of the kite decrees its bridling technique, and this may range from a one-legged bridle, so to speak, as used by Hargrave, to a hundred or more. The many lines that make up a multiple bridle are referred to not as legs but as shroud lines, though what quantity of legs are needed before they become shrouds doesn't appear to have been defined. The object of a multi-legged or shrouded bridle is not simply to hold the kite at its most efficient angle of attack, it also distributes stress evenly throughout the structure of the kite, helping it to retain its configuration under high wind velocity.

The accepted average setting for a bridle is arrived at by laying the kite upon its back, and, having attached the bridle line to the bridling points fore and aft of the spine, lifting the top end of the kite by suspending the bridle loop over one finger. By manoeuvring the line until the tail end of the kite is at an angle of between 20° and 30° from the floor (i.e. below the horizontal) the point on the bridle at which the kite now balances at this angle should be established. A towing ring should then be attached to this point by means of a lark's head hitch. Normally the towing point should be situated approximately one third down the length of the spine, and should stand away from the kite face about one half the total length of the spine. When the towing point is correctly situated the kite should rise sharply and straight when pulled forward, and should require only minimal re-setting at the flying site in order to trim the angle to the prevailing wind-speed.

The basic rule in bridle adjustment is: low wind-speed – high angle; high wind-speed – low angle. In other words, in a low wind-speed a greater angle of attack is needed than in a high

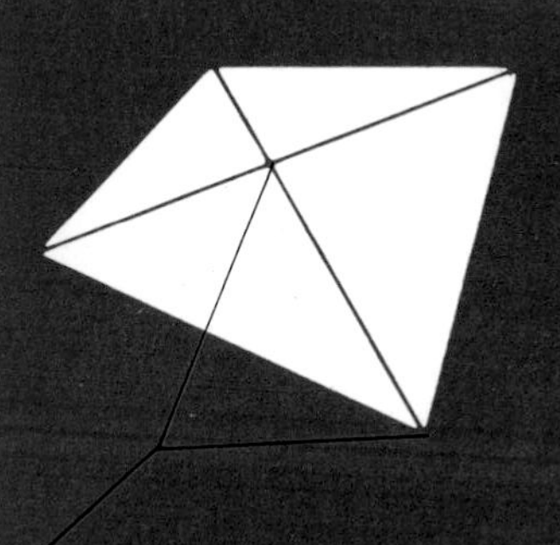

Two-legged bridle.

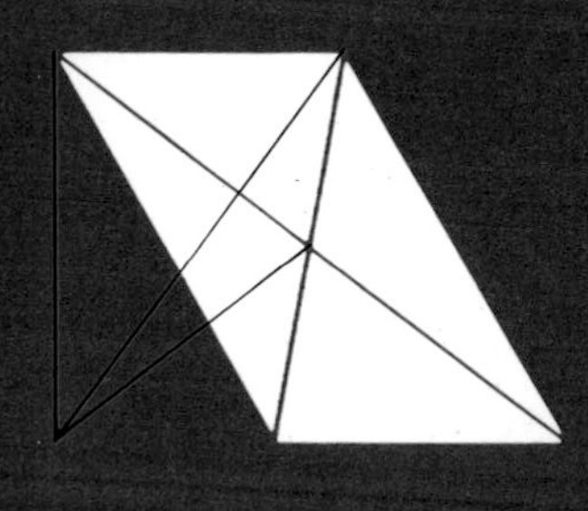

Three-legged bridle.

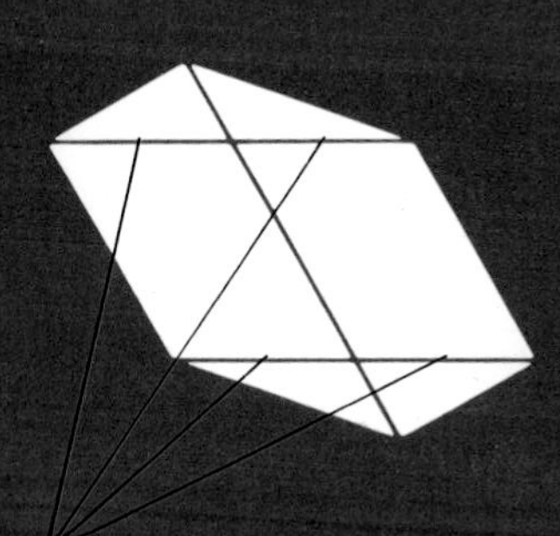

Four-legged bridle.

Compound bridle.

Box kite flown on edge with a two-legged bridle.

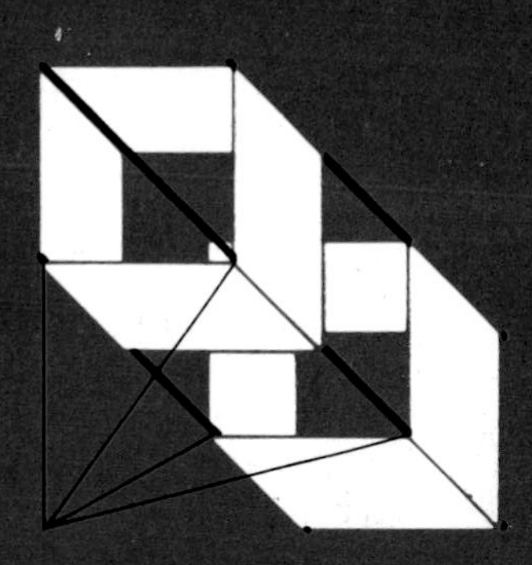

Box kite flown flat with a four-legged bridle.

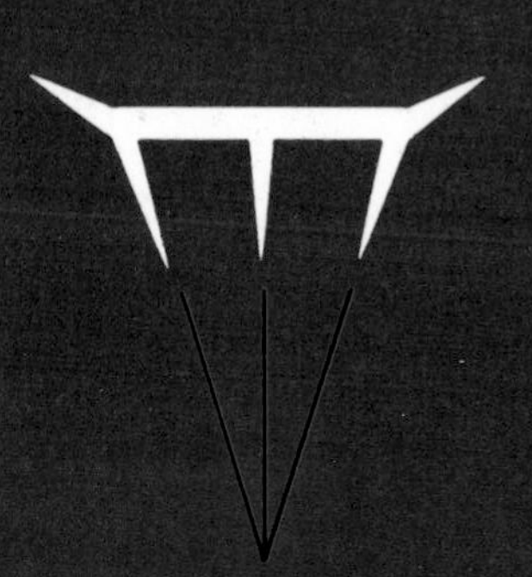

Front view of a multiple bridle on a multi-finned bow kite.

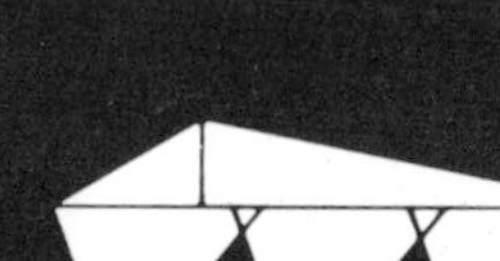

The same multiple bridle (nine shroud lines) seen from the side.

wind-speed. By exposing a larger area to a light breeze more wind is deflected over the face of the kite, at least at launching attitudes, helping it to pull against gravity until it reaches (hopefully) more lively air higher up. In a high wind velocity there is a good chance that the pressure of the air upon a surface set at too great an angle will break the spars before the kite leaves the ground; though if it's sturdily made and becomes airborne it will be very unstable as the wind pressure will override the stabilizing system, whether a tail, cells, fins or whatever. Herculean strength will be needed to hold a large kite if it *does* get into the air, and if it doesn't suffer a line break it will very possibly go into a series of tight lateral spins before crashing badly. A low angle of attack eliminates this by allowing greater air spillage around the kite, and with reduced pressure upon its face the stabilizers have a chance to take effect.

An extremely efficient bridling system, which also gives good stability, is the keel bridle. This is simply a normal two-legged bridle with the central triangle formed by the two legs and the spine filled in with fabric or paper. As will be realized, it is best to have two or three alternate towing points at the bottom tip of the keel in order to provide a degree of adjustment for various wind-speeds. Not only does a well-proportioned keel give good stability, but it also helps the kite to maintain an even form. By being sewn to the kite cover along the fore and aft spine line, the keel provides an overall downward pressure which also distributes stress along the entire length of the cover, lending it a uniformity and natural dihedral that contributes greatly to a smooth controlled flight. Most keels and rudders take advantage of the downward pressure exerted by the flying line to hold their form.

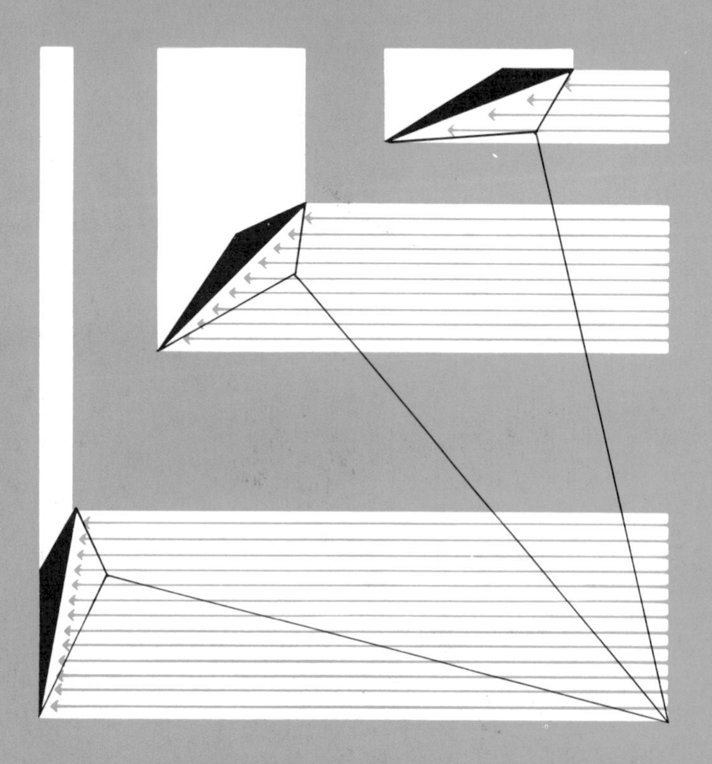

Lift and drag forces vary with angle of attack. A kite has reached its attitude of optimum performance when lift forces are at a maximum and its drag forces are at a minimum.

A fore-to-aft bridle line is of particular advantage in launching and climbing attitudes, for, as the kite climbs, the centre of pressure moves forward from the aft end.

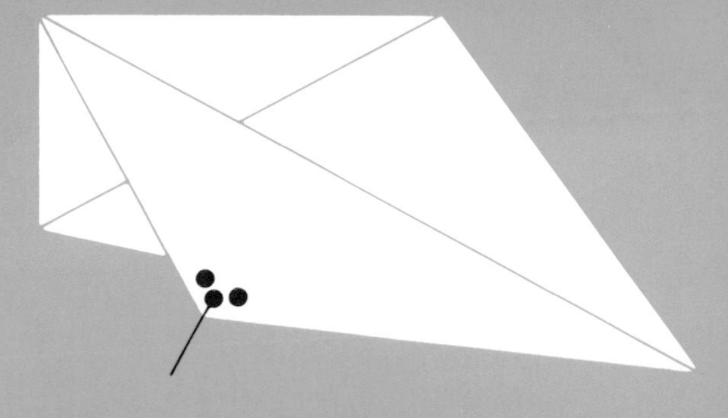

A keel bridle.

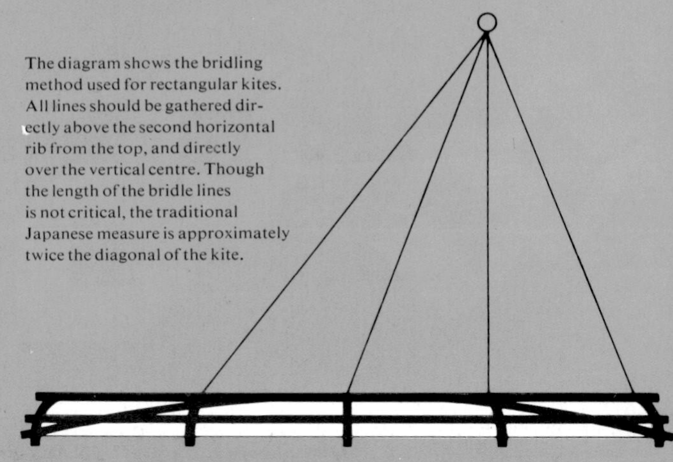

The diagram shows the bridling method used for rectangular kites. All lines should be gathered directly above the second horizontal rib from the top, and directly over the vertical centre. Though the length of the bridle lines is not critical, the traditional Japanese measure is approximately twice the diagonal of the kite.

Light wind kites are often constructed with a rudder low down at the aft end of the spine, lateral stability being provided in much the same manner that a rudder gives stability to an aeroplane. As with keels, a rudder should be carefully proportioned, as if it is too small it will be ineffectual, causing the kite to yaw badly, while if it is too large it will catch every stray breeze and will be blown all over the sky. As has been seen, when wind pressure increases upon the kite surface there comes a point at which this is capable of overriding the pressure upon the rudder, and stability is lost. A good way of spilling this unwanted pressure is the elastic, or spring-loaded bridle, capable of giving mid-air correction to the attack angle of the kite. A light spring, or elastic band is incorporated into the back leg of a two-legged bridle, causing the tail end of the kite to lift when the sail loading becomes too great. As the tail end lifts, air is spilled out at both the trailing and wing edges, allowing the rudder to remain effective in providing stability. As the wind pressure drops, so the spring contracts, trimming the kite to a more suitable angle. Much the same effect can be produced by either introducing a vent or a panel of low-porosity fabric into the tail end of the kite cover; or, and this applies to all aspects of kite design, a combination of all three systems.

A surprising number of kites are capable of being steered through the sky if flown on double, or even quadruple, lines. With the former the handler holds a line in each hand, and can cause his kite to dive, loop, rise, and fly to almost three points of the compass. The higher the wind velocity the more responsive the kite will be to line control. An aerodynamically efficient dirigible kite, with a skilled operator handling the lines, can be a very exciting sight and seldom fails to draw a

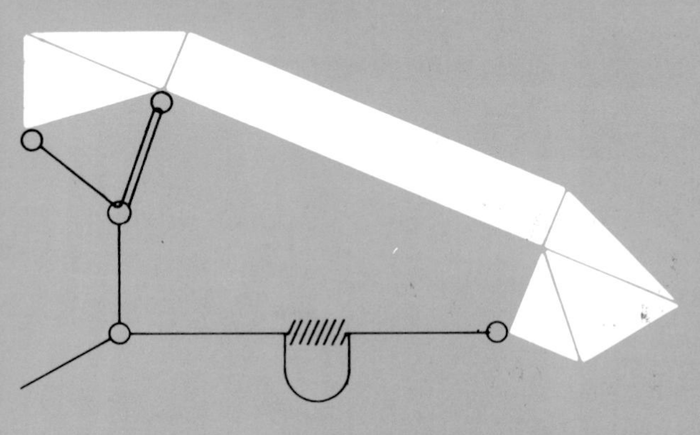

The spring-loaded bridle.

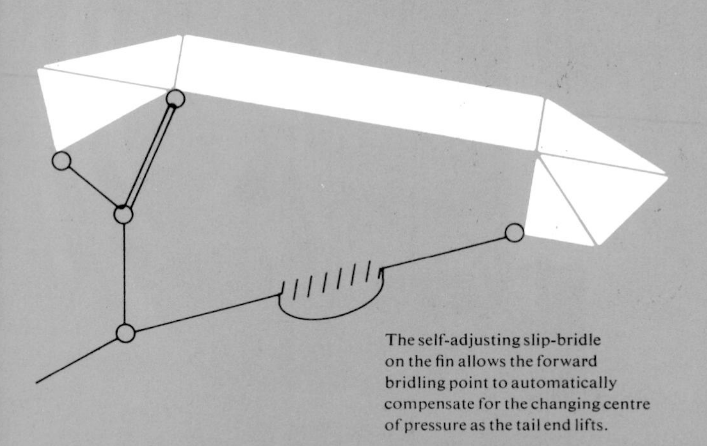

The self-adjusting slip-bridle on the fin allows the forward bridling point to automatically compensate for the changing centre of pressure as the tail end lifts.

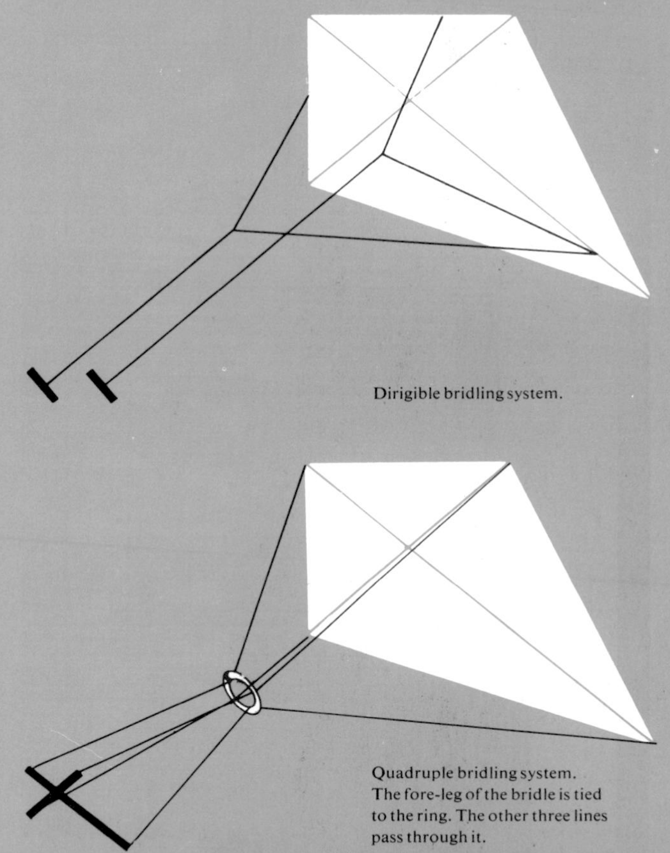

Dirigible bridling system.

Quadruple bridling system. The fore-leg of the bridle is tied to the ring. The other three lines pass through it.

crowd. George Pocock adopted four lined dirigible kites to haul his various kite-drawn vehicles across the otherwise peaceful countryside around Bristol in the early years of the nineteenth century. His four-way adjustable bridles gave him total control over his kites and, in his book *The Aeropleustic Art*, he describes in some detail his techniques for virtually sailing into the wind by deftly manipulating his quadruple lined monsters.

Flying Tails and drogues

Although a tail is theoretically inefficient inasmuch as it produces drag, this is what it is designed to do, and if the correct amount of drag is induced in the right place it can be turned from a negative to a positive force. Drag should not be confused with weight. Weight is concerned with vertical forces, and drag – in this application at least – is concerned with horizontal forces. The drag factor can be increased or reduced by either lengthening or shortening the tail. The dynamic forces acting upon the kite face are offset by means of the tail. These forces increase with wind velocity, and a correspondingly longer tail will be needed to offset them. Although the formula of seven times the length of the spine is a reasonable rule of thumb, the only way to assess properly the correct tail length is by a little trial and error. A tail of ideal

The running knot is a good choice for attaching tail bows, as it obviates the need to pull through the entire length of tail each time a knot is tied.

The clove hitch shares the same advantages of the running knot.

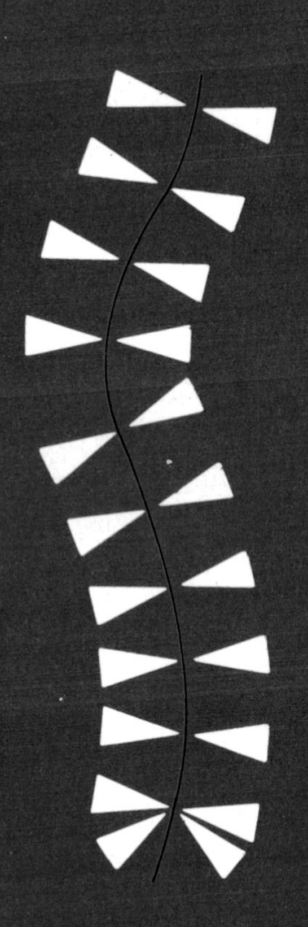

A traditional bow tail is equally effective in paper, or fabric.

A linen tape tail is run up in moments on a sewing machine.

Never throw off-cut away, it can always be used for tails.

length should, under normal conditions, not fly too straight (too long) neither should it be excessively skittish (too short); rather, it should sway gracefully and gently, literally computing – and counteracting – the movements of the kite. While flat kites are solely dependent upon the drag factor of a tail to provide directional stability, other kites, normally classifiable as tailless kites – and particularly kites with a high aspect ratio – may need the extra stabilizing influence of a tail in high winds.

As wind velocity tends to increase with height, maximum efficiency throughout a lift would depend upon a tail capable of automatically lengthening itself – or increasing drag – with altitude. In fact this effect is produced by the drogue, or wind cup, invented by Sir George Nares in the nineteenth century. The drogue, a conical sleeve usually open at both ends, acts as an extremely efficient self-regulating tail. It functions in much the same way as a funnel used for pouring liquid, inasmuch as when the input is slightly greater than the output the liquid gradually builds up until it overflows. So the drogue is capable of modifying the air flow and, even when spilling air, is producing maximum *relative* drag. The drogue governs the directional stability of a kite in a somewhat different manner from the normal tail. As a length of hanging string may be straightened either by smoothing it through its length or, more efficiently, by pulling at its end, so the latter applies to the drogue effect, which is no more than simple leverage; and just as longer levers are used for heavier weights, so longer drogue towing lines are used for heavier kites.

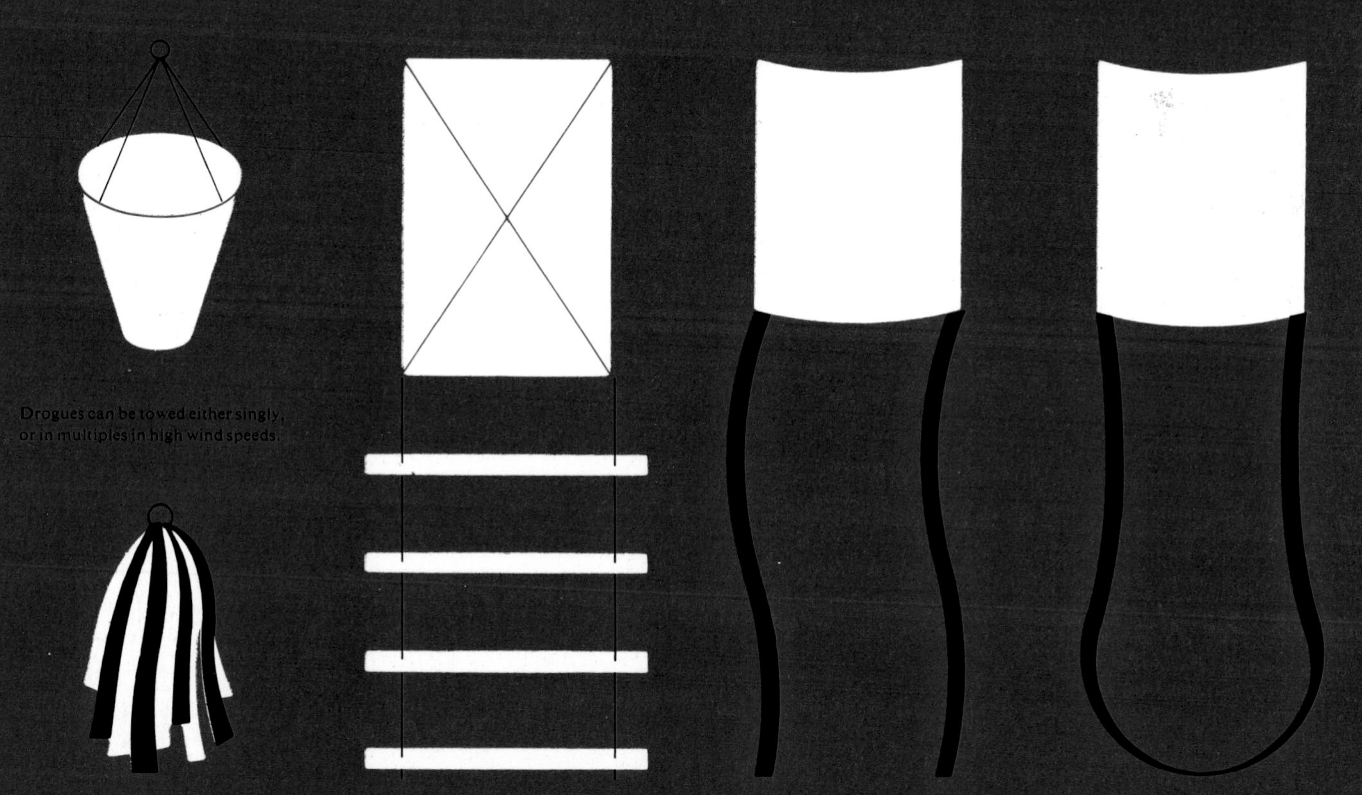

Drogues can be towed either singly, or in multiples in high wind speeds.

The donkey tail is recommended by Jalbert for his parafoils.

The ladder tail, made from thin card, is good for inducing considerable drag.

The Japanese ribbon tail should measure three times the diagonal of the kite.

The loop tail, simply a length of ribbon, is more effective than it looks.

Anybody who has put a lot of work into a kite will certainly want to minimize its chances of failure, and possible destruction, at launch or landing. These are the kite's most vulnerable moments, and there are a number of hazards to be avoided.

Terrain affects ground winds considerably and, even in a light breeze, the air above an uneven landscape is remarkably turbulent. Ground turbulence is caused not only by rugged terrain but also by trees and buildings, and it isn't until the kite is well up, say 150 ft or so, that it will settle down to its anticipated flying attitude. A flat, even and uninterrupted landscape such as the shores of large lakes, rolling moorlands or the sea shore are ideal. Beaches can be excellent flying sites, and a gentle onshore wind is invariably stable and laminar, the wind force increasing gradually and evenly as the kite gains altitude. However, because of variations between land and sea temperatures, an onshore wind can quickly turn into an offshore wind during the early evening. Coping with a relatively sudden turnround of 180° can be challenging to even the most experienced kite flyer, though to successfully negotiate such fickle winds brings its own rewards.

In the absence of such ideal locations there are a few points that should be considered. If the flying site is marred by tall buildings or trees be sure to launch upwind of them, and well away from them, as turbulence in even a light breeze can extend to twice the height of the obstacle, and occasionally a kite will be drawn towards the cause of the turbulence as though magnetized. If flying from a hillside it is better to

Even in a light breeze, turbulence created by an obstacle can extend downwind for a considerable distance.

Rotors are created on cliff tops, and downwind of even minor ridges in the terrain.

In a moderate wind, turbulence on the downwind slope can build up to effect the top of a hill. In anything over a light wind, a kite is best launched on the windward slope of a hill.

launch the kite from some way down the windward slope than the top. Not only will the updraught lend the kite additional buoyancy, but the top of the hill creates turbulence as does any other obstacle. Other more obvious hazards are electricity pylons, power cables and busy motorways. A maverick kite performing loops and general acrobatics low over traffic can be very distracting, and more than a little dangerous. Low-flying aircraft also constitute another very real hazard, and aeronautical administrations have strict regulations concerning the flying of kites in the vicinity of an airport. In England it is illegal to fly a kite within a three-mile radius of an airport, and there are invariably local regulations governing the height to which a kite may legally be flown.

Flying Launching, control and landing

Quite the most inefficient method of launching a kite is the old-fashioned technique of running. In a particularly light wind the kite will need a lot of coaxing to get it into the air, and the degree of attention that this requires cannot best be given while taking a cross-country run. If there isn't enough wind to take the kite from your hand as you offer it up, then a 'high-start' launch is needed. A high-start launch is easiest with two people; one holding the flying line, and the other positioned 45 m (say 150 ft) downwind of the handler. If the kite has a tail this should be laid along the ground towards the handler, so that as the kite is drawn up it takes immediate effect in stabilizing the kite as it rises. The handler should 'dump' the reel on the ground, taking hold of the line itself. The line should be taut, as a slack line reduces control over

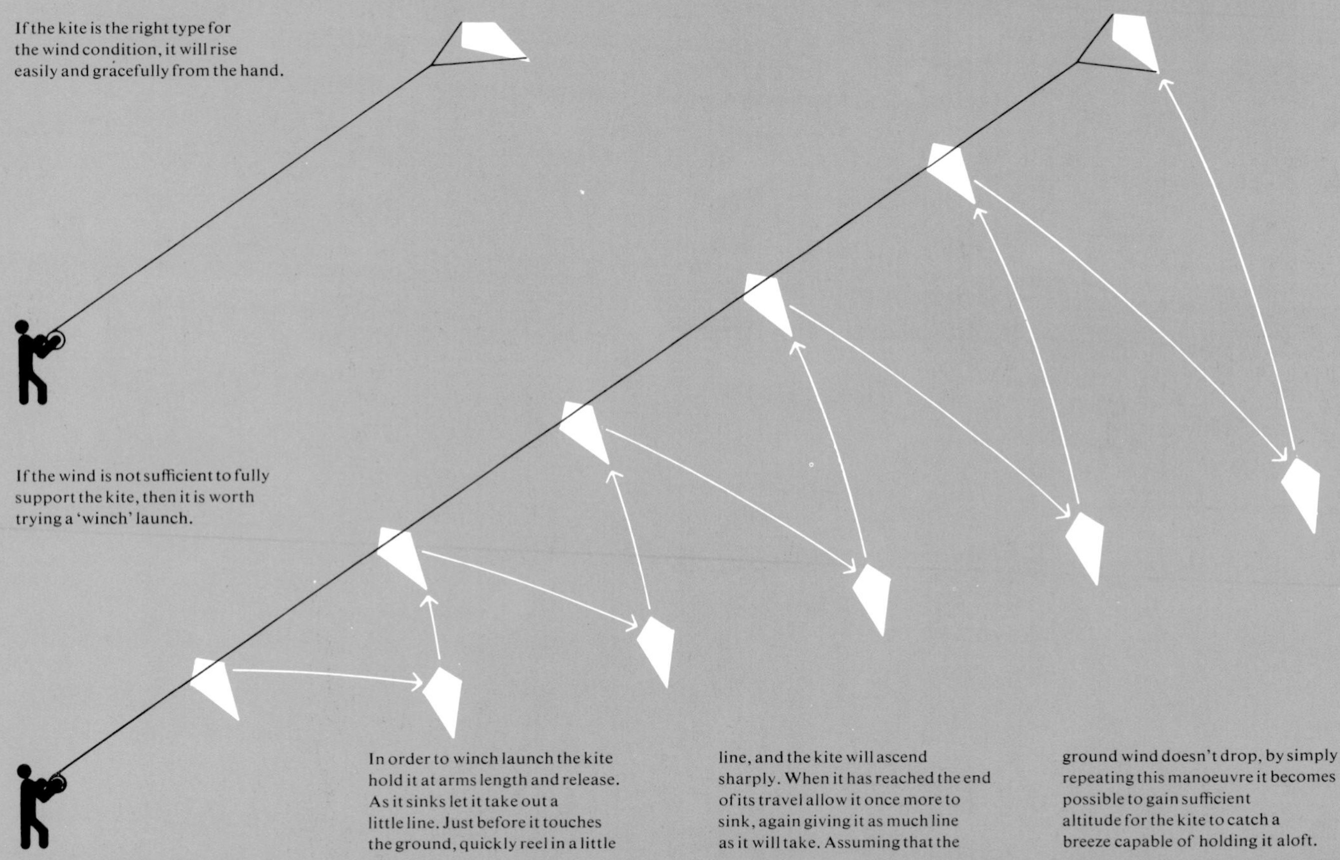

If the kite is the right type for the wind condition, it will rise easily and gracefully from the hand.

If the wind is not sufficient to fully support the kite, then it is worth trying a 'winch' launch.

In order to winch launch the kite hold it at arms length and release. As it sinks let it take out a little line. Just before it touches the ground, quickly reel in a little line, and the kite will ascend sharply. When it has reached the end of its travel allow it once more to sink, again giving it as much line as it will take. Assuming that the ground wind doesn't drop, by simply repeating this manoeuvre it becomes possible to gain sufficient altitude for the kite to catch a breeze capable of holding it aloft.

the kite, and all available control is needed, particularly at launching. After signalling to the launcher to release the kite the handler should take in line as quickly as possible – hand-over-hand is best unless a power winch is used – and the kite should rise steadily and evenly until it reaches more lively air, and 'catches', or pulls slightly on the flying line. With luck the kite will reach an altitude which allows it to maintain its correct attitude, when drag will be at a minimum and lift at a maximum, holding its position aloft, and tugging softly for more line. Very soon the line taken in at launch, which should be distributed neatly and evenly upon the ground, will be taken up, and the kite will be flying directly from the reel. If not so lucky, and the kite, having reached its flying attitude sinks towards the horizon, it should be given as much line as it will take, allowing it to fall as far away as possible, so setting up another high-start launch attempt, which should begin shortly before the kite reaches the ground. Again, take in line quickly until the kite catches the wind. If it still persists in sinking, another longer launch of about 100 m (say 330 ft) should be tried. If this fails also, and there is no lighter kite available, the alternatives are to either wait for more wind or abandon the attempt.

Assuming an efficient kite and a steady wind, the kite will take line out from the reel as it needs it, sinking backwards and downwards as it does so. Every 15 m (say 50 ft) or so allow the kite to climb back to its flying attitude by halting the line supply. By doing this the handler can constantly check that the kite isn't going to 'top'. A kite tops by flying so far through its arc of travel that it passes its intended flying angle, continues up to the zenith – with the flying line at 90° to the ground – and beyond, adopting a hopelessly negative

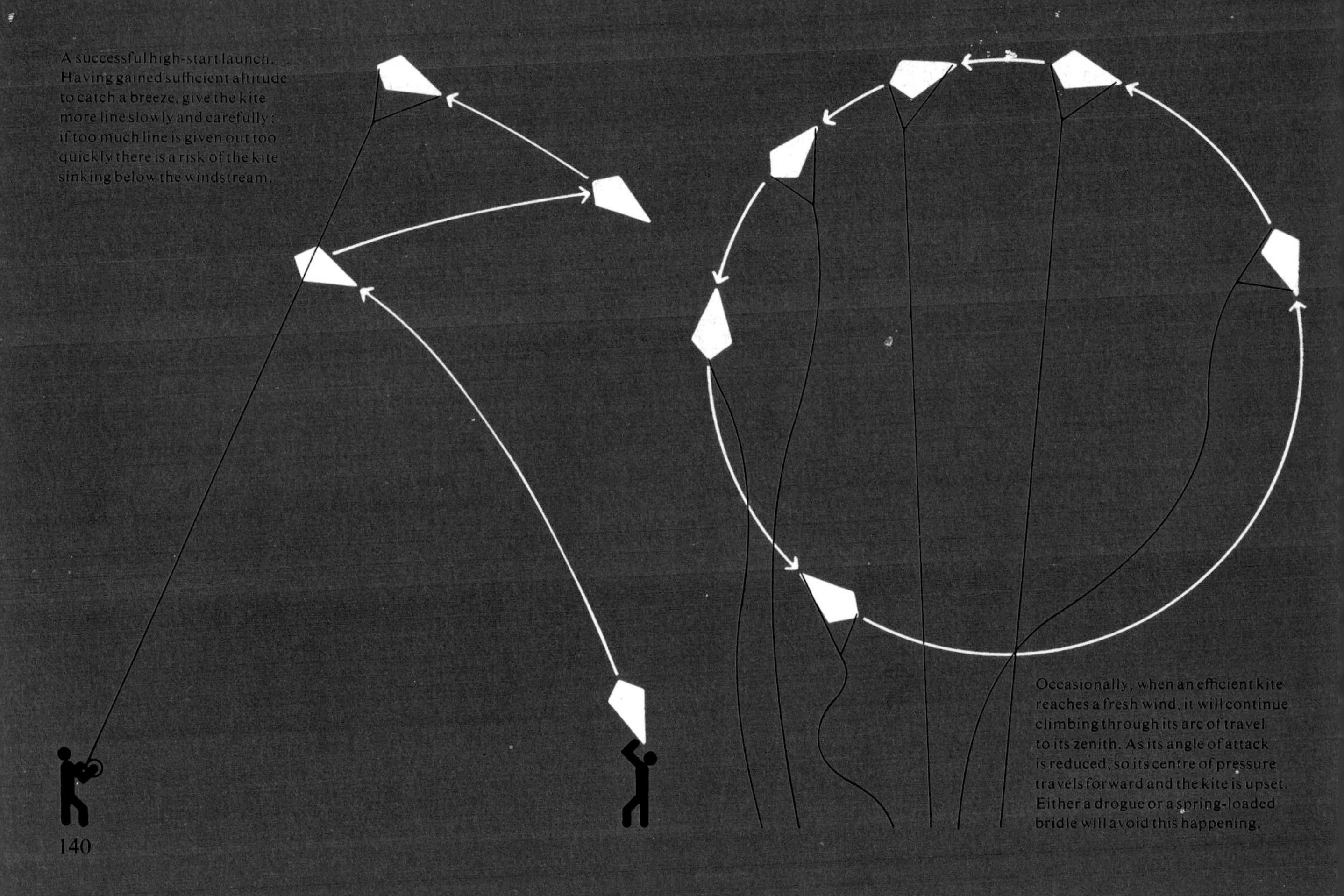

A successful high-start launch. Having gained sufficient altitude to catch a breeze, give the kite more line slowly and carefully; if too much line is given out too quickly there is a risk of the kite sinking below the windstream.

Occasionally, when an efficient kite reaches a fresh wind, it will continue climbing through its arc of travel to its zenith. As its angle of attack is reduced, so its centre of pressure travels forward and the kite is upset. Either a drogue or a spring-loaded bridle will avoid this happening.

angle of attack. At this point it will go into a series of wide lateral loops, which are more entertaining than alarming. If the conditions are right this can be checked by taking in line as slack becomes available. Each time the kite dives it gives line; and, by taking this up, it is usually possible to bring the kite down into lighter winds where control is regained. Should this happen close to the ground, however, there is a chance of not getting off so lightly, though serious damage can usually be avoided by simply giving the kite plenty of line just before impact with the ground.

If a kite develops excessive pull and it becomes difficult to retrieve, a good way of easing the pressure on the reel is to walk towards the kite while reeling in, towing it back to the starting point and repeating the process until the kite has reached more manageable wind-speed. If the pull is so great that this doesn't work, then the line will have to be 'under-run'. Under-running requires two people. While one holds the reel, a helper loops a piece of strong cloth – or a reel specially made for the purpose – over the kite line and walks out towards the kite, automatically pulling the line down as he walks. After reaching a reasonable distance he holds the line and walks back towards the handler, who takes in the line as he does so. Again, this operation has to be repeated until lower altitudes have been regained.

There is always a limit to which a single kite can be flown. This obviously varies, depending upon the size of the kite and the strength of the wind. When excess catenary, or sag, appears in the flying line this limit has been reached. Catenary is an undesirable feature and means that the kite simply cannot support the weight of the line. The lower the

Excess catenary in the flying line should be taken up by another kite if the lift is to be continued. Theoretically there is no limit to the quantity of kites that can be flown from a single line.

One of many methods of rigging a train of box kites.

Baden-Powell's double-sided bridle system for flying in train.

angle of flight, the more pronounced the catenary becomes, and vice versa. In order to continue sending the kite out it will be necessary to give the flying line extra support.

To do this, first take in the excess catenary onto the reel, launch a second kite on a couple of hundred feet of line, and attach the end of that line to the main line by slipping a ring on the flying line with a lark's head hitch, and securing the second line to it with a bowline. This is called flying in train and, with this technique, great altitudes can be reached. In 1919 a train of eight kites reached the record height of 9,740 m (31,955 ft).

Flying Wind conditions

Wind is caused by uneven atmospheric temperatures giving rise to differences in pressure and, as these imbalances naturally tend to even themselves out, so winds are formed. Winds are categorized into three main groups; local and regional persistent winds; global persistent winds; and episodic or maverick winds, such as cyclones, anticyclones, tornadoes and hurricanes. It is obviously the first of these groups, the local and regional persistent winds that are of interest to the average kite flyer, as they are small scale winds that are relatively shallow, and are seldom influenced by immense factors such as the rotation of the earth. On a world scale they are tiny eddies, simple wisps affected by nothing more than relative temperature differences between land and water, and the geographical relationships of mountains and

A returnable sail-driven messenger, or envoy, capable of climbing a kite line, releasing its payload, and returning to the operator.

Upon contact with a stop on the flying line the aluminium wire feeler is sprung, causing both the sail-securing line and the payload to be released.

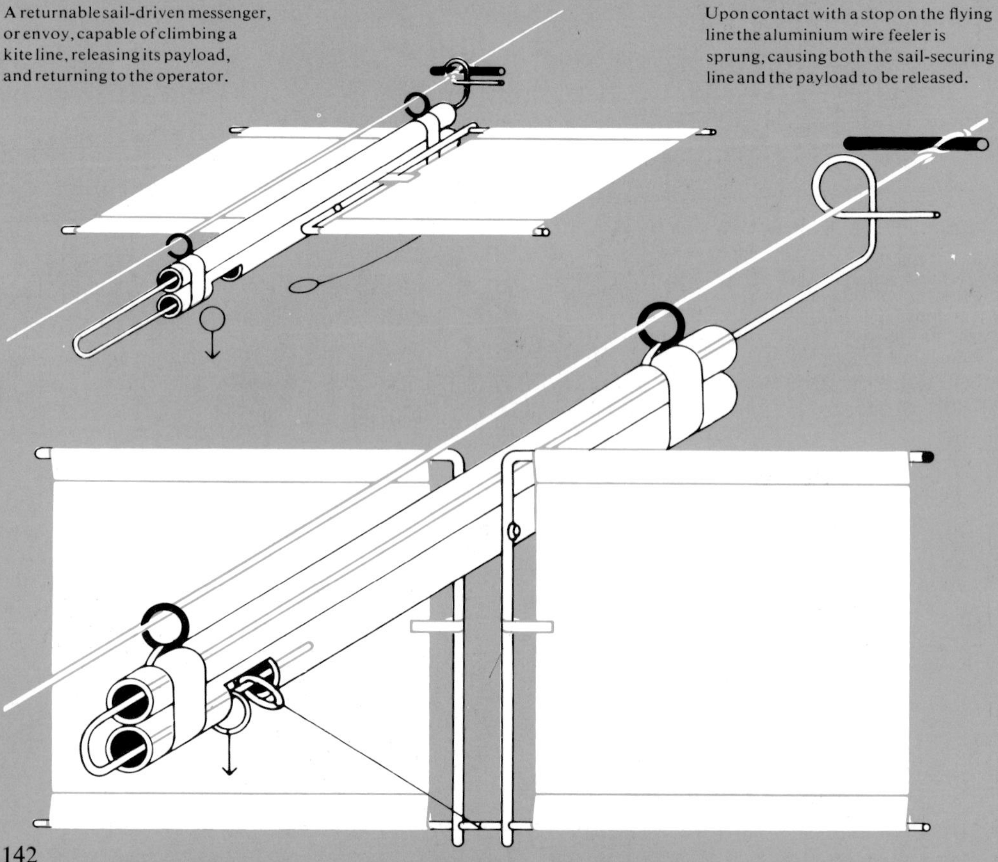

Parachutes make popular payloads.

Gliders are entertaining when released from a good altitude, though they are seldom retrieved. Consequently, folded paper versions are more generally used.

valleys. During early spring, about the time of the vernal equinox, extremes of temperature exist between the north polar regions and the equator, giving rise to the March winds so loved by kite flyers. March once heralded a quite definite kiting season, though these days enthusiasts tend to fly kites throughout the year. Whether this is due to more efficient kites or greater enthusiasm is difficult to say.

In 1806 Admiral Sir Francis Beaufort of the British Navy devised a wind velocity scale to enable the captains of sailing ships to accurately assess wind-speeds at sea. Though the original scale dealt with purely maritime effects, it has since been modified for landsmen in general, and kite flyers in particular. Assuming that even the most ardent enthusiast won't be flying kites when trees are being uprooted by the wind, the accompanying scale has been modified.

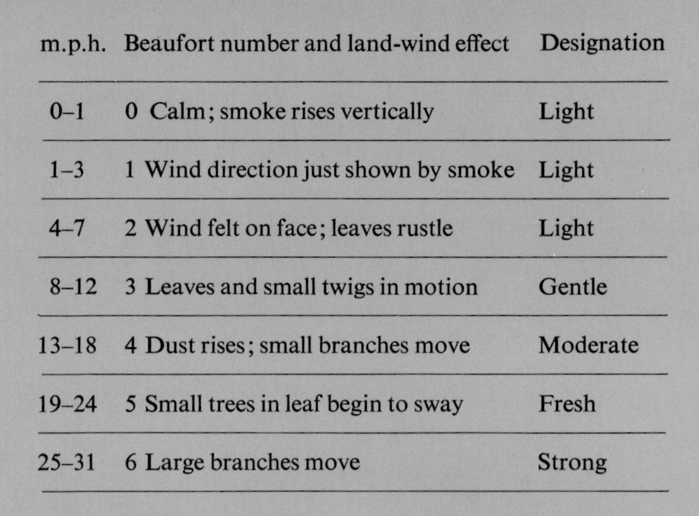

m.p.h.	Beaufort number and land-wind effect	Designation
0–1	0 Calm; smoke rises vertically	Light
1–3	1 Wind direction just shown by smoke	Light
4–7	2 Wind felt on face; leaves rustle	Light
8–12	3 Leaves and small twigs in motion	Gentle
13–18	4 Dust rises; small branches move	Moderate
19–24	5 Small trees in leaf begin to sway	Fresh
25–31	6 Large branches move	Strong

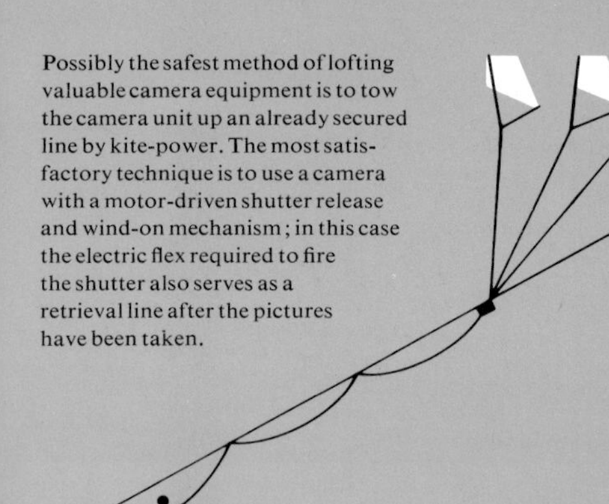

Possibly the safest method of lofting valuable camera equipment is to tow the camera unit up an already secured line by kite-power. The most satisfactory technique is to use a camera with a motor-driven shutter release and wind-on mechanism; in this case the electric flex required to fire the shutter also serves as a retrieval line after the pictures have been taken.

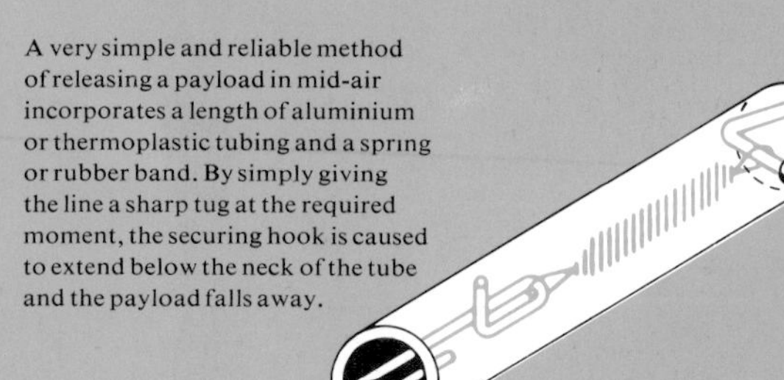

A very simple and reliable method of releasing a payload in mid-air incorporates a length of aluminium or thermoplastic tubing and a spring or rubber band. By simply giving the line a sharp tug at the required moment, the securing hook is caused to extend below the neck of the tube and the payload falls away.

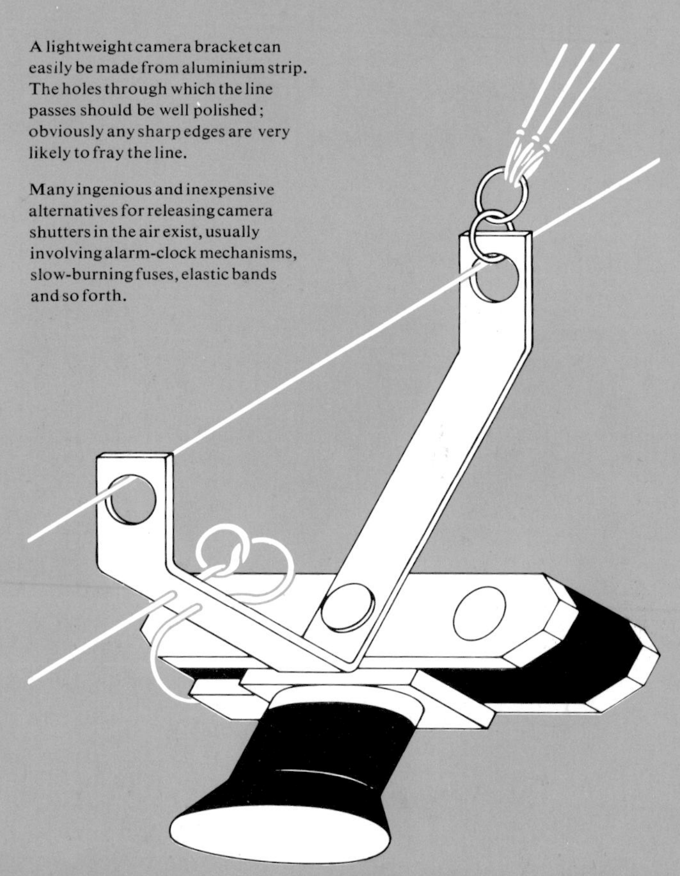

A lightweight camera bracket can easily be made from aluminium strip. The holes through which the line passes should be well polished; obviously any sharp edges are very likely to fray the line.

Many ingenious and inexpensive alternatives for releasing camera shutters in the air exist, usually involving alarm-clock mechanisms, slow-burning fuses, elastic bands and so forth.

The most comfortable wind velocities in which to fly are those between 8 and 16 m.p.h. Always remember, however, that even if the wind at ground level is light and manageable, a few thousand feet up it may not only be considerably stronger, but also blowing in a quite different direction.

One of the most exhilarating experiences in kite flying can be 'riding' a thermal or, more accurately, the thermal *effect*. A thermal is a somewhat elusive phenomenon to describe but is basically a rising current of warm air that occurs during late spring and summer, when a cool morning temperature gives way to a hot day. Most usually generated over large grassless areas, fields of dried grass, or even large flat concrete areas, the kite flyer's main difficulty is to position the kite high enough in the thermal for it to be affected by the current. Thermals gain velocity as they rise, so the kite must reach it at a reasonable altitude where there is enough velocity for lift. Soaring kites such as deltas, birds or rollers are needed to ride thermals, and the line is taken from the hand in a steady surge of energy rather than a noticeable tug. Thermals can also be formed in the areas beneath the outer edges of cumulus cloud. The air beneath the cloud, being shaded from the sun, is cooler than the surrounding atmosphere. This cool air spirals downwards, disturbing the warm air below, causing it to rise in a tubular effect around the column of cold air, and it is within the region of this rising air that the kite will be most likely to ascend, soaring and spiralling lazily as it does so. Though beware, even the slightest breeze is capable of gently blowing the thermal away, leaving the kite at a great altitude with no support; and the chances are that it will sink at a far greater rate than line can be taken in.

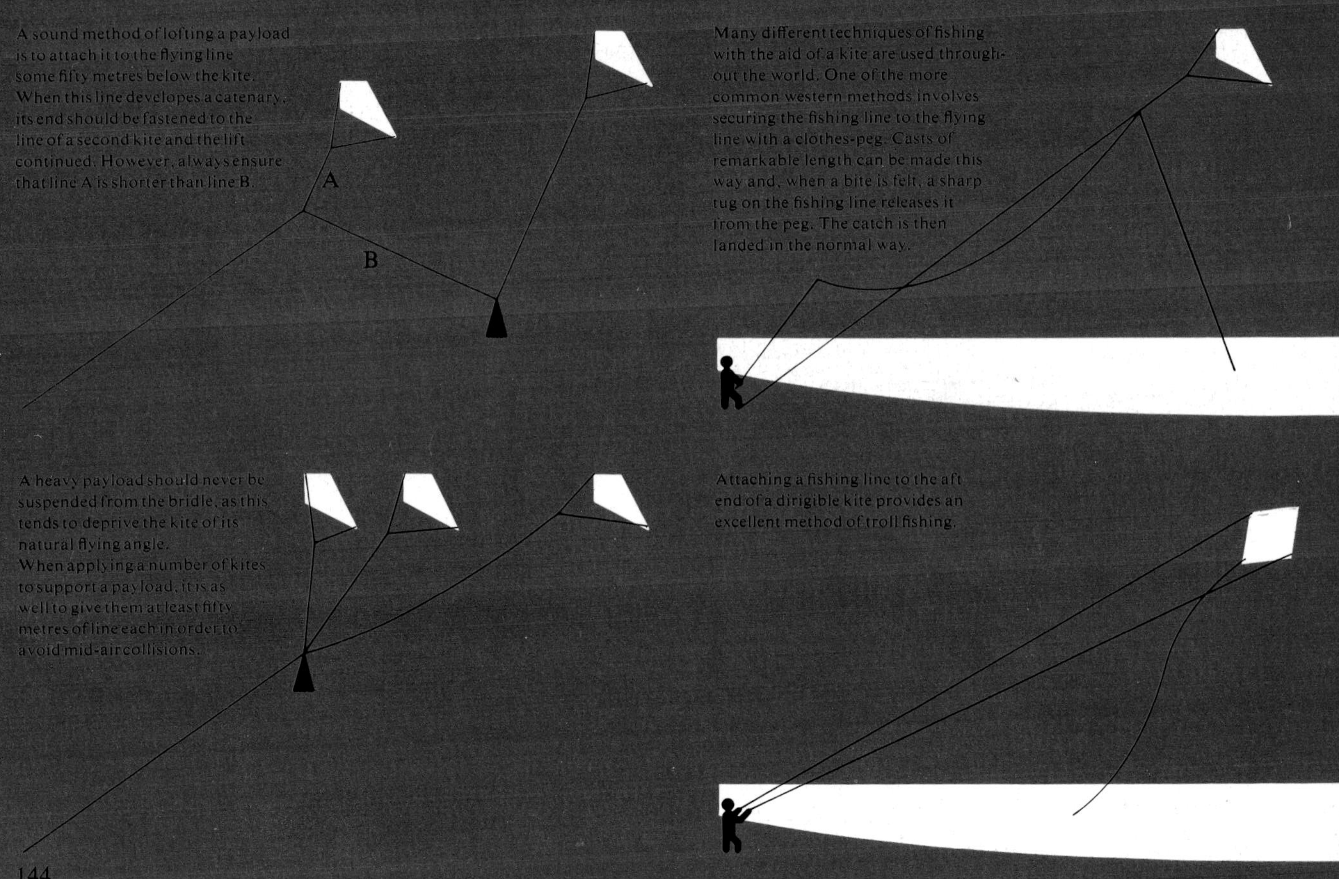

A sound method of lofting a payload is to attach it to the flying line some fifty metres below the kite. When this line develops a catenary, its end should be fastened to the line of a second kite and the lift continued. However, always ensure that line A is shorter than line B.

Many different techniques of fishing with the aid of a kite are used throughout the world. One of the more common western methods involves securing the fishing line to the flying line with a clothes-peg. Casts of remarkable length can be made this way and, when a bite is felt, a sharp tug on the fishing line releases it from the peg. The catch is then landed in the normal way.

A heavy payload should never be suspended from the bridle, as this tends to deprive the kite of its natural flying angle.
When applying a number of kites to support a payload, it is as well to give them at least fifty metres of line each in order to avoid mid-air collisions.

Attaching a fishing line to the aft end of a dirigible kite provides an excellent method of troll fishing.

A great deal of fun can be had from putting the wind to work. From great altitudes photographs can be taken, gliders launched, smoke bombs triggered, pamphlets can be distributed and lights can be flown at night. Many line climbers have been devised, ranging from simple discs of paper to ingenious envoys capable of carrying payloads up to the kite, releasing their burden and quickly returning for the next.

To a far greater degree than the sea, the air is terribly unforgiving of any carelessness, incapacity and neglect. Possibly the most attractive thing about flying kites is that it presents an opportunity of mastering the third element without actually entering it.

Flying   Rating a kite

Individual kites have a minimum and a maximum wind velocity at which comfortable flying can be performed; a kite's individual capabilities are dependent upon its 'rating'. The rating of a kite is simply the ratio of its weight to its sail-loading, or sail area. For instance, a fragile and highly rated lightweight with a large sail area will remain aloft in extremely light wind-speeds, while a low rated kite, being heavier, with a smaller sail area is capable of withstanding comparatively heavy winds. Because of such factors as the porosity and density of the cover fabric, it is not possible to arrive at a recognized standard rating; though one ounce to the square foot is considered to be average.

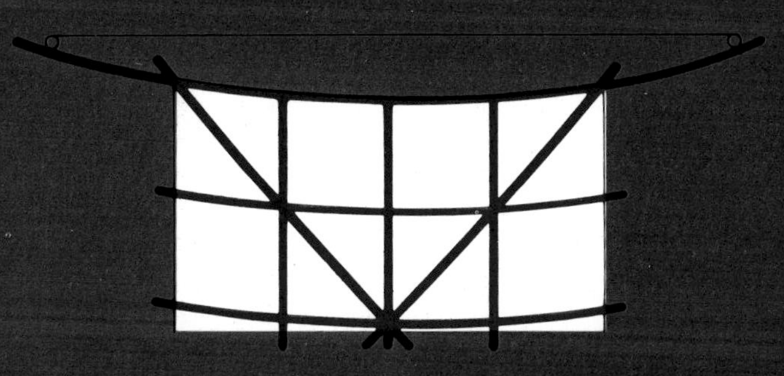

In the tradition of Huan Theng, eastern kites are frequently fitted with a hummer capable of emitting a rather mournful wail in the sky. A bamboo bow is fastened at the top of the kite, and is strung with a sliver of bamboo or rattan. In the west, old guitar strings suffice.

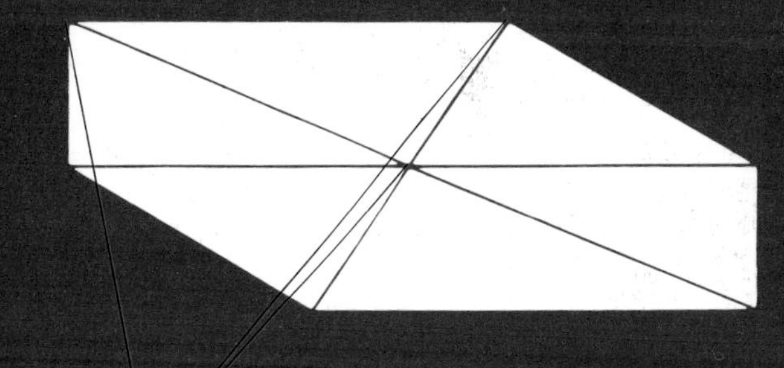

The aluminized surface of Mylar makes it an excellent cover material for night flying. Used as a reflector for a flashlight the kite becomes a U.F.O.

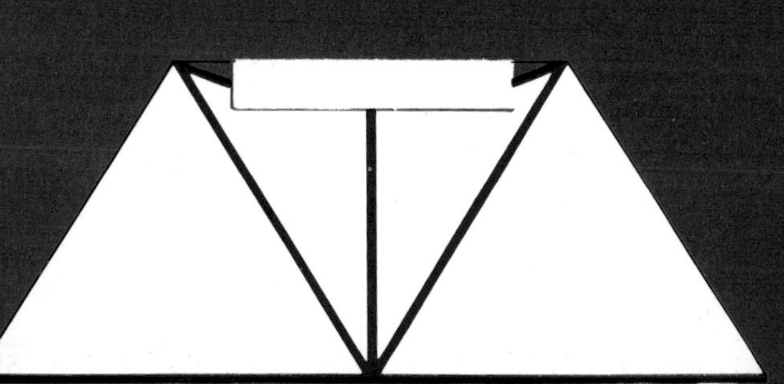

The paper buzzer is traditional to a number of ethnic kites, and is quite simply a strip of hard paper folded and glued around a taut line spanning two spar ends. A number of kite enthusiasts derive considerable pleasure from attaching a variety of noise producing gadgets to their kites.

This is a good way of mounting a banner on a kite line. A weight is necessary if light sticks are used.

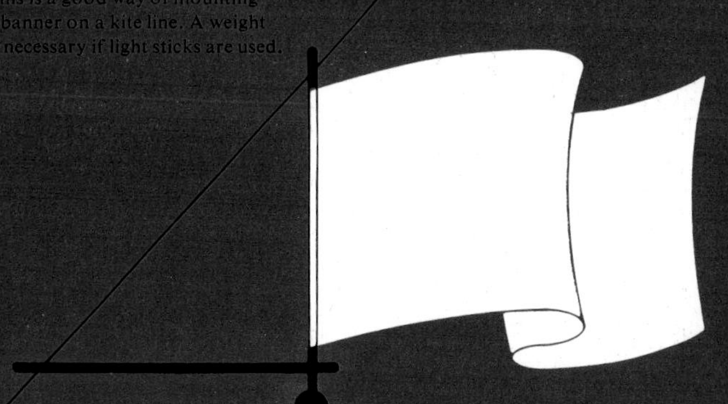

The satisfaction of determining the altitude of a kite is as great as the challenge that it represents. Calculating height is not a simple operation without a theodolite or an electronic rangefinder; but it can be done.

Referring to the right-angled triangle *ABC* below, a number of enthusiasts use commercial rangefinders to establish the distance between themselves and their kite *BA*, while others measure the flying line as it is taken off the reel, *BDA*. This is done in order to establish the length of the hypotenuse *BA* of the right-angled triangle *ABC*. Assuming *BC* to be horizontal, the angle *ABC* is measured, (52°) and its logarithmic sine (0·7880) is established. Having read the length of the hypotenuse *BA* with the rangefinder as 138 m (represented in the diagram at a scale of 1 mm = 1 m), by applying the formula: sine × hypotenuse = opposite, that is 0·7880 × 138 = 108·7 (say 109) the height of the kite is established as being 109 m above *C*.

As will be seen from the diagram, establishing the length of the hypotenuse by measuring the flying line tends to be unsatisfactory because of the catenary in the line.

Assuming that such sophisticated – and expensive – a piece of equipment as a rangefinder is not available, establishing the length of the hypotenuse becomes more difficult, more entertaining, and infinitely more satisfying.

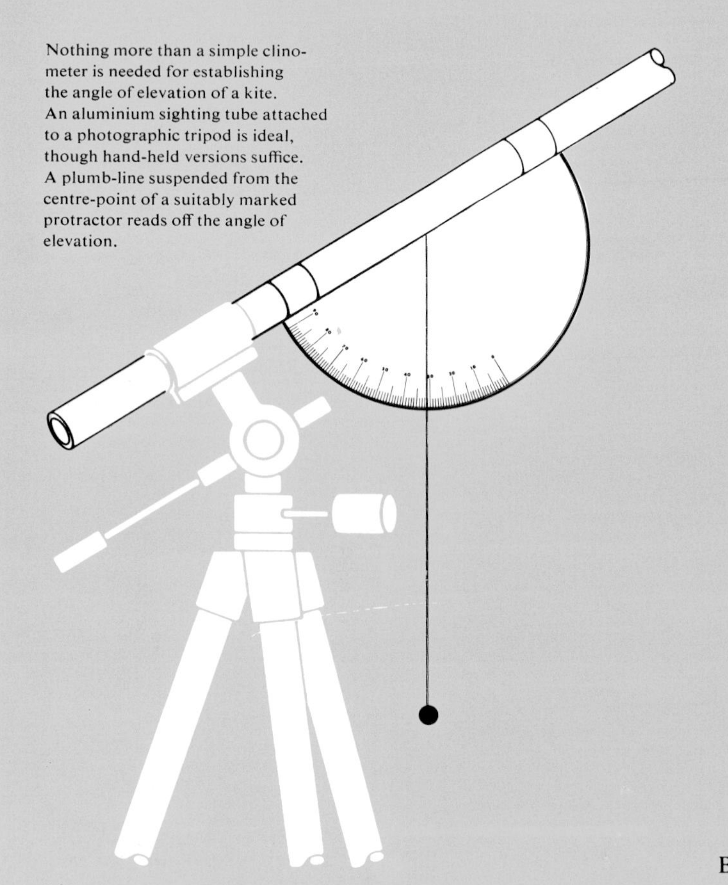

Nothing more than a simple clinometer is needed for establishing the angle of elevation of a kite. An aluminium sighting tube attached to a photographic tripod is ideal, though hand-held versions suffice. A plumb-line suspended from the centre-point of a suitably marked protractor reads off the angle of elevation.

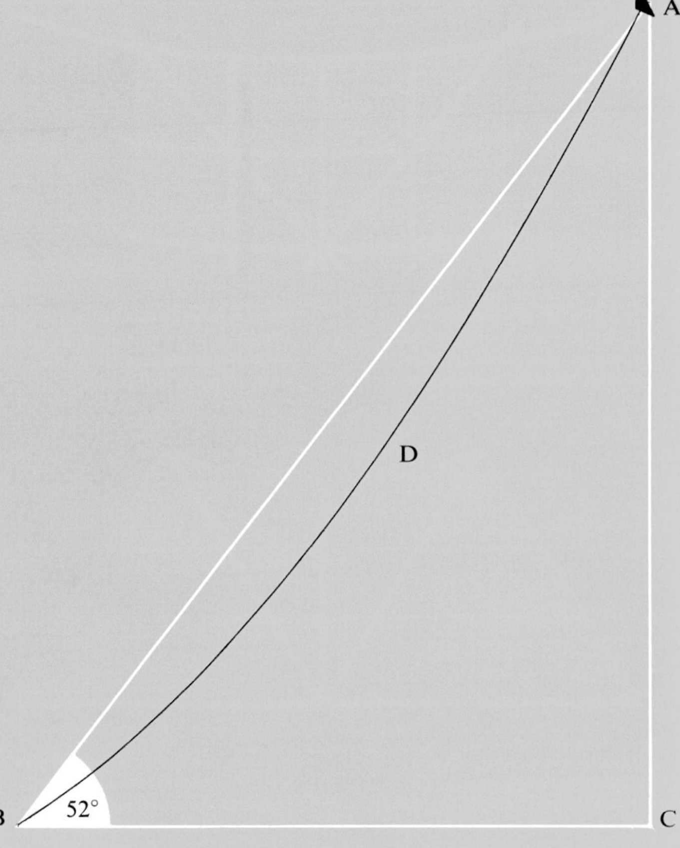

Referring to the main figure *ABD* below, tether the kite at any point, *E*. From a suitable point, *C*, angle *ACD* is measured by means of a clinometer, (71°). Then a distance *BC* is measured so that *B* and *C* are on the same horizontal plane as *D*, and the triangle *ABC* and *AD* are in the same vertical plane. Then measure angle *ABC*, (32°).

Therefore, in triangle *ABC*; *BC* is known; angle *ABC* is known; and angle *ACB* is known, being the supplement of angle *ACD*. Draw *BC* onto graph paper (at a scale of, say, 1 mm = 1 m). As angle *ABC* and angle *ACB* are known, construct the obtuse-angled triangle *ABC*, extending sides *BA* and *CA* to their point of convergence at *A*. Extend *BC* to *D*. By measuring *CA* (see caption) the length of the hypotenuse of triangle *ACD* is found (115 m). Reading the sine of angle *ACD* (71°) to be 0·9455, by applying the same formula: sine × hypotenuse = opposite, that is 0·9455 × 115 = 108·7 (say 109) it is again established that the kite is 109 m above *D*.

With the first of the above methods, however, the height of the rangefinder from the ground should be added to the final total: and with the second method, twice the height of the clinometer must be added, that is once for each reading. For maximum accuracy with such a simple measuring system, a second observation should be made simultaneously by a helper; the mean of the two results giving a tolerably accurate result.

Obviously any preferred unit of measurement, such as yards, may be substituted for metres in either system.

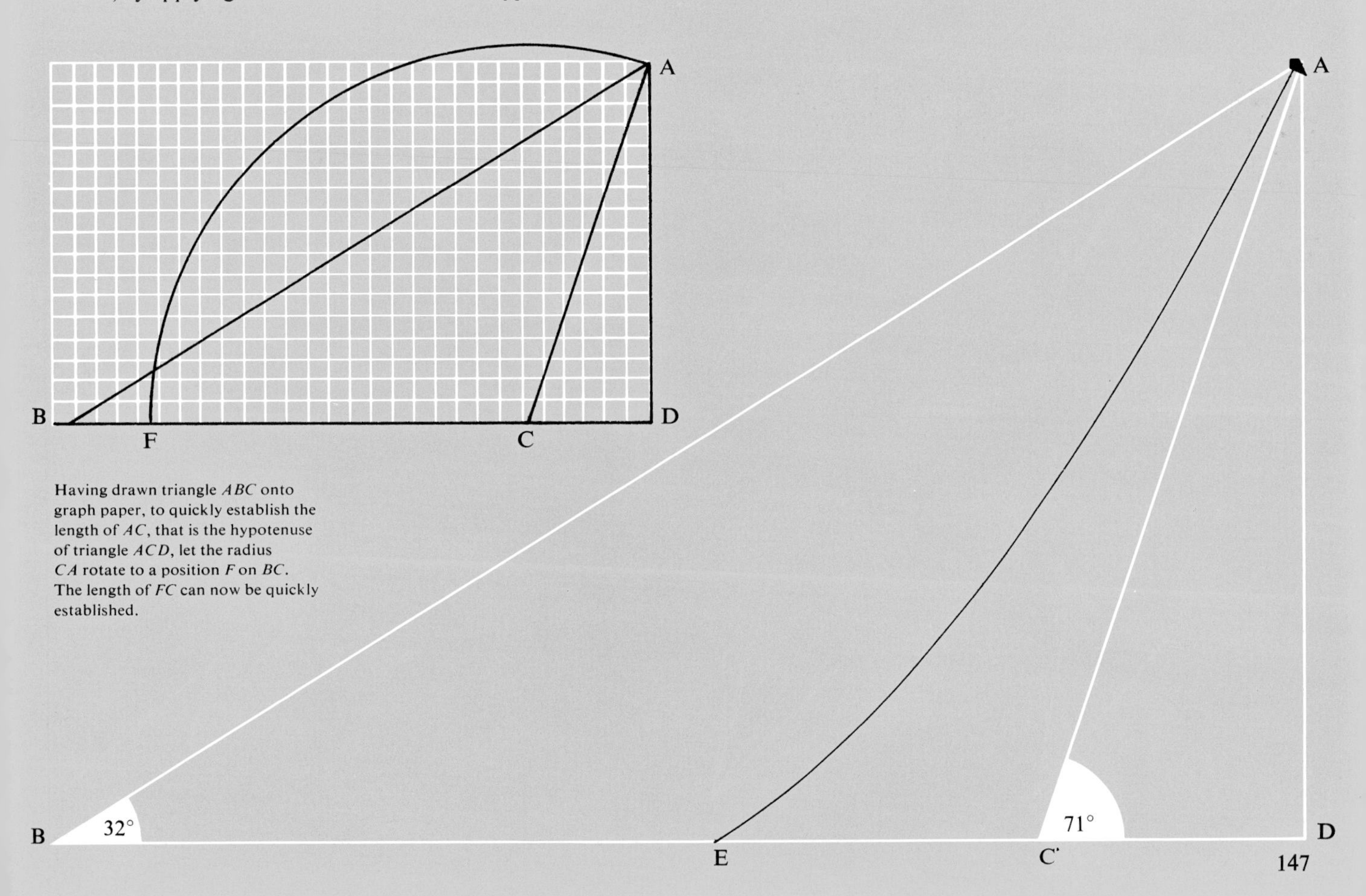

Having drawn triangle *ABC* onto graph paper, to quickly establish the length of *AC*, that is the hypotenuse of triangle *ACD*, let the radius *CA* rotate to a position *F* on *BC*. The length of *FC* can now be quickly established.

Kites fall into seven generic groups. The oldest and simplest type is the flat, or plane-surface kite, which, in its more impressive guises, can rival any of its successors for sheer spectacle. For example, the Thai Serpent is basically a flat kite, like the Chinese Centipede, which is no more than a series of circular flat kites flown in close train. The bowed kite has probably been flown in its many different versions for hundreds of years, though it was only around the turn of the nineteenth century that the reasons for its superior stability were understood. Most of the classic fighting kites may be included in this category. Another basic type is the box kite, comprised of pure cell combinations to provide lift and stability; these cell combinations, with wings added for extra lift, form the category known as compound kites. Three comparative newcomers to the old established kite family are canopy kites, such as sleds and parachutes, the soaring delta kites, which have evolved from Rogallo's original Flexible kite, and the parafoil, probably the most efficient application of tethered flight yet devised.

In an attempt to avoid obliterating detail with a mass of dimension marks, the following kite patterns are, wherever necessary, accompanied by a unit scale representing centimetres. To establish any dimensions quickly and accurately, simply span the measure required with a pair of dividers and read off the result against the corresponding scale. If dividers are not to hand, mark off the measures against the edge of a sheet of paper.

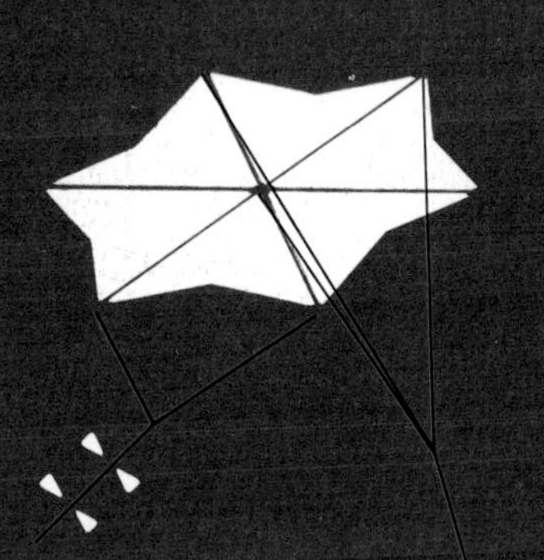

Flat, or plane-surface kite.

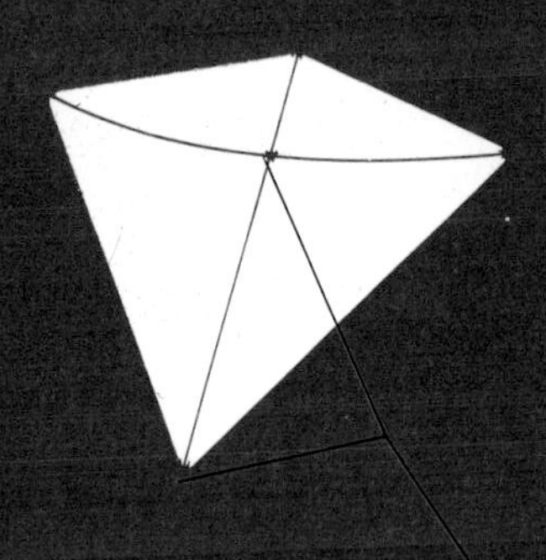

Bowed kite.

Box kite.

Compound kite.

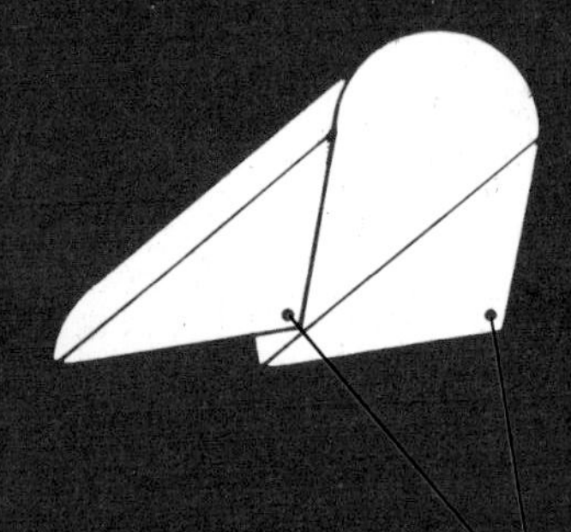

Sled.

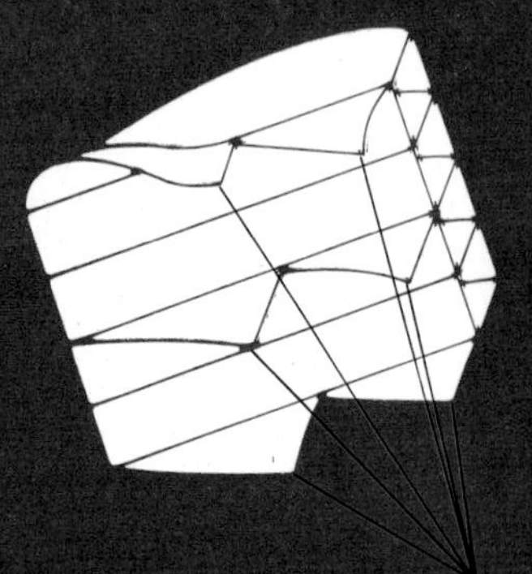

Parafoil.

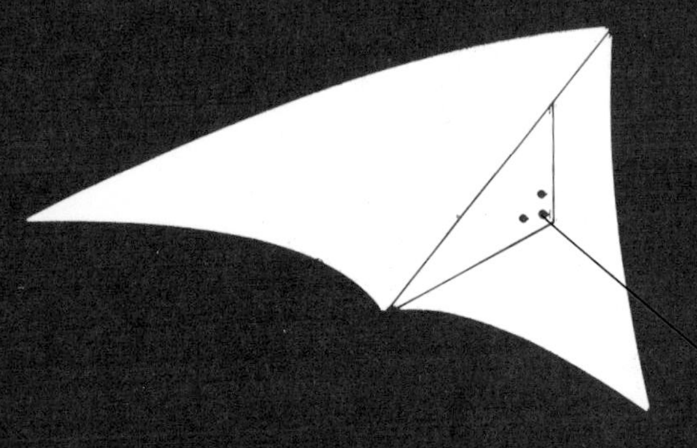

Delta kite.

It should be remembered that it is not so much the size, but the proportions of the kite that primarily dictate its performance. So long as a convenient size is arrived at, and the finished size is *proportionately* accurate – that is having lifting and stabilizing surfaces in ratio to those given in the pattern – then the kite should be efficient. Consequently, even though the unit scale that accompanies a pattern represents centimetres, the units may be read as inches, half inches or whatever. Nevertheless, the sizes given are recommended, as most of the western classics are based upon their original dimensions wherever these are still available. Sizes of the ethnic kites shown have been based upon either traditional working dimensions, or, where traditional versions appear discrepant, efficient and convenient working sizes have been arrived at by simple trial and error.

The materials given against the patterns are suggested rather than stipulated, as the permutations of materials are limitless. Because of reasons of availability and expense, a number of the materials used in the originals are no longer practical. Cover materials such as cedar veneer, goldbeaters skin, and silk have been replaced by natural and synthetic fabrics, and plastic film or sheet, while frames once made of hickory or young spruce are today fabricated from thermoplastic or fibreglass rod. The materials given tend to be those used *traditionally* for ethnic kites, and those used *originally* for western kites. If these seem impractical in some cases, it is as well to remember that an unexpected choice of material can occasionally yield surprisingly good results; consequently it is better to be open to experiment than to follow existing formulas slavishly.

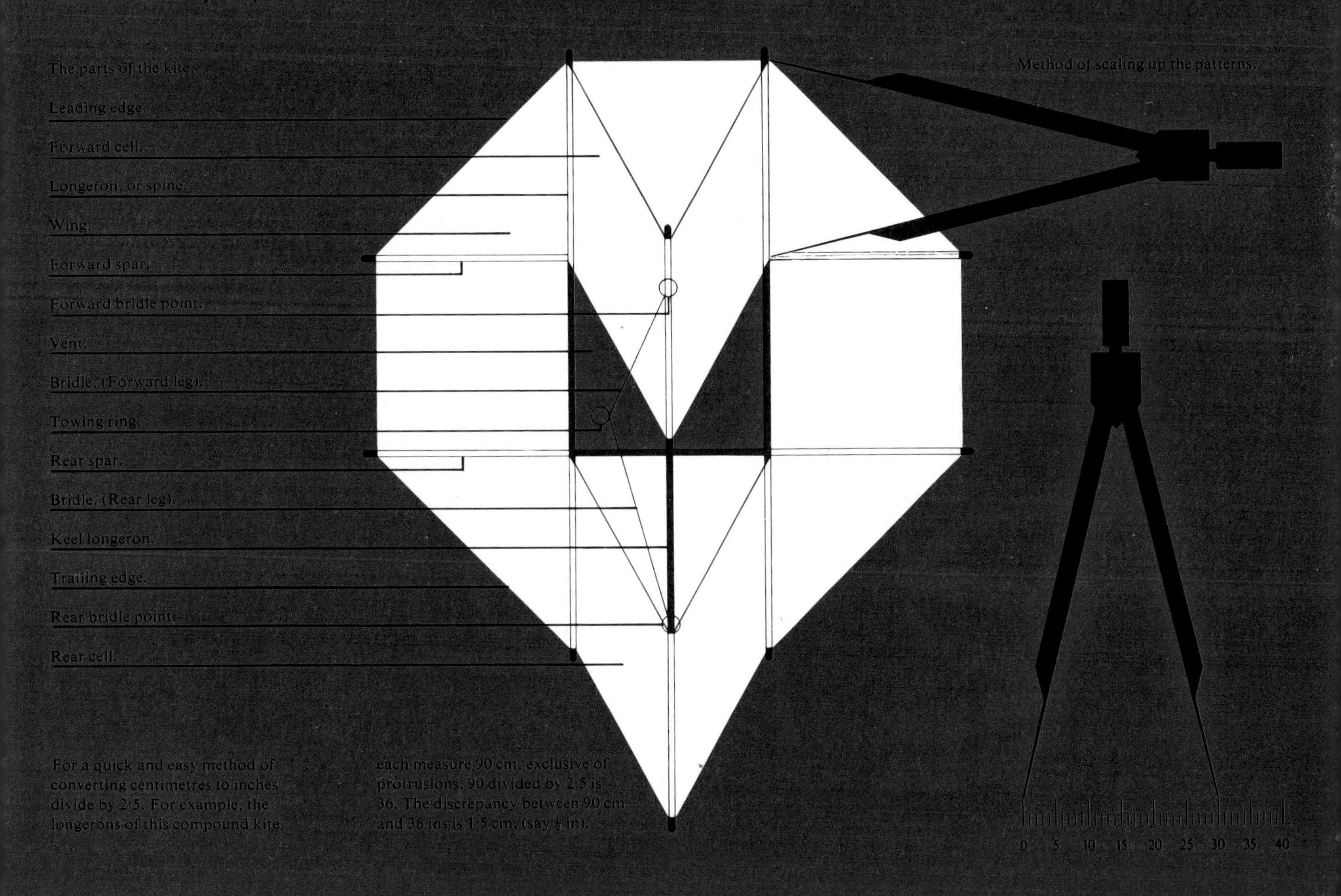

For a quick and easy method of converting centimetres to inches divide by 2·5. For example, the longerons of this compound kite each measure 90 cm, exclusive of protrusions. 90 divided by 2·5 is 36. The discrepancy between 90 cm and 36 ins is 1·5 cm, (say ½ in).

Chinese Centipede

Cover: paper.
Frame: split bamboo or rattan.
Bridle: two-leg.
Tail: paper streamers.
Wind: moderate.

In the classic Chinese version of the Centipede the head tends to be larger and stronger than the discs of the body. While some kite makers favour discs of uniform diameter, others tend to decrease the size through the length of the kite. Though the Centipede becomes progressively more difficult to fly as its length is increased, the longer the body the more striking the kite appears in flight. Individual discs should be balanced before assembly. To do this, place the vertical overlaps at the top and bottom of each disc onto two chair-backs, allowing a see-saw motion to occur in the horizontal plane. Trim the broom straws projecting from the horizontal stays until a good balance is achieved. Though sizes of the Centipede vary considerably, an average diameter for the leading disc is 40 cm (1 ft 3¾ ins.). Tie the discs at their tops and their sides, leaving 30 cm (1 ft) of line between the first two discs. This space should then successively be diminished by decrements of 1 cm (½ in) throughout the kite body. The Centipede kite is more spectacular than efficient.

Thai Serpent

Cover; silk.
Frame: split bamboo or rattan.
Bridle: two-leg.
Wind: light to moderate.

Traditionally made from silk, the Thai Serpent is extremely effective when covered with a fine gauge Mylar, though paper and plastic versions fly very successfully. The tail length is arbitrary, though the longer it is the more effective the spectacle.

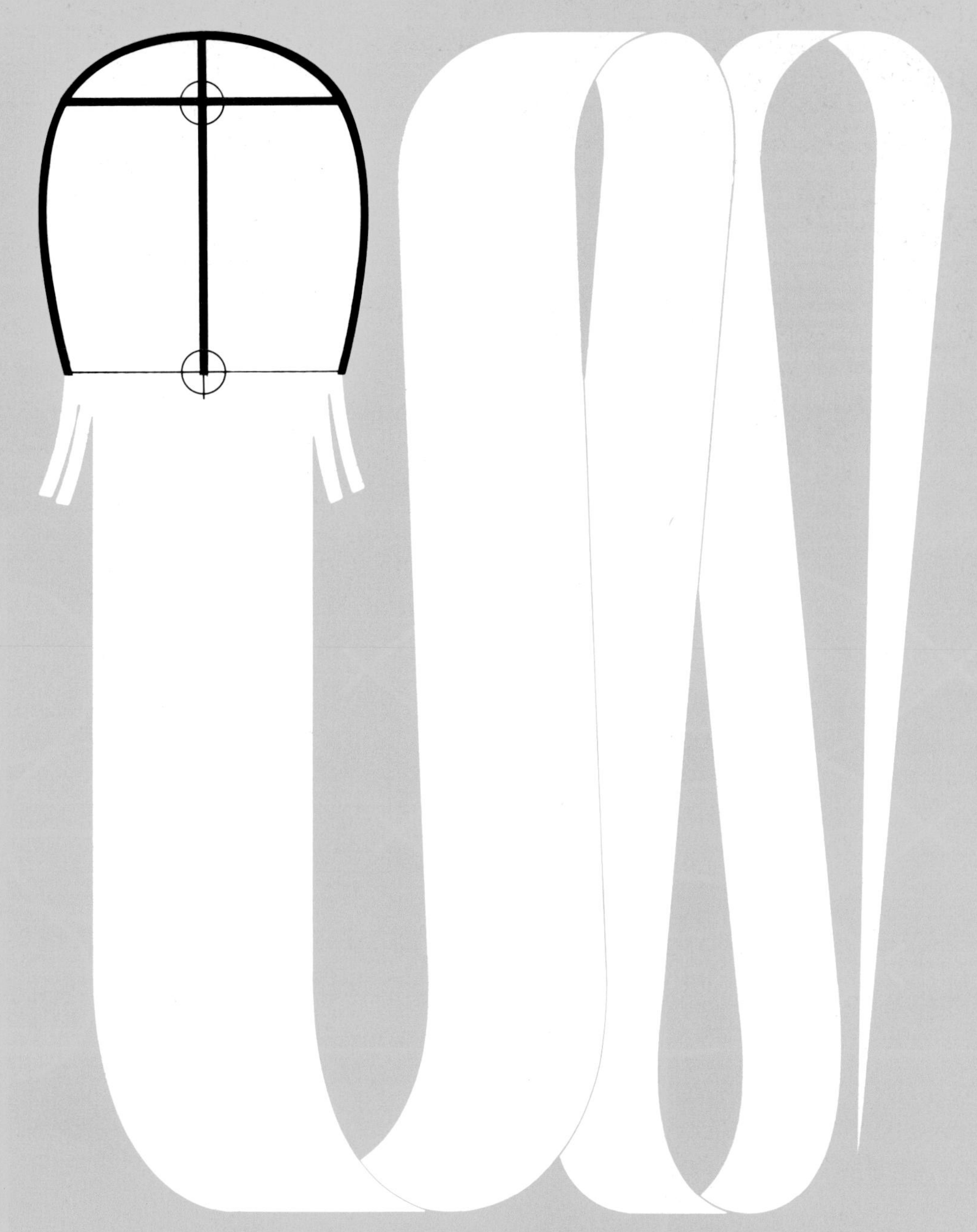

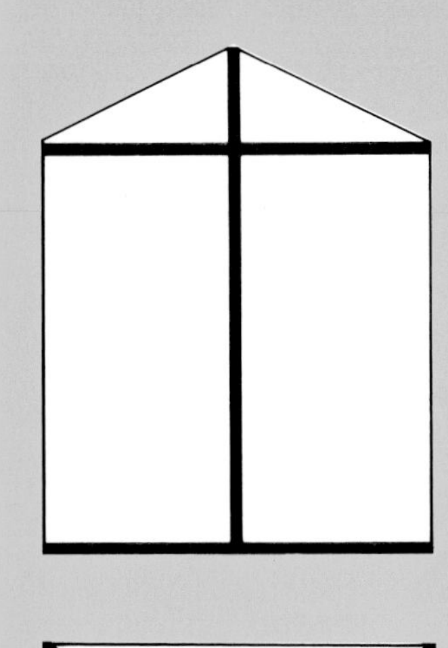

Alternate head-shapes for the Serpent.

Chinese fertility kite

Cover: paper.
Frame: bamboo.
Bridle: two-leg.
Tail: rice sheaves.
Wind: gentle to moderate.

The Chinese fertility – or rice – kite is traditionally flown over rice paddies with bundles of unthreshed rice attached to its wing tips and tail. The action of the wind upon the kite surface causes the rice grains to be shaken from the sheaves, scattering them in a symbolic fertilization process, in order to invoke an abundant harvest.

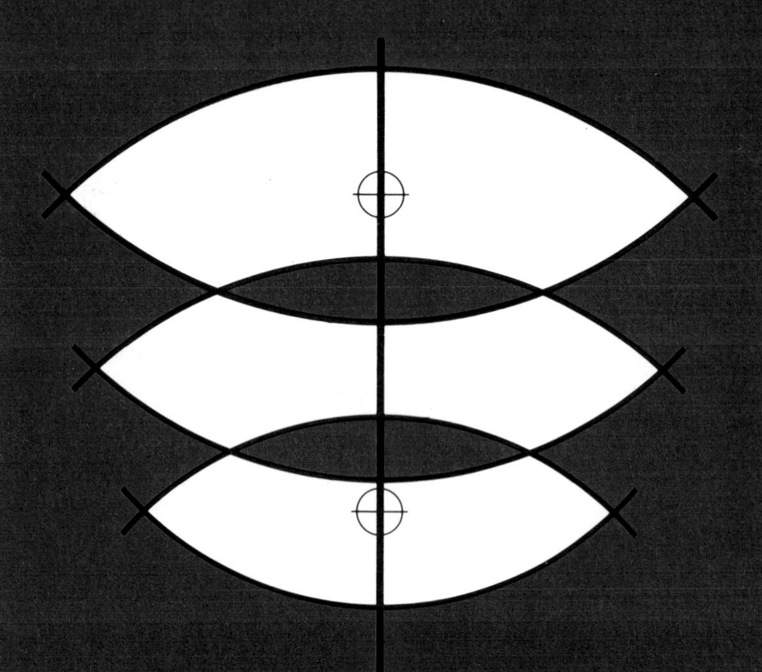

Hawaiian circle kite

Cover: paper.
Frame: split bamboo or rattan.
Bridle: three-leg.
Tail: single paper streamer.
Wind: light to gentle.

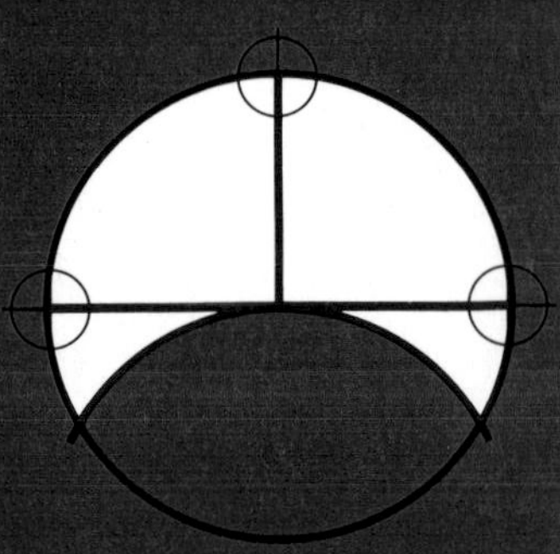

Chinese orange kite

Cover: paper.
Frame: split bamboo or rattan.
Bridle: two-leg.
Tail: paper streamers.
Wind: gentle to moderate.

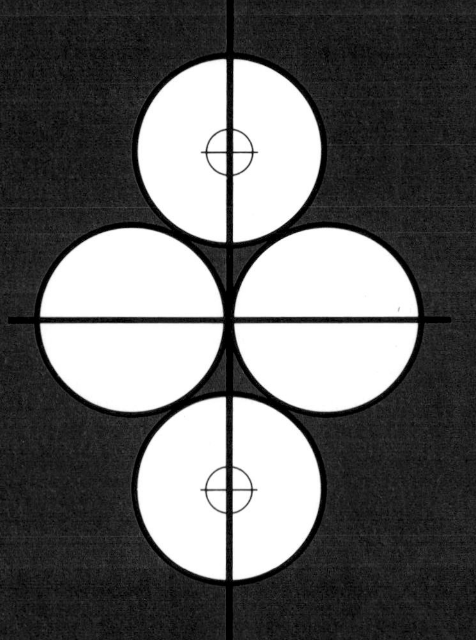

Iki Oniyocho kite

Cover: paper.
Frame: split bamboo.
Bridle: seven-leg (variable).
Tail: tasselled.
Wind: moderate to fresh.

Oniyocho kites are traditional to the islands in the Tsushima Strait, Western Japan. Individual islands each have their own version of the kite, such as the Goto Oniyocho and the Hirado Oniyocho. They commonly depict fearsome warriors or demons wearing elaborate helmets.

0 5 10 15 20 25 30 35 40 45 50 55 60 65 70 75 80 85 90 95 100 105

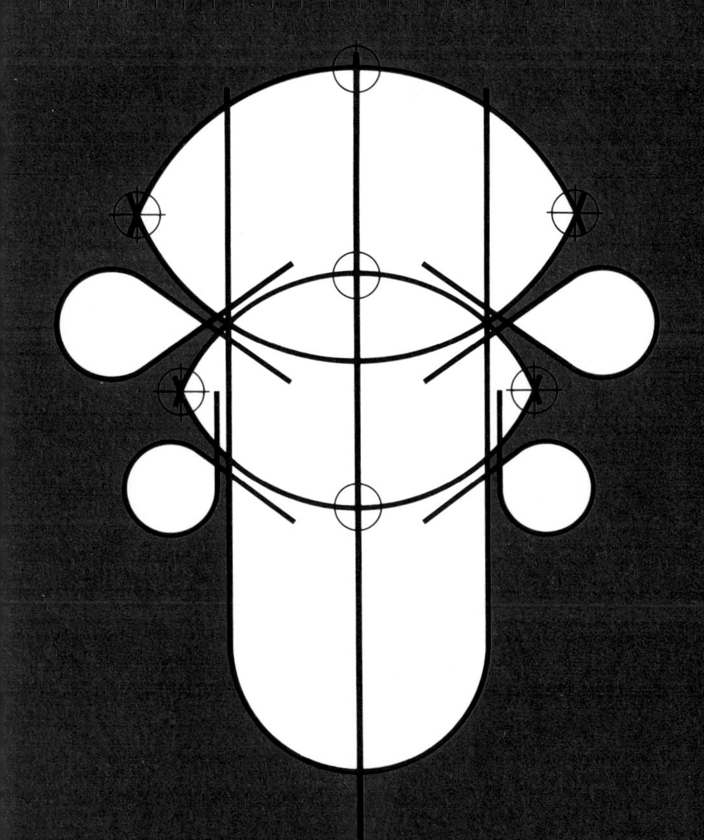

Semi kite

Cover: paper.
Frame: split bamboo.
Bridle: six-leg (variable).
Tail: tasselled.
Wind: light to gentle.

The Semi, or Cicada kite is one of Japan's many insect kites. Although known throughout Japan, the Semi kite is prevalent around Kita-kyushu.

0 5 10 15 20 25 30 35 40 45 50 55 60

Musha kite

Cover: paper.
Frame: bamboo.
Bridle: three-leg.
Tail: paper streamers.
Wind: light to gentle.

This is one of Japan's simpler rectangular kites, the sides of which are supported by cord only. The loose flap of cover paper at the trailing edge helps to induce stabilizing drag.

0 5 10 15 20 25 30 35 40 45 50 55 60 65 70 75 80 85 90

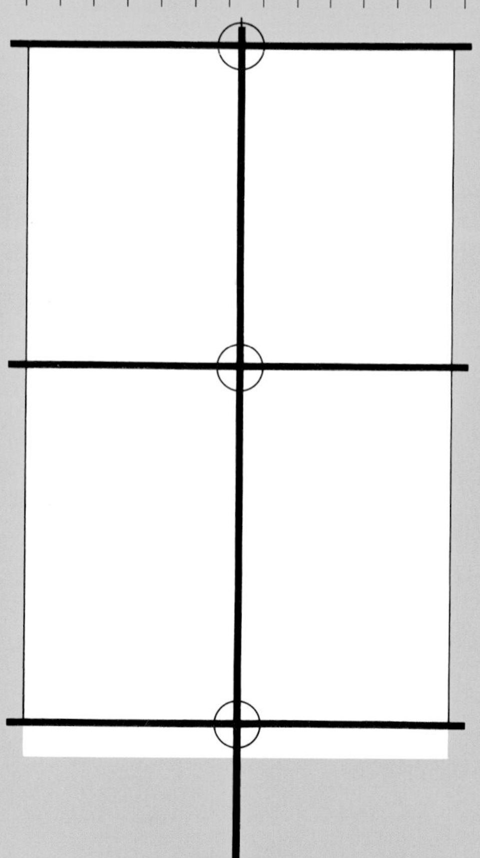

Wan-wan kite

Cover: paper.
Frame: bamboo.
Bridle: five-leg (variable).
Tailless.
Wind: gentle to fresh.

This is a scaled down version of the famous giant kites of Tokushima, said to be the largest kites ever built. The Wan-wan is flown heavily bowed.

0 5 10 15 20 25 30 35 40 45 50 55 60 65 70 75 80 85 90 95 100

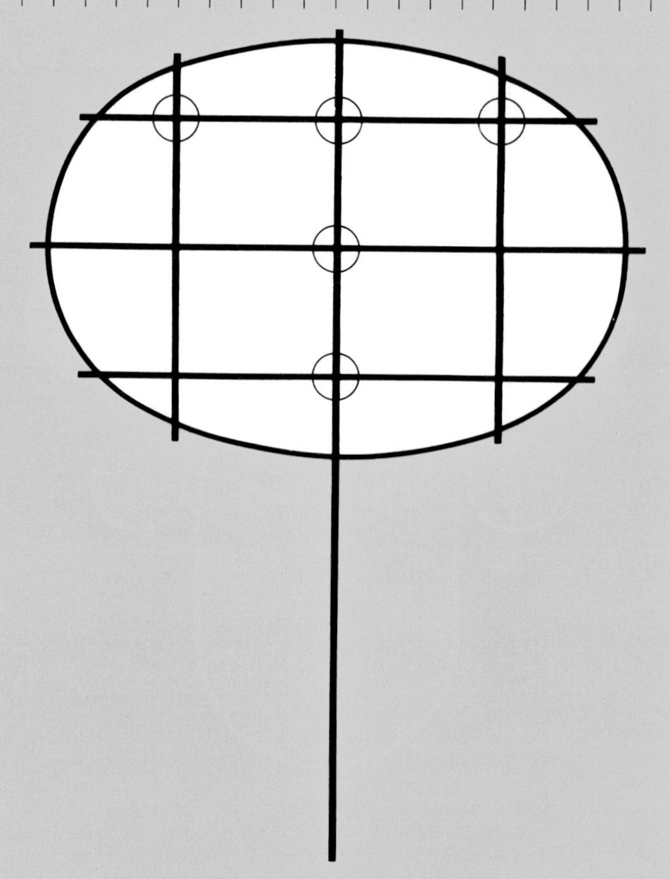

Machijirushi kite

Cover: paper.
Frame: bamboo.
Bridle: eight-leg (variable).
Tailless in light winds.
Wind: light to gentle.

The Machijirushi is a fighting kite flown in a variety of sizes at the annual Hamamatsu Festival.

0 5 10 15 20 25 30 35 40 45 50 55 60 65 70 75 80 85 90 95 100

Hakkaku kite

Cover: paper.
Frame: bamboo.
Bridle: five-leg.
Tail: paper streamers.
Wind: light to gentle.

This brightly painted eight-pointed star is a great favourite with Japanese children.

0 5 10 15 20 25 30 35 40 45 50 55 60 65 70 75

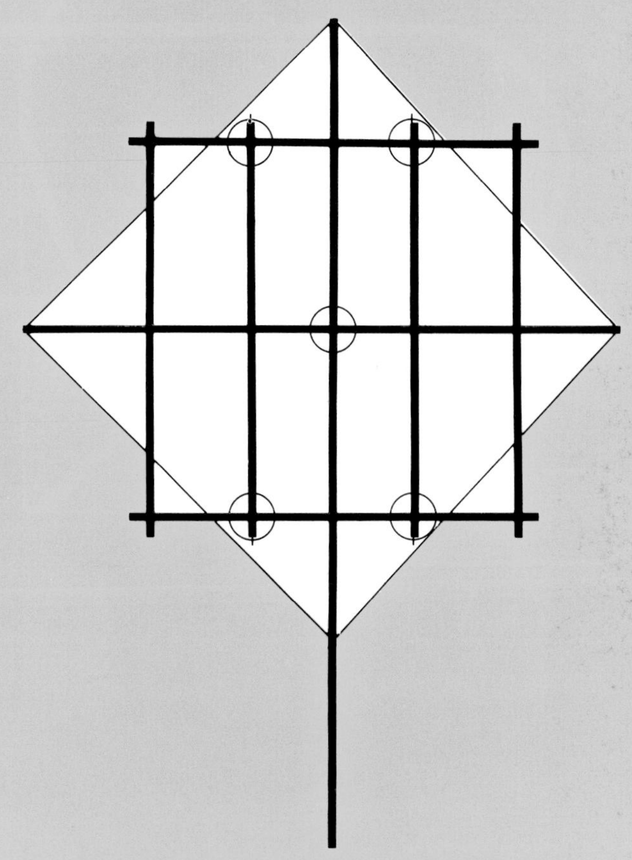

Yakko kite

Cover: paper.
Frame: split bamboo.
Bridle: three- or four-leg.
Tailless.
Wind: light to gentle.

The wing detail of the Yakko is of particular interest. The top and bottom edges of the wing cover are pasted to the curved frame in the manner shown below. As a result the excess paper at the wing tip is pushed upwards, giving a semi-tubular effect to the wing tip. The effect of this is similar in some respects to that of the dihedral in that, as the wind is streamed through the hole in the wing tip, it acts as a powerful stabilizing device.

Mikawa Tombi kite

Cover: paper.
Frame: split bamboo.
Bridle: three-leg.
Tailless.
Wind: light to gentle.

The Tombi, or Japanese Hawk, relies upon the same wing detail as the Yakko for its stability.

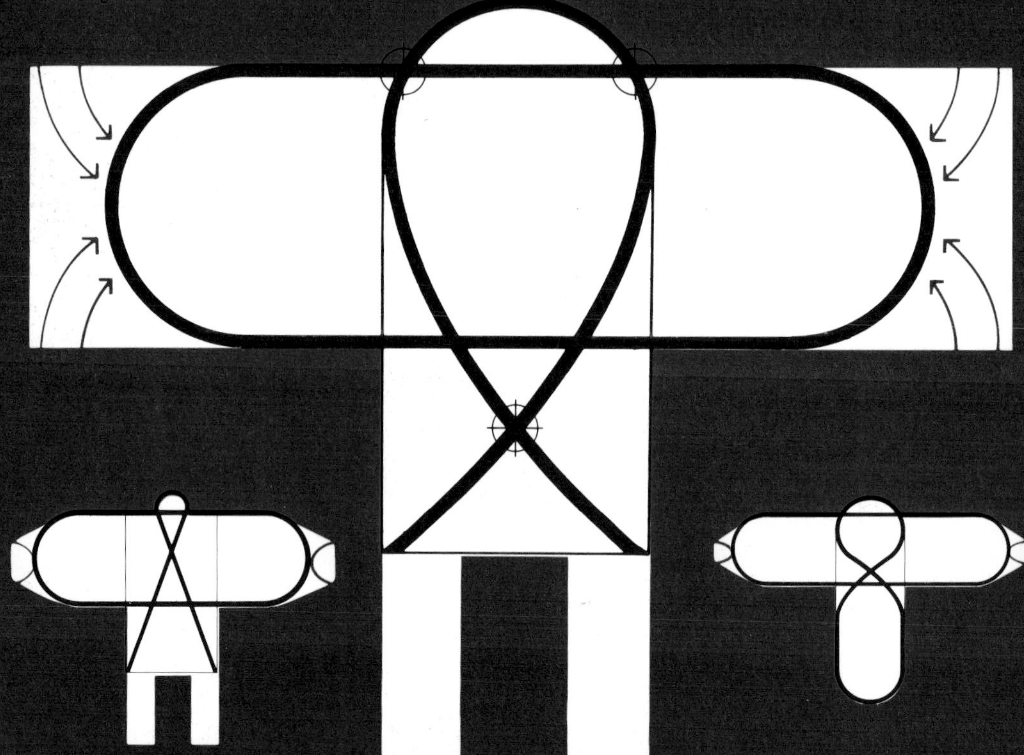

Alternate Yakko configurations.

Sode kite

Cover: paper.
Frame: split bamboo.
Bridle: two-leg.
Tailless.
Wind: light to gentle.

Also known as the Kimono kite, the Sode comes from Japan's Chiba Prefecture, and is so-called because of its obvious resemblance to the kimono jacket, or sode.

Suruga kite

Cover: paper.
Frame: split bamboo.
Bridle: four-leg.
Tailless.
Wind: light to moderate.

The Suruga kite derives its name from being first flown from the tower of Suruga Castle as a victory signal some four hundred years ago.

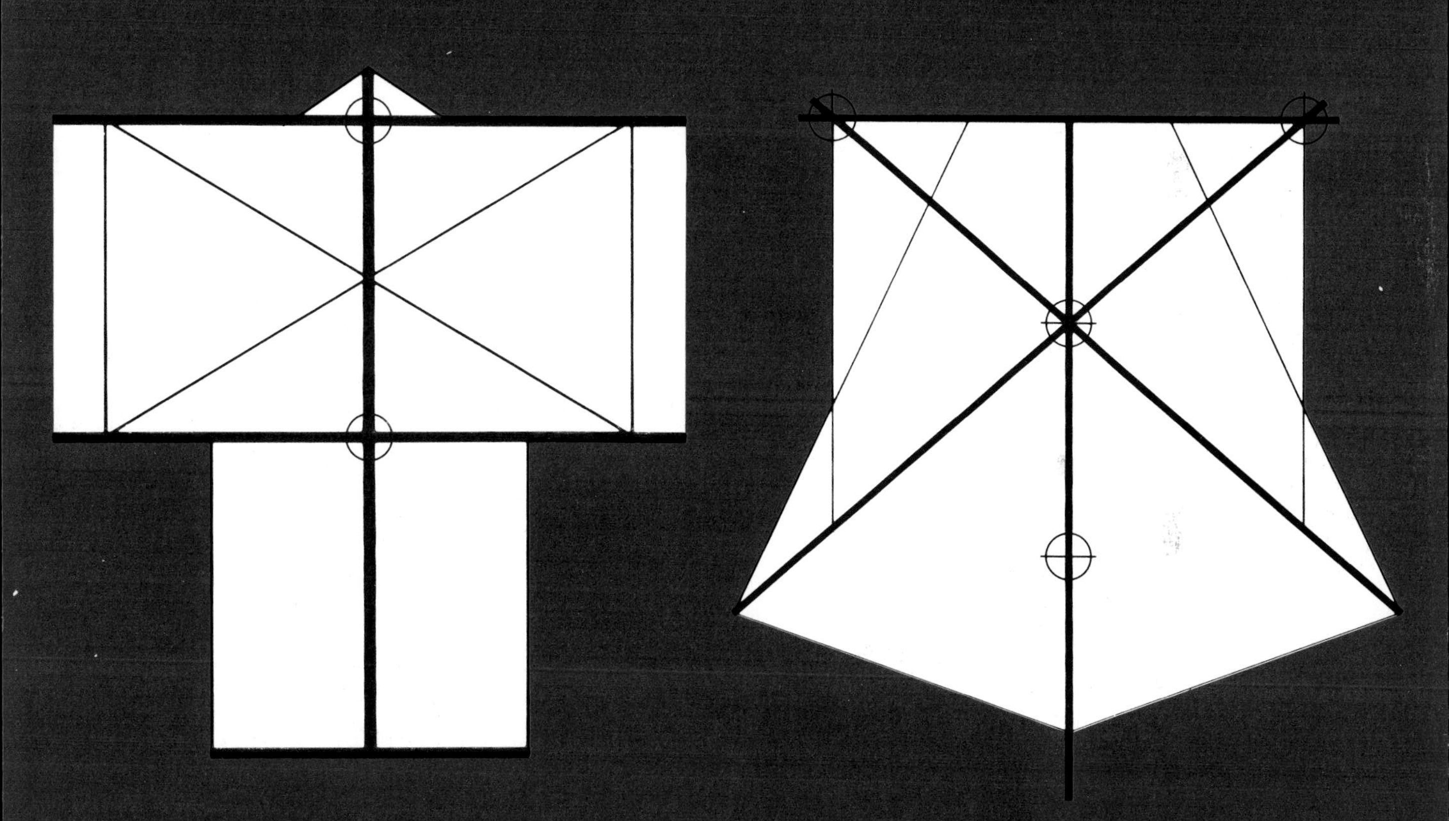

0 5 10 15 20 25 30 35 40 45 50 55 60

0 5 10 15 20 25 30 35 40 45 50 55 60 65 70 75 80 85 90

Chinese Hawk

Cover: paper or silk.
Frame: split bamboo.
Bridle: three-leg.
Tail: twin paper streamers.
Wind: light to moderate.

When made in silk, the framing lines of the Hawk are dispensed with in order that the trailing edges of the wings and the tail may flutter in the breeze.

Double Butterfly

Cover: paper.
Frame: split bamboo or rattan.
Bridle: two-leg.
Tail: paper streamers.
Wind: light to moderate.

Chinese Butterfly

Taiwan Butterfly

Cover: paper.
Frame: split bamboo.
Bridle: two-leg.
Tail: twin paper streamers.
Wind: light to gentle.

The spine, and all spars of the Taiwan Butterfly are pasted to the back cover of the kite. Spars are not lashed to the spine. As with the Chinese Butterfly (left), wing edges are supported with cord, though the Taiwan version also has cord supporting the spars within the area of the cover. This is pasted to the back of the cover with paper patches.

Nagasaki Hata

Cover: paper.
Frame: split bamboo.
Bridle: traditionally flown from an extremely long bridle approximately 2 m (say 6½ ft) in overall length.
Tailless.
Wind: gentle to moderate.

The fighting kite is an ultimate in kite design. A well-made fighter should be light, strong, highly balanced and perfectly symmetrical. The bow of the fighter is finely tapered towards its extremities and, when flexed between the hands, should fall into an even and resilient arc, if maximum response to line control is to be obtained. In skilled hands the fighting kite is exceptionally manoeuvrable, responding swiftly to even finger-tip control.

Indian Fighter

Cover: tissue paper.
Frame: split bamboo.
Bridle: two-leg.
Tail: small fin supported by two fine strips of split bamboo.
Wind: light to moderate.

When not held into the wind on a taut line, the fighting kite has no stability. Since it is flat and tailless, it relies upon the wind to give it a natural dihedral as its wing-tips are forced back by the pressure of the wind. The greater the pressure upon the surface the greater the dihedral angle becomes, thus always ensuring optimum stability. This characteristic is the secret of the Fighter's manoeuvrability and speed.

0 5 10 15 20 25 30 35 40 45 50 55 60 65 70

0 5 10 15 20 25 30 35 40 45 50 55 60 65 70

Thai Chula

Cover: paper.
Frame: bamboo.
Bridle: two-leg.
Tailless.
Wind: gentle to moderate.

Never an easy kite to launch, in light winds the fighter has to be given a high-start launch, the line being taken in as it rises, in order to maintain its dihedral in climbing. Once it has reached lively air it will remain stable so long as the flying line is kept taut. The moment the kite is given line the pressure against its surface diminishes, causing the kite to return to its normal flat surface, so losing its dihedral, and consequently its stability. The kite will begin to drop, making a series of lateral turns as it does so. When it is facing the required direction, gently take in line until the kite's dihedral again takes effect, and the kite will continue in that direction as long as its flying line remains taut.

0 5 10 15 20 25 30 35 40 45 50 55 60 65 70 75 80 85 90

Thai Pakpao

Cover: paper.
Frame: split bamboo.
Bridle: two-leg.
Tailless.

Although the rules of kite fighting vary throughout the east, in the main the objective is to cut free an opponent's kite by severing its flying line. For some distance below the bridle the line is rolled in, or drawn through, a preparation of adhesive and powdered glass or porcelain. Sawing this against a rival's line quickly results in a break, and the unfettered kite becomes the property of the victor.

0 5 10 15 20 25 30 35 40 45 50

Korean Fighter

Cover: paper.
Frame: split bamboo.
Bridle: three-leg.
Tailless.
Wind: gentle to fresh.

The classic Korean fighting kite has two horizontal spars only. The sides and trailing edge are supported by cord only, as is the central vent. Both spars are bowed; and this, together with the vent and the kite's characteristic 'ears' give remarkable stability even in strong winds.

0 5 10 15 20 25 30 35 40 45 50 55 60 65 70 75 80 85

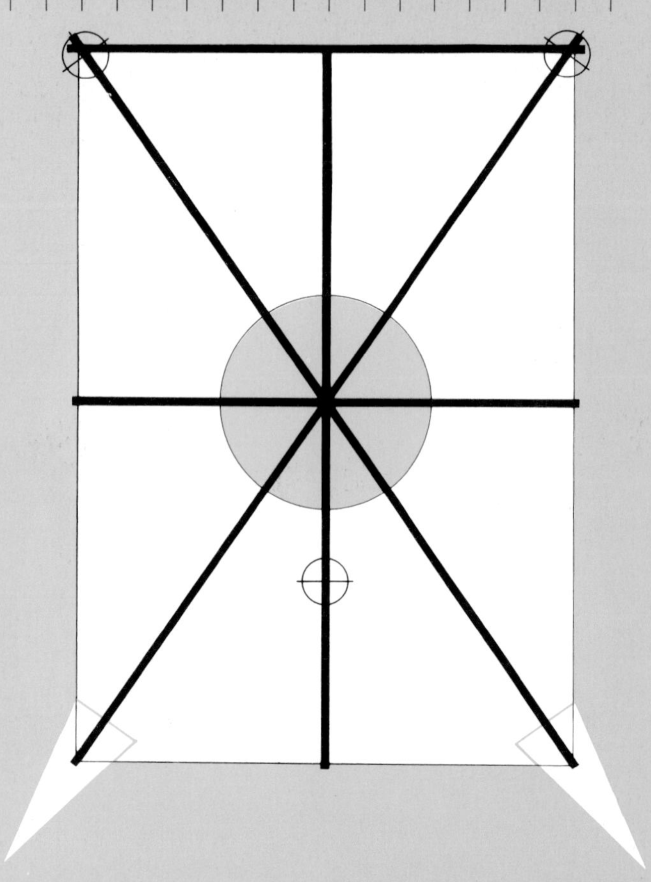

True Malay

Cover: silk.
Frame: bamboo.
Bridle: three-leg.
Tailless.
Wind: light to moderate.

Various forms of this classic kite have been flown throughout Malaysia and Indonesia for many centuries. Its close cousin the Javanese bow kite formed the basis of William A. Eddy's invention.

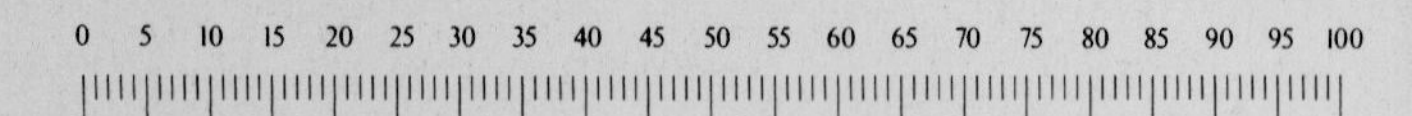

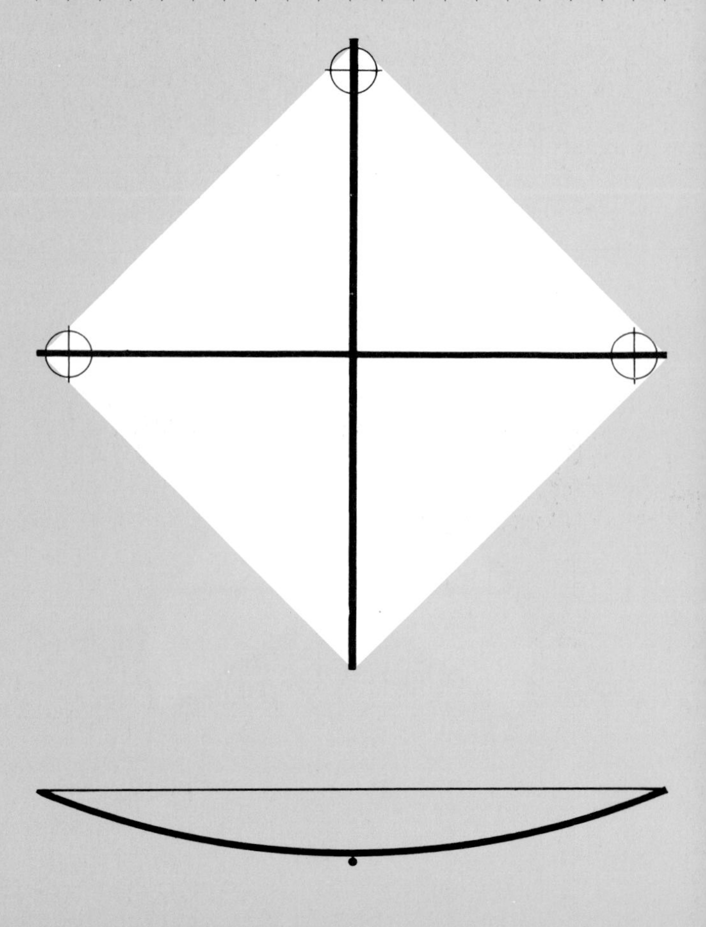

Sanjo Rokkaku

Cover: paper.
Frame: bamboo.
Bridle: four-leg.
Tailless.
Wind: gentle to moderate.

The face of the hexagonal Sanjo Rokkaku traditionally bears magnificent portraits of Japan's warrior heroes, though modern versions often carry advertising slogans. The spars should be fine enough to flex with the pressure of the wind.

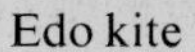

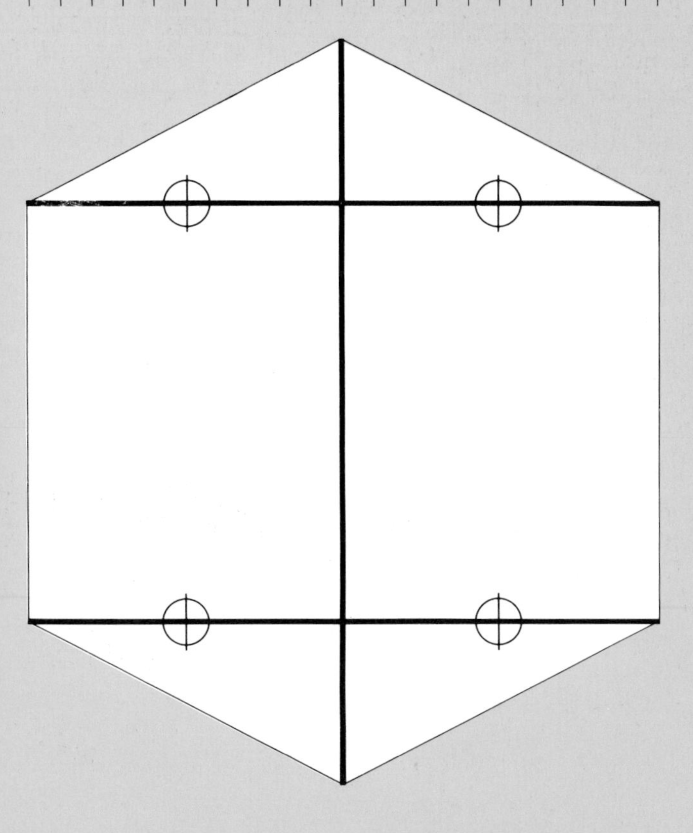

Edo kite

Cover: paper.
Frame: bamboo.
Bridle: multiple variants.
Tailless.
Wind: moderate to fresh.

The finest of all Japanese kites, the Edo kite develops tremendous lift; and in its larger versions is handled by well-drilled teams of flyers. It is flown with all spars bowed, and its sides supported with cord only. The sequence of laying the frame is: longerons first (supporting the face of the kite), then come the spars, and finally the diagonals.

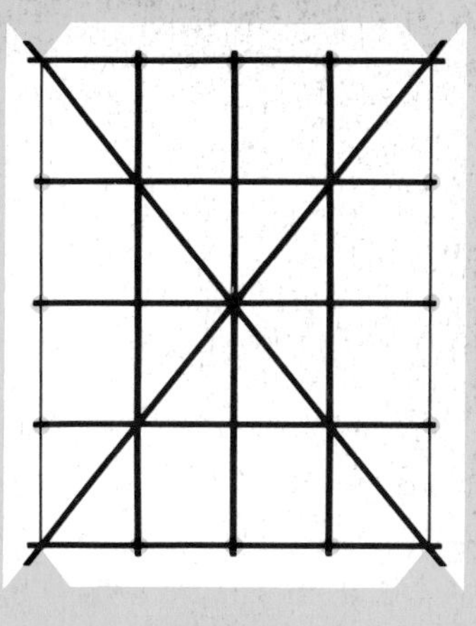

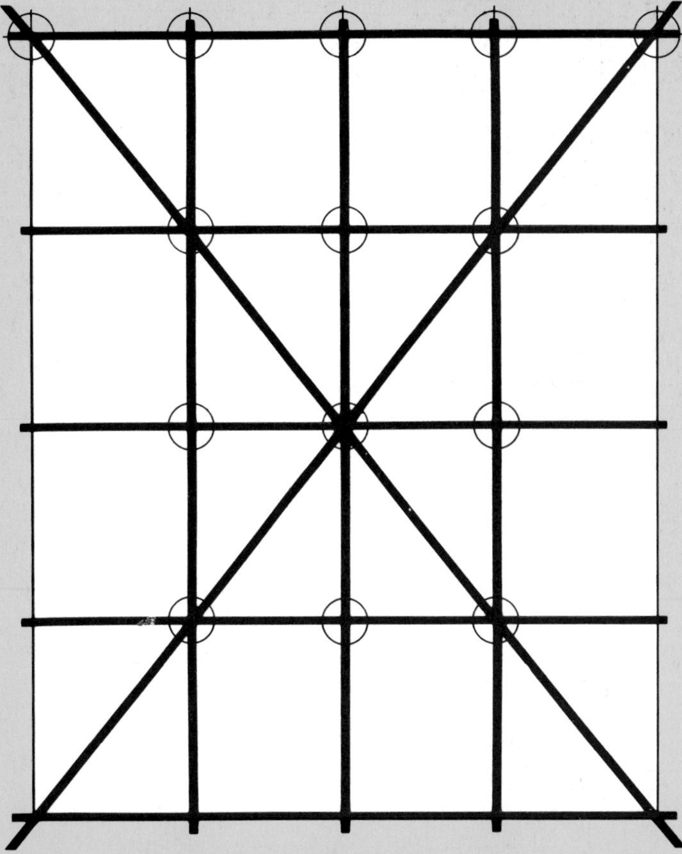

Star kite, five-point

Cover: paper.
Frame: bamboo.
Bridle: three-leg.
Tail: twin paper streamers.
Wind: light to moderate.

The framing lines running from the 'hands' and 'feet' of the star should be firmly secured at the points at which they cross the legs, or longerons. Framing lines that fall within the configuration must be secured to the back of the kite cover with paper patches.

Star kite, six-point

Cover: paper.
Frame: bamboo.
Bridle: two-leg.
Tail: single or triple streamers.
Wind: light to moderate.

0 5 10 15 20 25 30 35 40 45 50 55 60 65 70 75 80 85 90 95 100

0 5 10 15 20 25 30 35 40 45 50 55 60 65 70 75 80 85

Bermudan Octagon

Cover: tissue paper panels.
Frame: split bamboo.
Bridle: three-leg.
Tail: long single streamer.
Wind: light to moderate.

As with the Bermudan Three-stick, highly decorated versions of this kite are popular. Two or three of the spars are often extended and spanned with line. From these lines highly coloured paper streamers, fringes, flags and buzzers are flown, which, together with the traditionally long tail, can result in spectacular effects.
The basic double or single head-stick variations of the Bermudan kite allow for the attachment of paper buzzers or flags.

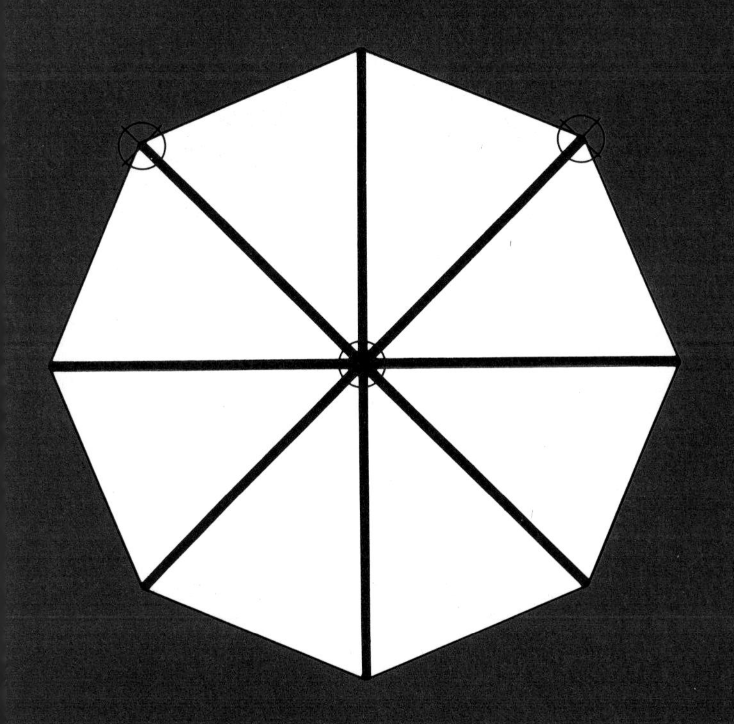

0 5 10 15 20 25 30 35 40 45 50 55 60 65 70

Bermudan Three-stick

Cover: tissue paper panels.
Frame: split bamboo.
Bridle: three-leg.
Tail: long single streamer.
Wind: light to moderate.

0 5 10 15 20 25 30 35 40 45 50 55 60

Batut camera kite

Cover: paper or cambric.
Frame: bamboo.
Bridle: compounded two-leg.
Tail: paper bows.
Wind: moderate.

This is a half-scale version of M.A. Batut's camera lifter, from which aerial photographs were successfully taken at Labruguière, France, during the last years of the nineteenth century.

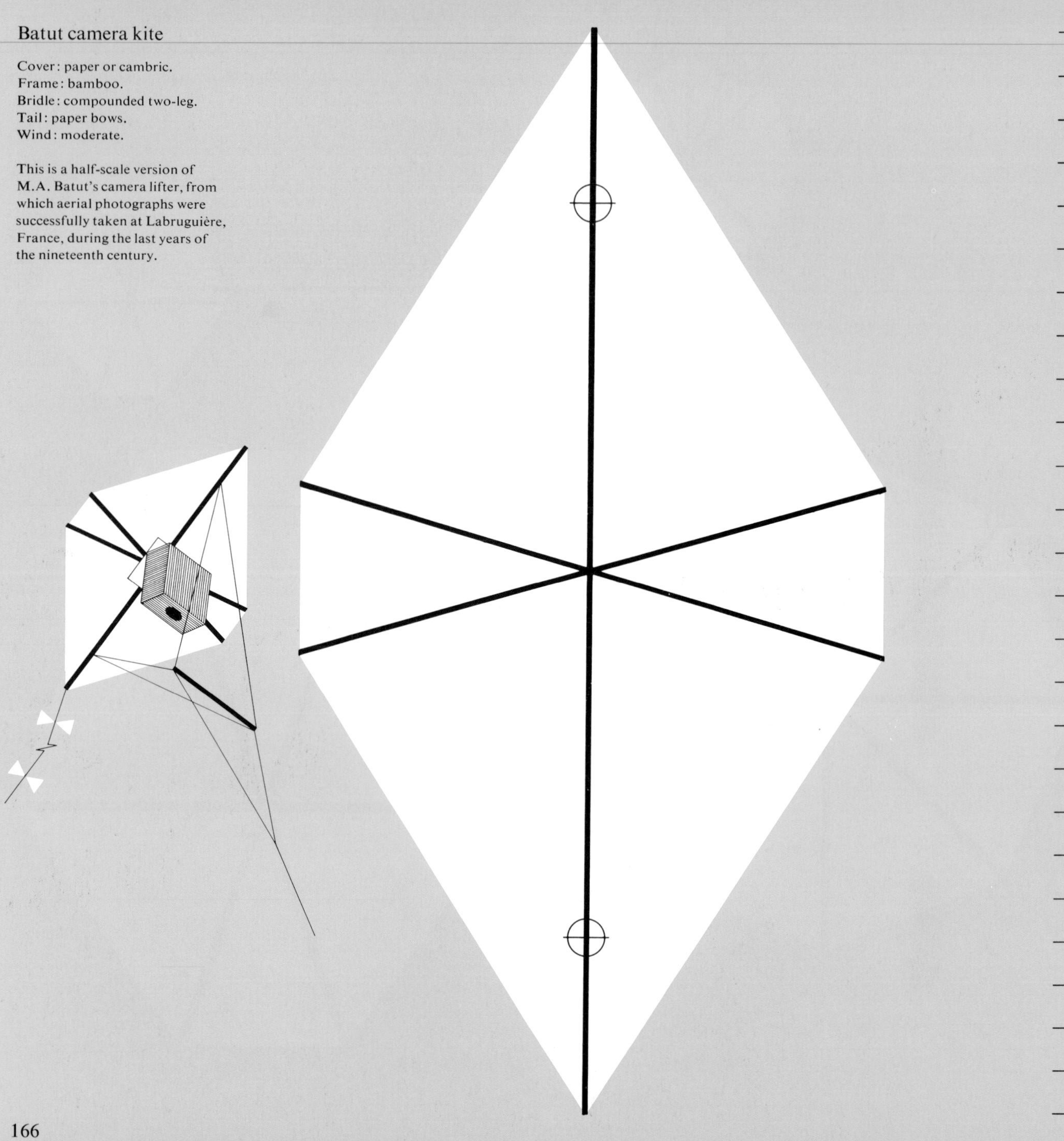

Barn-door kite

Cover: paper or fabric.
Frame: dowel.
Bridle: five-leg.
Tail: paper bows.
Wind: light to moderate.

Otherwise known as the American Three-stick, in its larger forms the spar is positioned slightly above or below the intersection of the diagonals, in order to give greater rigidity to the structure. The Barn-door kite is sometimes flown with a bowed spar for additional stability in fresh winds.

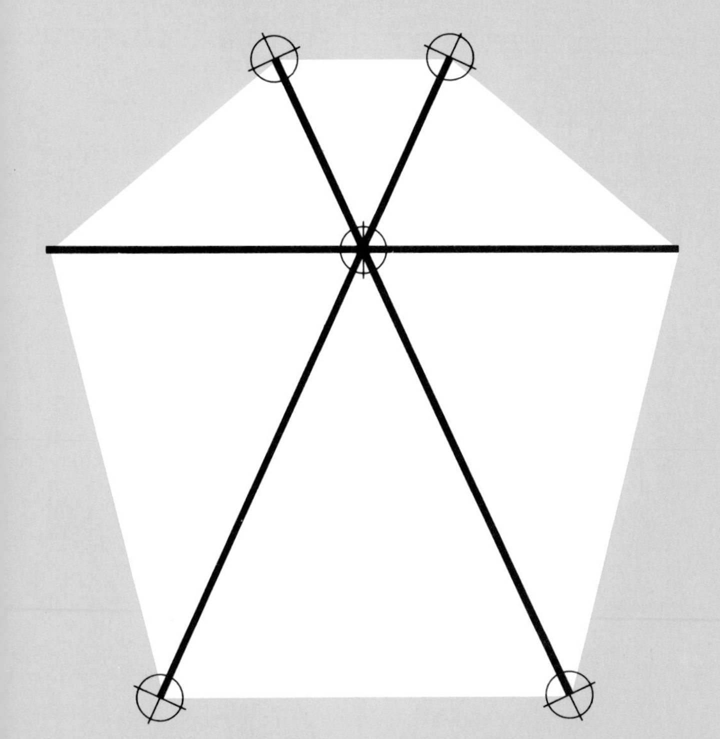

0 5 10 15 20 25 30 35 40 45 50 55 60 65 70 75 80 85 90

Hexagonal Three-stick

Cover: paper or fabric.
Frame: split bamboo.
Bridle: three-leg.
Tail: paper streamers or bows.
Wind: light to moderate.

A classic Chinese form, the Hexagonal may be flown flat – with a tail – or, if all sticks are bowed, tailless in light winds. For best results the length of the two forward bridle legs should be equal in length to the sides of the six equilateral triangles within the kite; and the rear leg four fifths of that length. The length of the tail towing lines should also be equal to the sides of the triangles.

0 5 10 15 20 25 30 35 40 45 50 55 60 65 70 75 80 85 90 95 100

English arch top

Cover: paper.
Frame: bamboo or dowel.
Bridle: two-leg.
Tail: paper bows.
Wind: light to moderate.

French pear top

Cover: paper.
Frame: bamboo or dowel.
Bridle: two-leg.
Tail: paper bows.
Wind: light to moderate.

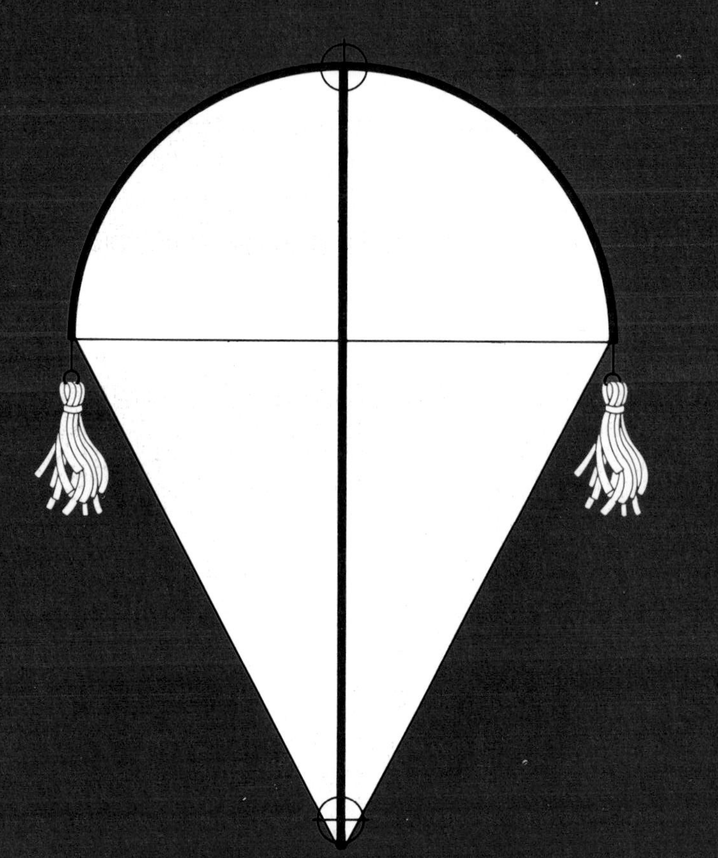

0 5 10 15 20 25 30 35 40 45 50 55 60 65 70 75 80

0 5 10 15 20 25 30 35 40 45 50 55 60 65 70 75 80

French pear top variant

Cover: paper.
Frame: dowel and split bamboo.
Bridle: two-leg.
Tail: paper bows.
Wind: light to moderate.

Eddy bow kite

Cover: cotton cambric.
Frame: rectangular section hardwood.
Bridle: two-leg.
Tailless.
Wind: light to moderate.

A high-water mark in western kite design, Eddy specified a cover wider along the line of the spar than the spar itself, resulting in a loose cover designed to divide into twin concaves either side of the spine. Although famous for its bowed spar, Eddy's specification stated no more than that the spar should be . . . 'preferably slightly curved'. It is an excellent kite for thermal soaring.

For a quick and secure means of adjusting the bow angle, the bow line – or guy – is fitted with a sliding guy adjustor or runner.

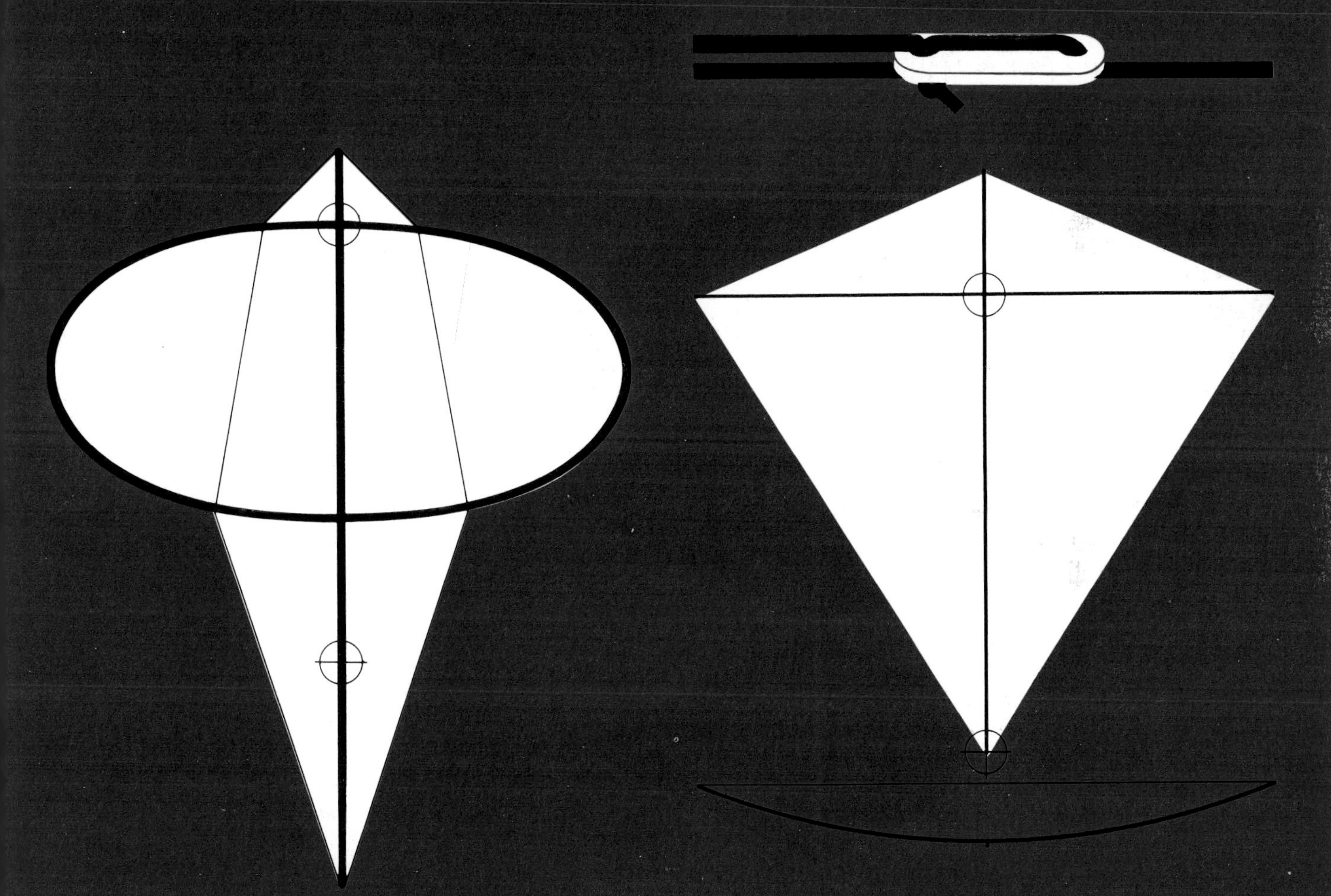

Double lozenge kite

Cover: paper or fabric.
Frame: dowel.
Bridle: two-leg.
Tail: paper bows.
Wind: light to moderate.

The tailless variant of the Double Lozenge has a stabilizing rudder dissecting the tail plane, and is flown with its wings either bowed or set at a dihedral angle.

Lozenge kite

Cover: paper.
Frame: dowel.
Bridle: two-leg.
Tail: paper bows.
Wind: light to moderate.

This is the basic European plane-surface kite illustrated in John Bate's *The Mysteryes of Nature and Art*.

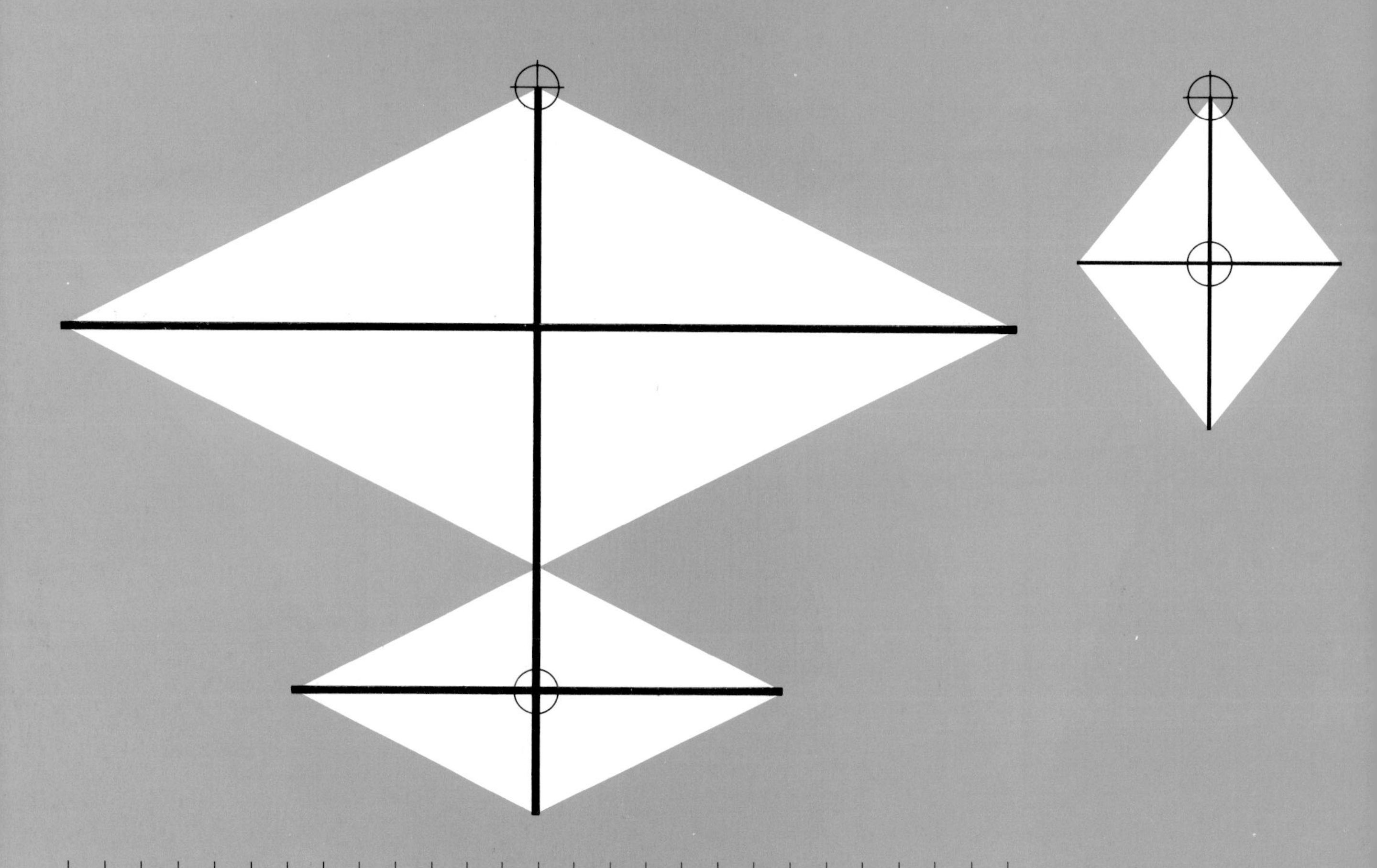

della Porta's kite

Cover: paper or silk.
Frame: dowel.
Bridle: three-leg.
Tail: twin streamers or ladder.
Wind: gentle to fresh.

The della Porta is a finely proportioned classic that develops considerable lift in fresh winds. A tail length of between three and four times the length of the diagonal is recommended.

Malay (variant)

Cover: nylon.
Frame: dowel.
Bridle: two-leg.
Tailless.
Wind: light to moderate.

Flown bowed, this is an excellent light-wind kite and thermal soarer. The proportions shown are based upon those favoured by the late Vasco van Blommestein, known to countless English kite flyers as 'Mr Van', who made and flew kites on London's Parliament Hill for over sixty years.

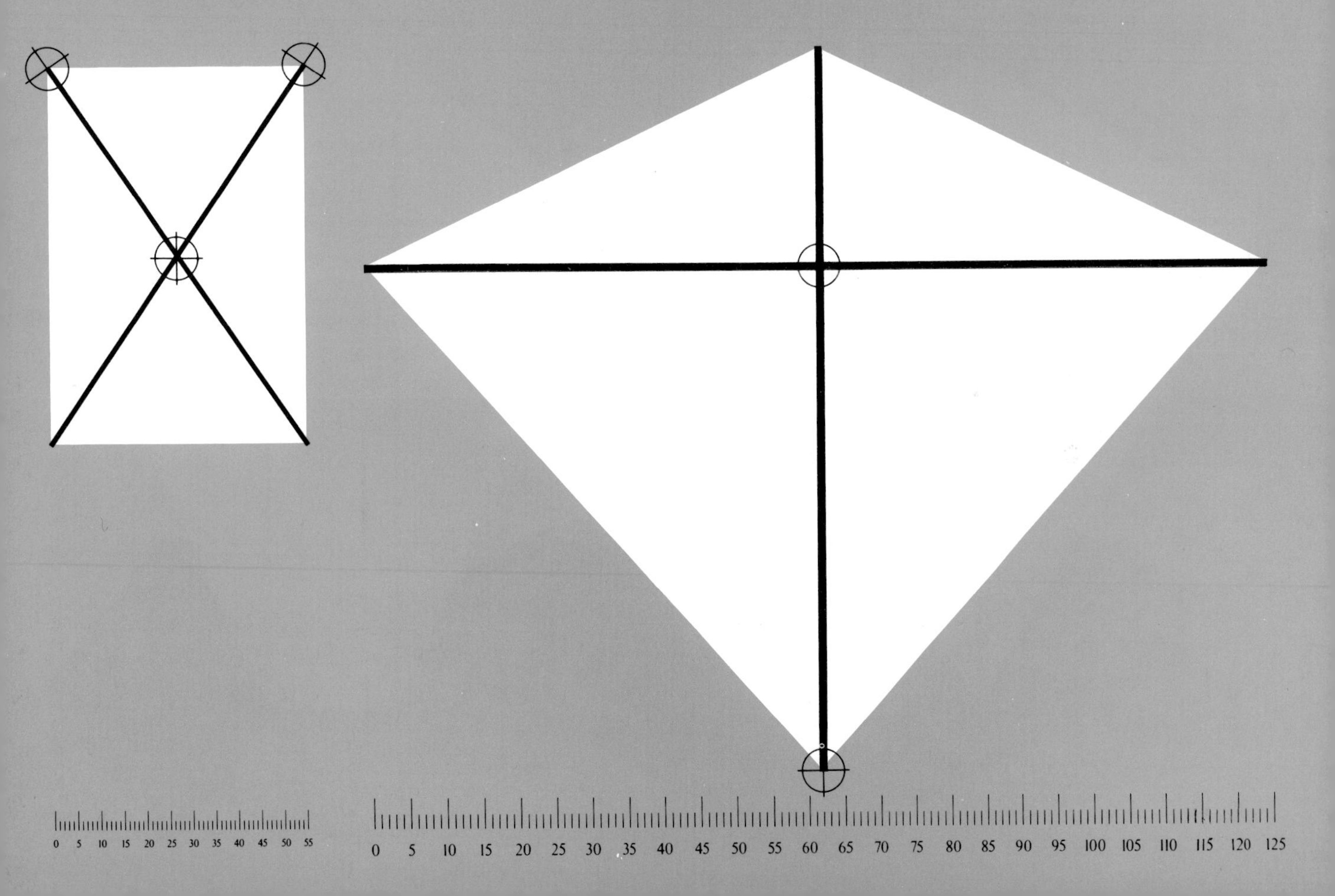

Classic Diamond

Cover: paper or fabric.
Frame: dowel.
Bridle: two-leg.
Tail: paper bows.
Wind: light to moderate.

H-form Three-stick

Cover: paper or fabric.
Frame: dowel.
Bridle: four-leg.
Tail: paper bows.
Wind: light to moderate.

The H-form is capable of being flown bowed and tailless in light winds; though if a single tail is used, tail towing lines should run as an extension of the trailing edges of the wings, i.e., a triangle should be formed by the wing tips and the point of convergence of the tail towing lines.

0 5 10 15 20 25 30 35 40 45 50 55 60 65 70 75 80 85 90 95 100 105 110 115 120 125 130 135 140 145 150 155 160 165 170 175 180 185 190

A-form Three-stick

Cover: paper or fabric.
Frame: dowel.
Bridle: three-leg.
Tail: paper bows.
Wind: light to moderate.

This kite may also be flown bowed and tailless in light winds. Again, if tail towing lines are used, the tail fastening should occur at the point of convergence of the trailing edges of the wings.

V-form Three-stick

Cover: paper or fabric.
Frame: dowel.
Bridle: three-leg.
Tail: paper bows.
Wind: light to moderate.

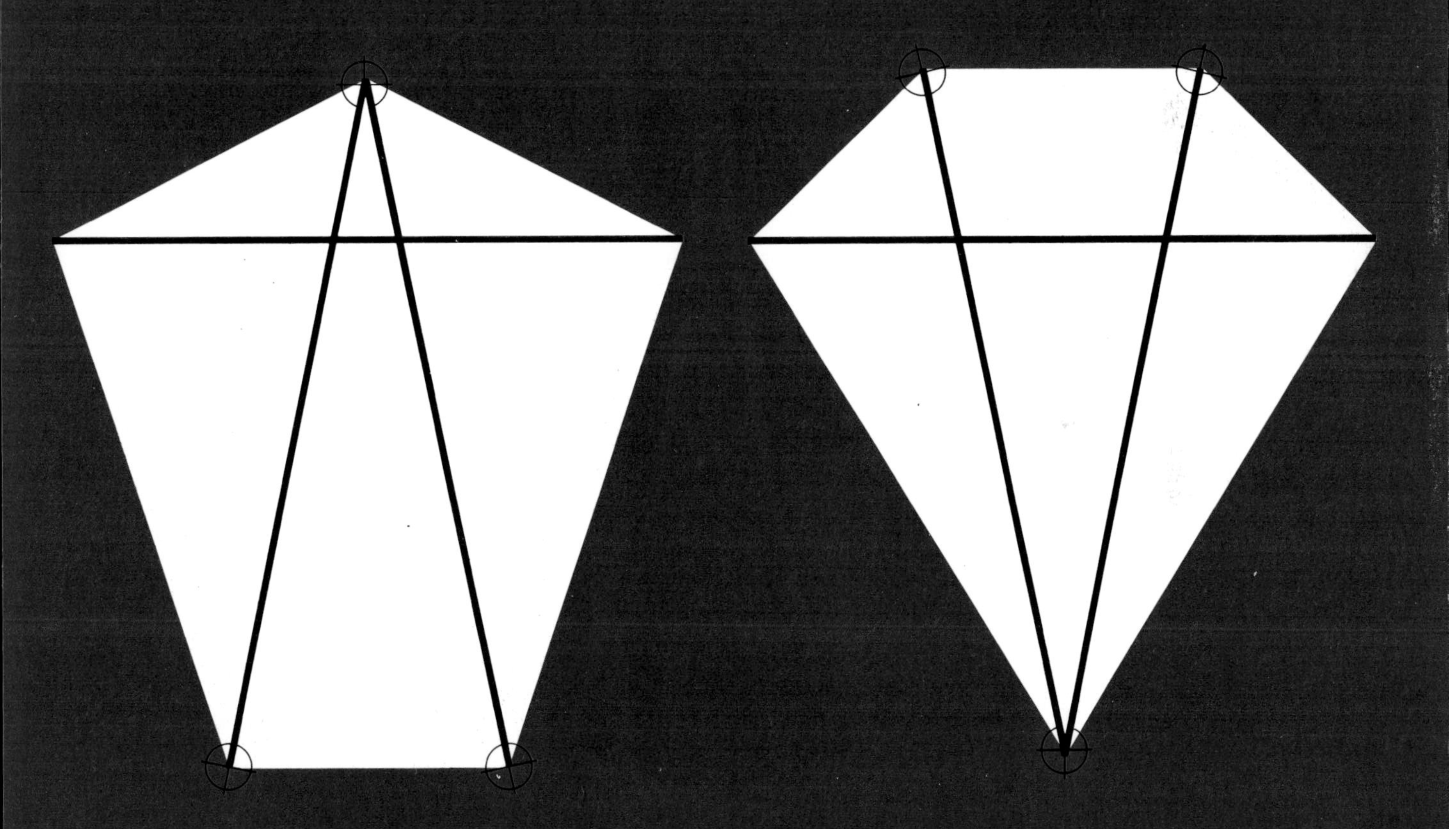

0 5 10 15 20 25 30 35 40 45 50 55 60 65 70 75 80 85 90 95 100 105 110 115 120 125 130 135 140 145 150 155 160 165 170 175 180 185 190

Brazilian Bird

Cover: silk or cotton.
Frame: dowel.
Bridle: four-leg.
Tailless with dihedral spar.
Wind: moderate to fresh.

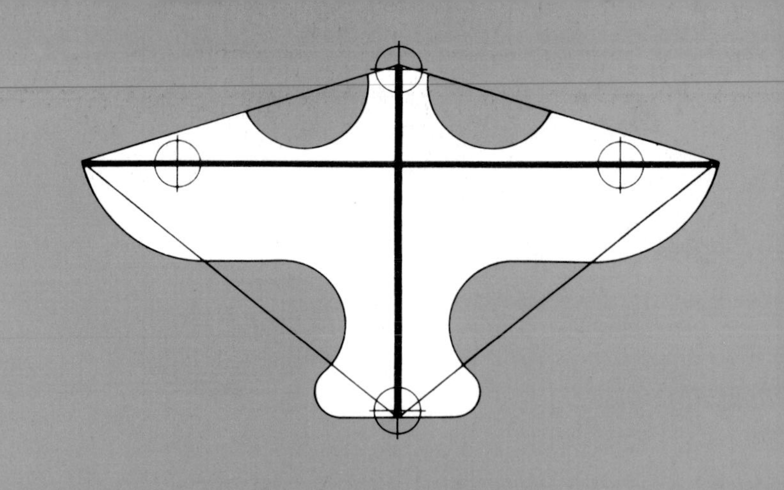

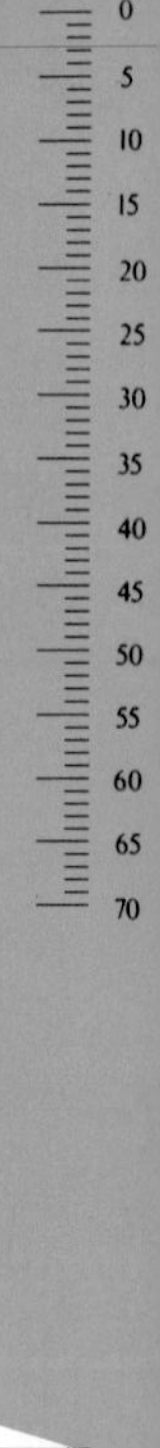

Double-spined Bird

Cover: silk or cotton.
Frame: dowel.
Bridle: six-leg.
Tailless with dihedral spar.
Wind: moderate to fresh.

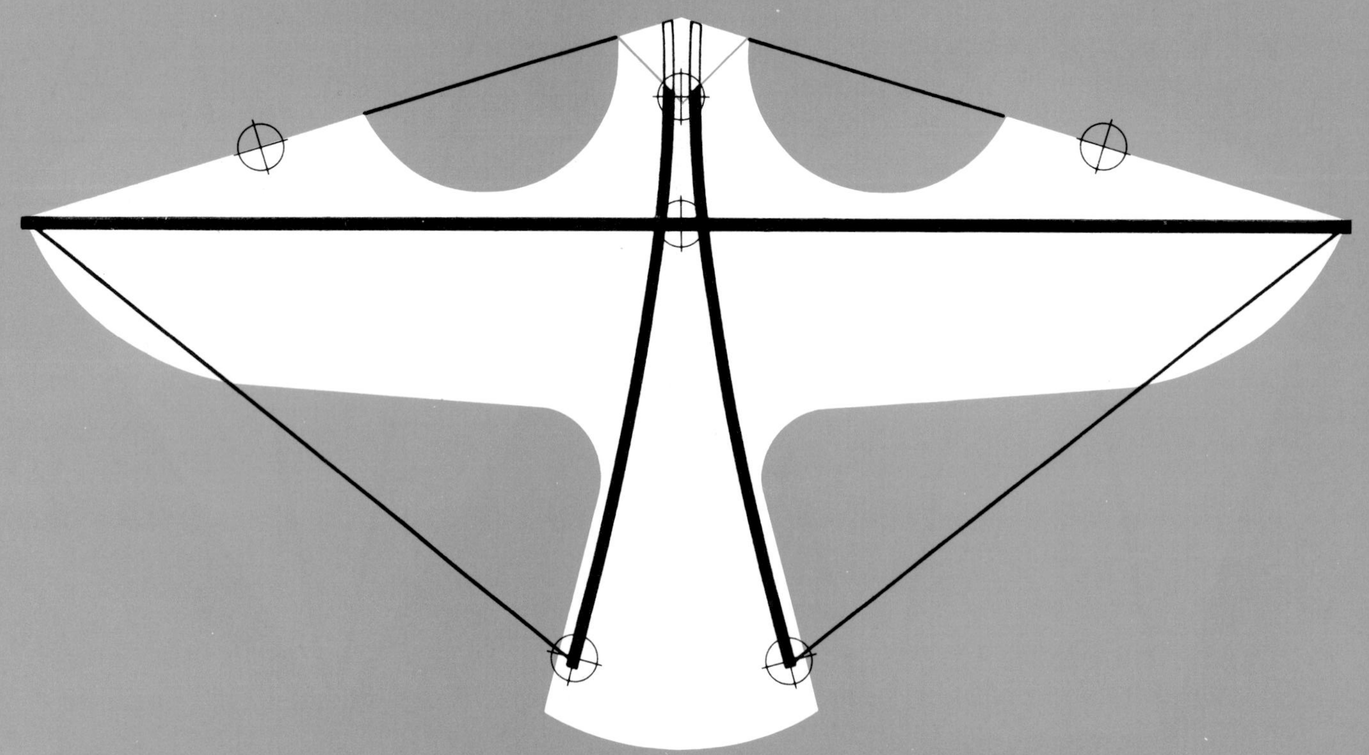

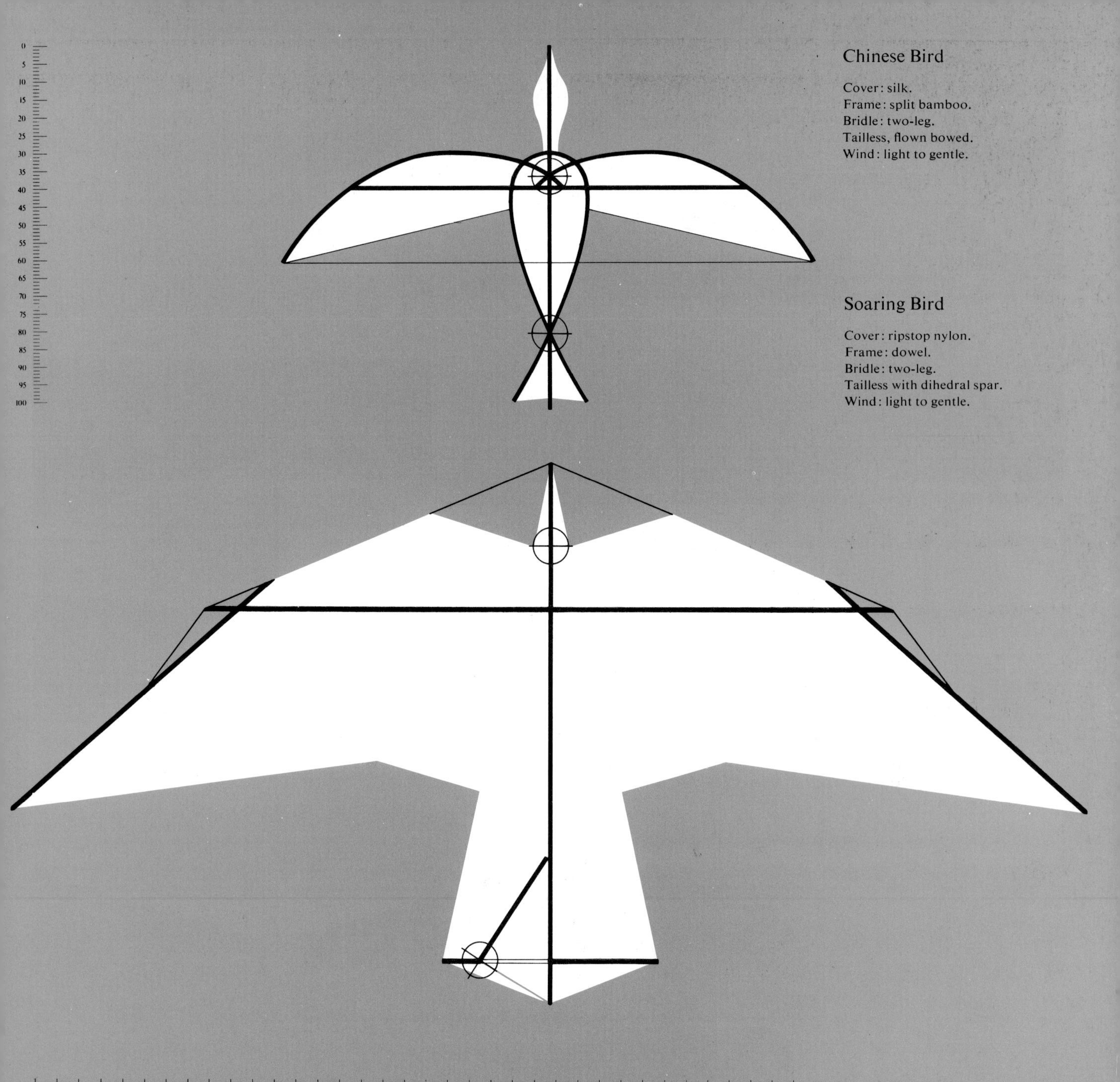

Chinese Bird

Cover: silk.
Frame: split bamboo.
Bridle: two-leg.
Tailless, flown bowed.
Wind: light to gentle.

Soaring Bird

Cover: ripstop nylon.
Frame: dowel.
Bridle: two-leg.
Tailless with dihedral spar.
Wind: light to gentle.

Baden-Powell's Levitor kite

Cover: cotton or linen cambric.
Frame: bamboo.
Bridle: four-leg.
Tail: see below.
Wind: moderate to strong.

Baden-Powell patented two versions of his Levitor kite in 1896, one rectangular, the other hexagonal. Although he specified that 'such a form of kite requires no such appendage as a tail', the four-legged bridle's tendency to hold the spars flat to the wind causes the Levitor to behave somewhat erratically, unless flown with some form of stabilizing system.

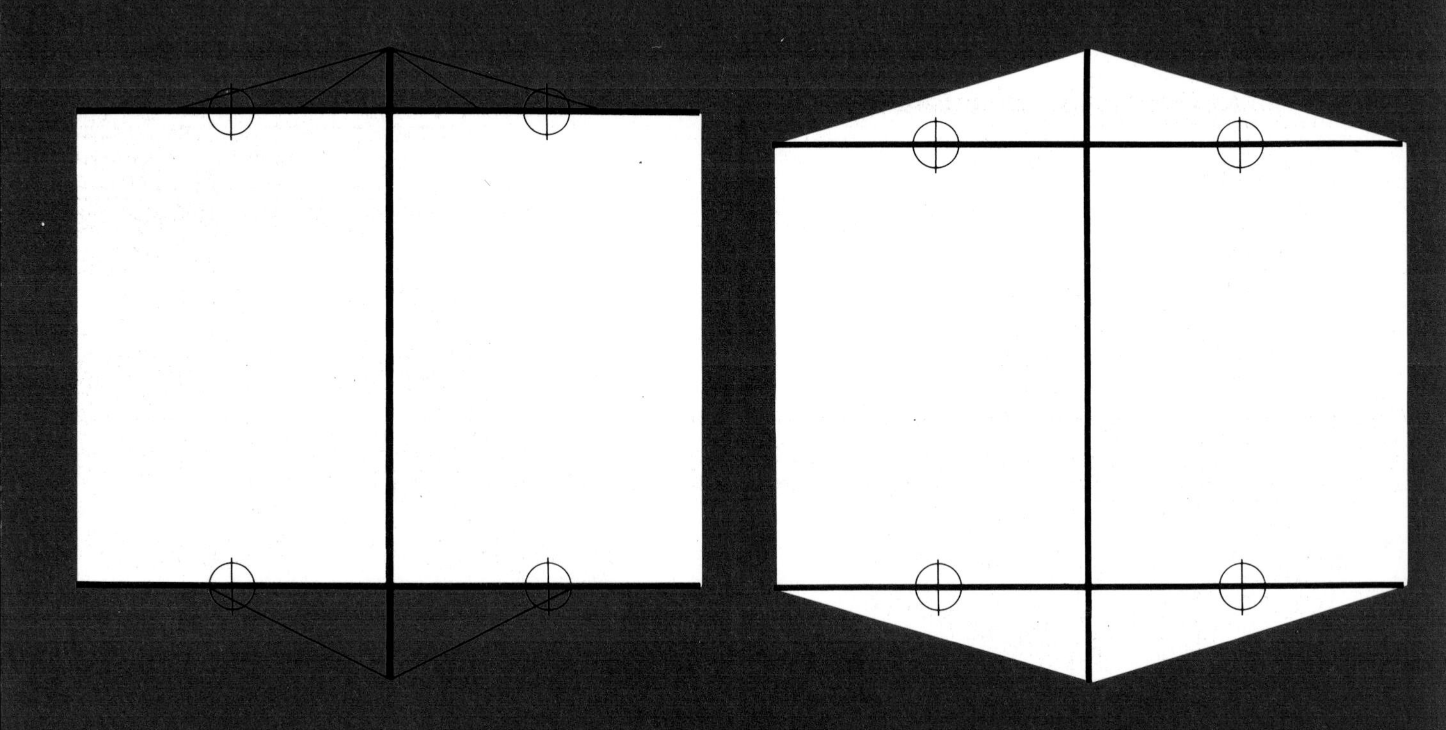

Keeled Diamond

Cover: paper, plastic or fabric
Frame: dowel
Bridle: keel or two-leg
Tailless, flown bowed
Wind: light to moderate

The two standard versions of the keeled kite are shown. The ventral keel is attached to the face, while the dorsal keel is secured to the back of the kite. When fitted dorsally, the keel requires a short mast protruding from the intersection of the spine and spar. This mast is held in position by a three-way joint at its base – see page 202 – and the bowing guys at its tip.

Hargrave's box kite

Cover: calico.
Frame: hickory or spruce.
Bridle: direct attachment.
Tailless.
Wind: fresh to strong.

Although originally covered in calico, a more modern material such as heavy gauge Tyvek makes an excellent alternative. This is certainly not a kite to be taken lightly, as in its full scale version the degree of lift that it develops in a fresh wind is frightening.

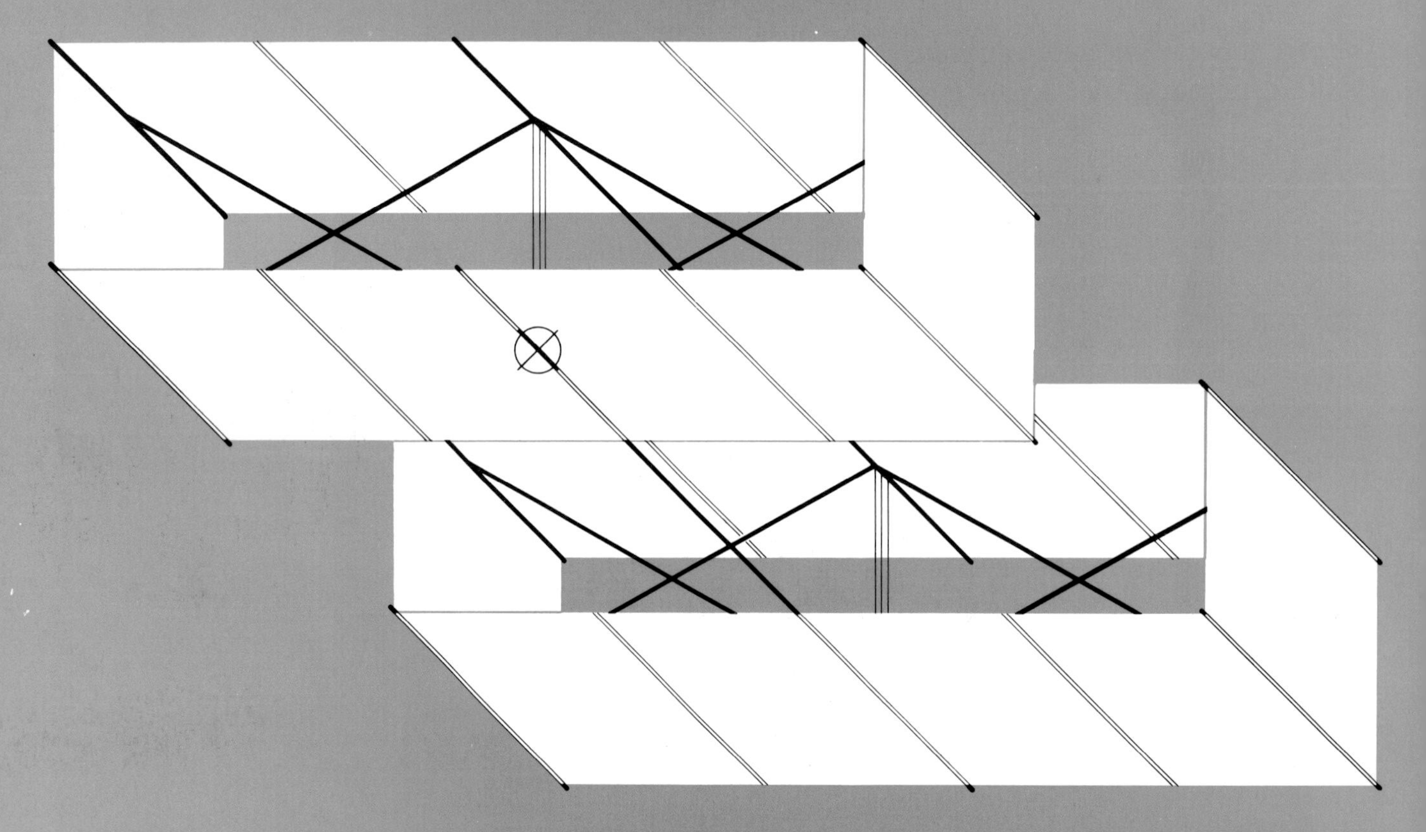

0 5 10 15 20 25 30 35 40 45 50 55 60 65 70 75 80 85 90 95 100 105 110 115 120 125 130 135 140 145 150 155 160

Blue Hill meteorological box kite

Cover: linen or cotton cambric.
Frame: hickory dowel or strip.
Bridle: direct attachment.
Wind: fresh to strong.

This is not an easy kite to make, as before frame assembly can begin a quantity of joint-holders have to be cut from metal sheet. Brass or copper was originally used. The nut and bolt which secures the joint-holder to the frame is also used as a shackle point for the bracing lines. Each cell should be diagonally braced as indicated, and fore-to-aft diagonal bracing (not shown) is also necessary. The cover is loop-stitched onto the frame, and its edges are laced together at the top centre of each cell.

Three-way joint-holder plate.

Joint-holder in position.

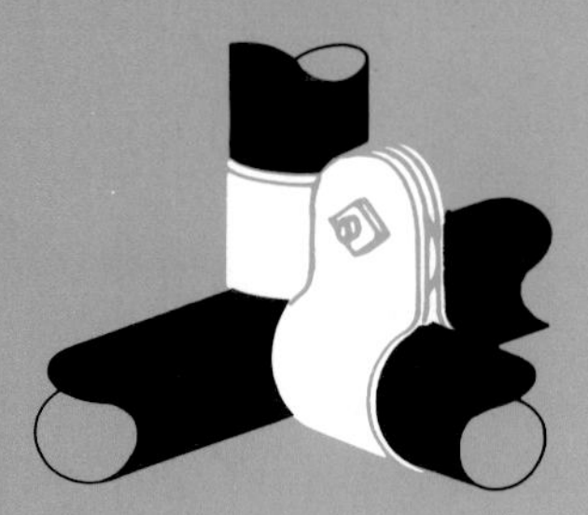

0 5 10 15 20 25 30 35 40 45 50 55 60 65 70 75 80 85 90 95 100 105 110 115 120 125 130 135

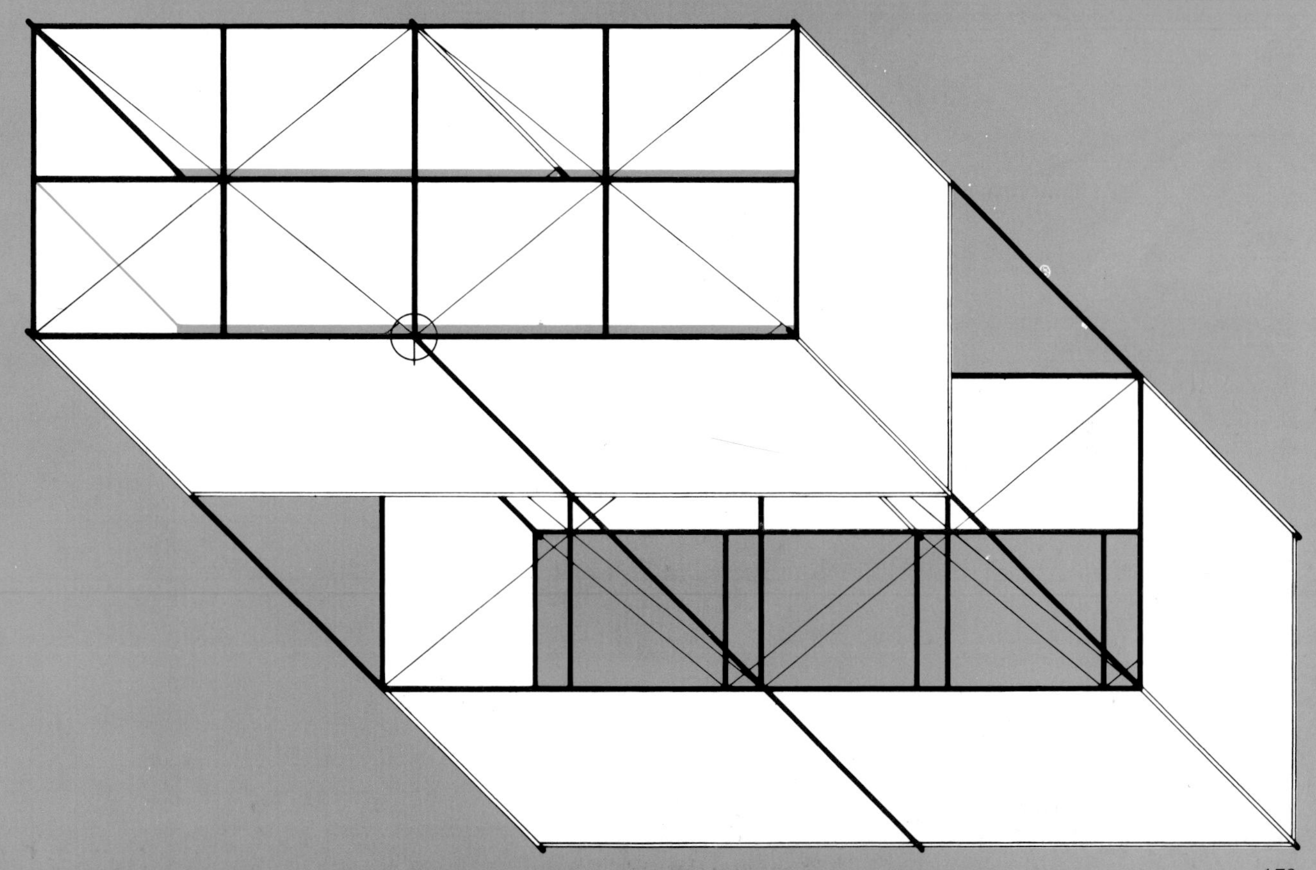

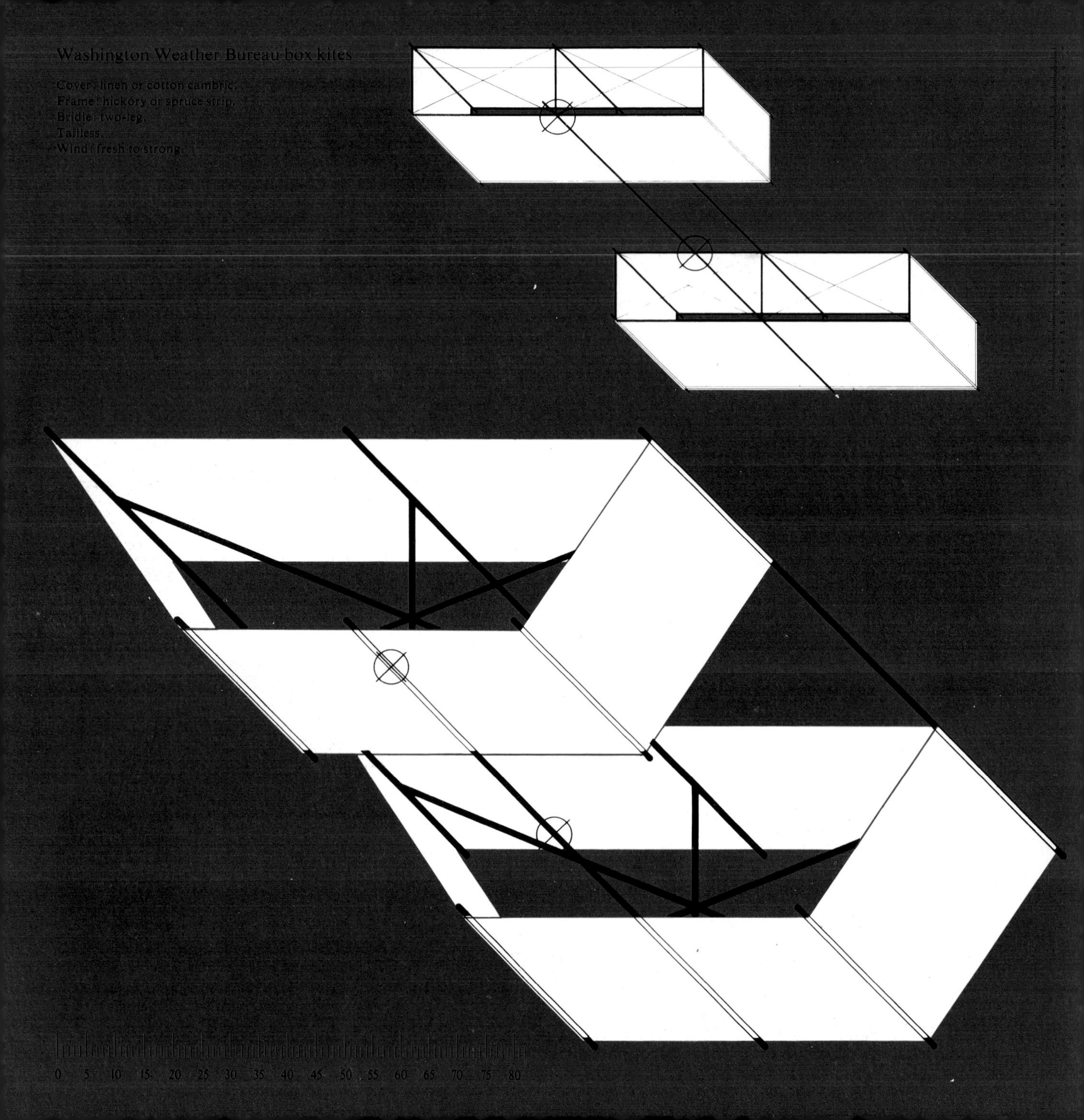
Washington Weather Bureau box kites
Cover: linen or cotton cambric.
Frame: hickory or spruce strip.
Bridle: two-leg.
Tailless.
Wind: fresh to strong.
0 5 10 15 20 25 30 35 40 45 50 55 60 65 70 75 80

Sauls' barrage kite

Cover: aircraft fabric.
Frame: spruce strip.
Bridle: five-leg.
Tailless.
Wind: fresh to strong.

When made to a reduced scale, the double set of wing bracers may be substituted for one set to each wing as in Hargrave's box kite. Each leg of the five-leg bridle is attached to the leading edge of the lower wing. The four outer legs are gathered to the central leg at a point one and a quarter times the length of the longerons.

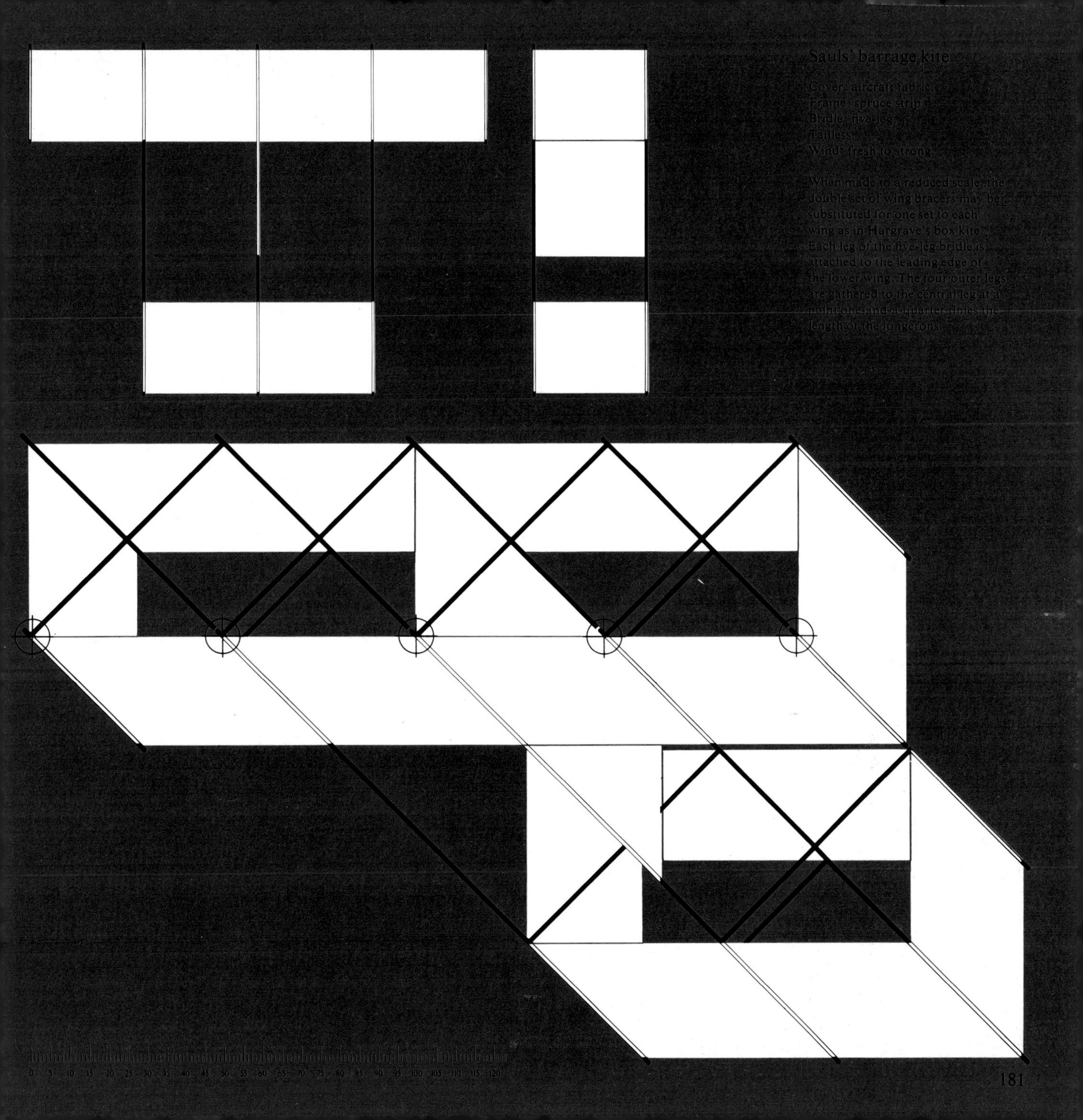

Dihedral-based box kite

Cover: ripstop nylon or Tyvek.
Frame: hardwood dowel or strip.
Bridle: two-leg.
Tailless.
Wind: moderate to fresh.

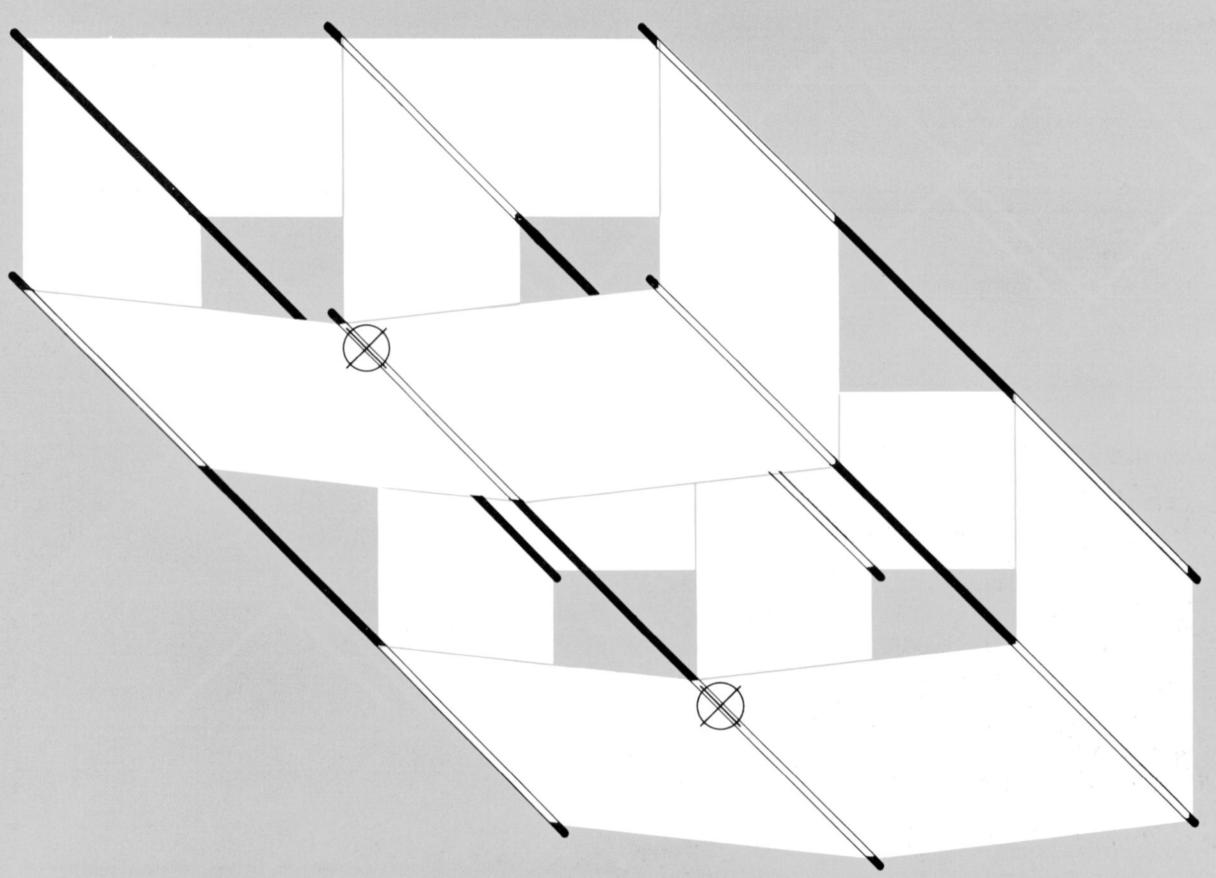

Four-winged box kite

Cover: ripstop nylon or Tyvek.
Frame: dowel.
Bridle: compound.
Tailless.
Wind: gentle to moderate.

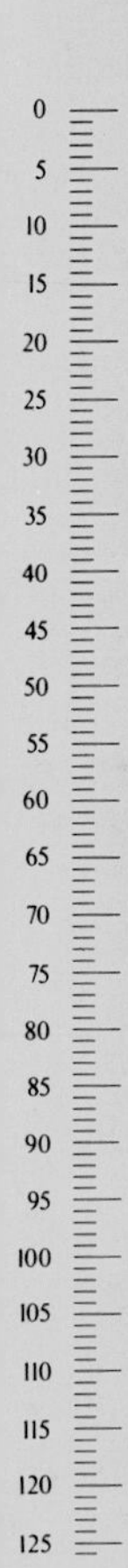

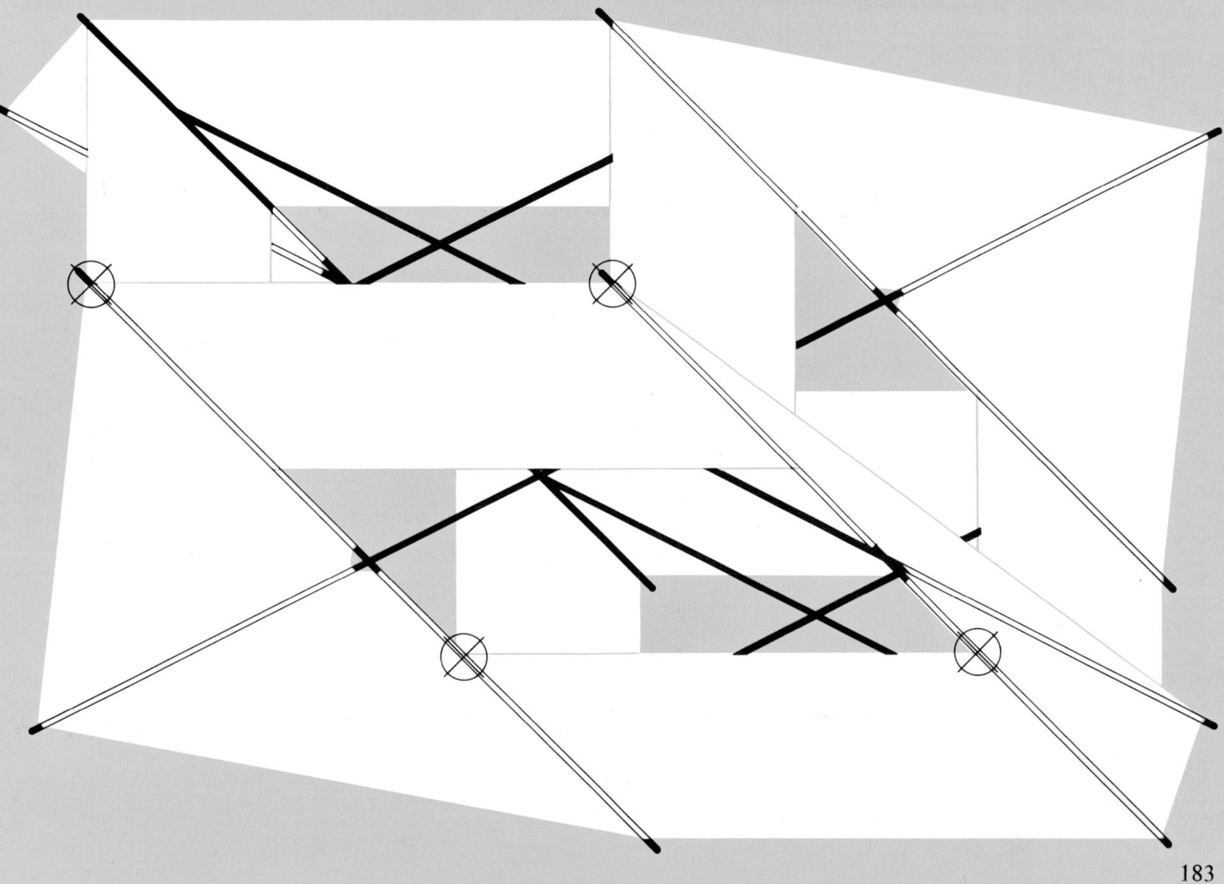

Cody's war kite

Cover: linen or cotton cambric.
Frame: hickory, bamboo or aluminium.
Bridle: compound.
Tail: flown drogued in high winds.
Wind: fresh to strong.

Cody usually worked in multiples of his favourite measurement, 6 ft. Consequently, the accompanying pattern, when measured in centimetres gives a span of 1.80 m (6 ft). This makes up a convenient scale-model of the original. However, in order to achieve a scale infinitely more acceptable to Cody, the units should be read off as representing inches; giving an overall width of 15 ft. At this span the width of the kite *body* measures 6 ft.

Cody appears to have had no strong feelings as to choice of cover material for his kites, suggesting silk, goldbeaters skin, and sheet aluminium amongst other choices. He considered tautness of the cover of prime importance, however, and achieved this in two ways. Firstly, by shaping all edges concavely – lending his kite the characteristic outline that earned it the nickname, 'The Bat' – he achieved extreme tautness at all edges. Secondly, by having the diagonal bracing struts protruding past the kite cover in all instances, it was possible for Cody to make correctional adjustments from all eight points of protrusion. Modifications in roll and pitch control could be made by adjusting the lengths of the wing-bracing lines.

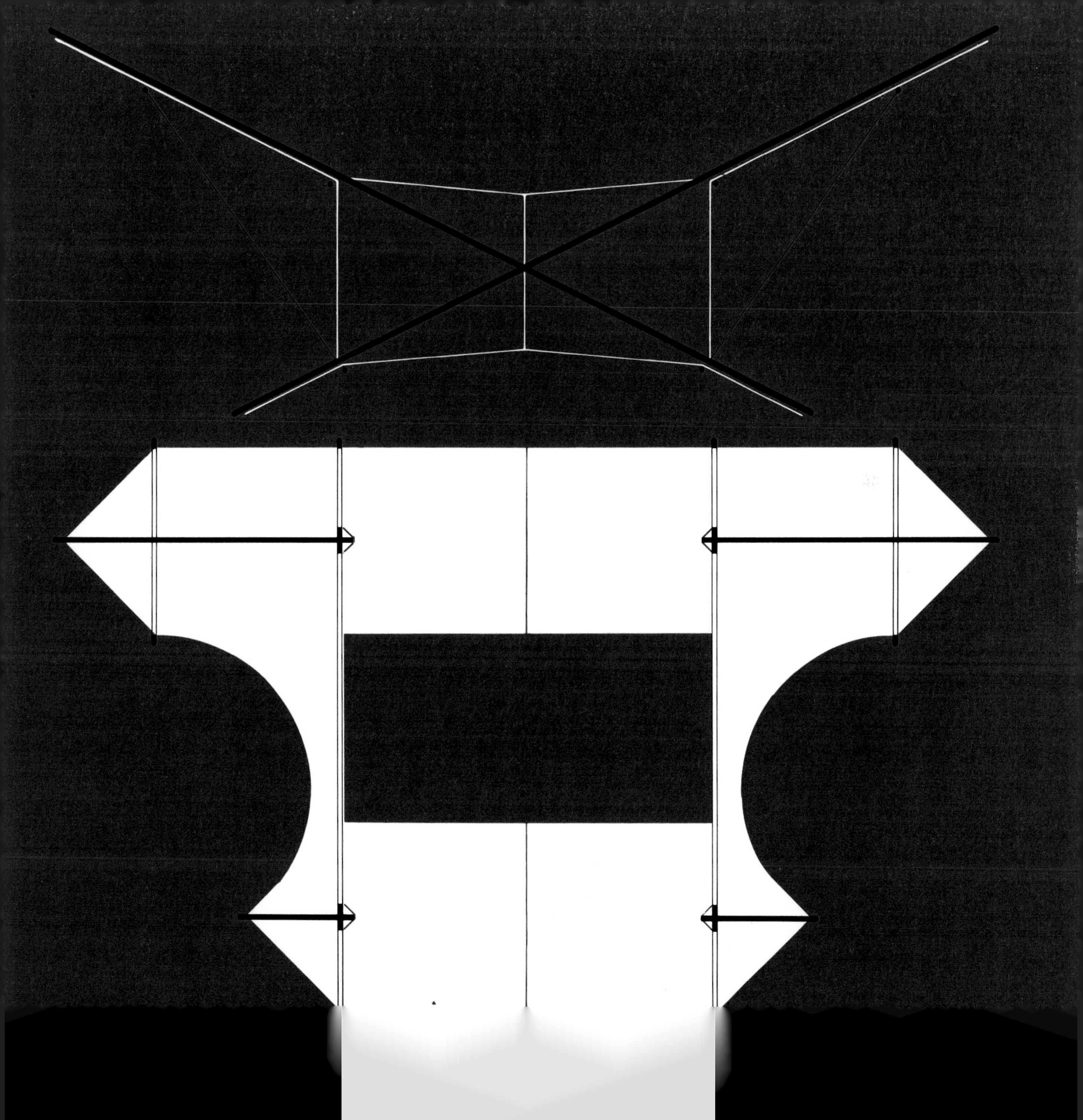

Double rhomboidal compound kite

Cover: ripstop nylon or Tyvek.
Frame: hardwood dowel or aluminium.
Bridle: compound.
Tailless.
Wind: moderate to fresh.

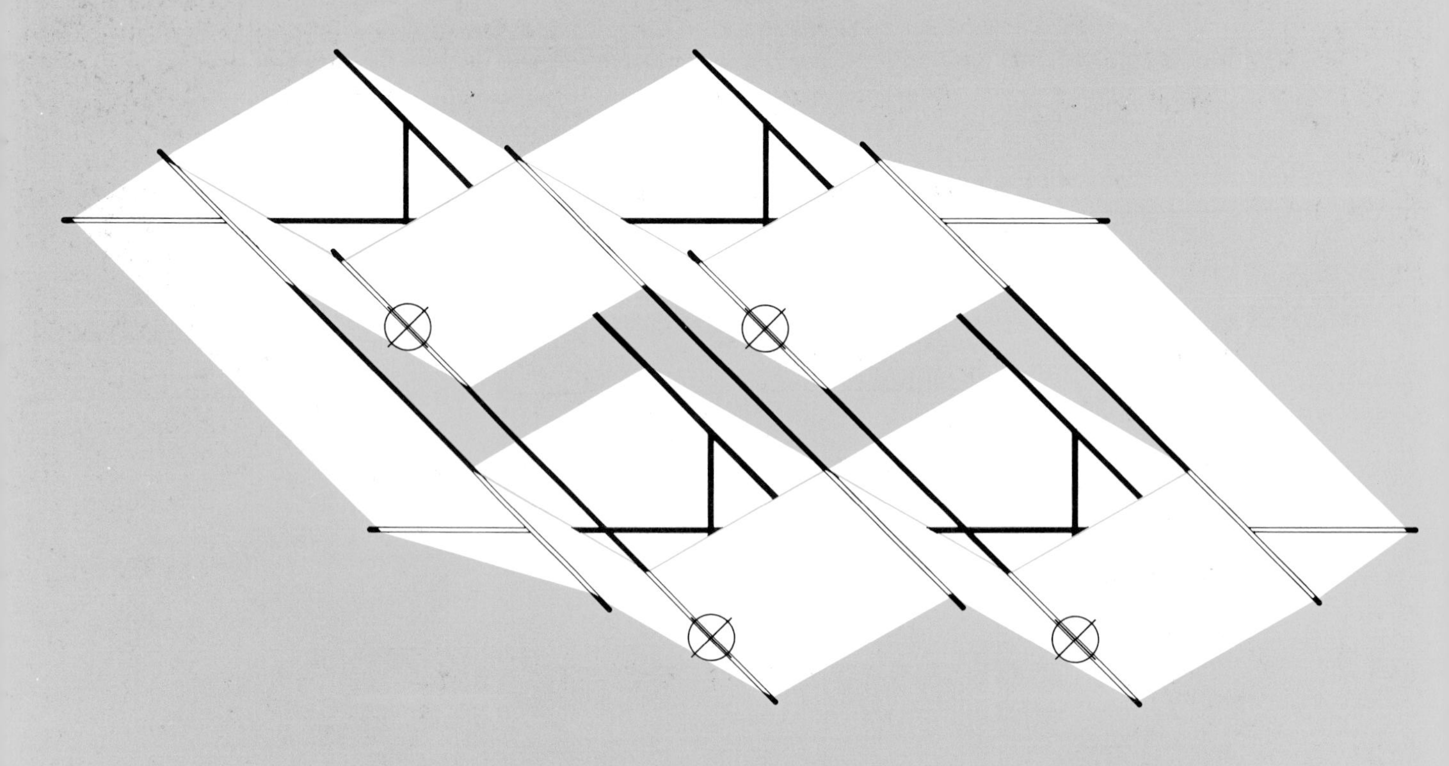

0 5 10 15 20 25 30 35 40 45 50 55 60 65 70 75 80 85 90 95 100 105 110 115 120 125 130 135 140 145 150 155 160 165 170 175 180 185 190 195

Early Cody compound kite

Cover: linen or cotton cambric.
Frame: hardwood dowel or aluminium.
Bridle: compound.
Tailless.
Wind: moderate to fresh.

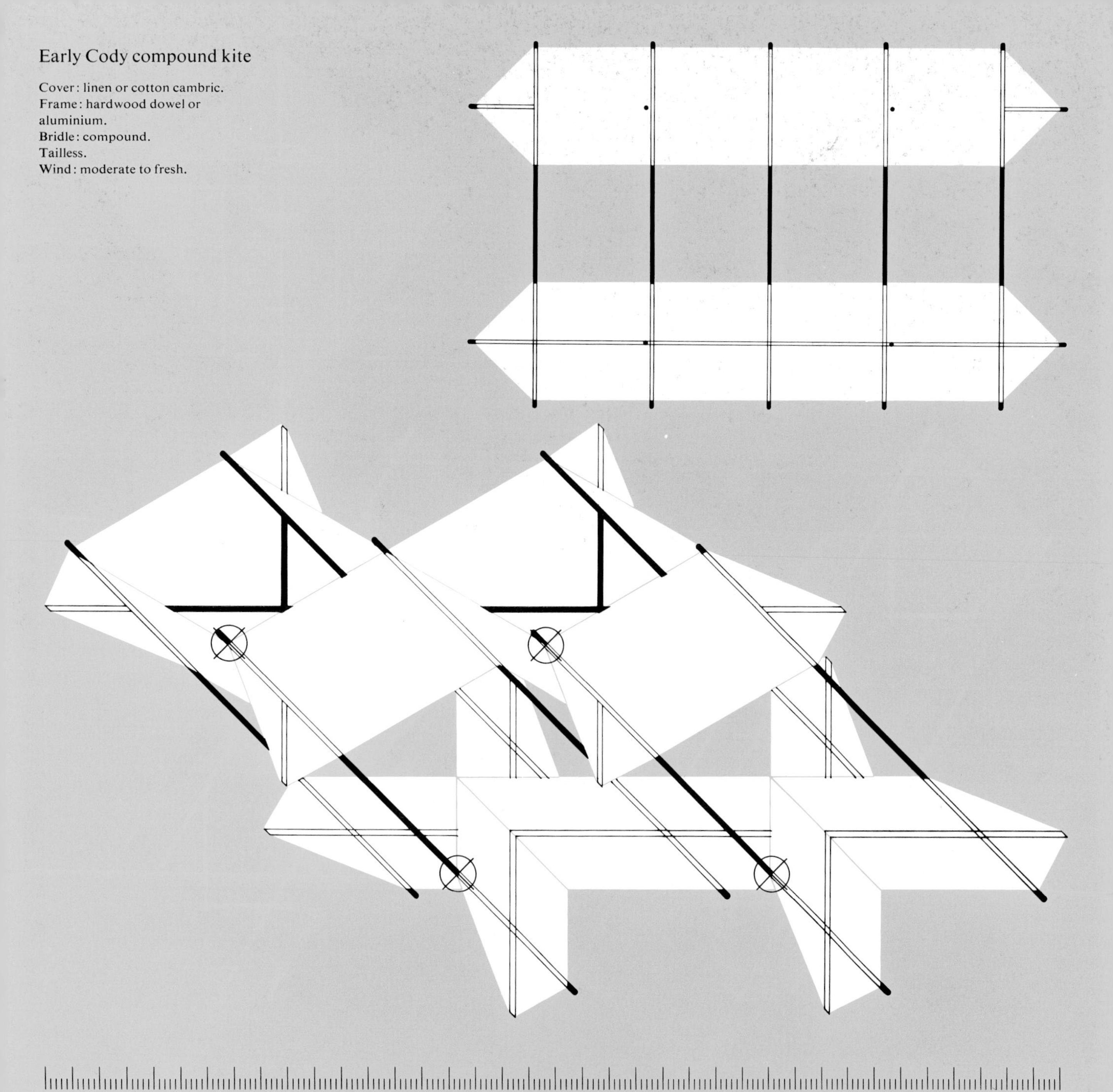

Basic box kite and compound variations

Cover: ripstop nylon or Tyvek.
Frame: dowel.
Bridle: two-leg.
Tailless.
Wind: box: moderate to strong.
Wind: compound: gentle to moderate.

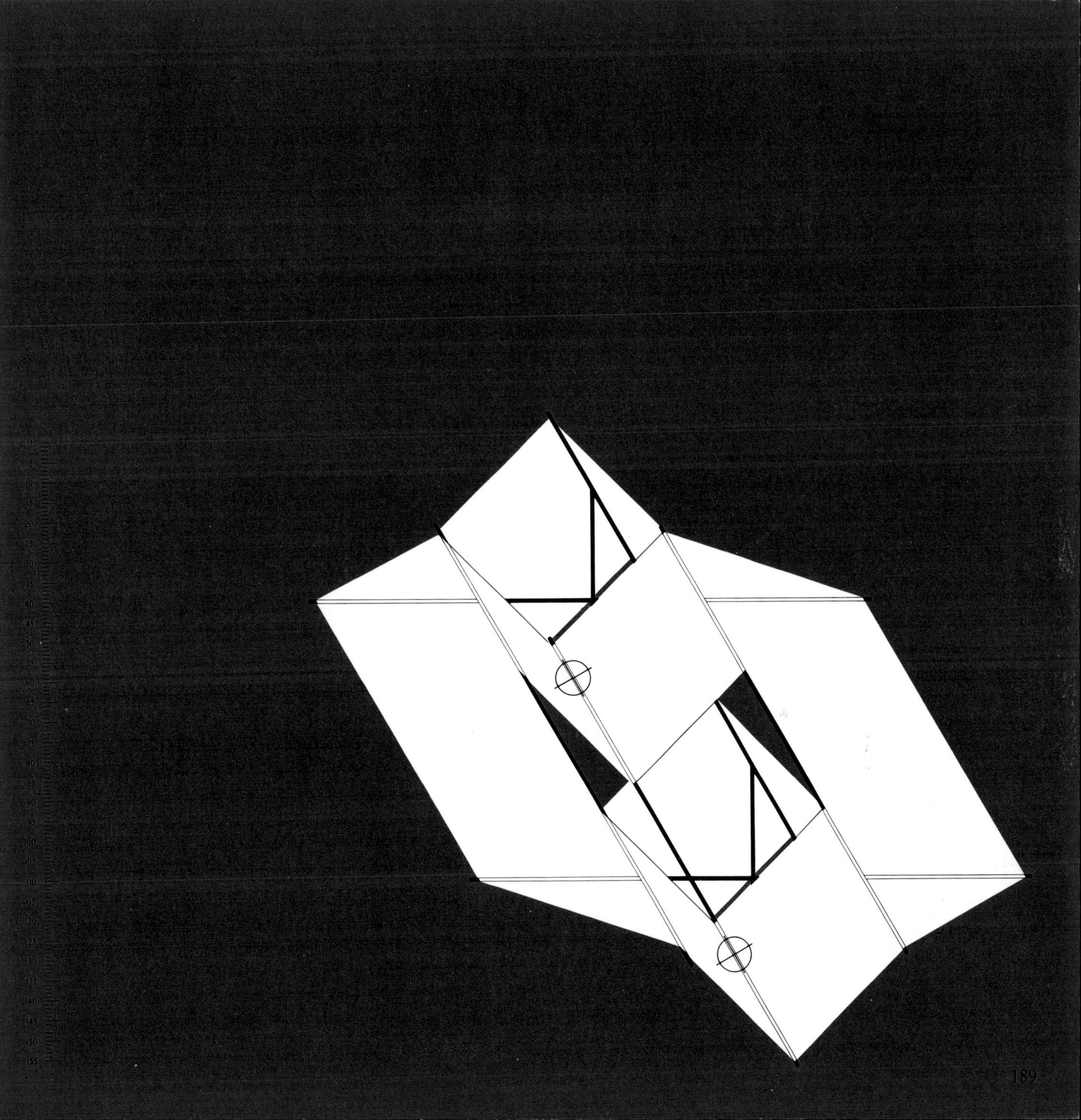

Salmon's multi-celled rhomboidal box kite

Cover: linen or cotton cambric.
Frame: hardwood dowel.
Bridle: tandem four-leg.
Tailless.
Wind: moderate to fresh.

In high winds the downward pull of the bridle lines may cause the cells to spread through their vertical plane, resulting in the loss of the vertical spreaders if they are only force-fitted.
To avoid this risk, secure the top longeron to the keel longeron by tapes positioned immediately above each bridling point.

If made to the given scale, each cell should be fitted with two sets of securely fastened bracers.

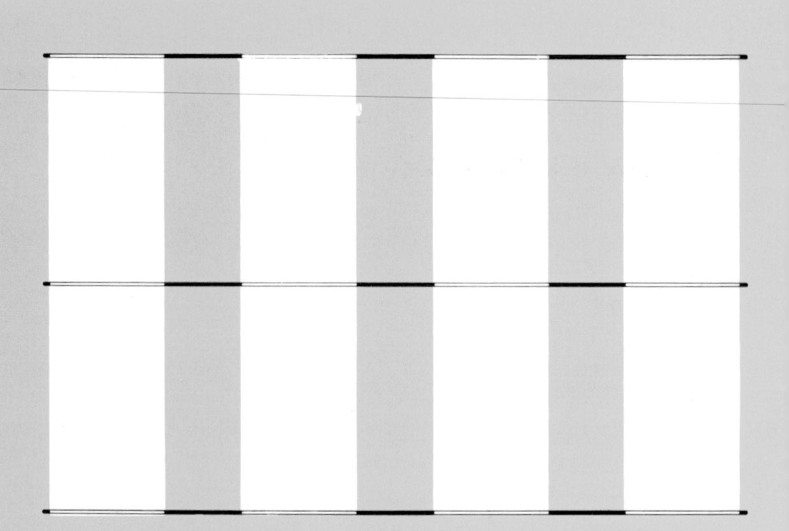

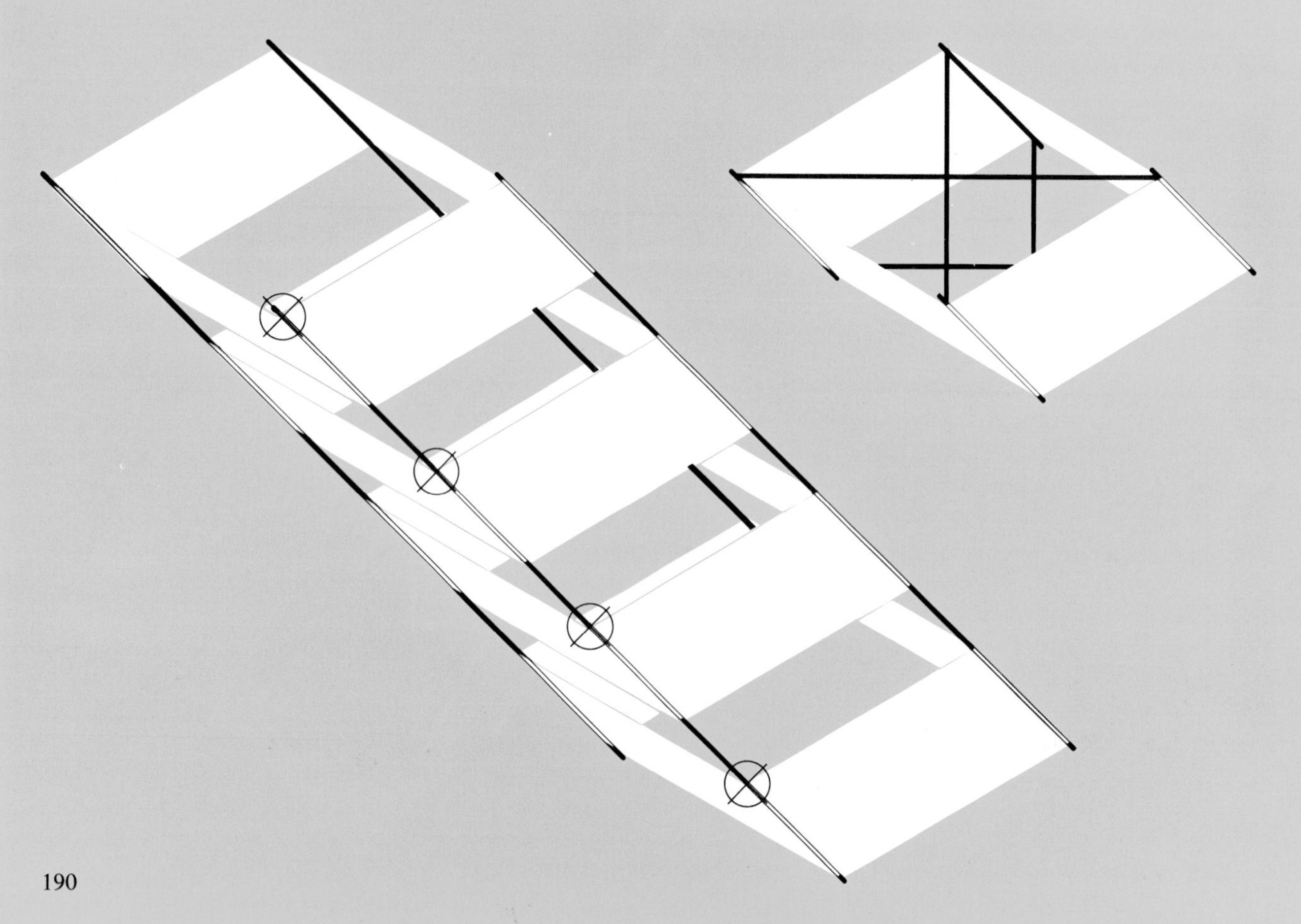

W-form kite

Cover: ripstop nylon or Tyvek.
Frame: dowel.
Bridle: compound.
Tailless.
Wind: moderate to fresh.

The three topmost longerons of this kite should be secured to the spars in order to establish its form.

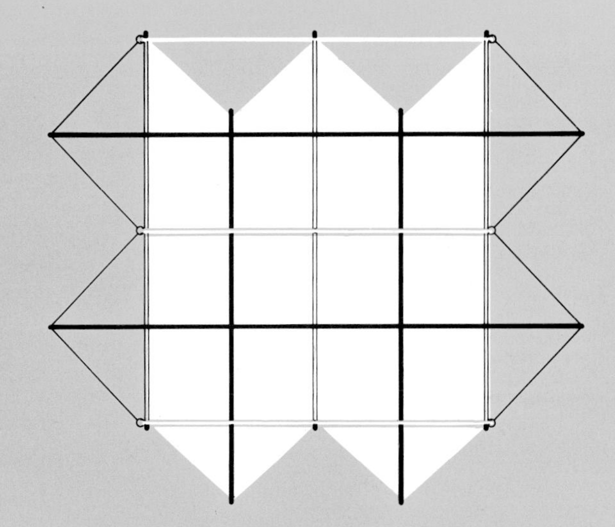

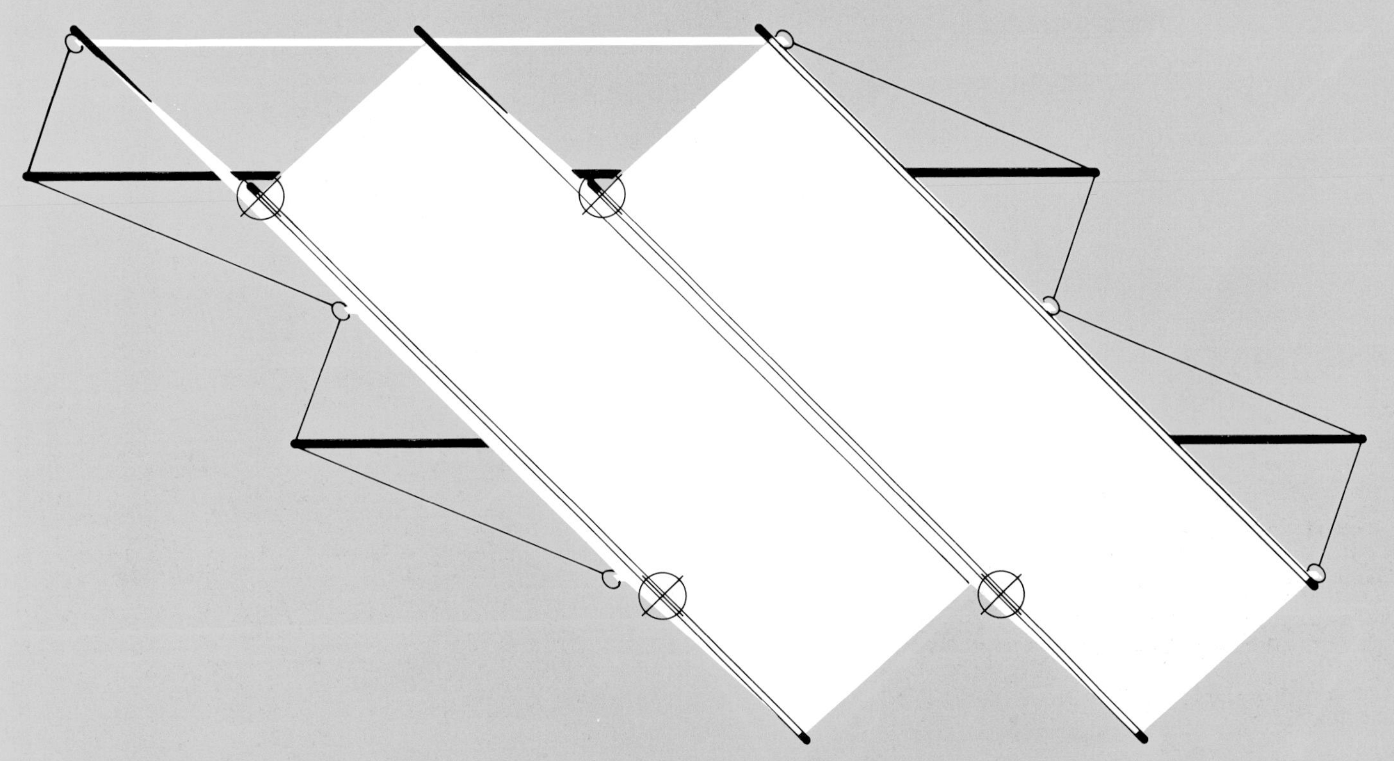

0 5 10 15 20 25 30 35 40 45 50 55 60 65 70 75 80 85 90 95 100 105 110 115 120 125 130 135 140 145 150 155 160 165 170

Bell's multi-celled triangular box kite

Cover: silk.
Frame: bamboo.
Bridle: two-leg.
Tailless.
Wind: fresh to strong.

This multiple version of Alexander Graham Bell's triangular-celled box kite (right) is not only designed to perform in high wind-speeds, but to an extent depends upon them to hold its form. As with the hexagonal box kite (opposite) this kite is locked into form by six bracing lines (not shown), which run diagonally fore-to-aft of the kite's length.

Triangular-celled box kite.

Bell's hexagonal box kite

Cover: cambric.
Frame: hardwood dowel.
Bridle: compound.
Tailless.
Wind: fresh to strong.

Like most of Bell's airborne creations this is an extraordinarily heavy kite best suited for high winds. It is also typical of Bell in that it is difficult to make, and is not easily collapsible; though for a reliable high-wind kite there are few finer.

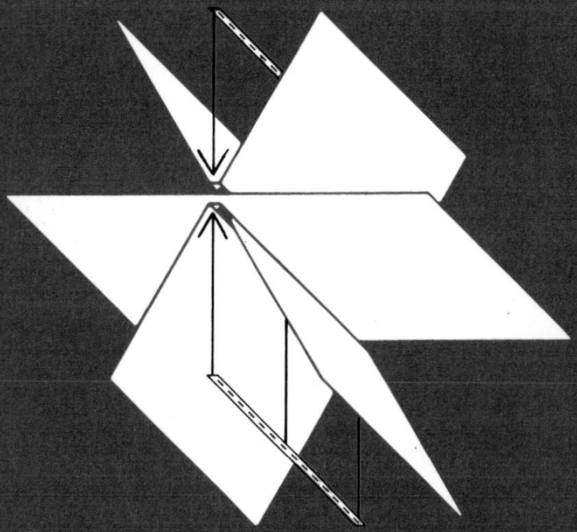

Cells are formed by double stitching binding tape onto both sides of the cell spokes (left), which should be prepared by having both their leading and trailing edges hemmed. The cell's outer cover is then double stitched to the free edges of the fabric spokes.

Four sets of cell bracers are pierced at either end by a metal pin, and are force-fitted against the double longerons fore-and-aft of each cell unit, holding the cells open (below). When assembled, the kite is locked into form by six diagonal bracing lines which run fore-to-aft of its entire length (not shown).

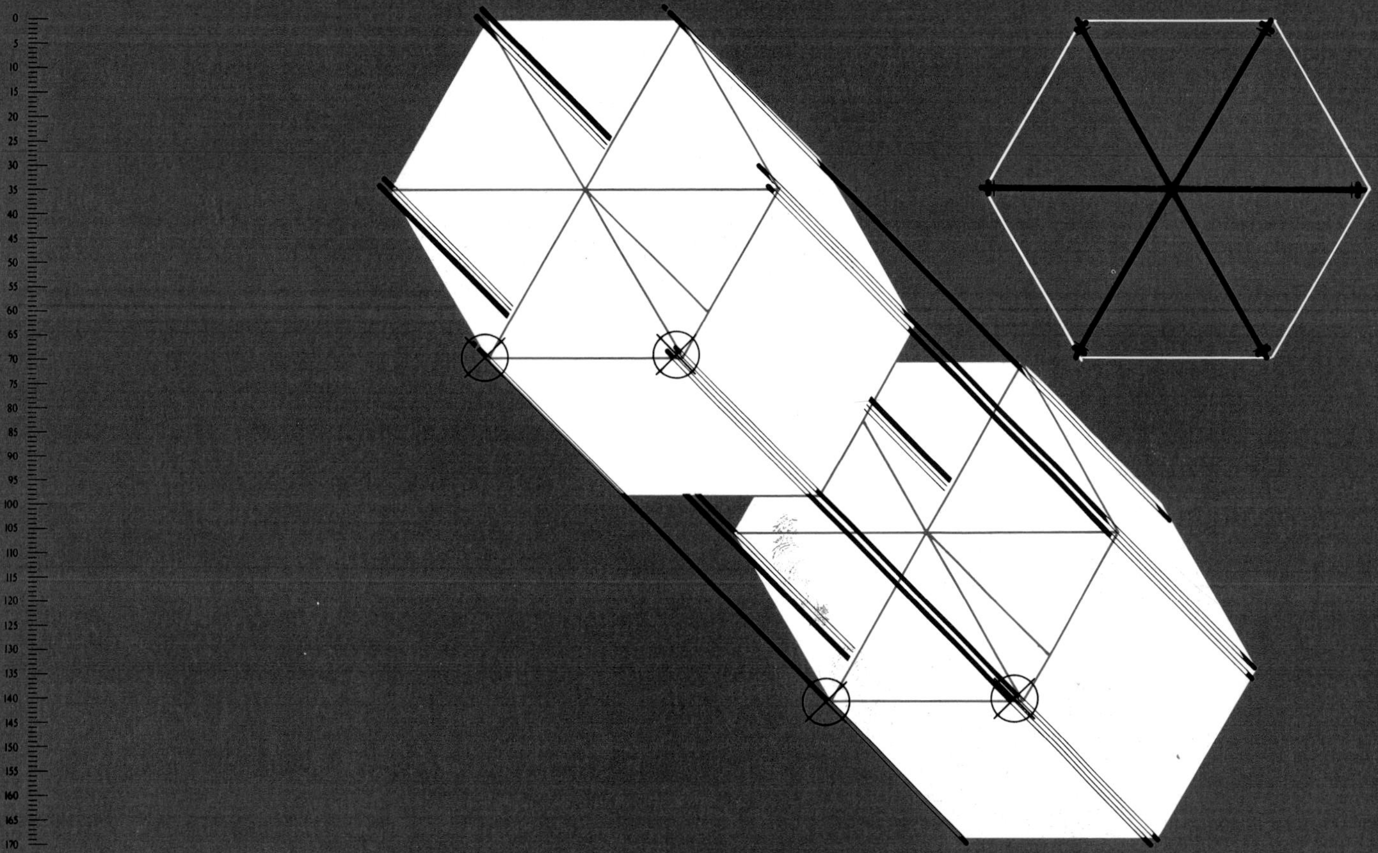

0 5 10 15 20 25 30 35 40 45 50 55 60 65 70 75 80 85 90 95 100 105 110 115 120 125 130 135 140 145 150 155 160 165 170

Bell's multi-celled tetrahedral kites

Cover: silk.
Frame: hardwood strip.
Bridle: two-leg.
Tailless.
Wind: moderate to fresh.

Within reason, the size of a tetrahedral kite is not important, though Alexander Graham Bell tended towards a norm of 25 cm (say 10 in). However the single cell tetrahedral needs to be of a reasonable size; about 1 metre in any direction gives a single cell good buoyancy.

Thermoplastic tubing is ideal for making the multi-cellular version: as it has an excellent strength to weight ratio, its ends can be easily flattened by heating, and securely bonded with an epoxy resin adhesive. Having first constructed the outer, or main tetrahedral, subsequent multiples within the structure can be glued into place. Plastic film is a perfect cover material for tetrahedral kites as, being air opaque, it gives maximum buoyancy, and each cover doesn't have to be hemmed. It can also be easily secured to the frame with waterproof adhesive tape.

When cutting the rhomboidal covers leave a suitable 'turn-over' on the appropriate sides.

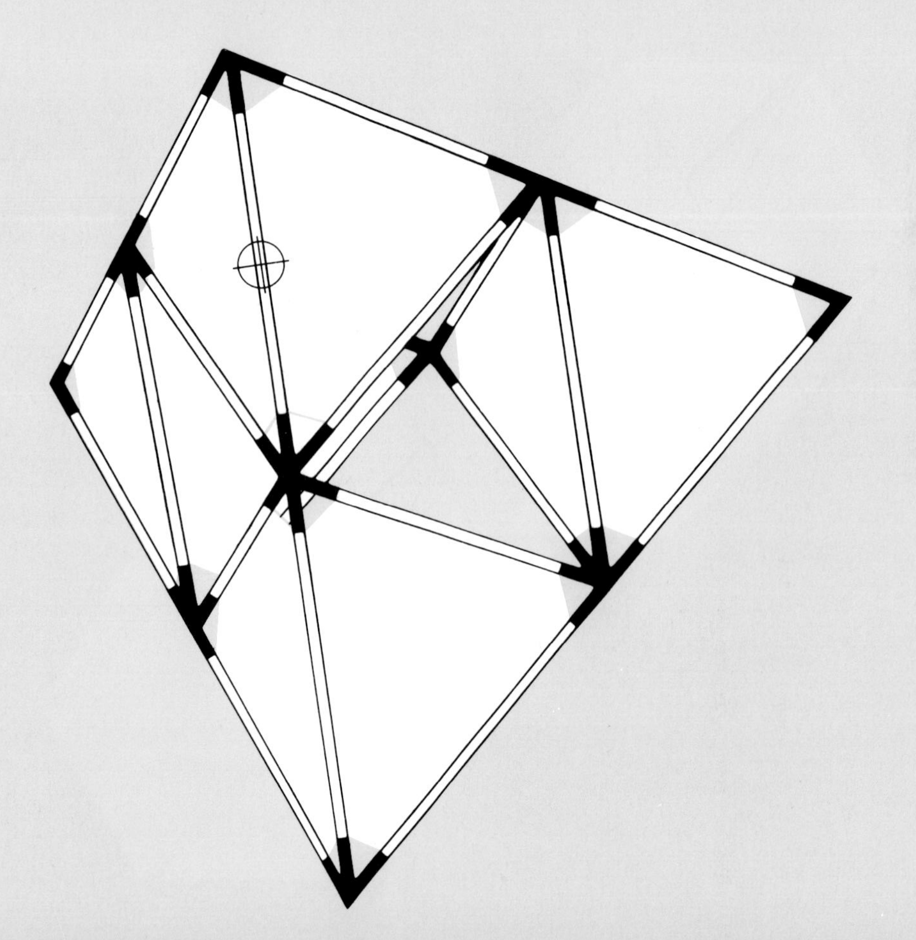

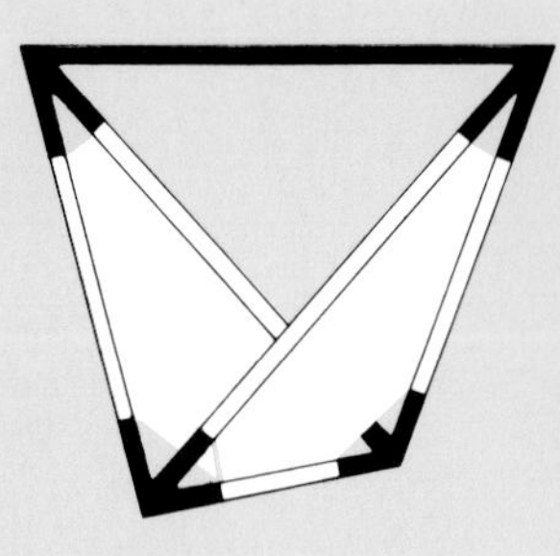

Single-celled tetrahedral kite.

Four-celled tetrahedral kite.

If thermoplastic tubing is not available, suitably formed aluminium fastenings provide an efficient method of securing the dowel ends. These may be riveted together, or tied with nylon line. The subsequent inner structure of dowelling can then be glued into position with U.F. (urea formaldehyde) resin, and faced with plastic, Tyvek or nylon covers.

Aluminium tubing is flattened and drilled through its end.

Each corner unit is made up of three of these pieces, two of which are bent to an angle of 30° each.

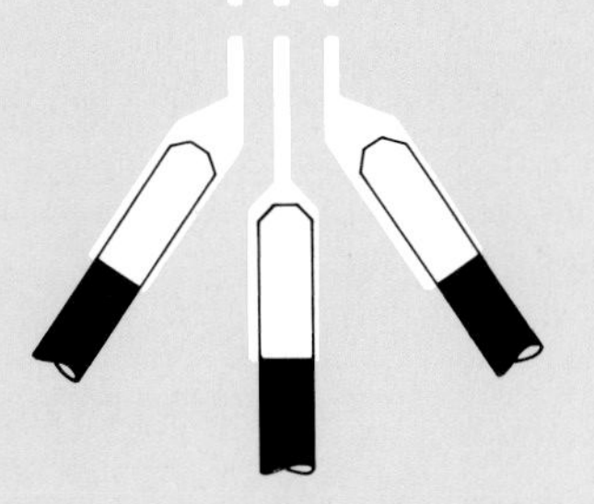

By lifting the centre piece 60° a tetrahedron corner unit is formed

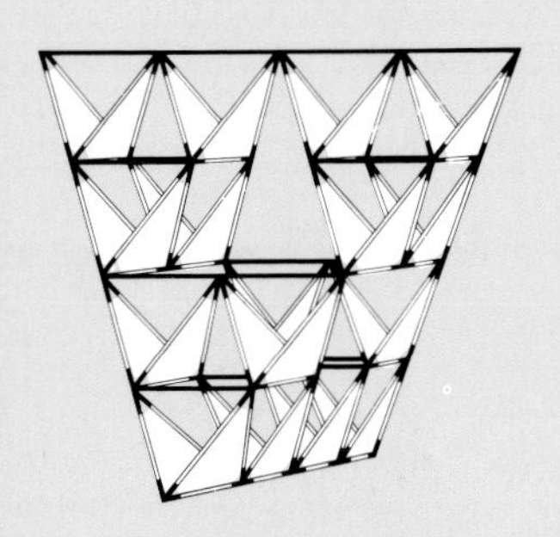

Sixteen-celled tetrahedral kite.

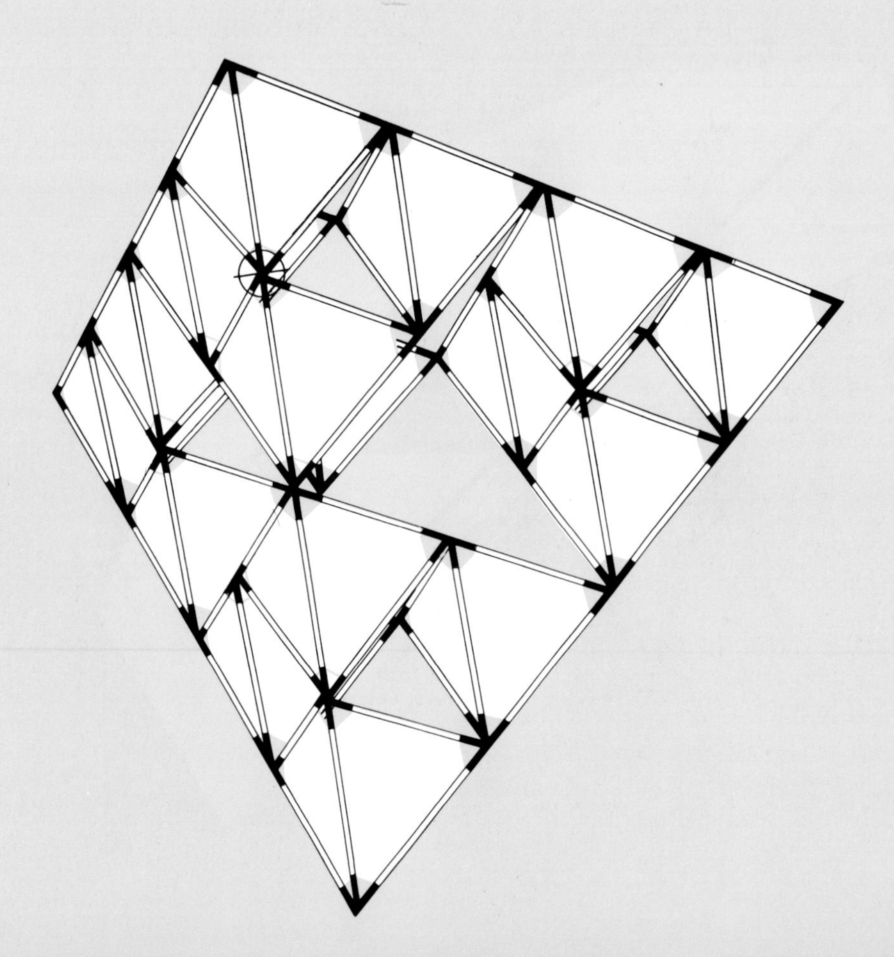

Conyne kite

Cover: cotton cambric.
Frame: spruce strip.
Bridle: two-leg.
Tailless.
Wind: gentle to fresh.

Better known as the French Military box, or Pilot kite, this is an excellent heavy weather flyer. For additional stability the spar may be lightly bowed.

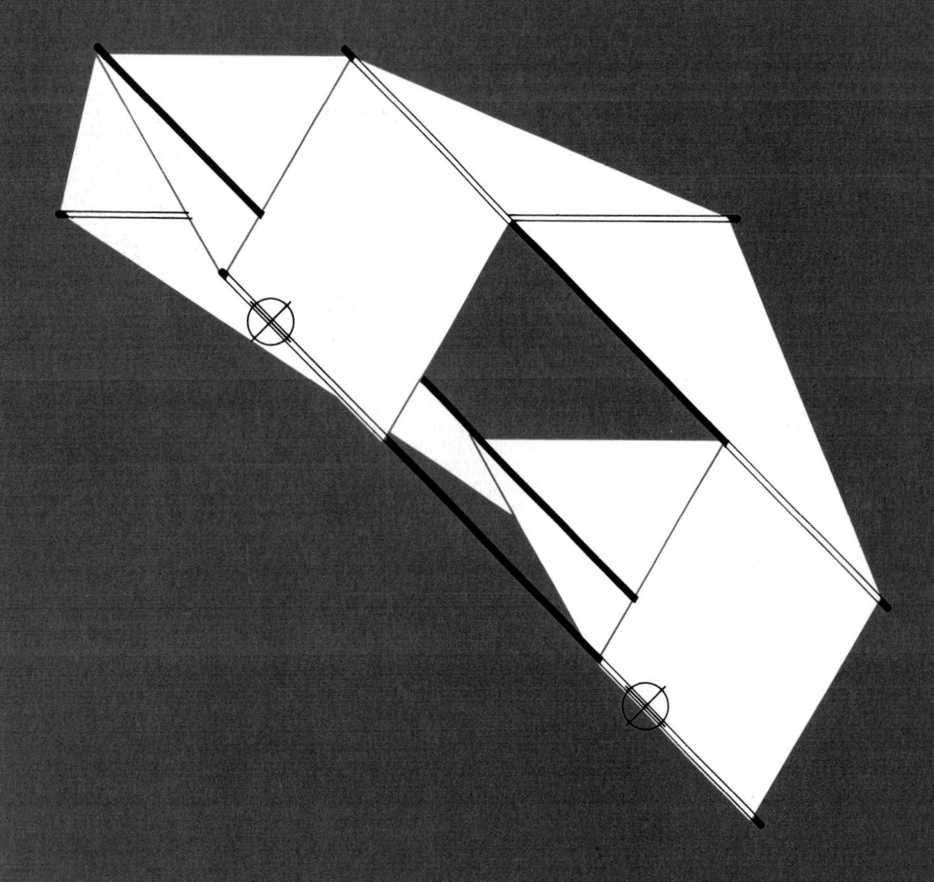

Double Conyne kite

Cover: cotton cambric.
Frame: spruce strip.
Bridle: compound.
Tailless.
Wind: light to moderate.

Also known as the Double Pilot or Double box kite, this variant of Silas J. Conyne's invention is much more buoyant and generally better behaved than its archetype.

A variable lifting surface can be given to a number of kites, and to Conyne's in particular, with simple detachable wind panels. Vents may be opened or closed, depending upon the suitability of the wind. Thus the range of winds in which the kite can be flown is increased. By being lightly fastened only, wind panels can be set to blow out when pressures upon the kite surface become excessive.

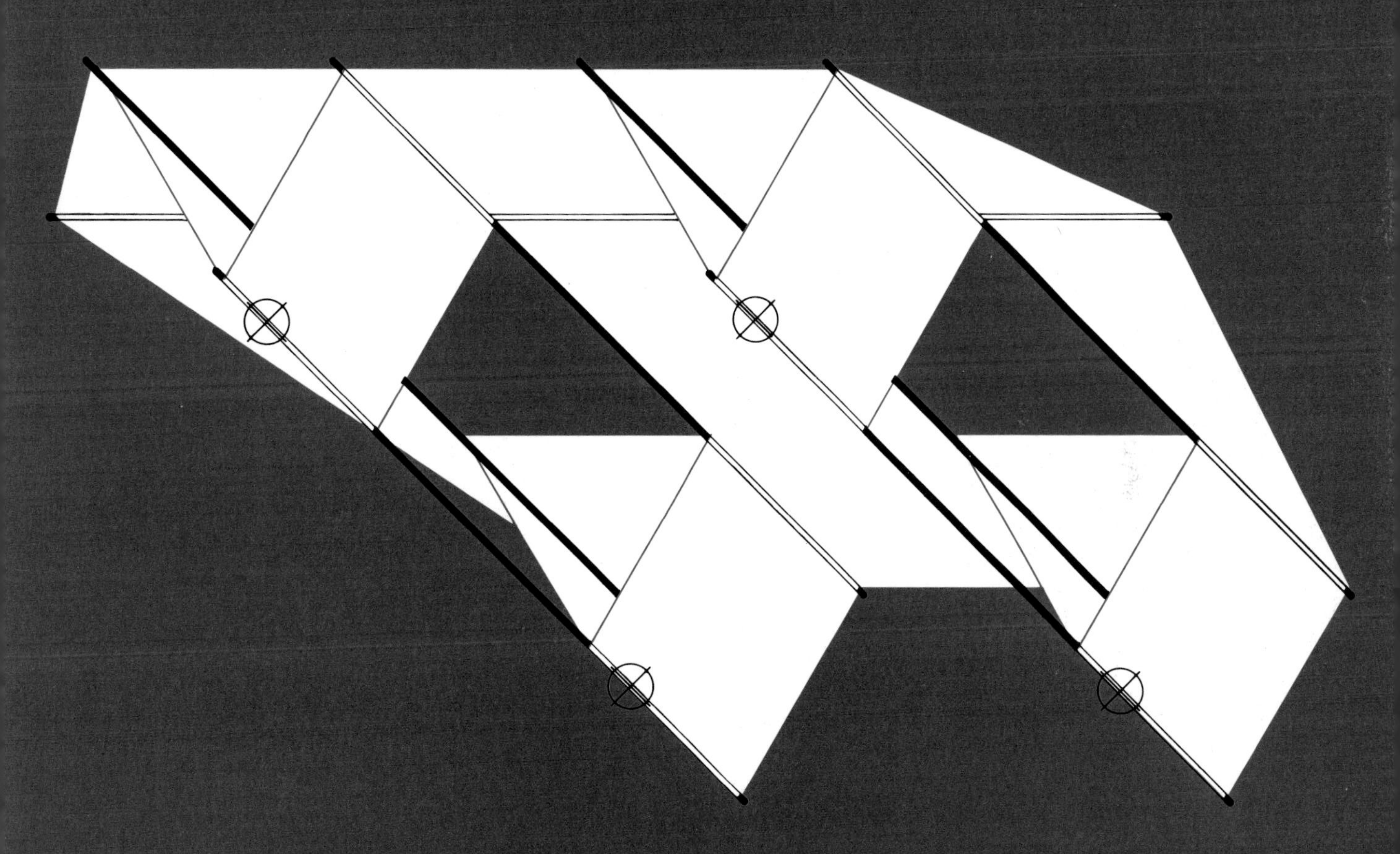

French Signal, or Rescue kite

Cover: waxed linen cambric.
Frame: bamboo.
Bridle: tandem three-leg.
Tailless.
Wind: moderate to strong.

A big, heavy and thoroughly stable craft, the Rescue kite was used by the French Military in experimental ship-to-shore rescue operations. Though generally flown tailless, in particularly heavy winds it was flown during its trials with a multi-pocketed fabric strip secured to its aft end. The pockets were filled with messages from the marooned, and with ballast for additional stability. For flying in more mundane circumstances, however, additional stability is achieved by lightly bowing the spar.

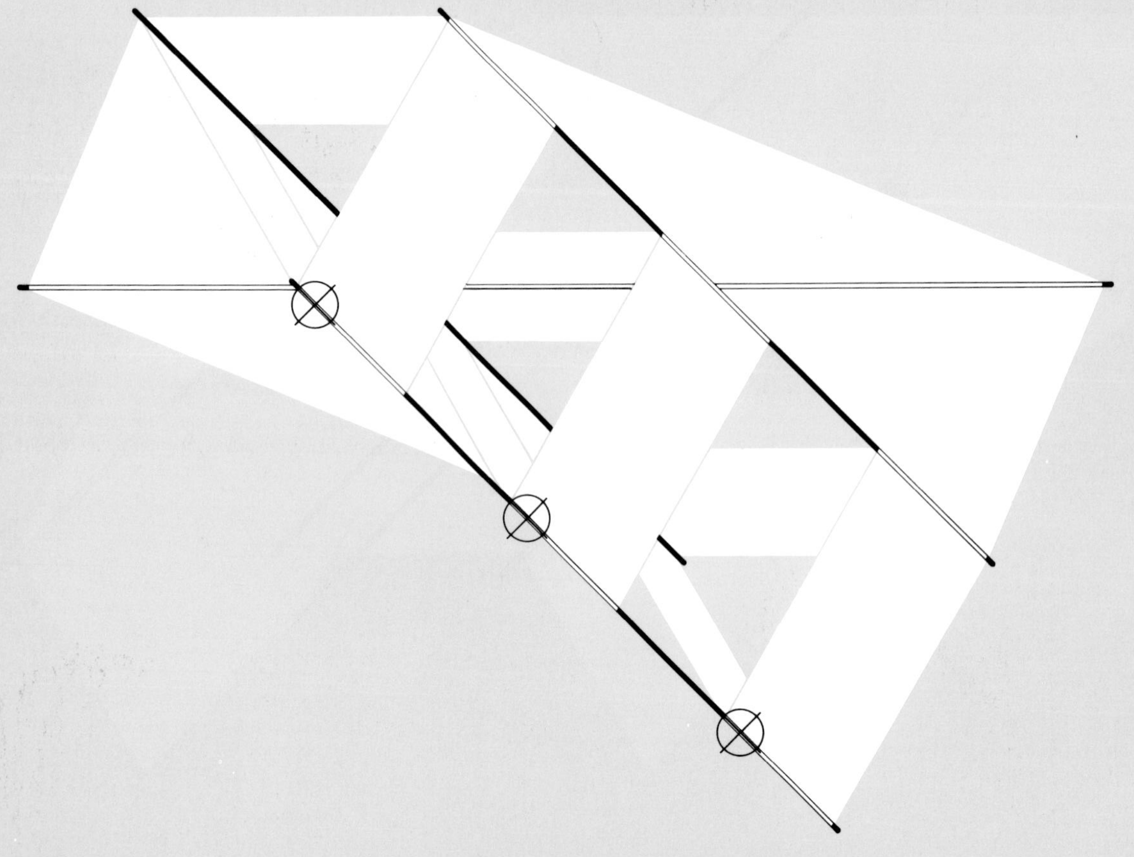

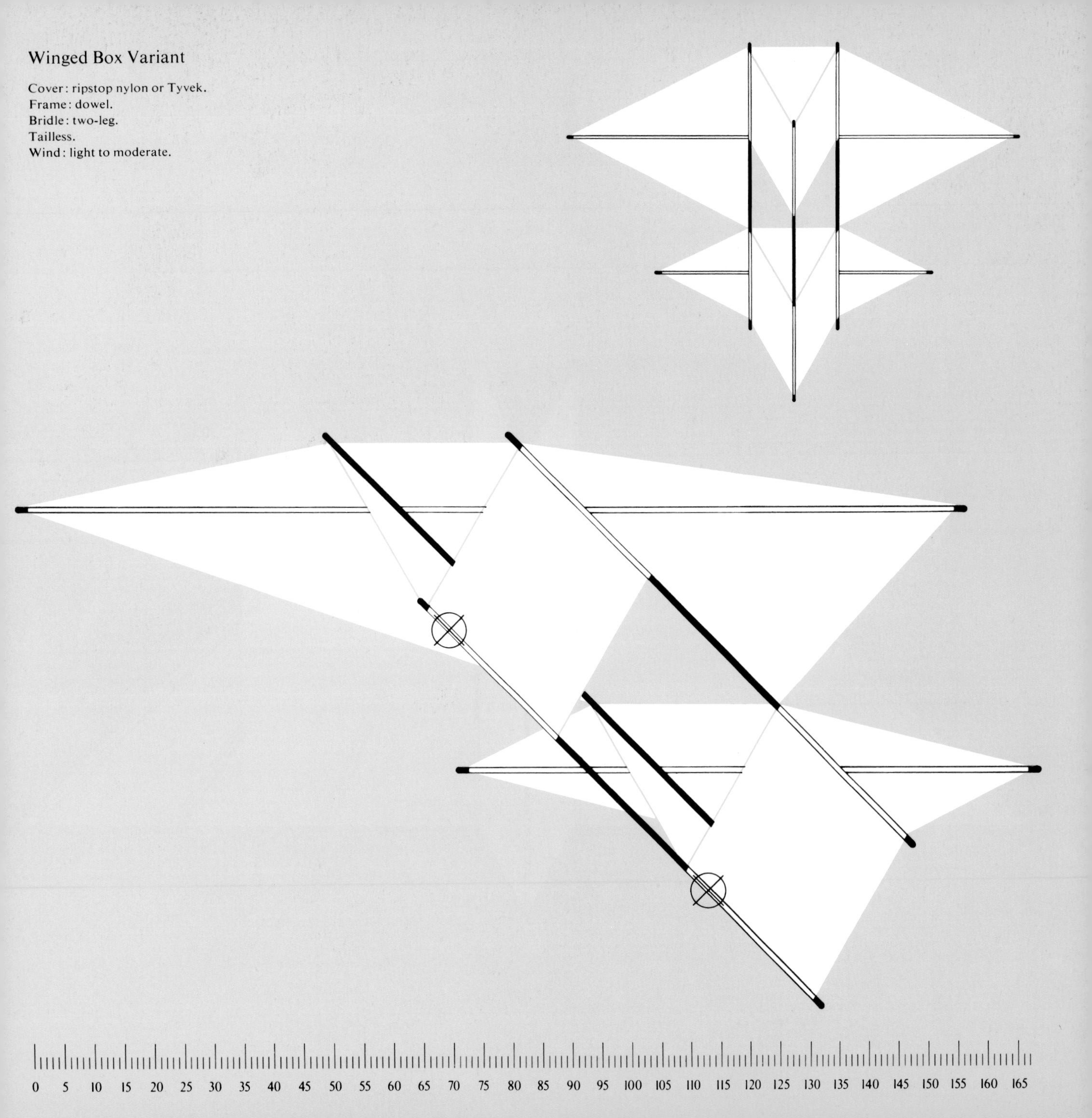
Winged Box Variant
Cover: ripstop nylon or Tyvek.
Frame: dowel.
Bridle: two-leg.
Tailless.
Wind: light to moderate.
0 5 10 15 20 25 30 35 40 45 50 55 60 65 70 75 80 85 90 95 100 105 110 115 120 125 130 135 140 145 150 155 160 165

Compound Bat kite

Cover: silk or industrial nylon.
Frame: dowel.
Bridle: two-leg.
Tailless.
Wind: light to moderate.

This is compounded from a triangular box kite and a Soaring Delta. The wing spreader is attached to the wing edges only; it is not secured to the longerons. This permits the wings to rise and fall independently, creating a strangely life-like impression. The illusion is heightened by introducing short lengths of fine dowel into the trailing edges of the wings. The weight of these, while helping somewhat towards stability, gives a convincingly bat-like edge.

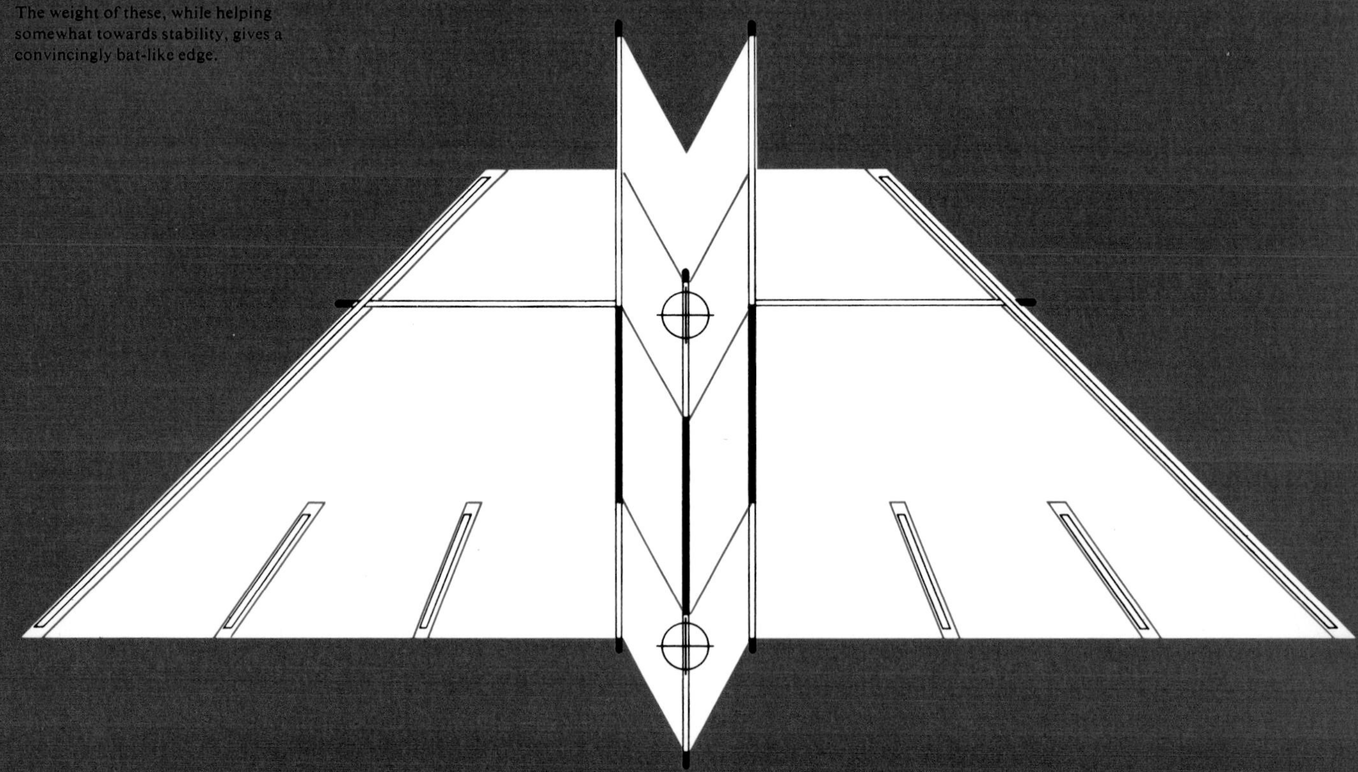

0 5 10 15 20 25 30 35 40 45 50 55 60 65 70 75 80 85 90 95 100 105 110 115 120 125 130 135 140 145 150 155 160 165 170 175 180 185 190 195 200

Compound Bird kite

Cover: silk or industrial nylon.
Frame: dowel.
Bridle: two-leg.
Tailless.
Wind: light to moderate.

As with the Bat kite opposite, the wings of the Bird are braced in such a way as to give them considerable freedom of movement in flight. This is a particularly graceful kite, most of all when made from silk. The diagonal wing bracers are not sewn into the wings, but are secured by pockets only.

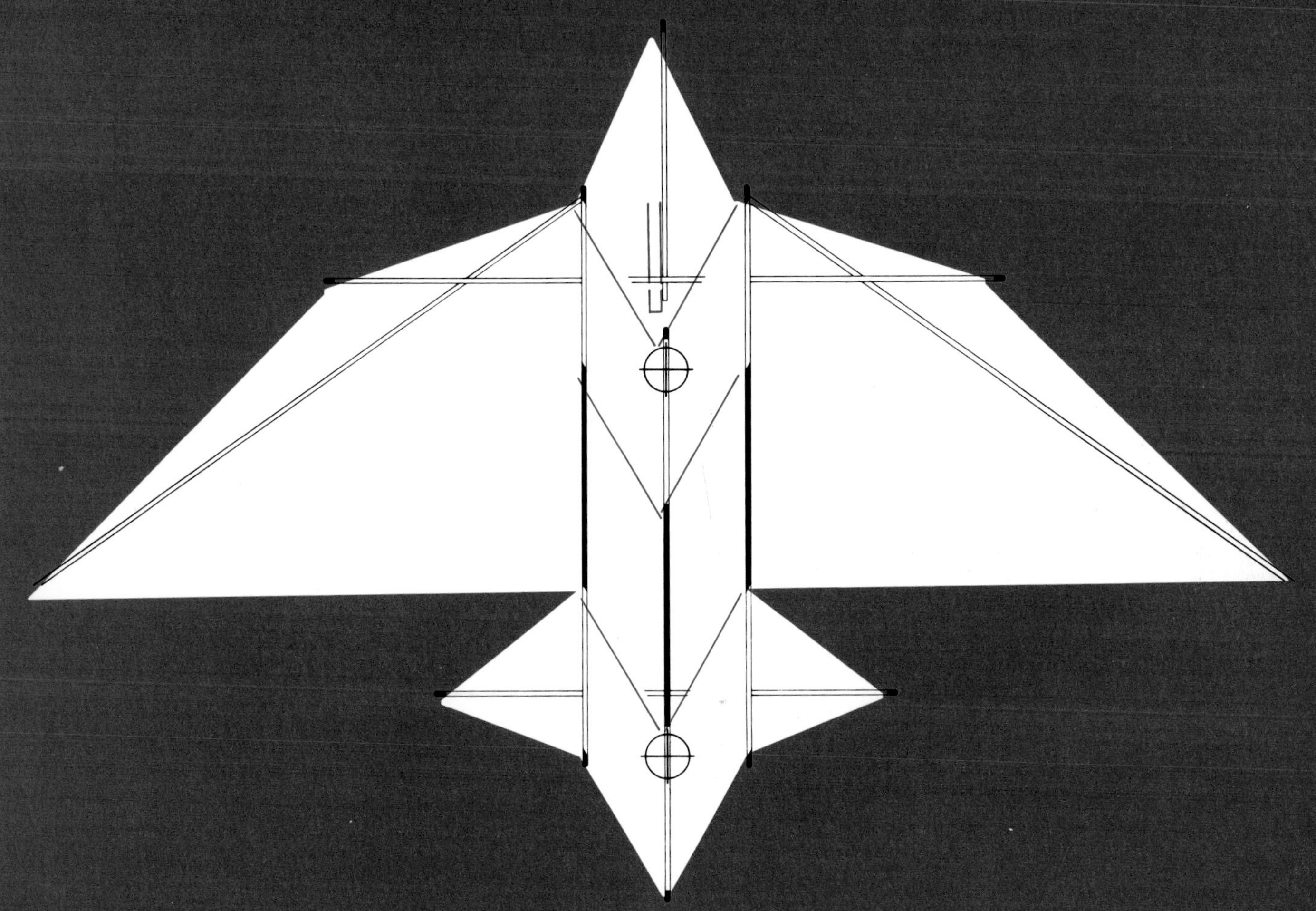

0 5 10 15 20 25 30 35 40 45 50 55 60 65 70 75 80 85 90 95 100 105 110 115 120 125 130 135 140 145 150 155 160 165 170

Marconi-rigged jib kite

Cover: cotton or industrial nylon.
Frame: dowel.
Bridle: four-leg.
Tailless.
Wind: moderate to fresh.

So-called because of its debt to the Marconi-rigged yacht, jib kites were prevalent in the forties. As in sailing, the twin jibs can be adjusted to suit a variety of wind-speeds. Loosely set for luffing in low winds, so they are set more tightly for flying in stronger winds. The forward-facing keel gives excellent directional stability by being positioned between the jibs.

It is important that the mainsail and the leading edges of the jibs are taut at all times; this is achieved by extending the edging tape to form loops, which are secured to the ends of the spar and spine.

The bridling of the Marconi is notoriously difficult to set, though, once a successful flying attitude has been achieved, bridle adjustment knots can be glued in place, as further modifications for wind variations are made with the jibs alone.

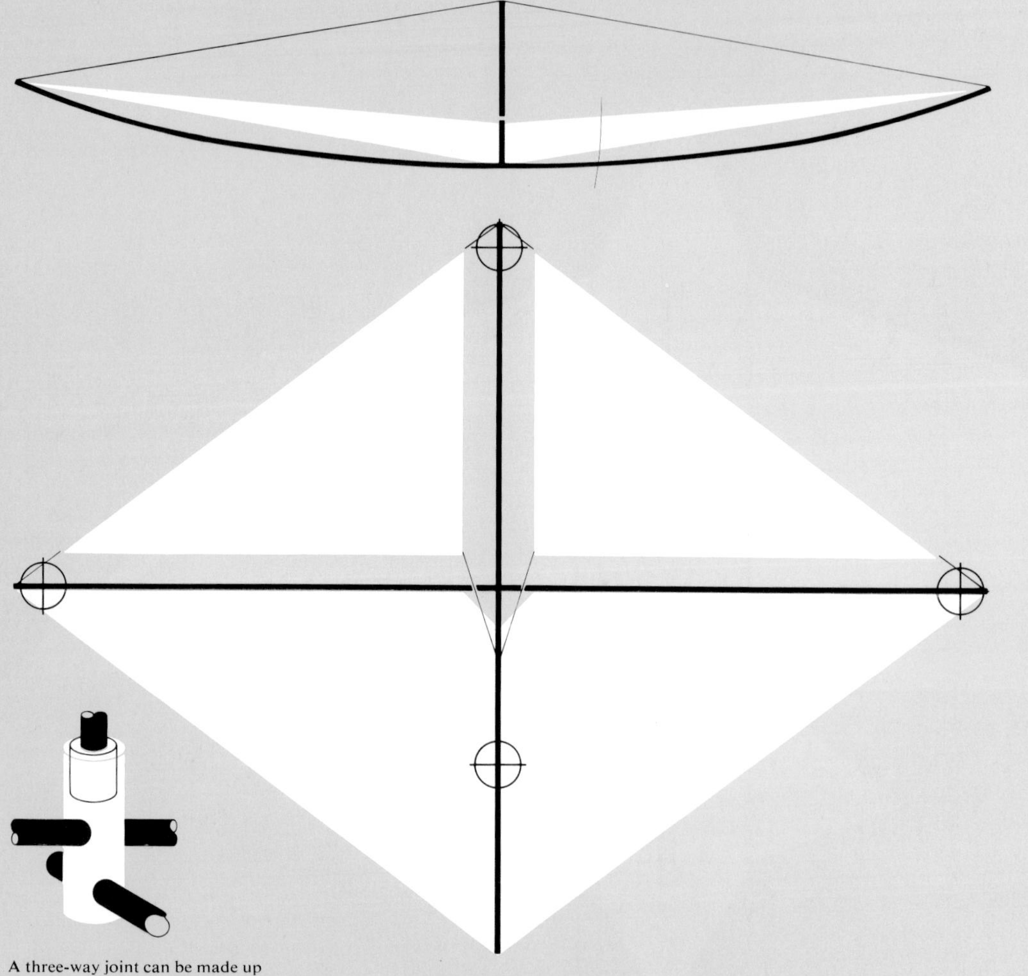

A three-way joint can be made up from a length of thermoplastic or aluminium tubing, suitably drilled and plugged. A balsa block makes a good alternative.

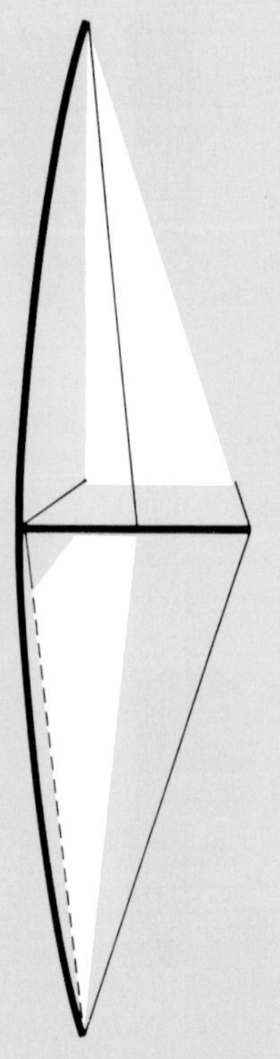

Jibs omitted for clarity (above).

Brogden's six-winged kite

Cover: cotton cambric.
Frame: spruce dowel.
Bridle: three-leg. (see below.)
Tailless.
Wind: light to moderate.

The original version of Charles Brogden's prize-winning kite was 5·18 m (17 ft) long, and proportionate to this pattern. The kite was originally an adaptation of part of an experimental flying machine built by Brogden in 1890, on which he apparently made glides of up to 7 m (20 ft) at a bound, on level ground.

Each wing is connected from its trailing edge to the leading edge of the wing below, directional stability being attained by regulating the lengths of the connecting lines. Brogden maintained that the spine should curve slightly forward at the tail end of the kite. This was apparently for reasons of stability. Whatever the reason, the rather unusual bridling method was devised in order to maintain this curve.

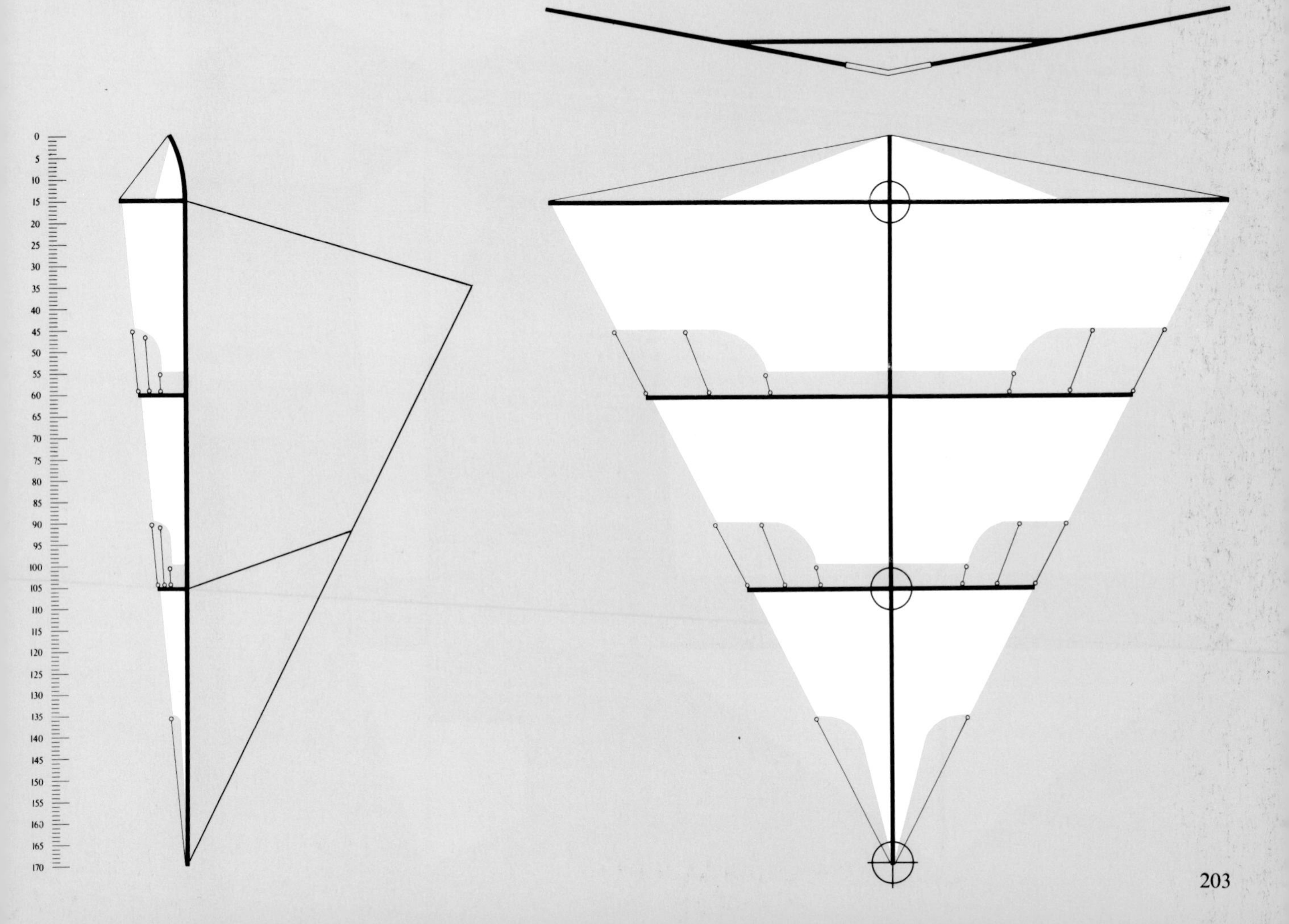

Double-sailed roller

Vented roller (right)

Cover: ripstop or industrial nylon.
Spine: aluminium rod.
Spars: dowel.
Bridle: slip-bridle (see page 135).
Tailless, flown with fin and rudder.
Wind: light to gentle.

Rollers are extremely graceful well-behaved kites, strictly for light-wind flying. Both spars of each kite are set at a dihedral angle.

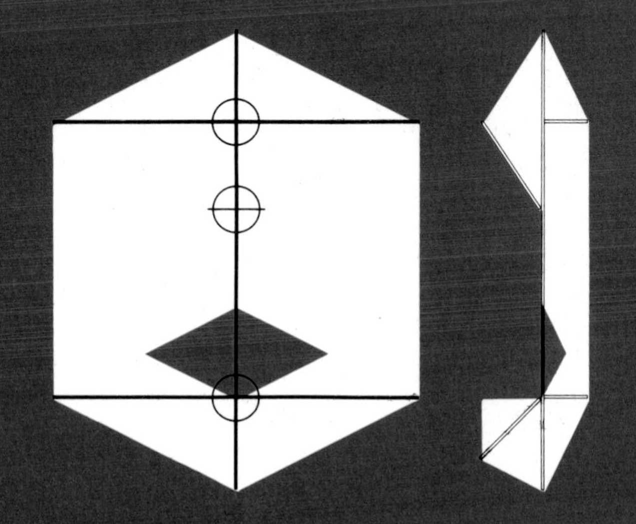

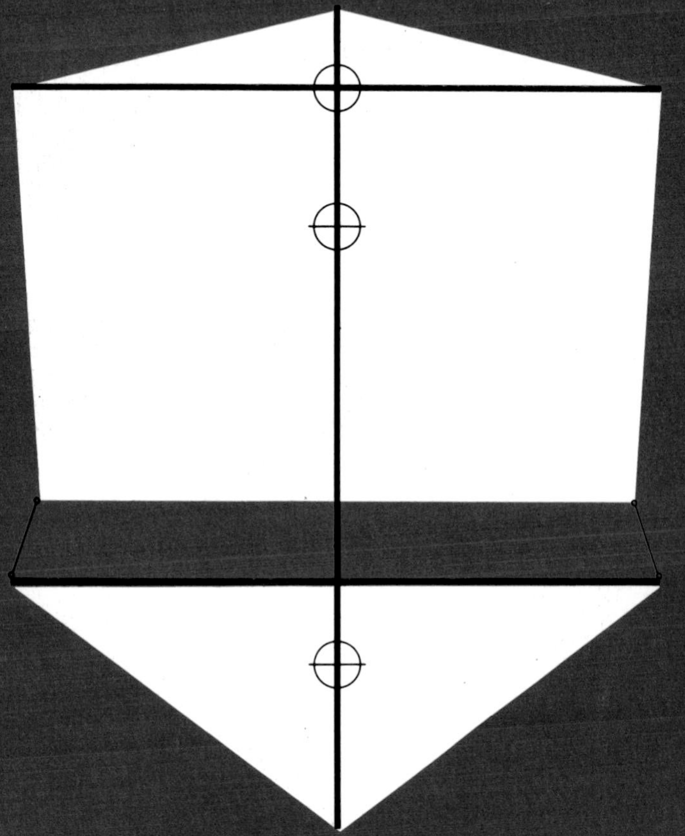

0 5 10 15 20 25 30 35 40 45 50 55 60 65 70 75 80 85 90 95 100 105 110 115 120 125 130 135 140 145 150

Hexagonal roller

Cover: ripstop or industrial nylon.
Spine: aluminium rod.
Spars: dowel.
Bridle: three-leg.
Tailless, flown with rudder.
Wind: light to gentle.

Both diagonal spars are set at a dihedral angle. Directional stability is governed by the setting of the guy lines connecting wing tips to the tail plane.

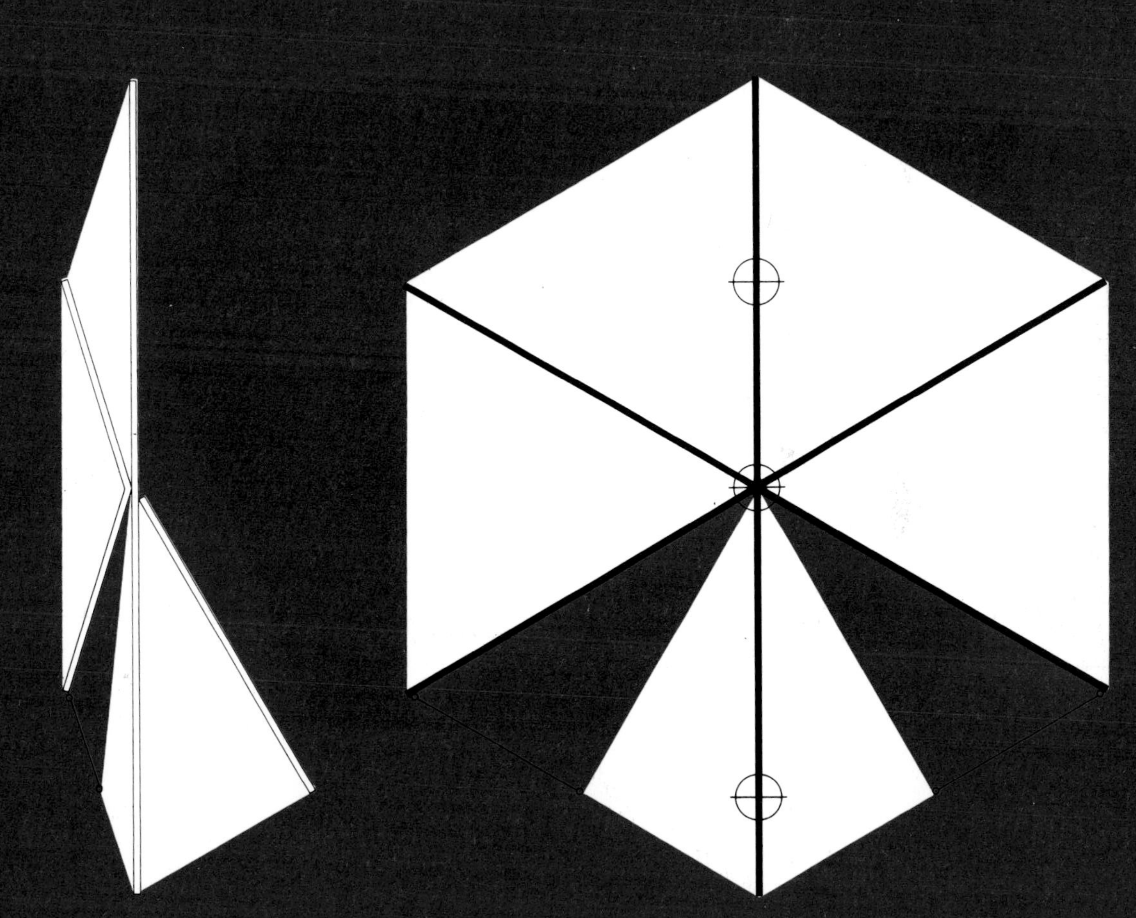

Multi-flare kite

Cover: fine gauge ripstop nylon.
Frame: thermoplastic tubing.
Bridle: twelve-leg.
Tailless.
Wind: light to gentle.

An excellent kite for high altitude soaring, the Multi-flare should be flown slightly bowed. The kite adopts an extremely high angle, developing considerable lift even in light winds. The gathering point of the shroud lines should fall slightly ahead of the spar, and should be slightly longer than the kite's length. If thermoplastic tubing is not available it may be substituted for 6 mm (¼ in) balsa wood dowel for the longerons, and 8 mm ($\frac{5}{16}$ in) dowel for the spar.

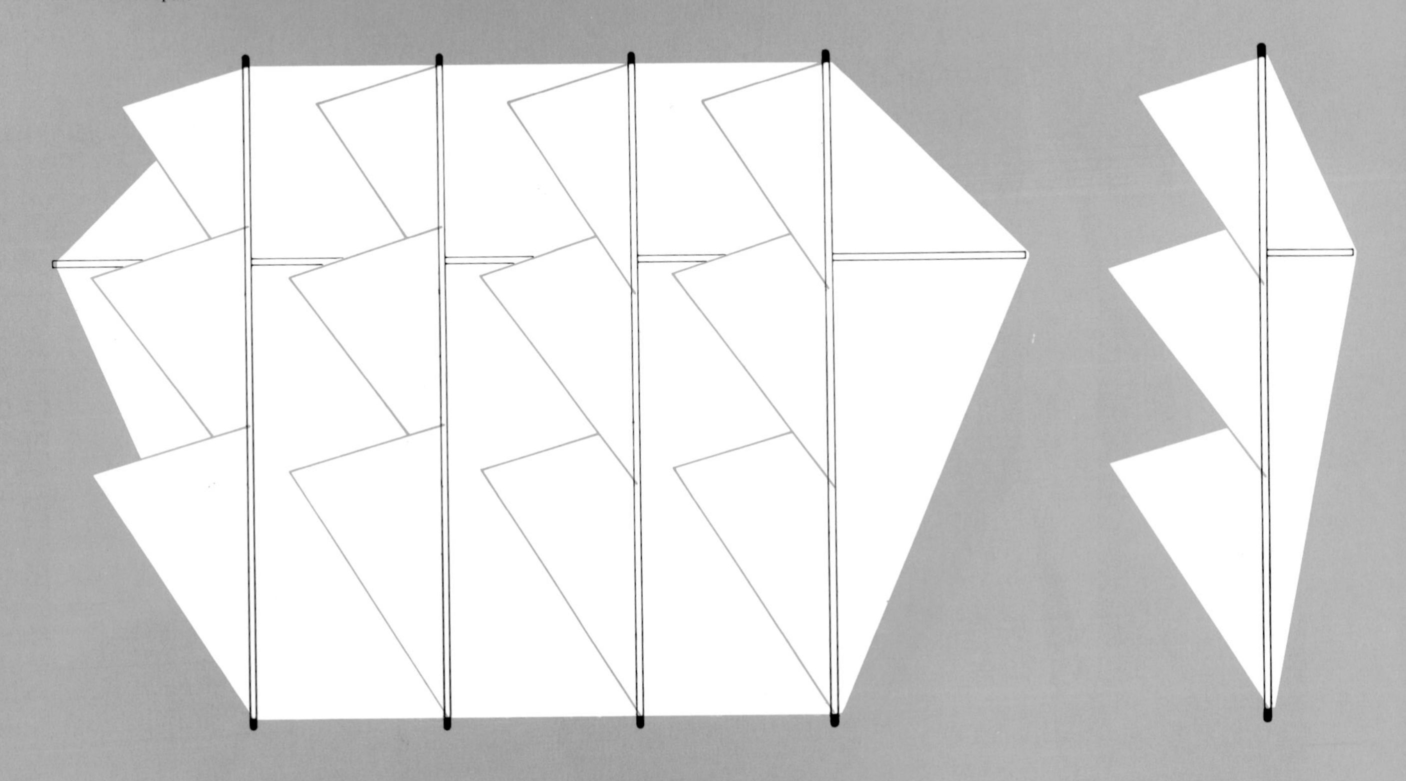

0 5 10 15 20 25 30 35 40 45 50 55 60 65 70 75 80 85 90 95 100 105 110 115 120 125 130 135 140 145 150

Flare kite

Cover: fine gauge ripstop nylon.
Frame: thermoplastic tubing.
Bridle: four-leg.
Tailless.
Wind: light.

This light-weight hybrid is flown with its spar bowed, and should be drogued in winds in excess of 5 m.p.h. The Flare kite is for extremely light winds only, as it becomes difficult to recover even in moderate winds.

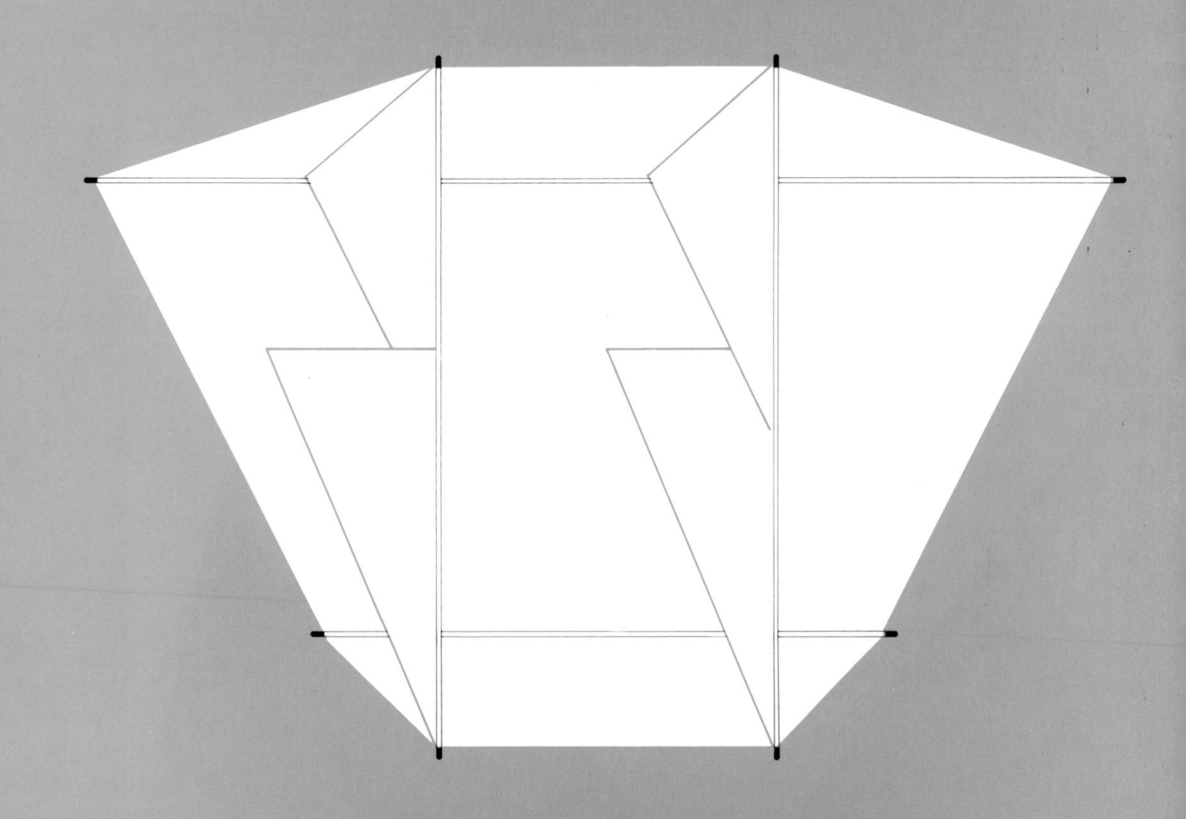

Stunter kite

Cover: medium gauge plastic sheet.
Frame: 6 mm (¼ in) aluminium tubing.
Bridle: double lined.
Tailless.
Wind: gentle to strong.

This is a highly efficient double-lined kite for performing aerobatics. Because of its flexible spar it is capable of being flown in a wide variety of wind-speeds, though the stronger the wind, the more responsive the kite is to the controls.
The bridles of this kite do not need to be adjusted for different wind-speeds.

The spring steel wire that forms the centre section of the spar should be set at a tension-free angle of 15° for maximum performance.
All joints and fastenings are formed from polyethylene tubing.
A good manageable length for lines is 60 m (say 200 ft) each; the kite is controlled simply by pulling on the right-hand line for a right turn and vice versa. An assisted launch is recommended for beginners.

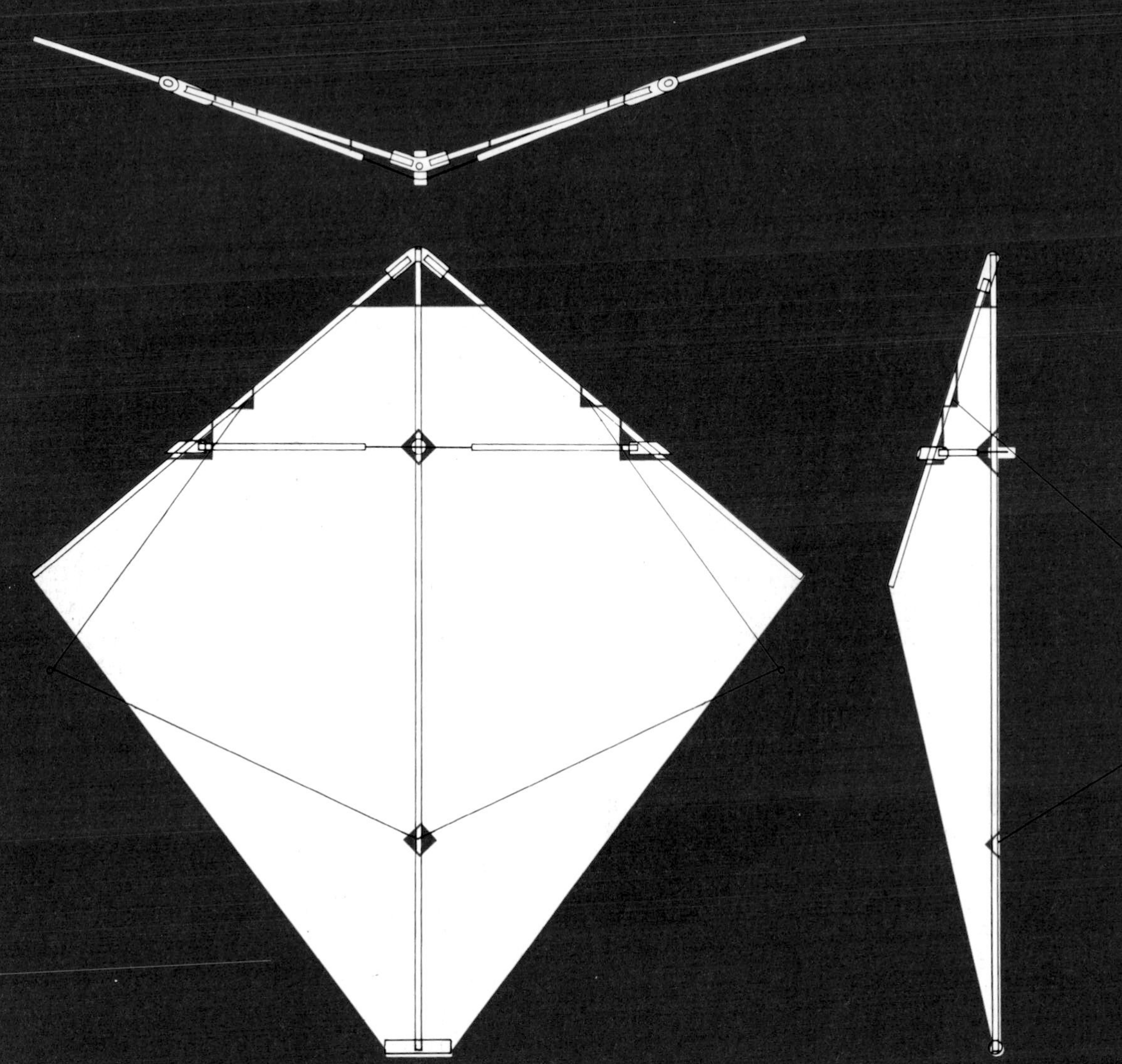

Rogallo Flexible kite

Cover: heavy gauge Mylar or similar flexible non-rigid fabric.
Frameless.
Bridle: six-leg.
Tail: Mylar streamer.
Wind: light.

The spine of the kite is nothing more than a diagonal fold which is held in position by the two centre legs of the bridle. When made in light gauge material this is usually supported by a fine strip of card or plastic. Button thread is sufficient for the bridles and flying line. Bridles are attached with adhesive tape. Tail measures 2·5 cm (1 in) × 80 cm (31½ in).

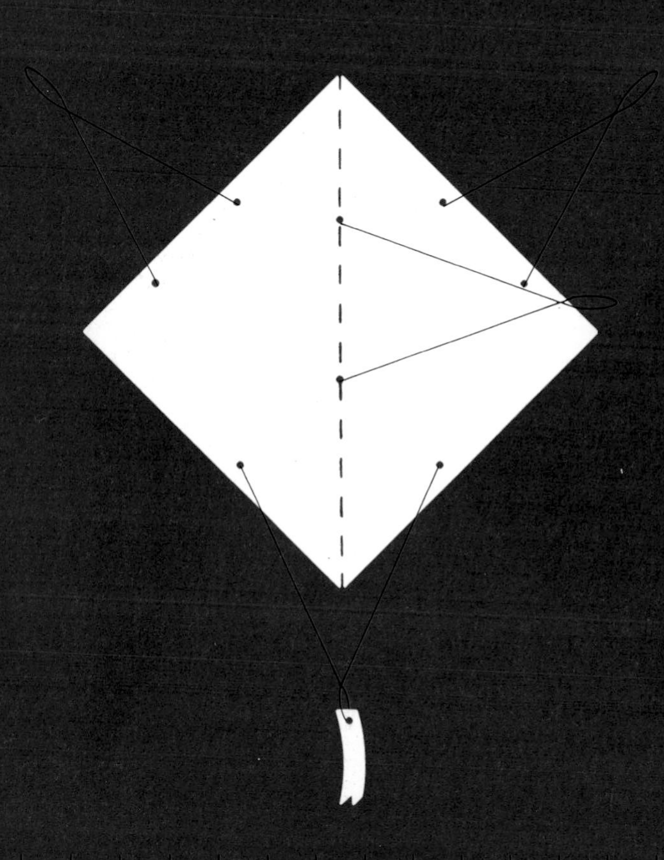

Semi-flexible soaring kite

Cover: medium gauge plastic or Tyvek.
Frame: dowel.
Bridle: keel.
Tailless.
Wind: light to moderate.

This is an efficient kite, and very simple to make in its plastic version, and has an extremely graceful movement in light winds.
The wing spreader should not be attached to the spine, but should move freely, allowing the wings to compensate interdependently for pressure changes upon their surfaces.
Though essentially a light-wind kite it can be adapted to fly in a wide range of wind-speeds if a flexible wing spreader is used.

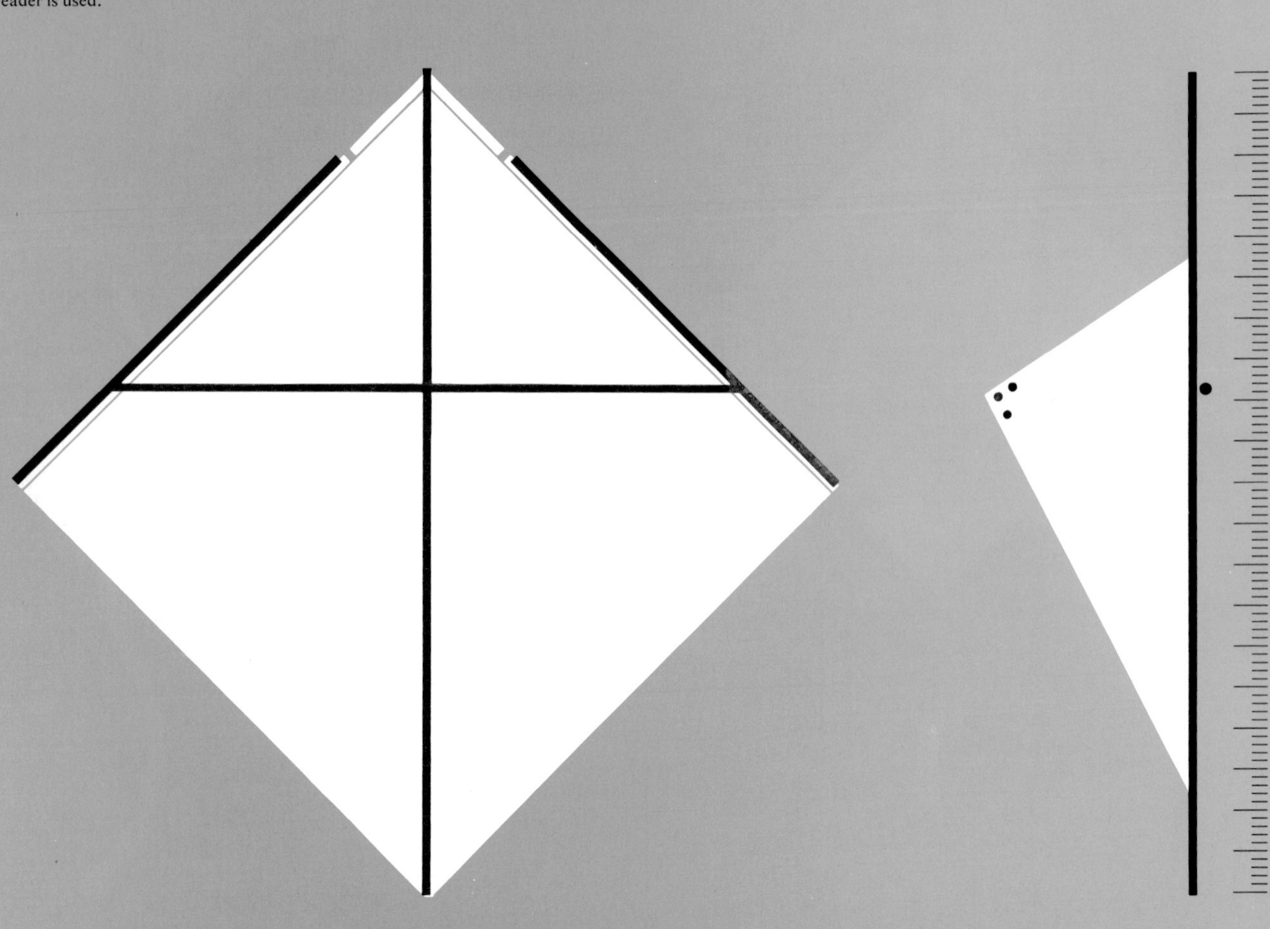

Russell Hall's kite

Cover: medium gauge plastic or Tyvek.
Frame: dowel.
Bridle: two-leg.
Tail: plastic streamer.
Wind: light to fresh.

The double parabolic cambers of Hall's kite give it excellent stability, and, if fitted with an elastic or spring-loaded bridle, it is capable of flying in a remarkable range of wind-speeds. The kite also has a tendency to adopt a very high angle of flight.

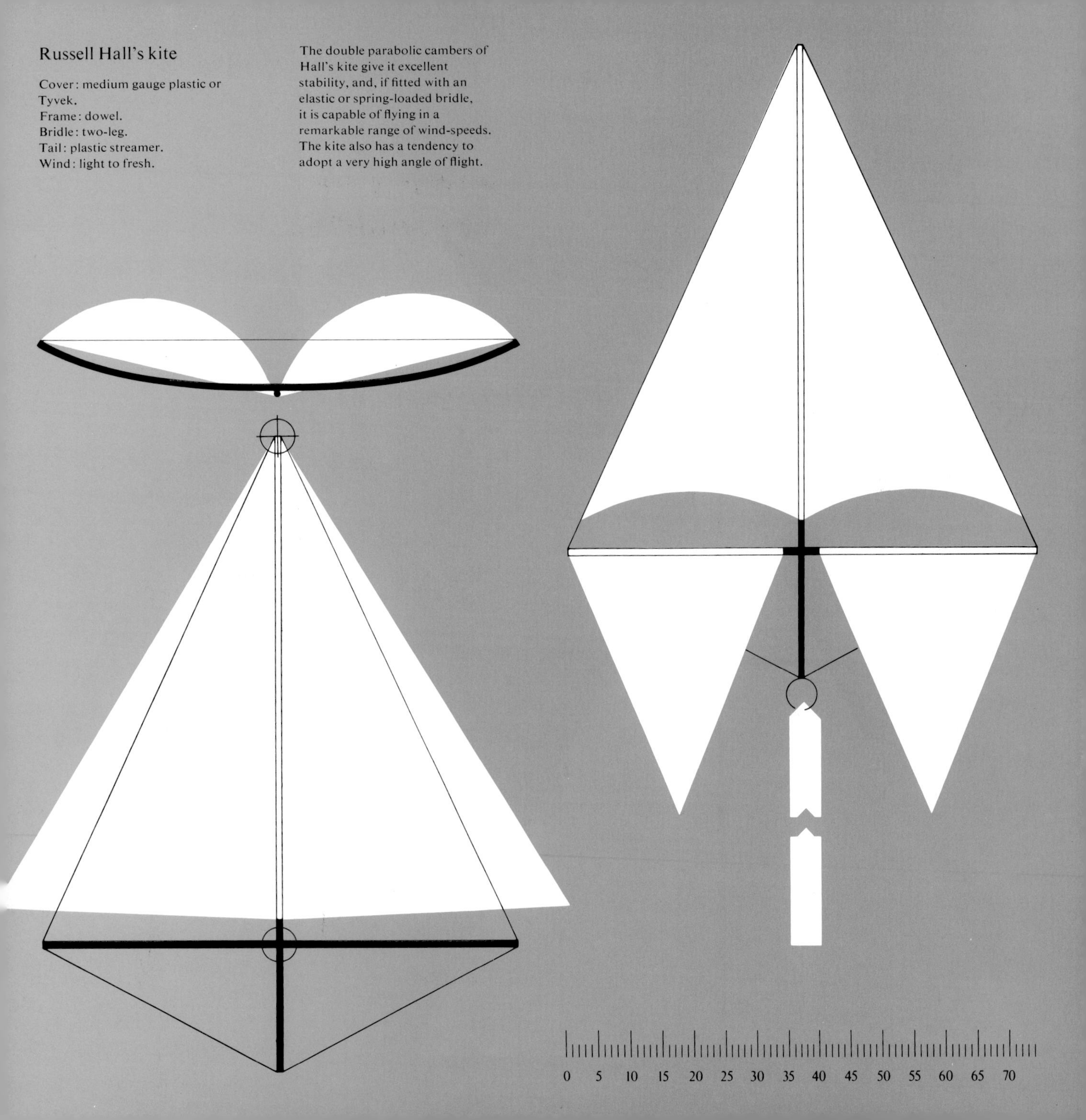

Modified Delta kite

Cover: plastic, Tyvek or nylon.
Spine: aluminium tube.
Spar: dowel.
Bridle: keel.
Tailless.
Wind: light to gentle.

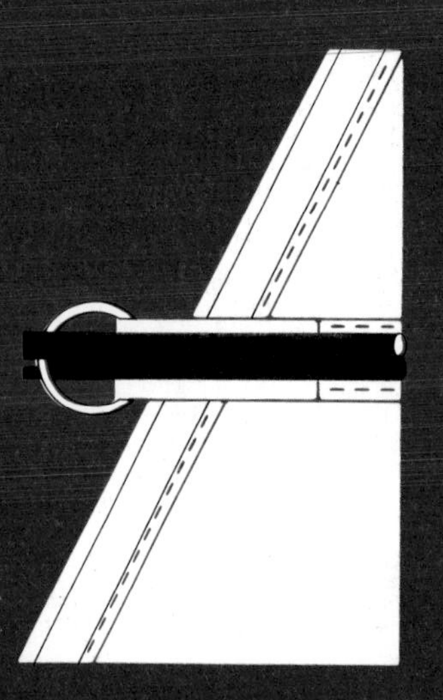

Detail of fastening method for the wing spreader of the Delta kite.

Soaring Delta kite

Cover: plastic, Tyvek or nylon.
Spine: aluminium tubing.
Spar: dowel.
Bridle: keel.
Tailless.
Wind: light to gentle.

The Delta is a fine thermal soarer. It is not a rigid kite, as its wings adjust themselves in flight. The Delta kite develops good lift in moderate winds. As the kite tends to be temperamental in difficult ground winds an aluminium spine is recommended: its tendency to nose-dive at launch and landing can result in breakage if a wooden spine is used.

For greater stability, the Soaring Delta is sometimes fitted with a loose 'apron' or fringes at its trailing edge.

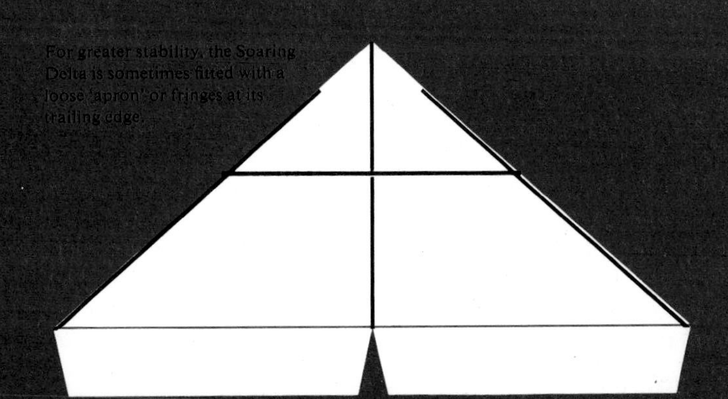

0 5 10 15 20 25 30 35 40 45 50 55 60 65 70 75 80 85 90 95 100 105 110 115 120 125 130 135 140 145 150 155 160 165 170 175 180 185

Sled kites

Cover: plastic, Tyvek or Mylar.
Spines: dowel.
Bridles: two-leg.
Tailless.
Wind: light to moderate.

Quickly cut from plastic sheet, the sled is amongst the easiest kites to make. Sleds may be flown without a vent in light winds, though they tend to become erratic as wind-speeds increase. The vent configuration devised by the well-known American kite flier/designer Ed Grauel gives excellent stability throughout a wide wind range, and is recommended as an excellent first kite.
Dowels are secured with waterproof adhesive tape, which is also used to reinforce the bridling points.
These points should also be pierced with eyelets to prevent tearing.
Bridle legs should each be approximately one-and-a-half times the length of the kite. The double sled has a three-leg bridle.
Circular vents are very easily cut out of polyethylene sheet or Mylar by placing the cover onto a smooth surface, securing it flat with small pieces of adhesive tape, and scoring round the centre point of the circle with a pair of dividers.

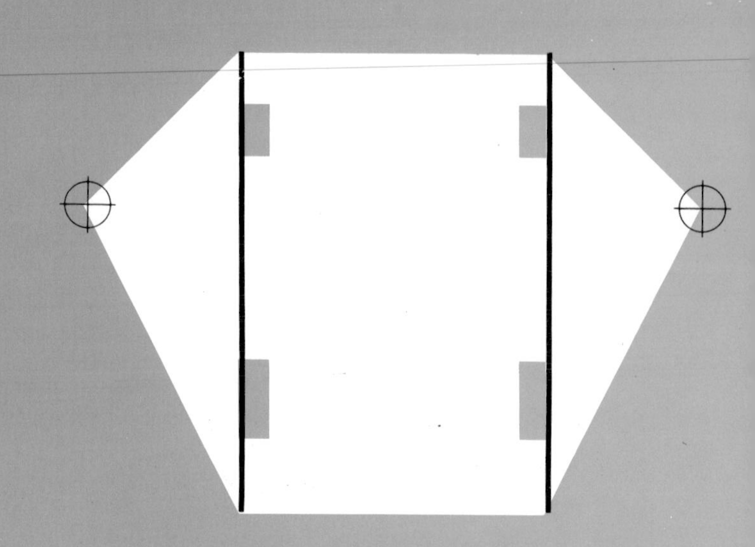

Scott sled.

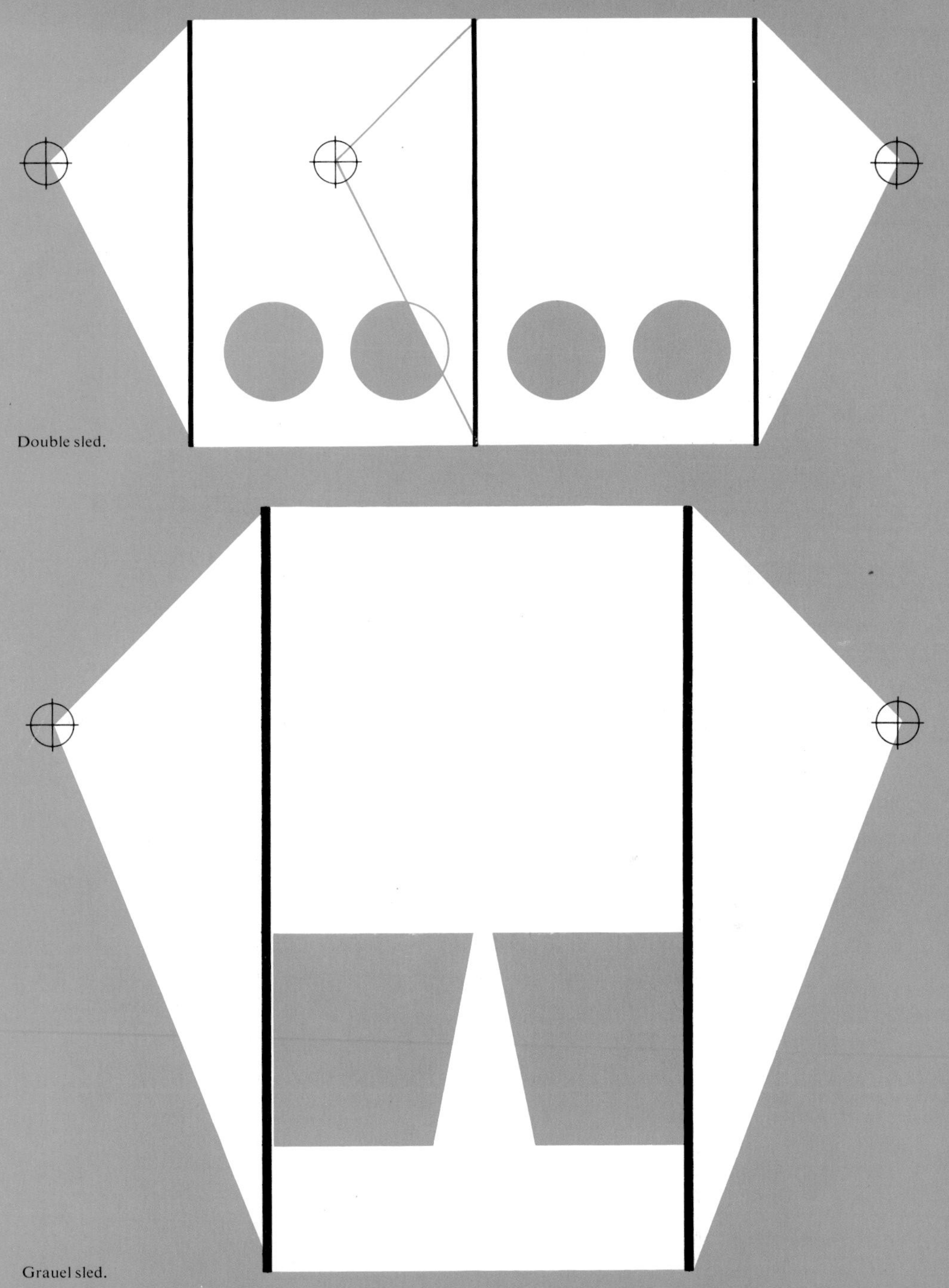

Double sled.

Grauel sled.

Jalbert's J-7·5 parafoil

The body and ventral fins, or flares, of the parafoil are constructed entirely from ripstop spinnaker nylon; and each individual piece, including the internal risers, must be carefully hemmed before assembly. At this stage also, ventrals should be fitted with tape tie-on loops.
All stitching on the parafoil should be secure, as the wind assiduously searches out defects; and should any unravelling occur within the cells the whole structure will need to be undone in order to carry out the necessary repairs.
Firstly, the risers are sewn into position onto the top side of the kite belly. Secondly, the ventrals are correspondingly sewn to the bottom side. After inspecting all seams thoroughly the top surface is stitched into place, working cell-by-cell from one side of the parafoil to the other. Finally, the trailing edge is turned over and hemmed, and a drogue towing loop is attached to its centre point.
The body of the parafoil is now ready for shrouding.

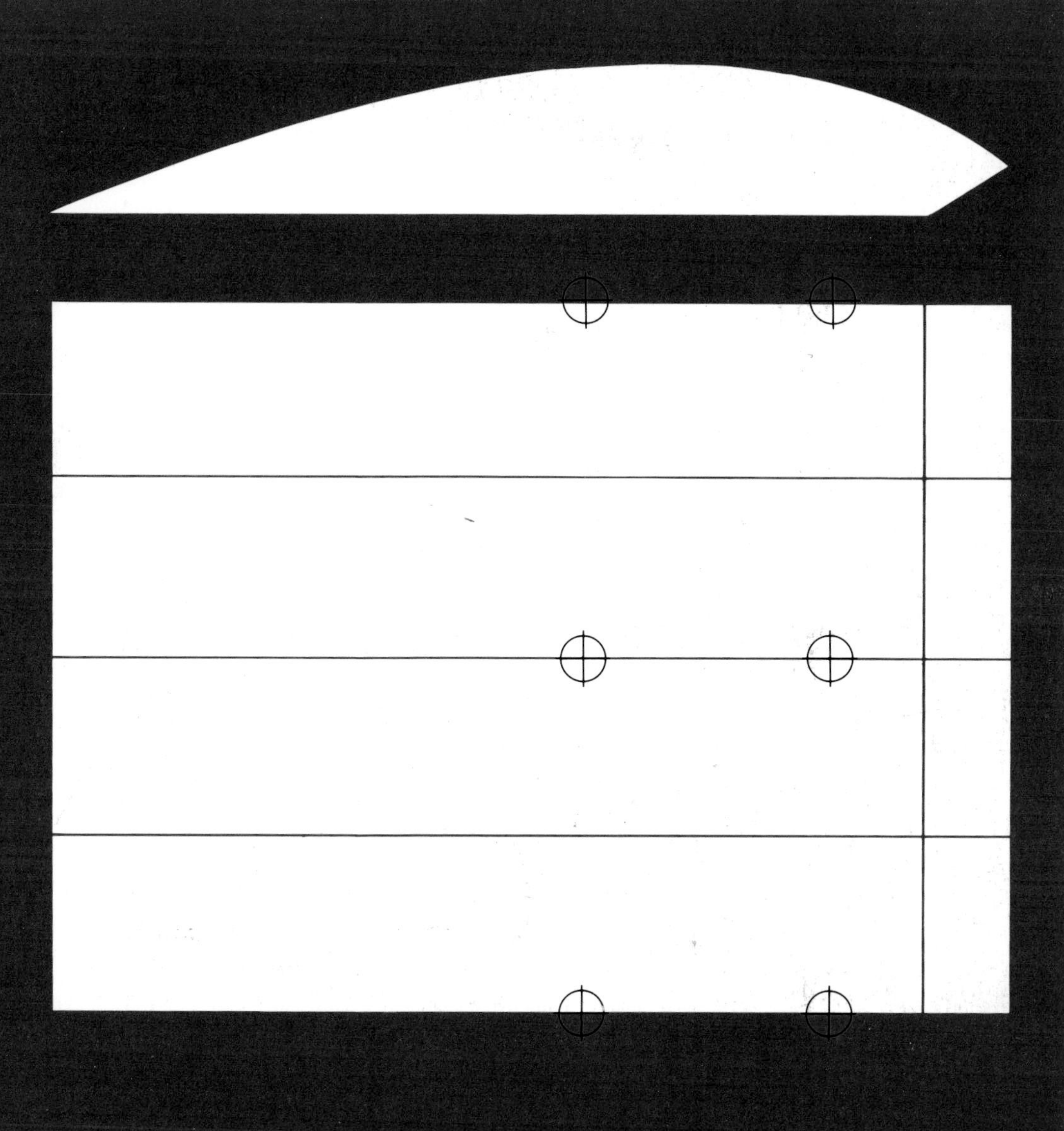

Large parafoil

Probably the simplest method of shrouding the parafoil body is to use continuous lengths of braided nylon line running from one ventral to its opposite counterpart. When securing these – a half blood knot is used for this – allow a reasonable length of excess line at the tie-on point for fine adjustment later on. Shrouding is most easily done by laying the parafoil on its back and weighting it flat. The centre point of each length of line should then be gathered at the longitudinal centre of the kite, at a point immediately above the front edge of the kite belly, and secured with a simple overhand knot. This provides a loop which becomes the towing point of the parafoil.
Large parafoils are best flown in moderate winds, and are launched by standing on the towing point and holding the leading edge open, allowing the wind to inflate the cells. When inflated, take the towing point and gradually give out line, holding the line taut; should the line be permitted to run slack, the ram-air principle is cancelled out and the parafoil will lose its shape.
Should the parafoil fly to one side, shorten the outer shroud lines on the side opposite to that which it favours.
The Jalbert parafoil is heavily patented throughout the world.

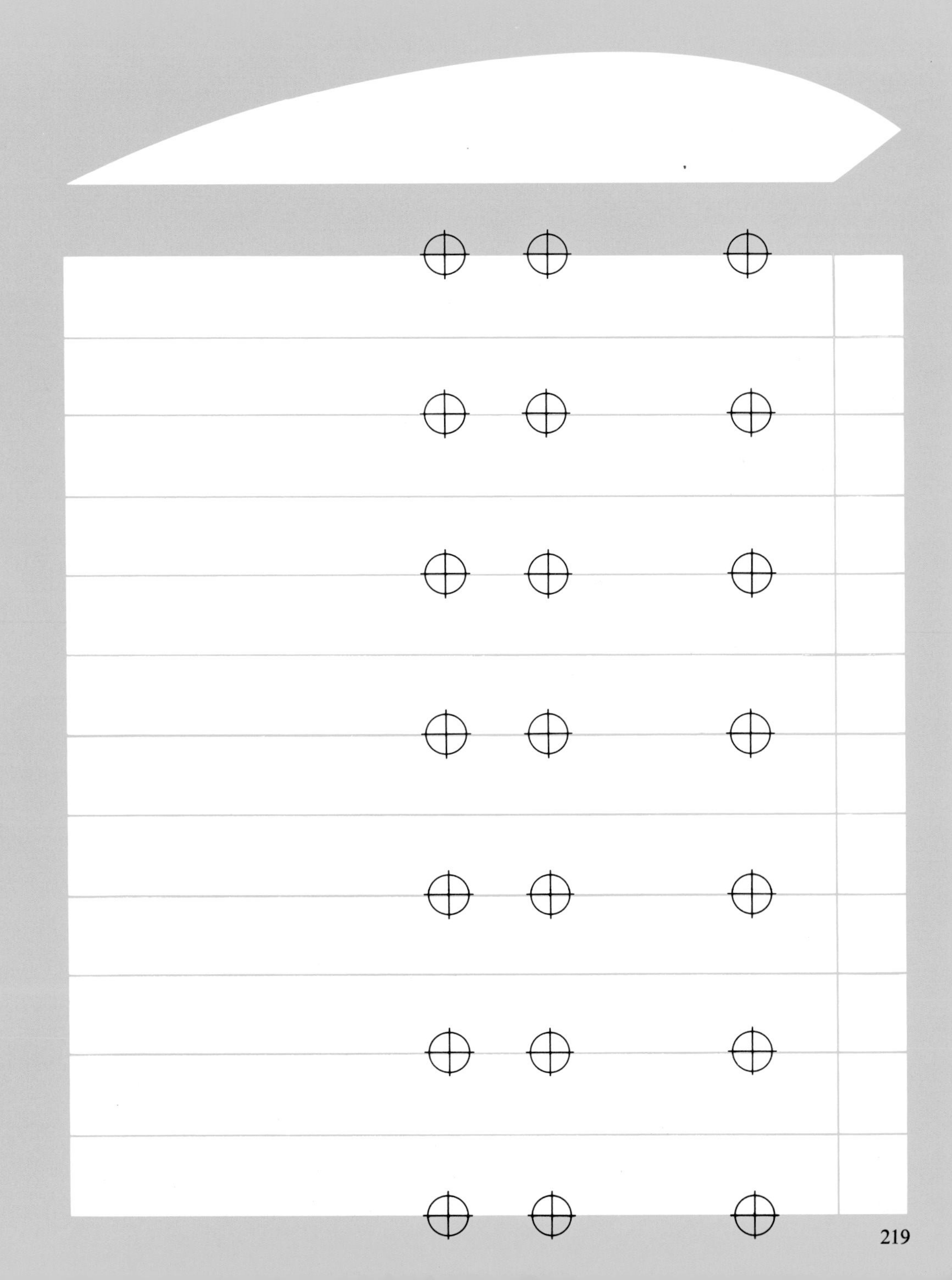

Paperfold kite

Many simple paperfold kites can be made in moments from good quality writing paper, and can be flown from cotton or button thread.
Fold a sheet of A4 writing paper in half (A), and mark off its diagonal (B) which should be offset by 1 cm (⅜ in). Fold the top leaf forward along this line (C) and the bottom leaf backwards (D) to form two wings and a keel (E).
Staple the keel together and punch holes against its edge. The wings are held flat by a small bamboo spar (F). Once the correct towing point has been found by a little trial and error, this will perform very well in gentle winds; particularly if bowed.

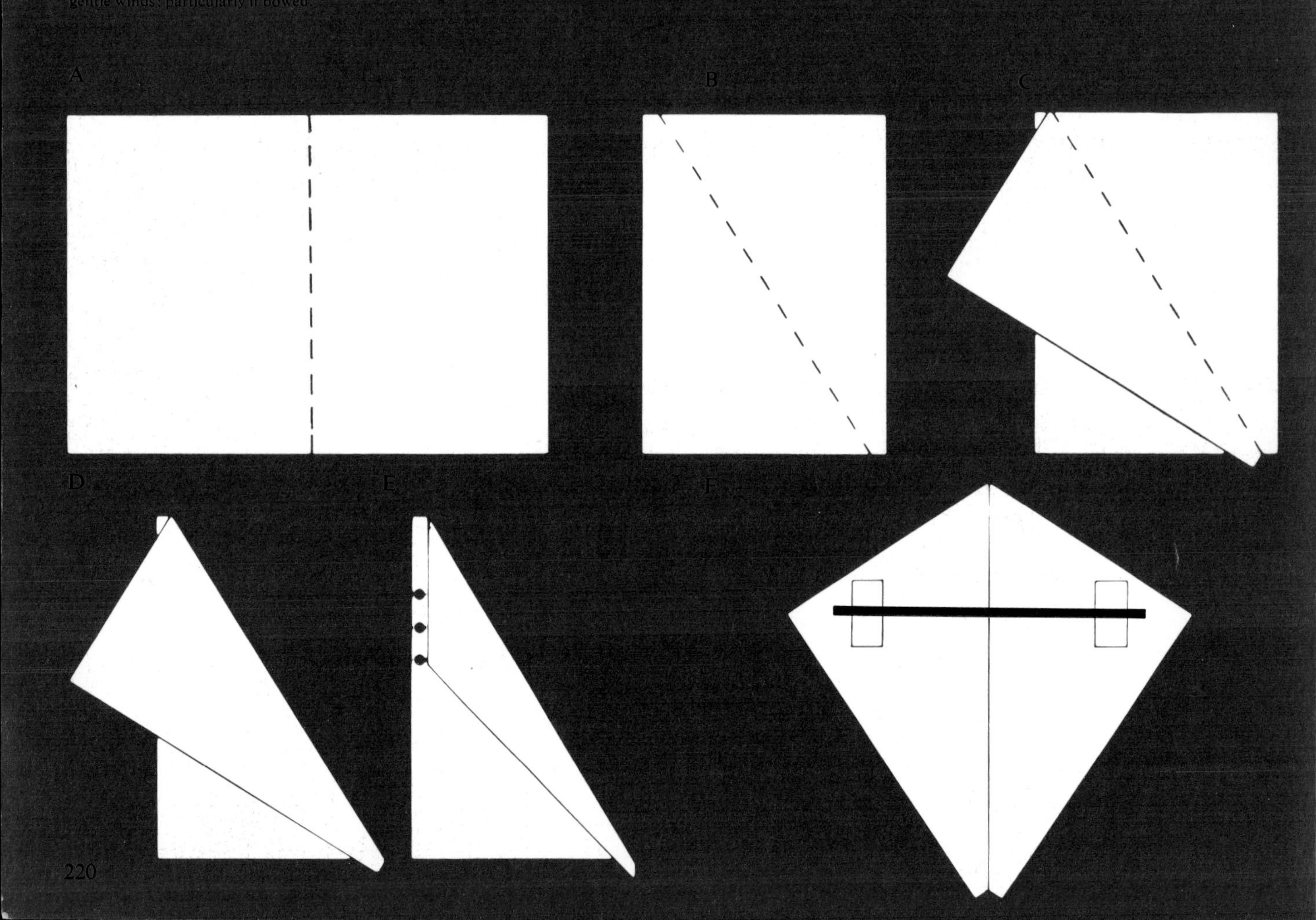

writing paper to find the square (A). Press in the diagonal fold and trim off the excess (B). Flatten out the square and place it diagonally (C), turning the outer edges inwards to meet the centre fold (D). The horizontal edges should now be folded against the outer edges (E). Reinstate the original fold, and cut 5 mm ($\frac{1}{4}$ in.) from top and bottom (F). Trim the off-cut (B) into four equal strips, join them with cellulose tape, and attach this as a streamer tail (G). With the centre fold now forming the keel base, sew on a button thread bridle, and the kite is finished.

Associations

American Kiteflyers Association
7106 Campfield Road, Baltimore, MD 21207, U.S.A.
The Association's magazine 'Kite Lines' is published quarterly and contains, news, views, and information on all aspects of kite flying.

British Kite Flyers Association
M.A.P. Ltd., P.O. Box 35, Hemel Hempstead, Hertfordshire.
The B.K.F.A. is a re-formation of the Kite and Model Aircraft Association, originally founded in 1902 by Marconi, Baden-Powell and Cody. The Association organises kite flying events, and publishes a bi-monthly news letter.
Founder: Ron Moulton

European Kiteflyers Association
Rushley Cottage, High Ham, Langport, Somerset
Editor: Nick Laurie

Kite shops: European

Der Drachenladen (Thomas Kibelksties)
Alter Postweg 45/Ecke Drakenbuger Str.
2800 Bremen 1, Germany

Harrods (Olympic Way)
Knightsbridge, London SW1 7XL

The Kite and Balloon Co (Colin Renwick)
613 Garrett Lane, London SW18 4SU

The Kite and Balloon Co Ltd (Colin Renwick)
27 Essex Street, Birmingham 3

The Kite Store (David Turner)
69 Neal Street, London WC2H 9PJ

Le Ciel est a tout le Monde
7 Avenue Trudaine, Paris, France

Malvern Kites (Peter Walters)
46 Ebrington Road, West Malvern, Worcs. WR14 4NL

Vincon, Paseo de Gracia, 96, Barcelona 8, Spain

Vlieger-Op (Gerard van der Loo)
Rijswijkseweg 74, den Haag, Holland

Kite shops: American

Above and Beyond (Timothy Burkhart)
Walnut Square, Berkeley, California 94709, U.S.A.

Aero-Foil Systems Inc (parafoils of all sizes)
7321 North Atlantic Avenue, Cape Canaveral
Florida 32920, U.S.A.

Come Fly a Kite Inc (Dinesh Bahadur)
900 North Point, Ghirardelli Square, San Francisco
California 94109, U.S.A.

Go Fly a Kite Store Inc (Andrea Bahadur)
1434 Third Avenue, New York, N.Y. 10028, U.S.A.

Hi Fli Kites (Reza Ragheb)
London Square, 12101C E. Iliff,
Aurora, Colorado 80014, U.S.A.

High as a Kite (John Harvey)
691 Bridgeway, Sausalito, California 94965, U.S.A.

International Kite Co
P.O. Box 3248, San Diego, California 92103, U.S.A.

The Kite Site (Charles Bernstein)
1075 Wisconsin Avenue, N.W., Georgetown
D.C., 20007, U.S.A.

The Kite Store
111 South 18th Street, Philadelphia, U.S.A.
2nd and Bay Avenue, Beach Haven, New Jersey, U.S.A.

Kiteworld Incorporated (Gordon Teekel)
540 De Haro, San Francisco, California 94107, U.S.A.

Let's Fly a Kite
13763 Fiji Way, Fisherman's Village, Marine Delrey
California 90291, U.S.A.

Let's Fly a Kite
1432 North Federal Highway, Dania, Florida 33004, U.S.A.

Outermost Kites (Dale Fleener)
Union Square, Provincetown, Massachusetts 02657, U.S.A.
Peacock Alley, Orleans, Vermont 05860, U.S.A.

Kite makers

Aero Kites Ltd (Brian Eccles)
P.O. Box 1, Pershore, Worcestershire

Airplane Kite Company
1702 West Third Street, Roswell, New Mexico, 8820

A.S.L. (Ace Kites)
Unit 12, Lansdown Industrial Estate
Cheltenham, Gloucestershire, GL51 8PL

Brookite Ltd
Francis Terrace, Junction Road, London N19

Cochranes of Oxford (Dunford Kites)
(Sqn. Ldr. Don Dunford, M.B.E.)
Fairspear House, Leafield, Oxford OX8 5NT

The Kite Factory
P.O. Box 9081, Seattle, Washington 98109, U.S.A.

Dan Leigh
54 Granville Terrace, Osborne Road, Pontypool,
Gwent, S. Wales

The Nantucket Kiteman
P.O. Box 1356, Nantucket, Massachusetts, 02554, U.S.A.

Peter Powell Kites Ltd
P.O. Box 1000, Cheltenham, Gloucestershire

Stratton Air Engineering
12821 Martha Ann Drive, Los Alamitos
California, 90720, U.S.A.

San Francisco Kite Factory
2231 Judah, San Francisco, California, 94122, U.S.A.

Skycraft (Nick Morse)
122–124 Cannon Street Road, London E1

Synestructics Inc
9559 Irondale Avenue, Chatsworth, California, 91311, U.S.A.

Vertical Visuals (Jilly Pelham)
95 Great Titchfield Street, London W1P 7FP

Cover materials

Cotton cambric: Louis Mankin Ltd
20 Charlotte Street, London W1P 1HJ

Paper of all kinds: Paperchase Products Ltd
216 Tottenham Court Road, London W1

The Kite and Balloon Co (Colin Renwick)
613 Garrett Lane, London SW18 4SU

The Kite Store (David Turner)
69 Neal Street, London WC2H 9PJ

The Kite Store (Martin Lester)
6a Boyces Avenue, Clifton, Bristol BS8 4AA

Frame materials

Aluminium: John Smith and Sons (Clerkenwell) Ltd
53–4 St John's Square, London EC1

Balsa Wood: Balsa Wood Supplies Ltd
Commerce Way, Lancing, Sussex, BN15 8TE

Bamboo: Bethal Brothers Ltd
87–9 St Paul Street, London EC2

Rattan Cane: Eaton
16 Manette Street, Soho, London W1V 5LB

Spruce: J. Brace and Sons Ltd
Saw Mills, High Ongar, Essex, CM5 9RU

Bibliography

Barwell, Eve, and Bailey, Conrad
How to Make and Fly Kites, Studio Vista, London, 1972.

Broomfield, G. A.
Pioneer of the Air: the Life and Times of Colonel S. F. Cody,
Gale & Polden, Aldershot, 1953.

Brummitt, Wyatt
Kites, Golden Press, New York, 1971.

Burkhart, Timothy
Kitefolio, Double Elephant, Berkeley, 1974;
Wildwood House, 1974.

Fowler, Haller
Kites: a Practical Guide to Kite Making and Flying,
Ronald Press, New York, 1953.

Franklin, Benjamin
The Papers of Benjamin Franklin (Vol. 4),
edited by L. W. Labaree, New Haven, 1961.

Geddes, Keith
Guglielmo Marconi: 1874-1937, H.M.S.O., 1974.

Gibbs-Smith, Charles H.
Aviation, H.M.S.O., 1970.
Sir George Cayley (1773-1857), H.M.S.O. 1968.
Sir George Cayley's Aeronautics, 1796-1855, H.M.S.O., 1962.
The Wright Brothers, H.M.S.O., 1963.

Hart, Clive
Kites: An Historical Survey, Faber & Faber, 1967;
Frederick A. Praeger, New York, 1967.
The Dream of Flight, Faber & Faber, 1972;
Winchester Press, New York, 1972.
Your Book of Kites, Faber & Faber, 1964;
Transatlantic Arts, New York, 1964.

Hiroi, Tsutomu
Kites, Mainichi Newspapers, Tokyo, 1973.

Houard, G.
Les Ascensions en cerfs-volants. Librarie Aéronautique,
Paris, 1912.

Hunt, Leslie, L.
25 Kites that Fly, Bruce Publishing, Milwaukee, 1929;
Dover Publications, New York, 1971.

Jouin, Colonel (ed.)
L'Aviation Militaire Française 1909-1969,
Ministère de la Défense National, Paris, 1969.

Jue, David
Chinese Kites, Charles E. Tuttle, Rutland, Vermont and
Tokyo, 1967.

Lecornu, Joseph
Les Cerfs-volants, Librairie Nony, Paris, 1902.

Lee, Arthur Gould
The Flying Cathedral: The Story of Samuel Franklin Cody,
Methuen, 1965.

Lloyd, Mitchell and Thomas
Making and Flying Kites, John Murray, 1975.

Miyawaki, Tatsuo
Tako, Biken-Sua, Tokyo, 1962.

Mouvier, Jean-Paul,
Kites, Éditions Gallimard, Paris, 1974;
William Collins, 1974.

Needham, J.
Science and Civilisation in China. (Vol. IV, Part 2),
Cambridge University Press, 1965.

Newman, Jay Hartley and Lee Scott
Kite Craft, Crown Publishers, New York, 1964.

Penrose, Harald
British Aviation: The Pioneer Years, Putnam, 1967.

Pocock, George
The Aeropleustic Art, or Navigation in the Air by the Use of Kites, or Buoyant Sails, 1827, second edition, 1851.

Polo, Marco
The Description of the World (Vol. 1),
Introduced by A. C. Moule, George Routledge, 1938.

Poujoula, R.
Le Cerf-volant de sauvetage, Librairie Aéronautique, Paris, 1913.

Poynter, Dan
Hang Gliding, Daniel F. Poynter, Massachusetts, 1973.

Ridgway, Harold
Kite Making and Flying, Arco Mayflower, 1962

Romain, C.
Les Cerfs-volants observatoires, Librairie Militaire, Paris, 1913.

Saconney, J. T.
Les Cerfs-volants militaires, Berger-Levrault, Paris, 1909.

Saito, Tadao
Colourful Kites from Japan, Japan Publications, Tokyo, 1969; Ward Lock, 1974.

Streeter, Tal
The Art of the Japanese Kite, John Weatherhill, New York, 1974.

Wagenvoord, James
Flying Kites, Macmillan, New York, 1968.

Walker, Frederick
Practical Kites and Aeroplanes, Guilbert Pitman, 1903.

Walker, Percy B.
Early Aviation at Farnborough, Macdonald, 1971.

Woglom, Gilbert T.
Parakites, G. P. Putnam, New York, 1896.

Yolen, Will
The Young Sportsman's Guide to Kite Flying, Thomas Nelson, New York, 1963.

Considerable reference has been made to the following journals:
The Aero Manual
L'Aéronaute
The Aeronautical Journal
Le Cerf-volant
Flight
Kite Tales
National Geographical Magazine
La Nature
Popular Science
La Revue Aérienne
Scientific American

David Pelham was born in Gloucestershire in 1938. He specializes in editorial design and has worked extensively in both magazine and book publishing. He has been Art Director of *Studio International* and *Harpers Bazaar*, and has designed books for Oxford University Press among other publishers. He has won several major design awards, and his work is represented in museums in Europe and the U.S.A. For twelve years he was Art Director of Penguin Books. He has been interested in kites since childhood.